Studies on the Origin of Harmonic Tonality

Studies on the Origin of Harmonic Tonality

Carl Dahlhaus

Translated by
Robert O. Gjerdingen

PRINCETON UNIVERSITY PRESS
PRINCETON, NEW JERSEY

Copyright © 1990 by Princeton University Press
Published by Princeton University Press, 41 William Street,
Princeton, New Jersey 08540
In the United Kingdom: Princeton University Press, Oxford

Dahlhaus, Carl, 1928–89
    [Untersuchungen über die Entstehung der harmonischen Tonalität.
English]
    Studies on the origin of harmonic tonality / Carl Dahlhaus ;
translated by Robert O. Gjerdingen.
        p. cm.
    Includes index.
    Translation of: Untersuchungen über die Entstehung der
harmonischen Tonalität.
    ISBN 0-691-09135-8 (alk. paper)
    1. Tonality. I. Title.
ML3811.D3913 1990
781.2′6—dc20   90-8696
                                                                        CIP
                                                                         MN

ISBN 0-691-09135-8

This book has been composed in Times Roman

Princeton University Press books are printed on acid-free paper,
and meet the guidelines for permanence and durability of the
Committee on Production Guidelines for Book Longevity of the
Council on Library Resources

Printed in the United States of America by Princeton University Press,
Princeton, New Jersey

Contents

TRANSLATOR'S PREFACE

In his book on architecture, the Roman scholar Vitruvius included a section on what we might now call the subject of acoustics, though he called it harmony. Forced to use the prevailing Greek terminology, he lamented that "harmony is an obscure and difficult aspect of music theory, especially for those not versed in Greek. If we wish to explain it, then we must make use of Greek terms because some of them do not have Latin equivalents" [Harmonice autem est musica litteratura obscura et difficilis, maxime quidem quibus graecae litterae non sunt notae. Quam si volumus explicare, necesse est etiam graecis verbis uti, quod nonnulla eorum latinas non habent appellationes (De Arch., 5.4.1)].

The modern writer on harmony faces similar if not greater problems, with the intervening centuries having added Latin, Italian, French, German, and English to the list of languages with important music-theoretical vocabularies. Professor Dahlhaus, in preparing the original edition of this work, wisely chose to let each source speak in its own tongue. He trusted his intended readers, European scholars in the humanities, to translate the various passages as they saw fit. For them, Rameau speaks in French, Zarlino in Italian, Tinctoris in Latin, de Santa Maria in Spanish, Lowinsky in English (with a slight accent, to be sure), and Riemann in German.

In preparing the English edition, my intent has been to make its contents accessible to as broad a spectrum of readers as possible. And, reasoning that if translating 20th-century German is helpful, translating 14th-century Latin is surely more helpful still, I have forced everyone in the book to speak English. As in the quote above, however, I include the original language after each quotation. So the expert, who might favor translating Vitruvius's *harmonice* as "harmonics" rather than "harmony," has the source at hand for direct comparison.

Vitruvius and other Latin authors translating musical terminology from the Greek had to contend with the Latin tongue's comparatively meagre vocabulary for matters musical. Two Greek terms with slightly different meanings often emerged as the same Latin word (e.g., the Greek φθόνγος [tone] and ψόφος [noise] could both become the Latin *sonus* [sound]). In musical vocabulary, especially on technical points, German and English stand in a similar relationship. Two German words expressing subtle distinctions often have a single English equivalent.

For example, Professor Dahlhaus illustrates a discussion of different historical concepts of musical intervals by contrasting the terms *Grossterz* [lit. "large third"] and *Durterz* [lit. "major-mode third"]. Both are normally translated as "major third." But this hopelessly obscures Professor Dahlhaus's point: the distinction between an interval as a size (a large size) and an interval as a component in a harmonic system (a major system). Another and more central distinction for the topic at hand is that between *Zusammenklang* and *Akkord*. In English, both can mean "chord." But as used in this study, the first term refers to a "sounding together" of many independent entities, while the second implies something perceived as one unit in a larger relational system. For the first, either "simultaneity" or "sonority" is possible in English, though neither is quite right. My choice in this book is predominately "sonority" because though less accurate in some instances, it better fits the overall semantic field to which Professor Dahlhaus applies *Zusammenklang*. For the second term, the ordinary word "chord" suffices, with the understanding that here it takes on an additional connotation: "*Akkord*, not *Zusammenklang*."

Other terms may lack native equivalents not because of an insufficient vocabulary, but because the ideas they represent may not survive the journey from one conceptual world to another. *Leittonwechselklang*, for instance, is a German word so deeply embedded in the concepts of Riemann's theory of functions that it requires an extended footnote even for German readers. In cases like this I have chosen to leave the word in the original language, since an awkward but legitimate borrowing seems preferable to the introduction of a spurious English neologism.

When Professor Dahlhaus wrote his *Studies* in the 1960s, it was a common practice to modernize the orthography of sources from earlier periods. Scholars who had grown up reading Cicero found Medieval spellings like *que* for *quae* or *michi* for *mihi* quaint and, in the minds of some, uncouth. Today the fashion has shifted toward preserving a text's original appearance. In reproducing the hundreds of citations treated by Professor Dahlhaus, my policy has been, where possible, to give them in their *Urtext* form. The tremendous amount of textual scholarship that has occurred since these *Studies* were written has also made it possible to present texts of greater authenticity than those based solely on the early though invaluable collections of Gerbert and Coussemaker.

Readers should note that textual authenticity is occasionally a mixed blessing. An author like Rameau can spell "subdominant," a word of his own coinage, three different ways in three different sources. And yet this too is a trait that warrants preservation, at least in small doses.

It shows us, in orthographic microcosm, something of Rameau the man—the 18th-century savant whose thoughts were always in flux, always seeking a better way to reduce the complexity of harmony to its *principes naturels*.

While I translated all quotes and citations independently, I have nevertheless gained much from consulting the extant translations of many of the texts touched upon in this volume. I owe a great deal to the work of Warren Baab on Guido d'Arezzo, Peter Berquist on Pietro Aaron, Philip Gosset on Rameau's *Traité*, Lawrence Gushee on Aurelian of Réôme, Deborah Hayes on Rameau's *Generation harmonique*, Jan Herlinger on Prosdocimo de' Beldomandi, Earnest Harris on Mattheson, Walter Hilse on Christoph Bernhard, H. Wiley Hitchcock on Caccini, Edward Lowinsky on Tinctoris, Guy Marco, Claude Palisca, and Vered Cohen on Zarlino, Clement Miller on Glarean and Gaffurius, Benito Rivera on Johannes Lippius, and Irwin Young on Gaffurius.

Misprints and other minor errors found in the German edition have been corrected without comment.

I would like to thank the National Endowment for the Arts for their original support of this project, the Mellon foundation and Harvard University for providing me time to revise it, and the staff of Harvard's Eda Kuhn Loeb Music Library for assisting with my many queries. I would like to thank my wife Catherine for her editorial assistance, Elizabeth Powers of Princeton University Press for guiding the book's production, and Dean Roy Elveton of Carleton College for supporting the project's last stages. Finally I must thank Professor Dahlhaus for his help, for his encouragement, and for his thought-provoking contributions to our understanding of the history of tonality in Western music.

Robert O. Gjerdingen
Cambridge, Massachusetts
1987

A NOTE ON PITCH DESIGNATIONS:

The pitches extending from the piano's middle C to the B a seventh above are represented as **c′, d′, . . . b′**. Pitches in the next higher octave are indicated by a double prime (e.g., **c″**). Pitches in the octave below middle C are represented by lower-case letters (e.g., **c**), and those in the octave below that by upper-case letters (e.g., **C**). In any octave, note names meant to specify particular pitches are set in bold type. Note names referring instead to a general class of pitches (e.g., all "c"s) are set in plain type.

Within the historical treatises cited by Professor Dahlhaus there are several divergent systems of designating pitches. Translated passages from these works use only the system described above. The original pitch designations, however, are preserved in the companion passages in the original languages.

A GUIDE TO THE TERMINOLOGY
OF GERMAN HARMONY

Robert O. Gjerdingen

It may strike some as odd that there could be such a thing as German harmony as opposed to English harmony. After all, the phenomena in question—chords, keys, progressions, modulations—are presumably perceived much the same in Bonn as in Boston. But the words used to describe these perceptions derive from different traditions, traditions influenced not only by different music theorists but also by famous pedagogues whose textbooks have consolidated divergent national terminologies.

At the core of present-day German terminology stands the colossus of Hugo Riemann, a musical scholar of vast erudition who produced work in practically every field of music history and theory. His writings, never timid, frequently created such a stir that they could still dominate discussions a generation after his death. In addressing the subject of harmony, Riemann set himself characteristically grandiose goals: to uncover the roots of "musical logic" and to discern the underlying dynamics of "musical syntax." Drawing on the scientific work of Helmholz, the dialectics of Hegel, and the speculative musical theories of Hauptmann and von Oettingen, he formulated his famous theory of functions. Its central claim is that every chord represents one of three functional categories: tonic, dominant, or subdominant. The categories themselves are of course shared in the English tradition, and their names go back to Rameau and the beginnings of modern harmonic theory. But what separates the German tradition is the extent to which these categories have reshaped the terms for other chords and their interrelationships.

The German names for triads on the so-called primary or tonal degrees of the major or minor scale (I, IV, V) are familiar to English-speaking musicians: "tonic," "subdominant," and "dominant." But the names for the so-called secondary degrees may strike the English reader as foreign in both sound and concept. In the major mode, triads on degrees two, three, and six—"supertonic," "mediant," and "submediant" in English—are known as the "subdominant parallel," the "dominant parallel," and the "tonic parallel," commonly abbreviated Sp, Dp, and Tp. Here one sees cast the long shadow of

Riemann. The name of each secondary triad connects it with a primary triad, and so with one of Riemann's three functional categories. The relationship supporting this connection, what the Germans call the "parallel" relation, is known in English as the "relative" relation: the association of major and minor scales sharing the same diatonic pitches (e.g., A minor and C major). To complete the reduction of the major-mode diatonic triads to the three harmonic functions, all that remains is to interpret the triad on the leading tone as an incomplete dominant seventh chord (often symbolized as "D^7" with a diagonal slash through the "D").

At this point German harmony still does not depart markedly from English harmony. Both traditions presume harmony to be "functional," though the meaning of this term is less clear in English than in German. Both are ultimately descended from Rameau, though filtered through various theories of fundamental progressions based on the primacy of root movement by fifth. Both are often expressed in terms of Roman numerals, writers in German using only upper-case letters, writers in English often using upper-case letters for major and augmented triads, lower-case letters for minor and diminished. And both traditions symbolize triadic inversion or chordal elements beyond the triad with the venerable figures of the thoroughbass.

Yet in its treatment of the minor mode, German harmony demonstrates the penchant for bold systematization that was a hallmark of later 19th-century German scholarship. While English harmony generally discusses the minor mode as an analogue of the major mode, German harmony has been greatly affected by Riemann's decision to treat minor as the inversion of major. The consequences of his decision have been far-reaching, and at one time, in the late 19th and early 20th centuries, resulted in a vast symmetrical constellation of chords and relationships known as "dualistic" harmony.

Riemann's goal was to provide for each chord or relation in the major mode a corresponding, and inverted, chord or relation in the minor mode. But the goal of thoroughgoing dualism conflicted with aspects of his own theory of functions, with factors of harmonic practice, and with major-minor relationships that are analogous and parallel rather than inverse and symmetrical. Several compromises were necessary, and their cumulative effect in the face of the continuing desire for symmetry was the creation of an entire new class of chords, the *Leittonwechsel-klänge* explained below.

From the perspective of dualistic harmony, the presence of the reference tone—the "root"—of a major triad at the *bottom* of both a perfect fifth and a major third (**c** in **c–e–g**) requires the reference tone of a minor triad to be located at the *top* of a perfect fifth and a major third (**g** in **c–e♭–g**). With this point in mind, let us create the three secondary triads in minor by inverting their major counterparts. In C major, the tonic parallel (Tp = A minor) differs from the tonic triad (T) by a single tone, an **a** one whole step *above* the fifth of the chord. So in C minor, the tonic parallel should differ from the tonic by a single tone one whole step *below* the fifth of the chord. The "fifth," however, is **c** itself, since the Riemannian root of this minor chord is **g**. The tone below the fifth is thus **B♭** and the tonic parallel of C minor is consequently E♭ major, symbolized as "tP" (upper case representing major, lower case minor). Following the same line of reasoning, the subdominant parallel in C major (Sp = D minor) has its C-minor counterpart in an A♭-major triad (sP), and the dominant parallel (Dp = E minor) its counterpart in a B♭-major triad (dP).

If one class of secondary chords—the parallel chords—could be formed by exchanging a primary chord's *fifth* for the tone above it in major or below it in minor, then a second class of chords could be formed by exchanging a primary chord's *root* for the tone below it in major or above it in minor. The tone involved in this exchange (*Wechsel*) is the leading tone (*Leitton*), either the tone a half step below the root in major or a half step above the "root" in minor. The result is a tonic *Leittonwechselklang*, customarily abbreviated Tl in the major mode, tL in the minor mode. As one might expect, there are also subdominant and dominant *Leittonwechselklänge*. In C major the complete set is Tl = E minor, Sl = A minor, and Dl = B minor. In C minor the inverted set is tL = A♭ major, sL = D♭ major, and dL = E♭ major. (One will occasionally see the term *Gegenklang* [lit. "contrast chord"] in place of *Leittonwechselklang*. The term *Gegenklang* emphasizes the contrast of mode and the major-third relationship between a function and its corresponding *Leittonwechselklang*.)

This is clearly not a simple system. Three functional categories can appear in any one of three chordal guises in either of two modes, eighteen possibilities in all: T, Tp, Tl, t, tP, tL, S, Sp, Sl, s, sP, sL, D, Dp, Dl, d, dP, dL. Why all this complexity? Perhaps the central reason is that this ingenious, occasionally convoluted system enabled Riemann to achieve a grand and masterful synthesis of both the old and the new in late 19th-century music. Ostensibly remote triads could be interpreted through the traditional terms of the I–IV–V–I, or now T–S–D–T, cadential schema. A sequence of A♭-major, B♭-major, and C-major chords, for example, could be neatly interpreted as a sub-dominant (sP) to dominant (dP) to tonic (T) progression in C-major, a reading of these chords not without support in certain late-Romantic cadences. And a chord that often perplexes harmony students, the Neapolitan chord of D♭ major in a C-major context, could be shown to be nothing more than a minor-mode subdominant *Leittonwechsel-klang* (sL).

The rise and partial fall of Riemann's system follows that of the late 19th-century harmony to which it was wedded. Thus in the first decades of the 20th century it was reaching new heights of complexity while simultaneously being undermined by doubts over its fundamental premises. In the course of this ferment several different symbolizations of the system arose. Today many are unfamiliar even to German musicians and are footnoted by Professor Dahlhaus where they occur. Two special symbols that nevertheless still retain some currency are the plus sign ($^+$) and the degree sign (°). The plus sign next to a note name or chord symbol indicates that the lower tone of the "fifth" is the reference tone. Thus "$^+$**d**" would mean that **d** is the reference tone of the major triad **d–f♯–a**. The degree sign indicates the inverse relationship—that the upper tone is the reference tone. Thus "°**a**" would mean that **a** is the reference tone of the minor triad **d–f–a**. Readers wishing a fuller account of the complete range of functional harmonic systems and their symbols should refer to the book by Renate Innig (*Systeme der Funktionsbezeichnung in den Harmonielehren seit Hugo Riemann* [Düsseldorf: Gesellschaft zur Förderung der systematischen Musikwissenschaft, 1970]).

The overtly dualistic elements of Riemannian harmony were among the first to fall out of favor, though earlier in this century their presence can still be strongly felt. For example, prewar German writers routinely used the term "dominant harmony" to refer not to a type of chord, V, but to a type of harmony based on a tonic with *two* dominants: an upper one, V, and a lower one, IV. And the notion of there being both a lower leading tone (**b** in C major) and an upper leading tone (**a♭** in C minor) is a matter of course for someone like Ernst Kurth. In more recent years the notion of *Leittonwechselklänge* has faded somewhat, but the concept of parallel chords remains strong and firmly entrenched in the standard terminology.

The remaining terms current in German writings on harmony have well-known English equivalents because they derive from a shared tradition antedating Riemann, that of *Stufentheorie* or "the theory of fundamental progressions." *Stufe* is an ambiguous term. Literally "step" or "scale degree," it connotes not only the diatonic triad on a particular scale degree but also that degree as the harmonic root of several possible chords and as a participant in one or more fundamental progressions, somewhat like a Roman numeral in English theory. The "IV" chord is thus the scale degree IV "writ large" (and in this sense one might view the theory of fundamental progressions, *Stufentheorie*, as the apotheosis of the thoroughbass).

Now just as in Riemann's theory of functions, the theory of fundamental progressions attempts to reduce the diversity of possible chord successions to an underlying model of one preferred progression, in this case V–I or the circle of fifths. The result, often achieved through "supposition" (=sub-posing; i.e., placing a conjectured bass a third or fifth below the real bass), is a profusion of "dominant" relationships. Those involving chromatic tones and known as "secondary dominants" in English are termed *Zwischendominante* or *Wechseldominante* in German and generally symbolized by a "D" in parentheses. A *Doppeldominante* is also a secondary dominant—the dominant of the dominant. It may be symbolized by two overlapping "D"s. (The fully dualistic system also requires the complementary symbol of two "S"s— the subdominant of the subdominant.) Finally, in cases where a dominant implies a tonic but the tonic is not realized in the music, the implied chord can be placed within square brackets. Thus, in a C-major context, (D)[Tp] might indicate an E-major chord *not* followed by an a-minor chord. That is, the square brackets indicate a missing tonic parallel (a-minor) which is preceded by its dominant (the major triad or dominant seventh chord on E).

Some may at first be put off by the overt theorizing apparent in German harmony, wishing perhaps that a choice be made once and for all between Riemann's *Functionstheorie* and the older *Stufentheorie*, or possibly believing that so-called linear theories have settled all earlier disputes. Yet this ongoing conflict between antithetical theories, with its attendant uncertainties and complexities, has special merits. In particular, whereas an English-speaking student may falsely believe that he or she is learning harmony "as it really is," the German student encounters what are obviously theoretical constructs and must deal with them accordingly. The sophisticated historical view of harmony that can arise within this tradition of competing theories is evidenced in Professor Dahlhaus's *Studies on the Origin of Harmonic Tonality*.

Studies on the Origin of Harmonic Tonality

INTRODUCTION

In 1844, F. J. Fétis defined "tonality," a term borrowed from Castil-Blaze, as the "set of requisite relationships, simultaneous or successive, among the tones of the scale" [collection des rapports nécessaires, successifs ou simultanés, des sons de la gamme].[1] A result of mankind's historical and ethnic diversity would, of course, be a multiplicity of tonalities (*types de tonalités*). But the theory that Fétis developed was restricted to *tonalité moderne*.

In contrast to Fétis, Hugo Riemann was convinced that the many *types de tonalités* could be reduced to a single *natürliches System*, that of the tonic, dominant, and subdominant chordal functions. The comprehension of tones as representatives of the tonic, dominant, or subdominant was to be taken as an innate norm of musical perception. But historians and ethnologists, shunning the forced constraints of systematization, rejected Riemann's thesis as empirically unsubstantiated. So "tonality," the phenomenon whose theory Riemann had developed, had to be more narrowly defined as "harmonic tonality" and removed from other *types de tonalités*. And in consequence, Riemann's "tonality" became a historical phenomenon whose origin could be described.

To be sure, it is a matter of dispute exactly when harmonic tonality—the representation of keys through chordal relationships—arose and developed. Many researchers seek its origin in the 14th (A. Machabey) or 15th centuries (H. Besseler), others in the 16th (E. E. Lowinsky) or 17th (M. Bukofzer).

The divergence of historical opinion rests to no small degree on contradictions between theoretical hypotheses. For this reason the first chapter, "The Theory of Harmonic Tonality," examines several systematic expositions of harmony: the fundamental-progression or "degree" theory [*Stufentheorie*] of Jean-Phillipe Rameau and Simon Sechter, the functional theory of Hugo Riemann, and the "energetic" theory of Ernst Kurth. To extract historically relevant criteria from theories that present themselves simply as universal musical systems, it is necessary first to narrow the range of their validity. Then an attempt must be made to resolve the contradictions between them.

Tonal harmony rests on two assumptions: first, that a triad constitutes a primary, direct unity; and second, that the progression of chordal roots establishes the key. In the second chapter, "Intervallic and Chordal Composition," conclusions about the development of a consciousness of chords and root progressions will be drawn from a study of modifications in compositional practice. Of course two preliminary conditions must be satisfied if the result is to be historically well founded: first, an attempt must be made to define the older principle of harmony that formed the backdrop for tonal harmony ("The Principle of Contrasting Sonorities"); and second, there is the unavoidable discussion of the thesis that tonal harmony originated in the 15th century ("15th-Century Harmony").

From musical notation alone it is not possible to make a direct determination of whether a vertical combination of tones was or was not intended to be a chord. Thus one must naturally combine several methods, not only assembling documentary evidence on the conception of polyphonic compositions ("Compositional Types and Formulas in the 15th and 16th Centuries") and the view of chords ("The Development of Chordal Theory") but also demonstrating, with analyses of compositional rules and procedures, the range of applicability of the traditional rules of counterpoint and the significance of deviations from the norm ("The Treatment of Dissonance," and "Figured-Bass Harmony").

From the 17th through the 19th century, the characterization of key and the grammar of chords were two sides of the same coin—tonality was determined harmonically, through chordal relationships, and harmony was defined tonally. By comparison, in music from the 14th through the 16th century the two factors are mutually independent—the method of linking vertical combinations of tones did not primarily serve the presentation of the mode. The third chapter, "Mode and System," describes the same development considered in the second chapter (there in terms of compositional practice) from the point of view of conceptions of key.

The underlying hypotheses are, of course, so unclear that a detailed presentation, sometimes appearing to stray from the subject, is unavoidable. First, the notion must be considered that the transition to harmonic tonality was connected with modifications in the tonal system ("The Evolution of the Tonal System"). And second, musicologists' opinions differ so fundamentally on the meaning of mode in 15th- and 16th-century polyphony that it would be arbitrary to accept any single such thesis as a point of departure ("Modal Polyphony").

The evolution toward harmonic tonality can best be observed in changes in the function and disposition of cadences ("Key Relationship and the Disposition of Clausulas"). In addition, an attempt will be made to describe the intermediate stage—that of the "no longer" and the "not yet"—that facilitated the transition to harmonic tonality ("Between Modality and Major-Minor Tonality").

In the fourth chapter, complete groups of works are analyzed. In the motets of Josquin des Prez, one can observe circa 1500 the significance of the c- and a-modes, proto-forms of major and minor. The analysis of some *frottole* by Cara and Tromboncino is motivated by the often-expressed thesis that it is in this genre that one can find the origin of tonal harmony. And finally, with reference to Monteverdi's madrigals, it will be demonstrated that the transition to tonal harmony was tied to changes in rhythmic organization and musical form.

. . .

The studies presented here were accepted as an inaugural dissertation in the winter semester of 1965/66 by the humanities faculty of Christian-Albrecht University, Kiel, West Germany.

I would like to thank both Professor Walter Wiora for including this manuscript in the *Saarbrücker Studien zur Musikwissenschaft* and the German Research Association for providing a publishing subvention.

CHAPTER I

THE THEORY OF HARMONIC TONALITY

Tonality and Harmony

Hugo Riemann defined "tonality" as "the special meaning that chords receive through their relationship to a fundamental sonority, the tonic triad" [die eigentümliche Bedeutung, welche die Akkorde erhalten durch ihre Bezogenheit auf einen Hauptklang, die Tonika].[1] Since Riemann termed these chordal meanings "functions," "tonality" is thus the embodiment of chordal functions.

The term, first coined by Castil-Blaze, was given formal definition by François Joseph Fétis. In conceiving the notion of tonality, Fétis experienced a dramatic enlightenment: "Suddenly the truth came to me; the issues were plainly set out, the darkness vanished, the false doctrines fell in shreds round about me" [Tout à coup la vérité se présente à mon esprit; les questions se posent nettement, les ténèbres se dissipent; les fausses doctrines tombent pièce à pièce autour de moi].[2] The mental image that Fétis connected with the term "tonality" is, of course, incompatible with Riemann's definition. To Fétis, the concept of functions was just as foreign as the idea of defining tonality primarily in terms of relationships among chords.

Riemann's system of tonality differs in four main points from the theory developed by Fétis: first, in the intellectual tradition in which the category "tonality" is based; second, in the designation of tonality's constituent features; third, in the conception of the relationship between the system of chords and the underlying scale; and fourth, in the determination of the theory's range of validity.

1. Riemann took over the thesis that tonality is based on acoustical fact from a tradition of "physicalism" (Jacques Handschin) extending back to Rameau. Thus the dominant tends toward the tonic because the dominant chord is contained within the harmonic series of the tonic chord's root.[3] But Fétis's concept of tonality represents the opposite thesis, the conviction that it is a mistake to explain musical relationships in terms of mathematics or acoustics. Fétis seized on the word "tonality" so as to have at hand a term expressing his view that scales and tonal systems are based not on the nature of sonic material but on diverse historical and ethnic circumstances. "For the elements of music, nature provides nothing but a multitude of tones differing in pitch, duration,

and intensity by the greatest or least degree . . . The conception of the relationships that exist among them is awakened in the intellect, and, by the action of sensitivity on the one hand, and will on the other, the mind coordinates the tones into different series, each of which corresponds to a particular class of emotions, sentiments, and ideas. Hence these series become the various types of tonalities" [La nature ne fournit pour éléments de la musique qu'une multitude de sons qui diffèrent entre eux d'intonation, de durée et d'intensité, par des nuances ou plus grandes ou plus petites . . . L'idée des rapports qui existent entre eux s'éveille dans l'intelligence, et sous l'action de la sensibilité d'une part, et la volonté de l'autre, l'esprit les coordonne en séries différents, dont chacune correspond à un ordre particulier d'émotions, de sentiments et d'idées. Ces séries deviennent donc des types de tonalités].[4] As a "purely metaphysical principle" (by "metaphysical" Fétis means "anthropological"), *tonalité* is the antithesis of the "natural principle" to which Rameau had reduced harmony. "But one will say, 'What is the principle behind these scales, and what, if not acoustic phenomena and the laws of mathematics, has set the order of their tones?' I respond that this principle is purely metaphysical. We conceive this order and the melodic and harmonic phenomena that spring from it out of our conformation and education" [Mais, dira-t-on, quel est le principe de ces gammes, et qui a réglé l'ordre de leurs sons, si ce ne sont des phénomènes acoustiques et les lois du calcul? Je réponds que ce principe est purement métaphysique. Nous concevons cet ordre et les phénomènes mélodiques et harmoniques qui en découlent par une conséquence de notre conformation et de notre éducation].[5]

2. According to Riemann, tonality is the embodiment of chordal meanings, and chordal meanings—subdominant, dominant, subdominant parallel, and dominant parallel—are based on "affinities between tones" [*Tonverwandtshaften*]. It was from Moritz Hauptmann that Riemann adopted the axiom that perfect fifths and major thirds are the only "directly intelligible" intervals,[6] and from the perfect fifth and major third Riemann deduced not only the structure of chords but also their relationship. Thus the major triad is composed of a perfect fifth and a major third above its root, the minor triad of a perfect fifth and major third below its fifth. And the relation between the tonic and dominant, or the tonic and subdominant, is due to the fifth-relation between the chordal roots in major or between the fifths in minor.

In contrast to Riemann, whose theory of tonality is a theory of "affinities between tones," Fétis saw the fundamental factor of *tonalité moderne* (the harmonic tonality of the 17th through the 19th century) residing in the contrast between triad and seventh chord, between the "consonant harmony called *accord parfait*, which has the quality of rest and conclusion, and the dissonant harmony, which causes tendency, attraction, and movement . . . Thus are determined the requisite relationships among tones that one designates, in general, by the name of tonality" [harmonie consonnante appelée accord parfait, qui a le caractère du repos et de la conclusion, et l'harmonie dissonante, qui détermine la tendance, l'attraction et le mouvement . . . Par là se trouvent déterminés les rapports nécessaires des sons, qu'on désigne en général sous le nom de tonalité].[7] The alternation of "rest" and "tendency" appears to be the governing principle of tonal relationship. Degrees I, IV, V, and vi of the major scale are "tones of rest" [*notes de repos*] and admit root-position triads. Degrees ii, iii, and vii, on the other hand, "cannot be considered tones of rest" [ne peuvent être considérées comme des notes de repos] and for that reason require a "derivative chord" [*accord dérivé*]—a sixth chord (**d–f–b**, **e–g–c'**, **b–d'–g'**). "Hence according to the tonal order, they can only be accompanied by derivative harmonies" [Suivant l'ordre tonal, ils ne peuvent donc être accompagnées que d'harmonies dérivées].[8] Fétis excludes the triads on degrees ii, iii, and vii from the *tonalité*. During chordal sequences that do include a triad or seventh chord on ii, iii, or vii, the feeling of tonality is suspended. "The mind, absorbed in the contemplation of the progressive series, momentarily loses the feeling of the tonality" [L'esprit, absorbé dans la contemplation de la série progressive, perd momentanément le sentiment de la tonalité].[9] Thus Fétis's concept of tonality does not comprise the totality of chordal relationships that are possible and significant in tonal harmony. Instead, it characterizes only a portion of them.

Fétis's theory seems irresolvably opposed to Riemann's. Yet a reconciliation is not out of the question. The assertion by Fétis that an *accord parfait* on the second or third degree of the scale is an exception to the rule of *tonalité* can be given the interpretation, without doing violence to his thesis, that a triad on the second or third degree *seems* to be an *accord parfait*, but is actually not. And the result of this "translation" is none other than Riemann's theory of "apparent consonances" [*Scheinkonsonanzen*]: the assertion that the apparent root of the subdominant parallel or dominant parallel is in fact a *sixte ajoutée*, a sixth added to the subdominant or dominant harmony. And conversely, Riemann's thesis that only the tonic, dominant, and subdominant are "consonances," while the tonic parallel, dominant parallel, and subdominant parallel are "dissonances," seems less strange if, following Fétis, one interprets "consonance" as *repos* and "dissonance" as *tendance*.

3. According to Riemann, tonality is a system of chords or "harmonies." The thesis of the primacy of the chord vis-à-vis the individual

tone, and of the chordal context vis-à-vis the scale, is one of the founding principles of the theory of functions. "1. We always hear tones as representatives of chords (i.e., consonant chords), of which there are only two kinds, namely the major chord (*Oberklang*) and the minor chord (*Unterklang*). 2. Similarly, we hear chord progressions (likewise melodies, which of course, following the first principle, represent chords in their simplest form) as a unitary relationship maintained with a principal chord (Rameau's *centre harmonique*, the tonic triad), against whose background the other chords are clearly understood and harmonically *related*" [1. *Wir hören Töne stets als Vertreter von Klängen*, d. h. konsonanten Akkorden, deren es nur zwei Arten gibt, nämlich den *Durakkord* (Oberklang) und *Mollakkord* (Unterklang). 2. *Akkordfolgen* (desgleichen Melodien, welche ja nach diesem Prinzip Akkordfolgen in einfachster Form darstellen) hören wir in ähnlicher Weise als eine Einheitsbeziehung auf einen Hauptklang (Rameaus *Centre harmonique*, die *Tonika*) wahrend, gegen welchem die andern Klänge wohlverständlich mit welchem sie harmonisch *verwandt* sind].[10] The major and minor scales are viewed as the result of disassembling the tonic, dominant, and subdominant chords into their constituent tones; the scale is secondary—a consequence, not a basis. The chordal context is independent of the scale.

As an extreme consequence of the hypothesis that the perfect fifth and major third establish "directly intelligible" tone and chord relationships there results the assertion that the A♭-major and E-major triads can be related directly to a C-major tonic. As an analog of the chord progression C–F–C–G–C, there appears C–A♭–C–E–C. "Hence the C-major tonality prevails as long as the harmonies are understood in their orientation to the C-major chord. For example, the admittedly audacious but effective and euphonious progression shown below

Example 1

defies definition in terms of an older doctrine of key. But in terms of a C-major tonality, it consists of the tonic triad, counter third-chord, tonic triad, plain third-chord, and tonic triad. That is, it consists only of closely related chords contrasted with the tonic triad" [So ist also die C-dur-Tonalität herrschend, solange die Harmonien in ihrer Stellung zum C-dur-Akkord verstanden werden; z. B. ist die zwar kühne, aber kräftige und wohlklingende Folge: (ex. 1), im Sinne einer Tonart älterer Lehre gar nicht zu definieren; im Sinne der C-dur-Tonalität ist sie: Tonika—Gegenterzklang—Tonika—schlichter Terzklang—Tonika, d. h. es sind der Tonika nur nah verwandte Klänge gegenübergestellt].[11] But the direct "third-relation" postulated by Riemann implies nothing short of suspending the distinction between diatonicism and chromaticism. If, in contrast to Riemann, one clung to the distinction, it would then be necessary to interpret the A♭-major chord as the parallel of the minor subdominant, and the E-major chord as a chromatic alteration of the dominant parallel. The A♭-major chord would be based on a "change of diatonic system" (an exchange of the C-minor for the C-major scale), while the E-major chord would be based on a chromatic alteration of the C-major scale. By contrast, an A♭-major or E-major chord related directly to C major is neither diatonic nor chromatic—the distinction is abolished. And it is in this suspension of diatonicism as the basis of chordal relationships that Riemann saw the distinctive feature of "tonality," as opposed to the "older doctrine of key" founded on the diatonic scale.

This is in glaring contrast to Fétis, who saw the prerequisite for tonality in the diatonic scale. "Tonality," wrote Fétis, "is formed from the set of requisite relationships, simultaneous or successive, among the tones of the scale."[12] To be sure, Fétis's account of the relationship between tonality and scale is contradictory, or at least appears to be. On the one hand, tonality is the "regulating principle" (*principe régulateur*) of relationships among tones: "Now the regulating principle of the relationships among tones, whether in the successive or simultaneous category, is generally designated by the name of tonality" [Or, le principe régulateur des rapports des sons, dans l'ordre successif et dans l'ordre simultané, se désigne en général par le nom de tonalité].[13] On the other hand, tonality "results" from the scale: "That which I call tonality is then the system of melodic and harmonic events that results from the arrangement of tones in our major and minor scales" [Ce que j'appelle la tonalité, c'est donc l'ordre de faits mélodiques et harmoniques que résulte de la disposition des sons de nos gammes majeure et mineure].[14] And a founding principle of tonal relationship— in addition to the scale—is also seen in the opposition between dominant seventh chord and triad, between "*tendance*" and "*repos*."[15] These contradictions are not, however, irresolvable. The various definitions of tonality, all of them well founded, come into conflict because they are formulated as if each were comprehensive, while in reality they constitute mere portions of a larger definition, a definition that Fétis had in mind but did not articulate. That is, *tonalité*—more precisely *tonalité moderne*—is a historically and ethnically conditioned way of hearing that comprehends tone and chord relationships under the categories of *tendance* and *repos*. It is most clearly marked in the contrast between dominant seventh chord and tonic triad, a contrast that stands in reciprocal relationship to the restriction of scales to major and minor. If Fétis alternately "defines" tonality as the result of historical and ethnic conditions (*le principe métaphysique*), as the relationships among tones (*les rapports nécessaires des sons*), as the contrast between dominant seventh chord and tonic, and as the major and minor scales, it is not that he involves himself in objective contradictions. Rather, he makes use of a rhetorical figure, claiming a part as the whole.

4. "If one asks," wrote Riemann, "wherein properly lies the task of a theory of art, then the answer can only be that it must fathom the selfsame natural lawfulness that consciously or unconsciously rules the creation of art and set it forth in a system of logically coherent theorems" [Fragt man sich worin eigentlich die Aufgabe der Theorie einer Kunst bestehe, so kann die Antwort nur lauten, daß dieselbe die natürliche Gesetzmäßigkeit, welche das Kunstschaffen bewußt oder unbewußt regelt, zu ergründen und in einem System logisch zusammenhängender Lehrsätze darzulegen habe].[16] The "system of logically coherent theorems" that Riemann had in mind is the theory of functions, and he had no doubt but that the "natural lawfulness" discerned through his theory was also "intuitively comprehended"[17] in ancient and medieval times, of course without becoming unambiguously formulated. "Even the simple monophonic melody set down in the preserved monuments of ancient art rests completely on a harmonic foundation" [Auch die einstimmige, einfache Melodie, wie sie in den erhaltenen Denkmälern antiker Kunst vorliegt, beruht durchaus auf harmonischer Grundlage].[18]

Fétis was more cautious. He mentioned different "*types de tonalités*"[19] without attempting to reduce them to a single principle. And in remarking about the "major scale of the Chinese" and the "minor scale of the Irish," he said, "Our harmonic progressions would be impracticable in these tonalities" [Les successions de notre harmonie deviendront inexécutables dans ces tonalités].[20] Still, for Fétis, just as for Riemann, *tonalité moderne* is the only system whose tonal relationships he could experience as "requisite." For him, even the *tonalité ancienne* of the 16th century was foreign and incomprehensible. To be sure, he defined *tonalité ancienne* as the "uni-tonic order" [*ordre unitonique*] and *tonalité moderne* as the "trans-tonic order" [*ordre transitonique*].[21] But the appearance that this definition is based on an explanation of *tonalité ancienne* is an illusion. The antithesis is incorrectly formulated, in fact even under Fétis's own assumptions.

For Fétis, the features of *tonalité moderne* are, first, the dominant seventh chord, and second, the method of using sixth chords to mark the half-step degrees 3 and 7 of the major scale as *notes de tendance*.

The definition of *tonalité moderne* as the "trans-tonic order" means no more than that the dominant seventh chord, which establishes the key, is at the same time a means for introducing a modulation. Thus *tonalité moderne* can be "trans-tonic," but need not be. As the earliest document of *tonalité moderne*, Fétis cites mm. 9–19 and 24–30 of Monteverdi's madrigal *Cruda amarilli*: "In the passage quoted here from Monteverdi's madrigal, one sees a tonality determined by the characteristic of the *accord parfait* on the tonic, by the sixth chord assigned to the third and seventh degrees, by the optional choice of the *accord parfait* or the sixth chord on the sixth degree, and finally, by the *accord parfait* and, above all, by the unprepared seventh chord (with major third) on the dominant" [On voit, dans le passage ici rapporté du madrigal de Monteverde, une tonalité déterminée par la propriété de l'accord parfait sur la tonique, par l'accord de sixte attribué au troisième et au septième degré, par la choix facultatif de l'accord parfait ou de l'accord de sixte sur la sixième; enfin, par l'accord parfait, et surtout par celui de septième sans préparation, avec la tierce majeure, sur la dominante].[22] Fétis characterizes *tonalité ancienne*, the harmonic language of Palestrina, only in a negative fashion—as a deviation from the norms of *tonalité moderne*. Since the dominant seventh chord is missing and the sixth chord is employed arbitrarily, it suffers from a lack of "*tendance*" and "*attraction*."[23] "There one finds nothing but a succession of mutually independent *accords parfaits*" [On n'y trouve qu'une suite d'accords parfaits indépendants les uns des autres].[24] The distinction that Fétis has in mind, but does not express, is that between what is well defined and what is undefined. *Tonalité ancienne*, as Fétis understands it, is vague, not "uni-tonic"; and the strongly outlined and, by means of the dominant seventh chord, unequivocally defined *tonalité moderne* can be either "trans-tonic" or "uni-tonic." Whether the key is varied, or a single key is maintained, is a secondary characteristic that Fétis interpreted as a primary one in order to formulate the antithesis between "trans-tonic" and "uni-tonic" and to avoid the admission that he was unable to define *tonalité ancienne*.

. . .

Nothing could be more wrong than to see the antitheses between Riemann and Fétis—the contrast between a "natural" and a "historico-ethnic" foundation of tonality, between the deduction of tonal contexts from "affinities between tones" and the appeal to the opposition of *tendance* and *repos*, between the claim of a comprehensive theory and the restriction of a theory to a limited range of applicability—as dead issues from the past. Three important questions remain problematical today: first, whether a "natural" foundation of harmonic tonality is possible; second, whether only chordal relationships, or also pitch relationships not based on chordal associations, should be termed "tonal"; and third, whether the centering of tone or chord relationships on a tonic pitch or triad should be considered an essential or incidental feature of tonality.

1. To avoid misunderstandings, one must differentiate the various aspects of Fétis's thesis that tonality is a "purely metaphysical principle" independent of natural constraints. He would not deny that consonance—more precisely, the ranking of intervals according to their degree of consonance—is a fact of nature and not merely the result of a "convention" [Setzung]. But according to Fétis, only the disposition of intervals falls under the concept of tonality, not their independent existence and individual characteristics. Not the fourth per se, but only the placement and function of the fourth in a scale is a "tonal" phenomenon. "The mathematical division of a string and the numerical ratios that determine intervallic proportions are powerless to form a musical scale because, in their numerical operations, intervals occur as isolated facts without requisite connections among themselves, and without anything that determines the order in which they should be linked together; whence he (Fétis) concluded that every gamut or musical scale is the product of a metaphysical law born of certain human needs or circumstances" [La division mathématique d'une corde et les rapports de nombres par lesquels se déterminent les proportions des intervalles, sont impuissants à former une échelle musicale, parce que, dans ses opérations numériques, les intervalles se présentent comme des faits isolés, sans liaison nécessaire entre eux, et sans que rien détermine l'ordre dans lequel ils doivent être enchaînés; d'où il conclut que toute gamme ou échelle musicale est le produit d'une loi méta-physique, né de certains besoins ou de certaines circonstances relatives à l'homme].[25] The perfect fifth and major third are facts of nature, but "isolated facts"; the connection of "isolated facts" depends on a "metaphysical law." By "metaphysics," Fétis means nothing more than anthropology: "Thus he (Fétis) came to see that the lascivious dis-positions of Oriental peoples gave birth to the small intervals of their languorous songs; that the discouragement of enslaved peoples created minor scales among them all" [C'est ainsi, qu'il fit voir que les dispositions lascives des peuples orientaux ont donné naissance aux petits intervalles de leur chants langoureux; que le découragement des peuples asservis a fit naître chez tous les gammes mineures].[26] To Riemann's system Fétis would object that although the perfect fifth and major third are "directly intelligible" intervals, even facts of nature, the decision to base a system upon them is still "metaphysical."

The "Lipps-Meyer law"[27] and Jacques Handschin's theory of "tone association" [*Tongesellschaft*] should be understood as attempts, based on the nature of acoustics or cognition, to account not just for the "isolated facts" but also for their "requisite connections."

a) The "Lipps-Meyer law" purports that the impression of closure, the "effect of finality," of a melodic interval depends on "whether or not the end tone of the interval can be represented by the number two or a power of two" [ob der Zielton des Intervalls durch die Zahl 2 bzw. eine Potenz von ihr repräsentiert wird oder nicht].[28] The law attributes an "effect of finality" to the melodic progressions **g–c**, **e–c**, **d–c**, and **B–c**, and an "effect of indicated continuation" to their inversions **c–g**, **c–e**, **c–d**, and **c–B**. The representatives of the number 2 are the lower tones of the perfect fifth (**c–g** = 2:3), the major third (**c–e** = 4:5), and the whole step (**c–d** = 8:9), and the upper tone of the diatonic half step in "just" intonation (**B–c** = 15:16). According to the Lipps-Meyer law, the Ionian, or major, mode is "natural," the Phrygian "artificial"; the Ionian tonic draws to itself "effects of finality" (**g–c**, **e–c**, **d–c**, and **B–c**), while that of the Phrygian "effects of indicated continuation" (**d–e**, **f–e**, **a–e**, **c–e**). Hence the Lipps-Meyer law implies a "natural" foundation for the major mode. The question must be left open, however, whether the law is a natural law of musical cognition, or whether, as a result of experiments with subjects brought up in the tradition of major-mode tonality, it assumes the very tonality it seems to prove. And even an attempt to support this law with historical arguments would be difficult, if not futile. From the 14th through the 16th century, it was possible to have not only the Ionian clausula

, to which the Lipps-Meyer law attributes an "effect of

finality," but also the Phrygian clausula , which according to

the same law has the character of "indicated continuation." Yet the presumption that the Phrygian clausula was perceived as a weaker cadence would be a historically relevant hypothesis only if there were special historical circumstances that it would be in a position to explain.

b) According to Jacques Handschin,[29] the set of seven diatonic pitches represents a closed system founded on the interval of a perfect fifth. A tone's position in the **F–c–g–d′–a′–e″–b″** circle of fifths determines its special character, the character of e being more like that of a or b than that of c or f. Thus the property of a tone that Handschin terms its "character" [*Charakter*] is an embodiment of relationships. The character of a tone is, as it were, its internalized position in the system, or conversely, its position in the system is the externalized representation of a tone's character. Handschin, however, defines a tone's character not only in terms of form, as a correlate of its position in the system, but also in terms of content—the "lower" tones of the circle of fifths, **F**, **c**, and **g**, are "steadier, more affirmative" [*gesetzter, affirmativer*] than the "upper" tones **a'**, **e"**, and **b"**.[30] And this characterization of inherent content implies a "natural" foundation for the major mode.

F, c, and g are the roots, a, e, and b the thirds, of the subdominant, tonic, and dominant triads in C major. For Handschin, major-mode tonality thus provides a striking illustration of the natural property of f, c, and g to be "steadier, more affirmative" than a, e, and b.[31] In C major, of course, a is directly related to f as a harmonic third, not indirectly as a tone four fifths away. And Handschin's interpretation of the major mode would be self-contradictory if it presumed that the tones' characters were bound solely to a conception of the diatonic set as a circle of fifths. Yet it seems that the difference between the **F–c–g–d'–a'–e"–b"** system of fifths and the **F–A–c–e–g–b–d'** system of fifths and thirds would not alter the fact that the similarity or dissimilarity in tone characters still depends on the proximity or remoteness of the tones in the series of fifths. Even in C major, which takes for granted the **F–A–c–e–g–b–d'** system of fifths and thirds, the chordal thirds a and e are more alike in their "characters" than the chordal third a and the subdominant root f. Thus the fifth-third system of tone relationships and the fifth system of tone characters are not mutually exclusive.

Minor-mode tonality, however, turns tone characters into their opposites. The assertion would be paradoxical that, as chordal thirds in A minor, f and c are "steady and affirmative." To be sure, f and c are, in minor just as in major, more alike than f and d, or c and a. Their similarity, whose index is the interval of a fifth, remains. Yet it changes its inherent content. Accordingly, only the formal definition of a tone's character as its "internalized" position in the system is irrefutable. But if the definition of inherent content is abandoned, then at the same time the "natural" foundation of the major mode is invalidated.

2. When Hugo Riemann spoke of tonality, he had in mind the same phenomenon as did Fétis. But in contrast to Fétis, he was convinced that the *types de tonalités* could be reduced to a single principle—the schema of three chordal functions: tonic, dominant, and subdominant. Historians and ethnologists, shunning the forced contraints of systematization, rejected Riemann's thesis as empirically unsubstantiated dogma. And the realization that the validity of the three-function schema was limited to the harmony of the 17th through the 19th century resulted in the concept of tonality losing its firmly drawn outlines. Scholars could have either reverted to Fétis's term, which included all

types de tonalités, and abandoned Riemann's interpretation, or, conversely, clung to Riemann's equation of tonality with the three-function schema and designated as "tonal" only the harmony of the 17th through the 19th century. But since neither possibility was dropped, the term "tonality" became ambiguous.[32]

If confusion is to be avoided, one must differentiate "melodic" tonality from "harmonic" tonality. Relationships among tones need not be reducible to chordal contexts in order to fall under the concept of tonality.

On the other hand, the tonality defined by melodic categories, which preceded the chordally based, harmonic tonality of the 17th century, can be defined as "modality." And, when intended as the opposite of "modal," it may be permissible to shorten the expression "harmonically tonal" to just "tonal." The concept of "tonality" therefore not only encompasses that of "modality," but can also become its opposite.

3. It is uncertain, or seems to be, whether the centering of tone and chord relationships around a tonic pitch or triad should be considered an essential or an incidental feature of tonality. Renouncing the defining feature "centering" causes "tonality" to fade into a general designation for relationships among pitches. "Tonality" and "tonal system" [*Tonsystem*; can imply only a "tuning system"] become synonymous expressions (provided one does not conceive of "tonality" as an "inner principle," and "tonal system" as its "outward manifestation"). "Tonality undoubtedly means that it is possible to establish a system of relationships and interdependencies between the harmonies that inhabit the area of a sound language."[33] Yet first, it is superfluous to use a second term to label the circumstance already referred to by the expression "tonal system." And second, renouncing the defining feature "centering" leads to linguistic fussiness: one must supplement the term "tonality" with a postscript expressing that one means contexts of tones and chords based on a center, or instead, following a suggestion by Rudolf Reti, speak only of "tonicality."

The renunciation of "centering" is, of course, not as unmotivated as it seems. It is negatively based: in the aversion toward naming "atonal" those tone and chord relationships that do not group themselves around a center. To avoid having to speak of "atonality," one stretches the concept of tonality until it means no more than that tones form an association and are not randomly juxtaposed.

The dilemma appears unavoidable. If Edward E. Lowinsky characterizes the harmonic technique of many 16th-century madrigals as "triadic atonality,"[34] and means by the term that chords were linked together without being related to a center, then there should be no logical objection to his usage. Lowinsky, however, fails to recognize that "tonality" is not only a theoretical, but also a historical category. The tonality of the 16th century and that of the 19th century are stages in a coherent development. But the "atonality" of the 16th century is in no way connected with that of the 20th century. In contrast to the two "tonal" situations just mentioned, those Lowinsky named "atonal" form no relationship that justifies their inclusion under the same category. Transferred from the music of the 20th century to that of the 16th century, "atonality" becomes an omnibus and perplexing concept without objective content.

. . .

The conclusions can be summarized in a few sentences.

1. The expression "harmonic tonality," synonymous with Riemann's *Tonalität* and Fétis's *tonalité moderne*, signifies the representation of a key by means of associations among chords related to a center—a tonic triad.

2. It must remain an open question whether, or to what extent, harmonic tonality is based on the nature of music or of man. The theme of this study, the origin of harmonic tonality in 16th- and 17th-century polyphony, can be treated without having to decide whether the "origin" should be interpreted as an exclusively historical occurrence or as the expression of a situation already pointed out by nature.

3. The centering of relationships on a tonic triad is taken to be an essential feature of harmonic tonality. On the other hand, when it is absent one should not speak of "atonality." The phenomena that E. E. Lowinsky calls "atonal" are, as will be shown, based on a principle that can be defined positively, making the negative characterization superfluous.

A Digression on the Concept of Harmony

While "counterpoint" is a concept and technical term of musical composition, "harmony" is a term taken from philosophy and less denotes than interprets specifically musical relationships.

"Harmony" implies an agreement [*Zusammenstimmen*] of disparate or contrasted elements. Up to the 17th century (following the Pythagorean-Platonic tradition), scholars looked to numerical proportion to provide an explanation of, and basis for, harmony. In music, the concept of harmony has included, since the early Middle Ages:[1] (1) the combining of tones into a sequence of tones, or even groups of tones into a melody; (2) the agreement of the two tones in a dyad, or of the tones and intervals in a triad; (3) the connecting of dyads into an intervallic progression; (4) the relationship among the voices of a polyphonic composition; and (5) the joining together of chords into a chord progression.

1. In the early Middle Ages, the application of the term harmony to melody, *modulatio*, meant no more than that the distances between tones were understood to be rationally determinable intervals— *consonantiae*. "Harmony, or ʽαρμονία, is the regulated motion of tones and the consonance of many sounds" [Harmonia est modulatio vocum et consonantia plurium sonorum vel coaptatio ("coaptatio" being an Aristotelian coinage for the Greek ʽαρμονία)].[2] But in the 15th century, melodies were defined as harmony not only because their tones formed rational intervals, but also because a melody was to be composed of disparate, not similar, sequences of tones. The complement of *harmonia*—the combining of contrasted elements—is *varietas* [variety]. If Tinctoris, in his *Diffinitorium*, uses the expressions *harmonia* and *melodia* synonymously, and in his *Liber de arte contrapuncti*[3] forbids repetitions of like sequences of tones, then through these apparently unrelated formulations he is able to show two aspects of the same thing. It is crucial not only that there be an agreement of elements, but also that the agreeing elements be disparate.

2. Since the 13th century, the concept of harmony has also been applied to simultaneous combinations of tones. Anonymous 1, who relies on Franco's *Ars cantus mensurabilis* in almost all the sections of his treatise (but not in the following definition), defines *concordantia* [consonance] as a "harmony of two or more sounds extended for the same length of time" [harmonia duorum vel plurium sonorum in eodem tempore prolatorum].[4] Gafurius, writing in 1518, admits as harmony only consonances of three tones, not of two. But this restriction does not imply an anticipation of the concept of harmony "in the modern sense."[5] "Hence those who held consonance and harmony to be the same should be judged wrong. For although a harmony is a consonance, not every consonance forms a harmony. Consonance is begotten from a high and a low sound, but harmony is brought about by a high, a low, and also a medial sound" [Hinc falso sunt arbitrati qui conso- nantiam & harmoniam idem esse posuerunt. Nam quamquam harmonia consonantia est: omnis tamen consonantia non facit harmoniam. Con- sonantia namque ex acuto et gravi generatur sono: Harmonia vero ex acuto & gravi conficitur atque medio].[6] The narrowing of the concept of harmony would appear to have been necessary because Gafurius, in order to categorize three-tone consonances as perfect or imperfect, needed a third determining factor. In addition to the greater or lesser variety of the tones, and the simplicity or complexity of the numerical

proportions, he required the superiority of "harmonic" over "arithmetic" and "geometric" proportion. With the theory of proportions, one could mathematically prove the imperfection of the fourth-octave chord (the arithmetic proportion 4:3:2 [e.g., c–f–c'; the ratios represent string lengths]) and the perfection of the fifth-octave chord (the harmonic proportion 6:4:3 [e.g., c–g–c']). "From the arrangement of three tones according to the harmonic mean . . . is then produced a *melodia* which we properly call a harmony. This of course consists of two unequal consonances that are brought together out of dissimilar proportions (the larger proportion from the larger numbers, the smaller proportion from the smaller numbers [e.g., in the harmonic proportion mentioned above, c–g–c', the larger numbers 6 and 4 represent the larger interval, the fifth c–g; the smaller numbers 4 and 3 represent the smaller interval, the fourth g–c'.])" [Dispositis vero tribus chordis secundum harmonicam medietatem . . . ea tunc producetur melodia: quam proprie harmonicam uocamus. Haec nempe duabus consonantiis inaequalibus constat: quae ex dissimilibus proportionibus majore quidem majoribus numeris: minore minoribus: conducuntur].[7]

Yet this principle, if one measures it by the musical reality of 15th-century counterpoint, is open to a *reductio ad absurdum*. For in the first place, Gafurius is compelled to declare the octave-twelfth chord perfect (the harmonic proportion 6:3:2 [e.g., c–c'–g']); but the fifth-twelfth chord imperfect (the arithmetic proportion 3:2:1 [e.g., c–g–g']); and the double-octave chord totally defective, representing as it does the geometric proportion 4:2:1 [e.g., c–c'–c''] and being composed of like, not disparate, intervals (thus not satisfying the prerequisite of the concept of harmony). And in the second place, by ancient tradition the intervallic proportions are invertible: the lower tone could correspond to the larger, but also to the smaller, number. [Thus an arithmetic proportion in one system could be mathematically transformed into a harmonic proportion in another.]

3. The application of the concept of harmony to dyadic interval progressions can be observed in the *Tractatus de contrapunctu* (1412) of Prosdocimo de' Beldemandi. Prosdocimo permits the parallel voice leading of imperfect consonances but limits their use because a succession of thirds or sixths not interrupted and articulated by an octave or fifth would create a harshness contradicting the harmony (harmony being the principle of combining disparate or contrasted elements). "The fourth rule is this: that we ought not to make counterpoints with unbroken combinations of imperfect intervals (no combination with a perfect consonance being interposed), since this would then be hard to sing, because by itself it will be found to have no harmony at all, the harmony in which is seen to exist the aim of all music" [Quarta

regula est hoc, quod contrapunctare non debemus cum combinationibus imperfecte concordantibus continue, nullam combinationem perfecte consonantem interponendo, quum tunc ita durum esset hoc cantare, quod in ipso nulla penitus reperiretur armonia, que armonia finis totalis musice existere videtur].[8] What is new is not the prohibition of an unbroken succession of thirds or sixths, but rather basing the prohibition on an appeal to the concept of harmony. The regular alternation between perfect and imperfect consonances is taken as a rule of composition: "In singing, consonance and dissonance should alternate . . . We can perform two, three, or more dissonances, and then there should follow a consonance . . . Consonance and perfect consonance are the same, and dissonance and imperfect consonance are taken to be the same" [Semper una consonantia et altera dissonantia cantari debet . . . Possumus facere duas vel tres ad plus dissonantias et postea sequi debet consonantia . . . Consonantia et consonantia perfecta idem sunt, et dissonantia et consonantia imperfecta pro eodem habentur].[9]

4. The 16th-century concept of harmony, as can be gathered from Zarlino's use of the word, embraces all the factors of polyphonic composition: the combining of tones into a sequence of tones; the agreement of the two tones in a dyad; the connection between successive dyads; the compounding of dyads into a triad;[10] and the relationship among the melodies and rhythms of different voices. The main principle of, the origin of, and the point of departure for musical harmony is the rationally determinable interval. "Thus it is clear that if someone hears a composition that expresses nothing save harmony, he takes pleasure in it only through the proportion that is found in the distances between the instrumental or vocal tones" [Come è manifesto: che se alcuno ode una cantilena, che non esprime altro che l'Harmonia: piglia solamente piacere di essa, per la proportione, che se ritrova nelle distanze de i suoni, o voci].[11] The prerequisite of a *harmonia* is a *varietà* or *diversità* [diversity]. According to Zarlino, not only parallel perfect consonances but also parallel imperfect consonances of equal size violate the principle of *varietà*, and thus also that of *harmonia*. "Because they well knew that harmony can arise only from things diverse, discordant, and contrary among themselves, and not from those things that agree in every respect. Thus if harmony does arise from such a variety, it will be necessary that in music not only the parts of the composition be separated from each other in highness and lowness, but even that their melodies be different in their movements, and that they include various consonances composed of diverse proportions" [Conciosiache molto ben sapevano, che l'Harmonia non può nascere se non da cose tra loro diverse, discordanti et contrarie et non da quelle ch'in ogni cosa convengono. La onde se da tal varietà

nasce l'Harmonia sara dibisogna che nella Musica non solo le Parti della Cantilena siano distanti l'una dall'altra per il grave et per l'acuto me etiandio che le lor modulationi siano differenti ne i movimenti et che contenghino varie Consonanze contenuti da diverse proportioni].[12]

Both successive and simultaneous intervals are viewed as different manifestations of the same harmony. In his explication of the rule that a composer wishing to express *asprezza*, *durezza*, and *crudeltà* [asperity, harshness, and cruelty] through a "harmony" should use intervals without a half step, Zarlino mentions not only harmonic intervals like the major thirteenth, but also melodic intervals like the whole tone.[13] And even rhythm is subsumed under the concept of harmony in the definition of counterpoint as a "type of harmony that contains in itself diverse variations of instrumental or vocal tones, with a sure law of proportions and measure of time" [modo di Harmonia, che contenghi in se diverse variationi di suoni, o di voci cantabili, con certa ragione di proportioni et misura di tempo].[14] The syntactic construction *non solamente*, *ma anco* [not only, but also] is characteristic of Zarlino's thought. And his concept of harmony, which embraces all the factors of composition, admits of no one-sided interpretations that allude to a precedence of voice leading or chord progressions, of dyads or triads.

5. D'Alembert, Rameau's exegete, termed as "harmony" not individual chords but their combination. "The mixture of several tones heard at the same time is called a *chord*; and harmony is properly a series of chords that, by their succession, please the ear" [On appele accord le mélange de plusieurs sons qui se font entendre à-la-fois; et l'harmonie est proprement une suite d'accords qui en se succédant flattent l'organe].[15] Consonance and dissonance are apparently intended to be the contrasted factors that unite into a harmony, for the change of chordal quality is one of the basic factors of tonal relationship in Rameau's system. The dominant and subdominant are primarily defined as chordal types, not as degrees of a key (V and IV). Every seventh chord is a *dominante*, every triad with a *sixte ajoutée* [added sixth, e.g., f–a–c′–d′], a *sousdominante* [subdominant]. The direct connection to the tonic is the feature by which one distinguishes a *dominante tonique* (V^7) from a *simple dominante* not immediately followed by the tonic (ii^7 and vi^7). The tonic is the goal and result of a resolution of dissonance, not a presupposed relational center: the seventh of the *dominante tonique*, by a descending step, and the *sixte ajoutée* of the *sousdominante*, by an ascending step, are both resolved to the third of the tonic triad. The unity of a key presented through chords is thus a harmony that arises out of an opposition, out of the contrast between a dissonant *dominante* or *sousdominante* and a consonant *tonique*.

ROOT PROGRESSION AND KEY

The fact that Jean-Philippe Rameau is the founder of modern harmonic theory seems so unequivocally established that one would attribute any doubt about it to a desire for paradox. "Rameau seized the initiative for the new treatment of harmonic theory as a theory of the significance of harmonies for the logic of musical composition. This honor remains his in any case, even if his system must be characterized as being in no way complete" [Die Initiative für die neue Behandlung der Harmonielehre als einer Lehre von der Bedeutung der Harmonien für die Logik des Tonsatzes ergriff Rameau; dieser Ruhm bleibt ihm auf alle Fälle, wenn auch sein System als ein keineswegs abgeschlossenes bezeichnet werden muß].[1] Both the theory of fundamental progressions and the theory of functions arose from fragments of the system outlined by Rameau. Yet the distinctive feature of Rameau's theory is neither the concept of fundamental progressions nor that of functions. Rather, it is the idea that chords, in order to form an association, must be linked by dissonances. And it is doubtful whether a theory that develops the "logic of musical composition" out of the simple opposition of dissonance and consonance represents a true theory of harmony in the 19th-century sense.

Rameau's fundamental idea is taken to be the reduction of all chords to triads and seventh chords—the differentiation of a *basse fondamentale* from the actual lowest voice, the *basse continue* [thoroughbass]. The *centre harmonique* of a chord is the lowest tone in its stack of thirds. "The basis of harmony resides not merely in the perfect chord, from which the seventh chord is formed, but even more precisely in the lowest tone of these two chords, which is, so to speak, the harmonic center to which all the other tones should be related" [Le principe de l'Harmonie ne subsiste pas seulement dans l'Accord parfait, dont se forme celuy de Septiéme; mais encore plus précisément dans le Son grave de ces deux Accords, qui est, pour ainsi dire, le *Centre harmonique*, auquel tous les autres Sons doivent se rapporter].[2] The progression of chordal roots—*centres harmoniques*—forms a *basse fondamentale* distinct from the actual bass voice (the *basso continuo*). And it is the *basse fondamentale* that must be understood as the hidden foundation of harmonic progression.

That the principle of chordal inversion had been anticipated in the 17th century by Johann Lippius,[3] Thomas Campion,[4] and Heinrich Baryphonus,[5] and in the early 18th century by Saint-Lambert[6] and Roger North,[7] is of little or at least of secondary importance—only through Rameau did it force its way into the general consciousness.

What is crucial is not that the idea was already old, but that in Rameau's theory it forms a dependent cofactor that cannot be plucked out of the context in which it is situated. The "tertian structure of chords," according to Hugo Riemann "the true system of Rameau the constructivist theorist" [das eigentliche System des konstruktiven Theoretikers Rameau],[8] is explained with a reserve that reveals that the principle of inversion is not self-substantiated, but obtains its meaning only from the system into which it fits. Both Rameau's confusions and the eventual disintegration of his system into antithetical theories—those of fundamental progressions and functions—are based on the difficulty of adequately representing a system of interrelated cofactors. "To make things more familiar, one may for the time being consider thirds as the sole elements of all chords: thus to form a perfect chord one third must be added to another, and to form all the dissonant chords three or four thirds must be added to one another" [Pour se rendre les choses plus familieres, l'on peut regarder à present les *Tierces* comme l'unique objet de tous les accords: En effet, pour former *l'accord parfait*, il faut ajoûter une *Tierce* à l'autre, & pour former tous les *accords dissonans*, il faut ajoûter trois ou quatre *Tierces* les unes aux autres].[9]

Rameau's system stems not from a rigid axiom, but from the notion that tonal harmony is based on the correlations between the resolutions of dissonance, the progressions of the fundamental bass, the meanings of chords, and the scale degrees of a key. In Rameau's presentation it remains an open question which of the factors (different aspects of the same thing according to Rameau) ought to be considered primary and fundamental. But this issue need not be resolved, because the essential feature of his system is the correlation of factors and not their unfolding from a single principle. Attempts to emphasize certain isolated components—the concept of the fundamental bass, or the categories of tonic, dominant, and subdominant—and to dismiss other components as incidental both miss and distort the sense of Rameau's theory.

The *double emploi* of the six-five chord **f–a–c′–d′** in C major is an exemplary case of the correlation that Rameau has in mind. The dissonance **c′–d′** is ambiguous. One can treat **c′** as a dissonant suspension resolving to **b**, or regard **d′** as a passing tone incorporated into the chord and continuing on to **e′**. The determination of the fundamental bass depends on the resolution of the dissonance. According to Rameau, a regular progression of the fundamental bass is by fifth or fourth, an irregular progression by second. "The real heart of composition, whether as regards harmony or melody, is chiefly (and above all for the time being) to be found in that bass which we term 'fundamental.' The bass should therefore proceed by consonant intervals, which are those of the third, the fourth, the fifth, and the sixth; so that each note of the fundamental bass can ascend or descend only by one of these intervals" [Le grand noeud de la Composition, soit pour l'Harmonie, soit pour la Melodie, consiste principalement & sur tout pour le present, dans la Basse, que nous appellons *Fondamentale*, & qui doit proceder en ce cas, par des Intervales consonans, qui sont ceux de *la Tierce*, de *la Quarte*, de *la Quinte*, et de *la Sixte*; sibien que l'on ne peut faire monter ni descendre chaque Notte de la Basse-fondamentale que par l'un de ces Intervales].[10] In consequence, Rameau bases the resolution 𝄢 on the root progression **d–g**, the resolution 𝄢 on the root progression **f–c**.

The resolution of dissonance and the progression of the fundamental bass determine a chord's meaning. In Rameau's system, a *dominante* is a seventh chord followed by a descending fifth in the fundamental bass (**d–G**); a *sousdominante* is a triad with an added sixth (*sixte ajoutée*) followed by an ascending fifth or a descending fourth in the fundamental bass (**f–c**). As an inversion of the seventh chord on the second degree, the six-five chord **f–a–c′–d′** is thus a *dominante*; as a triad on the fourth degree with *sixte ajoutée*, it is a *sousdominante*. "Only the tonic note supports the perfect or natural chord; the seventh is added to this chord in order to form dominants, and the major sixth to form subdominants. There is but a single tonic note in each mode or key; there is, moreover, but a single subdominant; and every other note of the fundamental bass is a dominant" [La seule Note tonique porte l'Accord parfait, ou naturel; on ajoute la Septième a cet Accord pour les Dominantes, & la Sixte majeure pour les Soudominantes. // Il n'y a qu'une seule Note tonique dans chaque Mode ou Ton; il n'y a, non plus, qu'une seule Soudominante; & toute autre Note de la Basse fondamentale est Dominante].[11] Chordal meaning and chordal degree do not necessarily coincide. There can be a *sousdominante* on the fourth degree, but also on the first degree.[12] And *dominantes* appear on the fifth, second, sixth, third, and even fourth degrees.[13] Rameau labels the seventh chord on the fifth degree the *dominante-tonique* to distinguish it from the other *dominantes*. "We shall distinguish the dominant of a tonic by the epithet 'tonic-dominant,' so that otherwise the single word 'dominant' will simply mean a dominant of another dominant" [Nous distinguerons la Dominante d'une Tonique par l'épithéte de *Dominante-tonique*; de sorte qu'autrement, le mot seul de *Dominante* signifiera simplement

une Dominante d'une autre Dominante].[14] Hence Rameau defines the
dominante and *sousdominante* not primarily in terms of tonality, but
in terms of compositional technique—as chordal types requiring a
specific resolution of dissonance and a corresponding progression of the
fundamental bass.

In Rameau's system, just as in the theories of fundamental progressions and of functions, the burden of establishing the key still falls
on chords. But in the presentation of a key, chords unite not as
representatives of fundamental progressions or of functions, but as links
in a chain of dissonances terminating in a consonance. The prototype
of an unbroken chord progression is the circle of seventh chords in
which the resolution of one dissonance coincides with the exposition
of another.

Example 2

"*A–A–A, D–E–F, S–T*: Evaded perfect cadences, in that neither the
false fifth nor the tritone is found in the first chord, that is, between
the third and the seventh of the note in the fundamental bass" [A.
A. A. D. E. F. S. T. Cadences parfaites évitées, en ce que la

fausse-Quinte ny le Triton ne se trouvent point dans le premier accord, entre la Tierce et la Septiéme de la Notte qui est à la Basse fondamentale]. The *cadences* are *parfaites* because of the descending fifth in the fundamental bass, *évitées* [evaded] because of the seventh in the second chord. The fundamental bass of chord *S*, the supposed third **D**, is an imagined root, not a real one [*supposition* connotes both abstract "imagining" and concrete "placing under"]. To make the chord progression *S–T* seem convincing, Rameau supposed the regular fifth-progression **D–G** under the irregular second-progression **F–G**.

"*B–C, O–P, R–S*: Deceptive cadences evaded by means of a seventh added to the second tone of the fundamental bass, that is, to notes *C*, *P*, and *S*. *B–C, R–S*: Perfect cadences evaded by means of a sixth added to the second tone of the thoroughbass" [B. C. O. P. R. S. Cadences rompuës évitées par Septiéme ajoûtée à la seconde Notte de la Basse fondamentale, c'est à dire aux Nottes C.P. et S.// B. C. R. S. Cadences parfaites évitées par une Sixte ajoûtée à la seconde Notte de la Basse continuë]. Rameau gives the *cadences B–C* and *R–S* dual and seemingly contradictory interpretations. On the one hand, they are deceptive cadences (C–d [V–vi]) with added sevenths (**c″** over **d**), on the other, authentic cadences (C–F [V–I]) with *sixtes ajoutées* (**d″** over **f**). Yet the actual circumstance that Rameau had in mind is unambiguous, even though he failed to articulate it clearly. When referred to the preceding chords *B* and *R*, *C* and *S* are triads with *sixtes ajoutées* (fundamental bass progression **C–F**). But in relation to the succeeding chords *D* and *T* they are seventh chords (fundamental bass progression **D–G**).

"*C–D*: Evaded deceptive cadence, in that neither the false fifth nor the tritone is to be found in the first chord of the fundamental bass, and that the seventh is added to the perfect chord on the note *D*" [C. D. Cadence rompuë évitée, en ce que la fausse-Quinte ny le Triton ne se rencontrent point dans le premier accord de la Basse fondamentale, & que la Septiéme est ajoûtée à l'Accord parfait de la Notte D]. The term *septième ajoutée* [added seventh] here means the tone **e**, not **d″**, because while **g′–b♭′–d″** is an *accord parfait*, **e–g′–b♭′** is not. Thus in relation to chord *C*, chord *D* is a triad with a supposed third (fundamental bass progression **D–G**), but when related to *E*, it is a seventh chord (fundamental bass progression **E–A**).[15]

It is the principle of the linkage of dissonance that distinguishes Rameau's theory from 19th-century theories of harmony. In these later theories, the hypothesis that a chord progression such as I–vi–ii–V–I establishes a key scarcely need be expressed, because the point is taken for granted. Rameau, however, left open the question of how one should understand a juxtaposition of simple triads. It even seems that he might interpret two triads not linked by a dissonance and its resolution as the tonic triads of different keys. "Every note that supports a perfect chord should be considered a tonic; thus one could say that in our first examples of the perfect chord there are as many different keys as there are notes [in the fundamental bass]" [Toute Notte qui porte *l'Accord parfait*, doit être regardée comme *Notte tonique*; ainsi l'on peut dire que dans nos premiers Exemples de *l'Accord parfait*, autant de Nottes, autant de *Tons* differens].[16] Of course the assertion that two simple triads represent two different keys is not made without some hesitation. And to avoid misunderstanding Rameau, one must bear in mind that the connecting dissonances need not actually be present in a composition, but can be added by the musical imagination. "Relative to what follows it, a tonic note can become whatever one wants; so that having arrived as if at a tonic, one can immediately name it the dominant or subdominant of that which follows it, even adding in the dissonance suitable at that point, though that is unnecessary—it is enough that the dissonance be implied" [Une Note-tonique peut devenir ce qu'on veut, relativement à ce qui la suit; de sorte qu'y étant arrivé comme à une Tonique, on peut l'appeler sur le champ Dominante ou Soudominante de ce qui la suit, en y ajoutant même la Dissonance qui lui convient pour lors, quoique cela ne soit pas nécessaire; il suffit de l'y sousentendre].[17] The absurd notion that the chord progression I–vi–ii–V–I implies a quadruple change of key can thus be avoided by means of simultaneously conceived [*mitgedachte*], tacitly implied dissonances, that is, by interpreting the progression as I–vi⁷–ii⁷–V⁷–I.

The recourse to imagined dissonances should be understood as a speculative hypothesis, not as the description of a musical reality. A musical reality includes, of course, not only actual pitches but also additional elements that are to be jointly heard without necessarily being acoustically present. Nevertheless, a supposed third (**d**) under the F-major chord *would* be hypothetically speculative. It does not have to be jointly heard, but need only be taken into consideration during analysis in order to comprehend why the F-major chord forms a convincing association with the following G-major chord. In his *Nouveau système*, Rameau cites the cadence I–V–I–IV–I–V–I (which he analyzes mathematically) in a simple, dissonance-free form.[18] And if it can be concluded from the mathematical demonstration that Rameau already saw the dissonance-free cadence as a paradigm of tonal harmony, the appeal to imagined dissonances does not imply doubt over whether triads as such *can* cohere. Rather, it appears as a speculative hypothesis meant to explain *why* they cohere. Therefore Rameau's notion of imagined dissonance, which would appear to involve a misunderstanding of the founding principle of tonal harmony [i.e., that triads form a context that establishes a key], ought, on the contrary, to be understood as a confirmation—or an attempt at a confirmation—of this principle.

Rameau does not expressly state that an imagined dissonance can be understood as a hypothetical factor and need not be deemed real or jointly heard. Yet this view can be indirectly inferred from his analysis of the following chord progression based on the *regola dell'ottava* [rule of the octave].[19]

Example 3

In the second measure, Rameau interprets the first-inversion C-major chord as a fragment of a seventh chord on **A** so that by a resolution of dissonance and a fifth-progression of the imagined *basse fondamentale* (**A–d**) he can link together the chords over **e** and **f** in the thoroughbass. According to Rameau's version of the figured bass, however, the resolution of the dissonance is irregular: the seventh (**g′**) over the imagined bass (**A**) progresses upward to the octave **a′** instead of downward to **f′**. And his apparent indifference toward an illegal resolution of dissonance may serve as an indication that Rameau understood an imagined, tacitly implied dissonance to be a conceptualized tone that did not have to be jointly heard.

Whether Rameau's theory is a theory of harmony in the 19th-century sense thus depends on the interpretation of imagined dissonances. A traditional component of Rameau's theory, the factor of linking chords by dissonances, is based on the principle of the variation of intervallic quality. And one of the basic ideas of contrapuntal theory from the 14th through the 17th century is that the variation of intervallic quality—the tendency of dissonance toward consonance, or of imperfect consonance toward perfect consonance—forms the driving force behind music's forward motion. A chain of sixths striving toward the perfection of an octave differs of course in degree, but not in principle, from Rameau's progression of seventh chords whose goal is a triad—an *accord parfait.*

On the other hand, the basic idea of the theory of harmony—the notion that triads as such, independent of the dissonances by which they might be linked, form a context that establishes a key—is only faintly expressed in Rameau's system. And to conceive of Rameau's theory as a theory of harmony one must give a speculative twist to the concept of imagined dissonance. The new and the old are therefore jointly entwined in Rameau's system. The traditional principle of contrapuntal theory, the variation of intervallic quality, fades from being a manifest factor of compositional technique to one that is imagined and tacitly implied—to a hypothesis that makes comprehensible the new and at first vaguely delineated principle of the theory of harmony, that of the tonal relationship between triads.

. . .

Hugo Riemann's thesis that Rameau was the founder of the theory of harmonic functions is based on a misconception. And it might not be superfluous to point out that the thesis is flawed, since it has been almost universally accepted, if not in every particular then at least in its main features.

1. Riemann[20] cites a sentence from the *Nouveau système* of 1726 to demonstrate that, in the seventh chord on the dominant and the six-five chord on the subdominant, Rameau had discerned "both of the only basic harmonies (besides the tonic) that exist for tonal logic" [beiden neben der tonischen allein für die tonale Logik existierenden Grundharmonien]: "We recognize only the dominant and subdominant as fundamental tones in the modulation from a given main tone, which, moreover, can exist as such only by means of its pure and perfect harmony" [Nous ne connaissons que la *Dominante* & la *Sous-dominante* pour Sons fondamentaux dans la *Modulation* d'un *Son principal* donné, qui d'ailleurs ne peut subsister comme tel qu'avec son harmonie pure et parfaite].[21] In his *Génération harmonique* of 1737, Rameau reiterates this thesis: "There are only three fundamental tones: the tonic, its dominant (which is its upper fifth), and its subdominant (which is its lower fifth, or simply its fourth)" [Il n'y a que trois Sons fondamentaux, la *Tonique*, sa *Dominante*, qui est sa Quinte au-dessus, & sa *Sous-dominante*, qui est sa Quinte au-dessous, ou simplement sa Quarte].[22] But the continuation of this passage indicates that Rameau, in contrast to Riemann, understood the term *dominante* to apply to seventh chords on all degrees, not just the fifth degree. "Only the tonic note supports the perfect or natural chord; the seventh is added to this chord in order to form dominants, and the major sixth to form subdominants. There is but a single tonic note in each mode or key; there is, moreover,

but a single subdominant; and every other note of the fundamental bass is a dominant" [La seule Note tonique porte l'Accord parfait, ou naturel; on ajoute la Septième a cet Accord pour les Dominantes, & la Sixte majeure pour les Sousdominantes. // Il n'y a qu'une seule Note tonique dans chaque Mode ou Ton; il n'y a, non plus, qu'une seule Soudominante; & toute autre Note de la Basse fondamentale est Dominante].[23] The *dominante* and the *sousdominante* are defined as chordal types, not as degrees or functions. And in Rameau's system, the thesis that the tonic, dominant, and subdominant establish a key means that in order to unite into a progression, chords must form a chain of dissonances that terminates in a consonance—the *accord parfait* of the *note tonique*.

2. "More than likely Rameau had already taken up even the concept of apparent consonance [*Scheinkonsonanz*]. Unfortunately, he neglected to express his thoughts on these 'secondary harmonies' in greater detail" [Es is mehr als wahrscheinlich daß Rameau auch der Begriff der Scheinkonsonanz bereits aufgegangen war; leider hat er es unterlassen, sich ausführlicher zu äußern, wie er über die 'Nebenharmonien' denkt].[24] According to Riemann, the chords on the second, third, and sixth degrees are "apparent consonances." The chord on the second degree in C major, **d–f–a**, consists of the root and third of the subdominant (**f** and **a**), and a sixth (**d**) that, as a dissonance, replaces the consonant fifth of the subdominant harmony. In Riemann's "harmonic logic," a chord on the second degree, the subdominant parallel, is thus a "conceptual dissonance" [*Auffassungsdissonanz*] even if it is acoustically an apparent consonance.

It is undeniable that Rameau's theory does imply the concepts of apparent consonance and conceptual dissonance. An F-major triad, under which Rameau supposes the lower third (**d**) as a "suppressed root" to convert the irregular fundamental bass progression of a second (**f–g**) into the regular progression of a fifth (**d–g**), is a conceptual dissonance that acoustically presents itself as an apparent consonance. But if one transfers these concepts from Riemann's theory of harmonic functions to Rameau's system, their meanings become reversed. Riemann defines the chord on the second degree as an apparent consonance because it is a subordinate form of degree IV. Rameau, on the other hand, treats the chord on the fourth degree, as long as it is followed by degree V, as an apparent consonance and bases it on degree ii, the "real" root even if "suppressed." While Riemann reduces "secondary harmonies" (ii, iii, vi) to "primary harmonies" (IV, V, I), Rameau reduces second-progressions of the fundamental bass to fifth-progressions.

The correlation between apparent consonance and secondary degrees postulated by Riemann does not exist in Rameau's system. Chords on both primary and secondary degrees are consonances in some contexts, apparent consonances in others. A chord on degree I, a consonance when preceding degree IV, is an apparent consonance when preceding degree ii (I–ii = vi⁷–ii). And a chord on degree vi, an apparent consonance in the deceptive cadence V–vi [= V–I with supposed third], is a consonance when serving as the *dominante* of degree ii.

Developing a theory of "secondary degrees" was superfluous in Rameau's system. Just like degrees I, IV, and V, degrees ii, iii, and vi were all *sons fondamentaux* [fundamental tones] of a key. Rameau calls a chord progression that presents a key a *modulation*, "since modulation is nothing but the progression of fundamental tones, and that of the tones included in their chords" [Comme la *Modulation* n'est autre chose que le progrès des Sons fondamentaux, et celui des Sons compris dans leurs Accords].²⁵ And concerning the *modulation* of a key, Rameau unambiguously states that, besides the tonic, it comprises five *sons fondamentaux*. "Setting sol . . . as the main tone, and having arrived at the modulation of do, its subdominant . . . , at that time I fancy this do as the new main tone, then picture to myself the five other fundamental tones of its modulation by thinking do, re, mi, fa, sol, la, just as I had to think sol, la, si, do, re, mi with regard to sol" [Posant *Sol* . . . pour *Son principal*, & étant arrivé à la *Modulation* d'*Ut* sa *Sous-dominante* . . . , j'imagine pour lors cet *Ut* comme premier *principal*, puis je me represente les cinq autres *Sons fondamentaux* de sa *Modulation*, en disant *Ut. Re. Mi. Fa. Sol. La.* de même que j'ay du dire à l'égard de Sol, *Sol. La. Si. Ut. Ré. Mi*].²⁶

3. According to Riemann, Rameau's system suffers from an internal contradiction. Although Rameau recognized "the six-five chord on the fourth degree of the scale as a fundamental chord" [den Quintsextakkord auf der vierten Stufe der Tonart als Grundakkord], nevertheless he "always cast a sidelong glance toward the seventh chord on the second degree as its 'real' foundation (so as to maintain his first principle—the tertian structure of chords)" [schiele er doch mit einem halben Seitenblick immer auf den Septimenakkord der zweiten Stufe als 'eigentliche' Grundlage hin (um sein erstes Prinzip—den Terzaufbau—zu wahren)].²⁷ The tertian structure of chords is, however, not Rameau's "first principle." Rather, his first principle is the correlation between the resolution of dissonance and the progression of the fundamental bass. And it is on this correlation that the dual interpretation of the six-five chord is based. This *double emploi* does not mark a flaw in the system; instead, it is a direct consequence of a fundamental idea, one that Riemann failed to appreciate.

. . .

Theories of tonal harmony are attempts to substantiate why chords form an association that characterizes a key. And it is the founding principles on which these theories base tonal chord relationships—not single theorems or categories—that determine the degree of connection or divergence between the theories.

Simon Sechter's theory of fundamental progressions [*Stufentheorie*][28] was developed from Rameau's theses. Yet it renounced the characteristic feature of Rameau's theory: the motivation of chord progressions by dissonances. Thus Sechter's theory, since it establishes a mutual relationship between triads *per se* (and not as mere fragments of seventh chords), is a theory of harmony in a narrower, more precise sense than is Rameau's system. But on the other hand, by suspending the correlation between the progression of the fundamental bass and the resolution of dissonance, Sechter runs into considerable difficulties.

Sechter's doctrine is partly a theory of chordal scale degrees and partly a theory of fundamental progressions, without the exact relationship between these two factors having been resolved. As a theory of chordal scale degrees, it is based on the idea that chords establish a key because the key's scale forms the material out of which they are composed. "As is familiar from elementary knowledge, it is from this scale that the intervals, the chords, and the just discussed progression of the same receive their first and most natural definition" [Wie aus den Elementarkenntnissen bekannt ist, erhalten von dieser Tonleiter die Intervalle, die Accorde und die erst abzuhandelnde Folge derselben die erste und natürlichste Bestimmung].[29]

Sechter supplements the theory of chordal scale degrees with the method of reducing second-progressions of chordal roots to fifth-progressions. Beneath the ascending second-progression I–ii, Sechter, just like Rameau, supposes the descending fifth vi^7–ii. "For example, in order to make the progression from the triad on the first degree to that on the second conform to what is natural, the seventh chord on the sixth degree must either actually be introduced between them, or be inwardly imagined" [Um zum Beispiel den Schritt vom Dreiklang der 1sten zu jenem der 2ten Stufe naturgemäß zu machen, muß dazwischen der Septaccord der 6ten Stufe entweder wirklich gemacht oder hinein gedacht werden].[30] And Sechter interprets triads whose roots progress down a second, ii–I or vi–V, as fragments of ninth chords, V^9–I or ii^9–V. "In order to make as natural as possible apparent descending second-progressions of two triads, one avails oneself of the expediant of treating the fifth of the first triad as a ninth, the third of the same as a seventh, and the root and its octave as a fifth. This first triad is then an incomplete nine-seven chord from which the root and third are missing" [Um die scheinbaren Schritte in die Untersecunde mit zwei Dreiklängen möglichst naturgemäß zu machen, bedient man sich des Mittels, die Quint des ersten Dreiklangs als Non, die Terz desselben als Sept und den Grundton und dessen Verdoppelung als Quinten zu betrachten, welches sodann ein unvollständiger Septnonaccord ist, welchem die Terz und der Fundamentalton fehlen].[31]

Example 4

Sechter's system, of course, suffers from the defect of juxtaposing, without a clear connection, the characterization of key by chordal scale degrees and the reduction of root progressions of a second to those of a fifth. It lacks the very factor that secured the connection in Rameau's theory: the linking of chords by dissonances.

According to Rameau, the function of a dissonance lies in its *liaison en harmonie* [providing harmonic connection]. "The rules established for dissonance give proof of the connection [*liaison*] of which we wish to speak. For when one says that it is necessary to prepare a dissonance, that means that the tone which it forms in one chord must have been part of the chord immediately preceding it. And when one says that it is necessary to resolve it, that means that it must have a definite progression of a type that we naturally desire, after having heard it" [Les regles établis pour la *Dissonance*, prouvent la *Liaison* dont nous voulons parler; car, lorsqu'on dit qu'il faut *Préparer* une Dissonance, cela signifie que le Son qui la forme dans un Accord, doit avoir fait partie de l'Accord qui la précède immediatement; & quand on dit qu'il faut la *Sauver*, cela signifie qu'elle doit avoir un progrès fixé, & tel que nous se souhaitons naturellement, après l'avoir entenduë]. A dissonance is subject to a pressure to resolve that determines the chord progression. "Now nothing can better give the impression of a harmonic connection than the same tone which serves two successive chords, and which at the same time makes one desire the tone, not to say the chord, that ought immediately to follow" [Or rien ne peut mieux faire sentir une *Liaison* en Harmonie, qu'une même Son qui sert à deux Accords successifs, & qui fait souhaiter en même tems le Son, pour ne pas dire, l'Accord qui doit suivre immediatement].[32] In Rameau's system, the factor that binds together the progression of chordal roots and the characterizaton of a key is the resolution of dissonance. The model of a chord progression is the sequence of seventh chords whose goal and conclusion is the *accord parfait* of the tonic: "a simple dominant . . . followed by another dominant, and so on from one to another until a tonic-dominant is reached, after which the tonic ought naturally to follow" [Simple dominante . . . suivie d'une autre dominante, & ainsi d'une à autre jusqu'à une Dominante-tonique, après lequelle doit naturellement suivre la Tonique].[33]

Sechter abandoned the principle of linking chords by dissonances. (The imagined dissonances resulting from the addition of "suppressed roots" are, in the theory of fundamental progressions, a secondary and incidental factor.) What establishes a relationship between chords is not dissonance, whether real or "tacitly implied," but both the progression of chordal roots and the fact that the chords belong to the same scale. Yet one can imagine the characterization of a key by chordal scale degrees without the precedence of the fifth progression, and vice versa. Both factors—the complete scale and the progression by fifths—are in fact included in the sequence I–IV–vii–iii–vi–ii–V–I, the conceptual model of Sechter's theory.[34] But the external coincidence establishes no internal connection. And Sechter himself seems to have sensed the deficiency, for in a distant passage in a chapter on "The Laws of Meter" he outlines an idea to reconcile these factors: the closer a root progression in the sequence approaches the concluding tonic, the more "decisive" [*entscheidend*] it is. "So [it] is important to observe that the progression from the fifth to the first degree is the most decisive, the progression from the second to the fifth degree less decisive, still less that from the sixth to the second, still less that from the third to the sixth, still less that from the seventh to the third, and still less that from the fourth to the seventh . . . If, however, one starts out with the progression from the first to the fourth degree, and lets the seventh degree follow accordingly, then it carries still less weight than the progression from the fourth to the seventh degree" [. . . so ist nöthig zu bemerken, daß der Schritt von der 5ten zur 1en Stufe am entscheidendsten, minder entscheidend der Schritt von der 2ten zur 5ten Stufe, noch minder jener von der 6ten zur 2ten, wieder minder jener von der 3ten zur 6ten, noch minder jener von der 7ten zur 3ten, noch minder jener von der 4ten zur 7ten Stufe ist . . . Fängt man aber sogleich mit dem Schritte von der 1ten zur 4ten Stufe an, und läßt darnach die 7te Stufe folgen, so ist er noch minder an Wert, als der Schritt von der 4ten zur 7ten Stufe].[35] The importance, the "weight" [*Wert*], of a root progression and the degrees it connects therefore depends on its proximity or remoteness to the tonic, as measured by fifths.

This thesis, of course, is flawed in two respects. First, explaining the fourth degree as the "most remote" does violence to common sense. And second, the "decisive" root progressions are really I–IV, vii–iii, vi–ii, and V–I. Between IV and vii, iii and vi, and ii and V, one perceives caesuras—in fact, one does so independently of the metric placement of the chords. One uses upbeat phrasing if the sequence begins with an upbeat (I–|–IV vii–|–iii vi–|–ii V–|–I) and downbeat phrasing if the beginning falls on the stressed part of the measure (I–IV | vii–iii | vi–ii | V–I). The progression IV–vii—"more decisive" than I–IV according to Sechter—is actually a dead interval.

To live up to the promise of its name, the "theory of fundamental progression" had to characterize chordal scale degrees (beyond merely numbering them) in terms of their relationships both to each other and to the tonic. A series of Roman numerals is no theory at all, and the theory of functions seems to supply what the theory of fundamental progressions lacks: an unequivocal, firmly outlined characterization of chordal scale degrees. In the theory of functions, I is defined as the tonic, ii (in major) as the subdominant parallel, iii as the dominant parallel or the tonic *Leittonwechselklang*, IV as the subdominant, V as the dominant, vi as the tonic parallel or the subdominant *Leittonwechselklang*, and vii as a fragment of the dominant seventh chord. The theory of fundamental progressions would accordingly come into its own through the theory of functions. The theory of functions would be the true theory of fundamental progressions. Yet chordal scale degrees, as scale degrees, are abolished by the principle underlying this characterization. When understood as a subdominant parallel, a ii ceases to be a ii, because according to Riemann, the apparent root—the very tone that establishes the chordal scale degree as a scale degree—is a dissonant *sixte ajoutée*.

On the other hand, it would be a mistake not to recognize that the theory of fundamental progressions implies the beginnings, even if hidden, of a theory of functions. According to Sechter, a "suppressed root" is an "inwardly imagined" tone. And the distinction between what is real and what is imagined has relevance for compositional technique. Sechter interprets the progression I–ii as vi^7–ii. The fifth of degree I is thus "really" a seventh. It can, nevertheless, serve as the preparation of a four-three suspension over the second degree, and as the preparation of a dissonance, it is a consonance. "If the preparation of a suspension must be accomplished by means of the seventh above a root, then the root is thereby suppressed so that the rule [of consonant preparation] should remain unbroken" [Wenn die Vorbereitung eines Vorhaltes durch die Sept eines Fundamentes geschehen muß, so wird das Fundament dabei verschwiegen, damit die Regel keinen Abbruch erleide].[36] The fifth, which represents a dissonant seventh, is treated like the consonance it appears to be. Sechter's reductive method thus assumes a distinction fundamental to a theory of functions: the differentiation between appearance and significance, between what is presented and what is represented.

In these competing theories, the criteria underlying the separation of appearance and significance are, of course, so dissimilar that their reconciliation seems impossible. First, the theory of fundamental progressions differs from the theory of harmonic functions in its concept of ambiguity, the *double emploi*: in the I–IV–V–I cadence, IV is both IV (I–IV) and ii[7] (ii[7]–V) at the same time. Second, the supposition of fifths permitted by Sechter (along with that of thirds) contradicts the fundamental idea of the theory of functions. According to that theory's criteria, the notion that ii before I should be taken as V[9], and vi before V as ii[9], is absurd, since it leads to a confusion of antithetical extremes—the subdominant (subdominant parallel) with the dominant, and the tonic (tonic parallel) with the dominant of the dominant. And third, the reduction of one degree to another is reversible in the theory of fundamental progressions, but not in the theory of functions. According to the latter theory, one can only reduce vi to I, iii to V, and ii to IV, while in the former theory the reverse is also possible—I to vi, V to iii, and IV to ii. Yet these antitheses are not irresolvable.

1. To support the thesis that IV in the progression IV–V–I should be understood as ii[7], Sechter writes, "The cross-relation also makes it clear that when the root appears to ascend one degree, the fifth of the first root forms a seventh with the fifth of the second, and for that reason the fifth of the latter root should itself be considered the root of the former" [Auch das macht der Querstand klar, daß, wenn das Fundament um eine Stufe zu steigen scheint, die Quint des ersteren zu der Quint des zweiten eine Sept bildet, und daher die Quint des zweiten Fundamentes früher selbst als Fundament betrachtet werden müsse].[37] The second between the fifths of IV and V is to be perceived as an implicit dissonance that one explains as a seventh (**d–c′**), thus as ii[7], and that one resolves to a third (**g–b** = V). But if, according to Sechter, the chord's fifths form a contrast of a second, then there seems no reason why the same interpretation should not apply to the roots of IV and V. And the resolution of this contrast between subdominant and dominant is the tonic: the IV–V–I cadence appears as the exposition and resolution of a dissonance. But the fact that the relationship between IV and V is understood as a dissonance that resolves to I means that IV, in order to be linked with V and I, need not be interpreted as a fragment of ii[7]. When transferred from chordal fifths to roots, this concept of a contrasting second-relation makes the supposition of a

suppressed root, for whose justification Sechter thought up the concept in the first place, superfluous. In the cadence I–IV–V–I, IV is not IV from one view and ii[7] from another, but simply IV.

2. The theory of fundamental root progressions suffers from the defect of considering only the direct connections between chords and neglecting the indirect ones. By means of a slight revision, however, the supposition of lower fifths, the reinterpretation of ii before I as V[9], or vi before V as ii[9], can be made superfluous, so that even the second difference is resolved between the theories of fundamental progressions and of functions. Specifically, in progressions such as ii–I–IV and vi–V–I, degrees ii and vi, rather than being related directly to I and V as fragments of V[9] and ii[9], can be indirectly linked with IV and I as parallel chords.

3. In the theory of fundamental progressions, the method of reducing not only vi to I, iii to V, and ii to IV, but also I to vi, V to iii, and IV to ii, loses its *raison d'être* owing to the concept of the contrasting second-relation. If one grants that IV–V, I–ii, and V–vi are contrasts reconciled by I, V, and ii, then it is superfluous to interpret IV–V–I as ii[7]–V–I, I–ii–V as vi[7]–ii–V, and V–vi–ii as iii[7]–vi–ii.

The only difference left between the theories is in their interpretations of the second degree. While the theory of fundamental progressions asserts the autonomy of the second degree, the theory of functions denies it. And, as an analysis of the concept of functions will show, this difference can be resolved only through a reformulation of the theory of functions itself, not by a revision of the theory of fundamental progressions. At the same time, it will become clear that the concept of functions can be separated from Riemann's method of demoting secondary degrees to dissonant variants of primary degrees, so that one can retain the concept of fundamental progressions without giving up the concept of functions.

INTERPRETATIONS OF THE CADENCE

"The triad on the tonic," writes Sechter, is "in a reciprocal relationship with the triad or seventh chord on the fifth degree, or with the triad on the fourth degree" [Der Dreiklang der Tonica (ist) mit dem Dreiklange oder Septaccord der 5ten oder mit dem Dreiklang der 4ten Stufe in Wechselwirkung].[1] Each chord is what it is—tonic, dominant, or subdominant—in relation to the others. And the result of this reciprocal relationship is the cadence, the model of tonal harmony.

With respect to the cadence, that is, the context of the progression I–IV–V–I or the functions T–S–D–T, one can differentiate five features that, in varying assortment and with varying emphasis, have defined interpretations of tonal harmony since the 18th century, interpretations that did not, however, unequivocally set forth the interdependence of the cofactors (and the attendant futility of the search for a single fundamental principle). The five features are: (1) the progressions I–IV and V–I are based on fifth progressions of the *basse fondamentale*; (2) an inclination toward the tonic is aided by "characteristic dissonances," the *sixte ajoutée* of the six-five chord on the subdominant and the seventh of the dominant seventh chord; (3) the second-relation between IV and V appears as a contrast resolved by I; (4) degree I is connected to degree IV, and degree V to degree I, by leading-tone progressions; and (5) in the cadence, there still operates the memory of a historical

proto-form, the discant-tenor clausula . "Concerning

this primitive pattern [i.e., the basic cadence] much must of necessity be said, for it is precisely this pattern that contains most of the others. Indeed the 'cadence,' properly understood, is the foundation and archetype of music making in general" [Über dieses Primitive werden viele Worte unvermeidlich sein, denn gerade dieses enthält das Meiste; ja, die 'Kadenz' ist, richtig verstanden, Grundlage und Urbild des Musizierens überhaupt].[2]

1. In Rameau's *Traité de l'harmonie* it is said of the fifth that, in the V–I cadence, it seems to return to its source. "We are fully satisfied only when we hear a final cadence formed from this progression, when it seems that the fifth returns to its source in passing to one of the tones of the octave from which it was generated (for here to ascend a fourth or descend a fifth is the same thing" [Nous ne sommes pleinement satisfaits, que lorsque nous entendons une Cadence finale formée de cette progression, où il semble que la Quinte retourne à sa source, en passant à l'un des Sons de l'Octave dont elle est engendrée (car monter de Quarte ou descendre de Quinte s'est icy la même chose)].[3] And in his *Nouveau système*, Rameau writes, "Therefore we well observe that the title of perfect cadence is attached only to a dominant that progresses to the main tone, because this dominant, which is naturally contained within the harmony of the main tone, seems, when it progresses to it, to return as if to its source" [Remarquons donc bien que le titre de *Cadence parfaite* n'est annexé à une *Dominante* qui passe au *Son principal*, qu'en ce que cette *Dominante* qui est naturellement comprise dans l'Harmonie du *Son principal*, semble retourner comme à sa source, lorsqu'elle y passe].[4] The similarity of these formulations conceals a difference in the premises on which they are based. In the *Traité de l'harmonie*, Rameau's thesis is mathematical, in the *Nouveau système*, physical and acoustical. The

source to which the fifth returns in the *Traité de l'harmonie* is the octave (whose harmonic division results in the fifth), while in the *Nouveau système*, it is the tonic (whose harmonic series includes both the fifth and the dominant triad).

Between the appeal to the harmonic series and the notion expressed by the name "dominant," there persists a contradiction that Rameau left unresolved. The concept of the dominant purports that the dominant actively determines the tonic chord, and that the tonic is passively determined by the dominant chord. "In the bass, the first of the two notes that form a perfect cadence is called 'dominant' [in the sense of 'governing' or 'having dominion over something'], because it must always precede the final tone and therefore governs it" [On appelle *Dominante* la premiere des deux Nottes qui dans la Basse, forment la cadence parfaite, parce qu'elle doit préceder toûjours la Notte finale, & par consequent la domine].[5] On the other hand, the conceptual model of the harmonic series makes the tonic appear as the fundamental factor, the dominant as the dependent factor. The notion that the dominant chord is implied by the tonic certainly makes intelligible the progression from I to V, but not the return from V to I. For this reason Arnold Schoenberg believed that the expression "dominant" was, "strictly speaking, not entirely correct." "Thus it is more a dependence of the fifth on the tonic that is characteristic of the relationship than the contrary, the domination of the fundamental by the fifth" [Es ist also für das Verhältnis eher eine Abhängigkeit der Quint vom Grundton charakteristisch als das umgekehrte, das Beherrschtwerden des Grundtons von der Quint].[6] And Heinrich Schenker defined I–V as a "natural" progression prescribed by the harmonic series, but V–I as an "artificial inversion."[7]

The attempt, however, to establish an acoustical basis for the relationship contradicts the musical experience expressed by the name "dominant," the experience that V–I is a "natural progression" and not an "artificial inversion." And it suggests a return to the mathematical formulation hinted at by Rameau in his *Traité de l'harmonie*. Rameau's thesis that the fifth arising from the harmonic division of the octave will gravitate back to its source can be understood as a rudimentary version of the "Lipps-Meyer law"—that the impression of closure, the "effect of finality" [*Finaleffekt*], of a melodic interval depends on "whether or not the end tone of the interval can be represented by the number two or a power of two" [ob der Zielton des Intervalls durch die Zahl 2 bzw. eine Potenz von ihr repräsentiert wird oder nicht].[8] The mathematical formulation is, of course, less an explanation than a "symbol."[9]

2. In Rameau's theory, *dominante* and *sousdominante* are names for specific chordal types: the *cadence parfaite*, D^7–T, is characterized by the seventh chord, the *cadence irrégulière*, S_5^6–T, by the six-five chord.[10] Indeed, according to Rameau the progression I–V–I–IV–I is ambiguous. (The fact that the fifth degree precedes the fourth, instead of the reverse, is motivated less technically than didactically; the external order of succession is meant to express an internal precedence of the *cadence parfaite* over the *cadence irrégulière*.)

Example 5

Rameau defines the first phrase as $\begin{matrix} \text{I} & \text{V} & \text{I} & \text{IV} & \text{I} \\ \text{T} & \text{D}^7 & \text{T} & \text{S}_5^6 & \text{T} \end{matrix}$. "Note *A* is the given main tone, on which the perfect cadence from *B* to *A* and the irregular cadence from *C* to *A* conclude" [La Note {*A*} est le *Son principal* donné, où se terminent la *Cadence parfaite* {de *B* à *A*} & la *Cadence irréguliere* {de *C* à *A*}]. In the second phrase the functions change places: $\begin{matrix} \text{I} & \text{V} & \text{I} & \text{IV} \\ \text{S}_5^6 & \text{T} & \text{D}^7 & \text{T} \end{matrix}$. "Note *B* is the dominant that becomes, in turn, the main tone of its modulation when the irregular cadence from *A* to *B* ends there, at which point the given main tone then becomes the subdominant. Note *C* is the subdominant that becomes, in turn, the main tone of its modulation when the perfect cadence from *A* to *C* ends there, at which point the main tone then becomes the dominant" [La Note {*B*} est la *Dominante* qui devient à son tour *Son principal* de sa *modulation*, lorsque la *Cadence irréguliere* s'y termine {*A* à *B*}; où le *Son principal* donné, devient pour lors *Sous-dominante*. // La Note *C* est la *Sous-dominante*, qui devient à son tour *Son principal* de sa *modulation*, lorsque la *Cadence parfaite* s'y termine {d'*A* à *C*}; où le *Son principal* devient pour lors *Dominante*].[11] The difference that Rameau describes (without giving reasons for it) is based on the metric placement of the chords. The dissonant chords appear on weak beats, the consonant chords on strong beats.

The antithetical explanations of the I–V–I–IV progression juxtaposed by Rameau—T–D–T–S and S–T–D–T—were melded together by Moritz Hauptmann. Hauptmann's interpretation of the cadence is in the form of a dialectic. "For the sake of the octave unity of the triad, the fifth-concept will be constituted anew, so that this triad might be at variance with itself, might appear to itself in opposing definitions. This occurs by means of two other triads, the subdominant [*Unter-*

Dominant] and the dominant [*Ober-Dominant*], of which the first contains the root of the given triad as its fifth, the second the fifth of the triad as its root. In this way the initially established triad is brought into self-contradiction or opposition, for in the first situation it becomes itself a dominant chord, and in the second a subdominant, and in this way changes itself from the autonomous octave-unity into the significance of the fifth-duality. The uniting, contradiction-resolving concept of the third then allows the triad, divided against itself into opposing definitions, to at the same time include within itself these oppositions, and to change itself from a passive being-a-dominant to an active having-a-dominant, so that the triad might set the two disuniting unities outside of itself and become itself a unity from this duality: the unity of a triad of triads" [Der *Quint-Begriff* für die Octav-Einheit des Dreiklanges wird wieder darin bestehen, daß dieser sich in sich selbst entzweie, in entgegengesetzte Bestimmungen zu sich trete. Dies geschieht durch zwei andere Dreiklänge, dem der *Unter-Dominant* und dem der *Ober-Dominant*, von denen der erste den Grundton des gegebenen als Quint, der andere dessen Quint als Grundton enthält. Dadurch kommt der zuerst gesetzte Dreiklang mit sich selbst in Gegensatz oder Widerspruch, denn er ist in der ersten Stellung selbst Oberdominant-, in der andern Unterdominant-Accord geworden, und ist damit an sich aus der selbständigen *Octaveinheit* in die Bedeutung der *Quintzweiheit* übergegangen.—Der verbindende, den Widerspruch aufhebende *Terzbegriff* läßt nun den in entgegengesetzten Bestimmungen von sich geschiedenen Dreiklang diese zugleich in sich zusammenfassen, das passive Dominant-*sein* in das active Dominant-*haben* an sich übergehen, daß er die beiden ihn entzweienden Einheiten als Zweiheit außer sich setze und selbst Einheit dieser Zweiheit werde: *Einheit eines Dreiklanges von Dreiklängen*].[12] The expressions "octave," "fifth," and "third" are used metaphorically: Hauptmann terms direct unity "octave," contradiction—the separation leading to opposite definitions—"fifth," and the resolution of the contradiction into a reconciled unity "third." Degree I, initially "asserted" [*behauptet*] as tonic but not "proven" [*bewiesen*], runs into an internal contradiction, its bifurcation into antithetical relationships: on the one hand, I is the dominant of IV, on the other, it is the subdominant of V.

August Halm seems to have a similar understanding of the cadence. In the beginning, the tonic is an unreconciled assertion [*Setzung*], at the end, a reconciled result. "The totality begins with the tonic chord given by the assertion of a key; this same triad leads out from itself, becomes productive, and as a dominant gives rise to the lower chord (IV) that naturally follows. In this way a contrasting element, dissonance in the sublime sense, comes to the fore and finds resolution in a return to the tonic, which has now become a goal and point of rest after being a point of departure and motion. Out of the disturbed unity of the tonic triad, cleft by motion, is born the far superior unity of the key" [Das Ganze hebt mit dem durch die Setzung einer Tonart gegebenen Grundaccord an; derselbe geht aus sich heraus, wird produktiv, führt als Dominant den natürlich folgenden tieferen Accord (IV) herbei. Ein gegensätzliches Element, Dissonanz im sublimen Sinn, ist damit aufgetreten, und kommt zur Lösung bei der Rückkehr zur Tonika, welche nun Ziel- und Ruhepunkt geworden ist, nachdem sie Ausgangspunkt und Bewegung war. Aus der gestörten Einheit des sich in der Bewegung spaltenden Tonika-Dreiklangs wird die weit höhere Einheit der Tonart geboren].[13] The easily overlooked difference that while Hauptmann describes the I–IV–I–V–I cadence, Halm describes the I–IV–V–I cadence, is, however, an indication of an opposition between their respective explanations.

According to Hauptmann, degree I is exposed to a contradiction, to the double definition of I as dominant of IV and subdominant of V. According to Halm, the contradiction is the difference between "assertion" [Setzung] and "reconciliation" [Aufhebung], between I as tonic and I as dominant of IV. Halm constructs the cadence out of two descending fifth progressions; Hauptmann regards it as the intersection of descending and ascending fifth progressions. For Halm, the restoration of degree I as tonic depends on the fifth progression V–I; for Hauptmann, it depends on the changeover of degree I from "being-a-dominant" (I–IV = D–T and I–V = S–T) to "having-a-dominant" (IV–I = S–T and V–I = D–T). Hauptmann interprets the change from "being-a-dominant" to "having-a-dominant" as a transition from passivity to activity; being-a-dominant is passive, having-a-dominant is active. Thus Hauptmann perceived the beginning of a progression (the dominant or subdominant) as the dependent factor, the conclusion or goal (the tonic) as the determining factor. In contrast, in the beginning of a progression, in the dominant, Halm discerned the determining factor, and in the result, in the tonic, the dependent factor. Hauptmann thinks "teleologically," Halm "energetically."

For Halm the driving force behind chordal progression is the fifth progression, "the axiom of motion";[14] for Hauptmann it is the dialectic between division and restoration. The changeover from "being-a-dominant" to "having-a-dominant" is, however, a fiction; the antithesis that Hauptmann took to be dialectical is merely a contrast. The metric placement of chords suggested by Rameau—separating the interpre-

tation of $\begin{array}{c|cc|c} \text{I} & \text{V} & \text{I} & \text{IV} \\ \hline \text{S} & \text{T} & \text{D} & \text{T} \end{array}$ from that of $\begin{array}{cc|cc} \text{I} & \text{V} & \text{I} & \text{IV} \\ \hline \text{T} & \text{D} & \text{T} & \text{S} \end{array}$ —proves Haupt-

mann's dialectic of the cadence to be imaginary. According to Hauptmann, the accented part of the measure is the determining factor, the unaccented part the dependent factor.[15] Since a "passive" chord corresponds to the unaccented part of the measure, degree I as a "passive being-a-dominant" would be rhythmically presented as I | IV I | V I, and as an "active having-a-dominant," by contrast, as I IV | I V | I. But the permutation of strong and weak beats does not conform to musical reality.

3. The whole-tone contrast between IV and V is the external correlate of the internal contradiction that characterizes the cadence—the separation of degree I into the opposite definitions of being dominant to IV and subdominant to V. According to Jean Baptiste Mercadier, the subdominant and dominant form a dissonance that is resolved by the tonic. "In fact the lack of consonance prevailing between the dominant and the subdominant, far from obliging us to separate these two roots, does it not, on the contrary, induce us to place them one after the other, so that the ear should discover that neither of them is the term to which the other refers, and so that it should thus sustain and strengthen its attention on the tonic? Is not this selfsame harshness the only means of determining this tonic?" [En effet le défaut de consonance qui règne entre la dominante et la sous-dominante, bien loin de nous obliger à séparer ces deux sons fondamentaux, ne nous engage-t-il pas au contraire à les mettre de suite; afin que l'oreille s'apperçoive qu'aucun d'eux n'est le terme auquel on rapporte l'autre, et qu'elle soutienne et fortifie ainsi son attention sur la tonique? N'est pas même la rigueur le seul moyen de déterminer cette tonique?].[16]

4. According to Ernst Kurth, the tonal connection between tonic and subdominant, and dominant and tonic, is based primarily on the leading-tone progression from the third of the tonic to the root of the subdominant, and from the third of the dominant to the root of the tonic. "Thus, with regard to that force of reverting from the dominant to the tonic (moreover the general tendency of a triad to go to its subdominant), one also can now speak of an 'original tonal energy,' alongside an original melodic energy, as an element in the play of harmonic-tonal forces, a tonal energy, however, that still has its origin in melodic energy" [So kann man neben einer melodischen Anfangsenergie nun auch hinsichtlich jener Rückschlagskraft von Dominante zur Tonika, des weitern der Tendenz eines Durdreiklangs überhaupt zu seiner Subdominante von einer "tonalen Anfangsenergie" als Element des harmonisch-tonalen Kräftespieles sprechen, die aber eben auf die melodische ursächlich zurückgeht].[17] The tendency inherent in the leading tone is to be viewed as the cause, the impression produced by the dominant as the effect. "But one must always bear in mind that the leading-tone tendency of the third (in alliance with the force of the seventh), set out in the rules of musical progression (e.g., of the

dominant seventh chord) and already taken into consideration by theoretical works from the distant past onward, itself first established the specific, fixed tendency of the dominant" [Nur muß man sich immer vor Augen halten, daß die in den musikalischen Fortführungsgesetzen (z. B. des Dominantseptakkords) schon von sehr alten theoretischen Werken an berücksichtigte Leittontendenz der Terz (im Verein mit der Schwerkraft der Sept) erst selbst die spezifische, bestimmte Dominanttendenz begründet].[18]

The leading tone is undeniably one of the constituent features of the cadence. But "original tonal energy," which is to be understood as "melodic"—Kurth speaks of a "penetration of the leading-tone effect into the major third" [Eindringen der Leittonwirkung in die Durterz][19]—is a questionable hypothesis. An ascending half step can connect a seventh with an octave, or a fifth with a sixth. And while the leading tone is indeed the seventh of the scale, it is not the fifth. The leading-tone effect is thus dependent upon the context, upon the system of tonal relationships. Rather than being a basic phenomenon, it is itself based on other phenomena.

According to Kurth, the "explanation of leading-tone tension by appeal to the effect of the dominant" [Erklärung der Leittonspannung aus Dominantwirkung] is "erroneously reversed" [verkehrt];[20] it mistakes a cause for an effect. First, however, Kurth's attempt at a causal interpretation aims at an empty target. The leading-tone tendency is only a cofactor in the effect of the dominant, an effect based on the correlation between a leading-tone progression, a descending fifth, and a dissonant seventh. And just as a cofactor is not the cause of the whole in which it participates, but is what it is only as constituted within that whole, so conversely the whole arises out of the reciprocal action of the cofactors. Thus if the dominant character of degree V is bound up with the leading-tone tendency of the third, then outside of the correlation with the descending fifth and dissonant seventh, the leading tone lacks the "original tonal energy" that Kurth ascribes to it.

Second, leading-tone tension, rather than being immutable, is a historically variable phenomenon. The half-step progression can be perceived not only as "urging" [drängend], but also as "indistinct" [undeutlich]. The progression from the dominant chord to the tonic chord is open to an "energetic" interpretation; one can conceive of the tonic as the result of an "original energy" emanating from the dominant. Yet the tendency of imperfect consonances to move to perfect consonances, the basic factor of 14th- and 15th-century counterpoint, is of quite a different nature. An imperfect and a perfect consonance face each other as dependent and independent dyads respectively, not as determining and determined elements; the progressions are established more "teleologically" than "energetically." "Imperfect consonance is deservedly named on account of its instability, because it moves from place to place, and because *per se* it is found among none of the fixed proportions. Such [imperfect consonances] are, namely, the minor third, the major third, and the major sixth" [Imperfecta concordantia ab instabilitate sua merito denominatur, quae de loco movetur in locum et per se inter nullas certas invenitur proportiones. Tales enim sunt semiditonus, ditonus et tonus cum diapente].[21] Perfect consonance is *clara* [clear, bright, manifest], imperfect consonance *minus clara*[22] [less clear]; and the striving of the sixth toward the octave, or of the major third toward the fifth, is the tendency of the cloudy and muddled to move toward what is clear and firmly outlined. The character of the interval progression, however, determines the character of the leading tone. The leading tone filled with "original energy" forms the correlate to a dominant cadence, the indistinct, unstable leading tone the correlate to imperfect consonance.

5. Heinrich Schenker developed the I–IV–V–I cadence from an *Urlinie* [fundamental line], that of the *Terzzug* [third-progression] e′–d′–c′. The lower voice, the "counterpoint," sets c–g–c against the *Terzzug* of the upper voice, with f–g in the bass being a "prolongation" of g. "Thus in foreground cadences the IV–V second-progression arises from considerations of counterpoint! And so the question is finally answered about the origin of the wondrous second-progression: the fact that the spirit of fifth-relations can make itself master of chordal degrees, even degree IV, only through a fifth (or fourth as inversion) does not invalidate the contrapuntal origin of the IV–V second-progression!" [Der Sekundschritt IV–V in den Kadenzen des Vordergrundes kommt also vom Kontrapunktischen her! Damit is die Frage nach der Herkunft des wundersamen Sekundschrittes endlich beantwortet: daß sich der Quintengeist der Stufen auch der IV. Stufe nicht anders als durch eine Quint (oder Quart als Umkehrung) bemächtigen kann, hebt den kontrapunktischen Ursprung des Sekundschrittes IV–V nicht auf!].[23] Hence according to Schenker, the second-progression is primary, the descending fifth (I–IV) secondary.

Schenker's hypothesis seems to be supported by the memory of one of the proto-forms of the I–IV–V–I cadence. The *Terzzug* is the tenor formula of the discant-tenor clausula . And for the discant-tenor suspension and its resolution, not only G but also the second-progression F–G can form the supplementary bass (the *contratenor bassus* served the discant-tenor framework as an added voice). The F then originates through the "prolongation" of a "counterpoint."

The historical proto-form is, however, neutralized in the I–IV(or

ii_5^6)–V–I cadence. For reinterpretating the modal clausula as a cadence in major means that the bass progression, and not the discant-tenor formula, must be understood as the compositional foundation. Thus, on the one hand, as the relational center of a cadence, the *Terzzug* is a historical manifestation rather than a "basic phenomenon" [*Urphänomen*]. And on the other hand, as the chordal cadence arose, the *Terzzug* lost the very relevance that Schenker tried to deduce from it.

THE THEORY OF HARMONIC FUNCTIONS

In an 1890 essay entitled "Tonality," Heinrich von Herzogenberg mentions the comma difference between the tuning of **f♯–a–c′–d′** as V_5^6 in G major, and as V_5^6 of V in C major. "On an instrument tuned with pure thirds" the difference "can be heard quite clearly, though it must always be an *intentional object of consciousness*" [Auf einem mit natürlichen Terzen gestimmten Instrumente . . . sehr deutlich zu hören, immer muß er aber g e d a c h t werden]. Von Herzogenberg italicized the phrase "intentional object of consciousness," but he wrote it with hesitation. An apologetic remark reveals that he feared the reproach of *Begriffsrealismus* ["conceptual realism"; a neo-Kantian term]: "Please excuse my use of this somewhat scholastic expression" [Diesen etwas scholastischen Ausdruck bitte ich mir zu Gute halten zu wollen].[1] A generation that had grown up in awe of the natural sciences viewed with suspicion the realization that musical tone relationships could not be reduced to the given acoustical data. Even though this realization forced itself on von Herzogenberg, he still mistrusted it.

The fundamental idea of Hugo Riemann's theory of functions is "that the act of listening to music is not a passive sufferance of the effects of sound on the organ of hearing, but is much more a highly developed application of the logical functions of the human mind" [Daß das Musikhören nicht nur ein passives Erleiden von Schallwirkungen im Hörorgan sondern vielmehr eine hochgradig entwickelte Betätigung von logischen Funktionen des menschlichen Geistes ist][2]—thus that the relationships between tones are not learned from the acoustical substrate, but on the contrary, are expressed in it. In contrast to the passively borne "sensation of tone" [*Tonempfindung*], Riemann sets up an actively constituted "conceptualization of tone" [*Tonvorstellung*]· "If one has grasped these fundamental notions, then it is clear that from the very first the inductive method of the physiology and psychology of music proceeds down the wrong road if it takes as its point of departure the investigation of the elements of music as sound, instead of the establishment of the elements of music as conceptualized in the mind" [Hat man diese grundlegenden Gedanken begriffen, so leuchtet ein, daß die induktive Methode der Tonphysiologie und Tonpsychologie von Anfang an auf einem verkehrten Wege geht, wenn sie ihren Ausgang nimmt von der Untersuchung der Elemente der klingenden Musik, statt von der Feststellung der Elemente der vorgestellten Musik].[3]

The "elements of conceptualized music" are the major and minor triads. "Harmonic relatedness (not 'relatability'), the representation of a chord, is, in fact, a primary feature of every perceptible tone, that is, of every tone heard in a musical context. Depending on how a tone is conceived—as 1, 3, or 5 of a major chord, or instead as 5, 3, or 1 of a minor chord—it becomes something essentially different, it has an entirely distinct expressive value, character, and content" [Tatsächlich ist die harmonische Bezogenheit (nicht 'Beziehbarkeit'), die Klangvertretung, eine Haupteigenschaft jedes konkreten Tones, d. h. jedes musikalisch gehörten Tones. Jenachdem ein Ton als 1, 3 oder 5 eines Durakkords oder aber als I, III or V eines Mollakkords vorgestellt wird, ist er etwas wesentlich Verschiedenes, hat er einen ganz anderen Ausdruckswert, Charakter, Inhalt].[4]

. . .

Using the chord progression C–A–d–G–C = T–(D)–Sp–D–T as an illustration, Riemann demonstrates the independence of a musical conception of tone from the given acoustical data. Acoustically, the tone **d** is doubly determined: it is both a fifth below **a**, the third of the subdominant (or two fifths below **e'**, the third of the tonic), and a fifth above **G**, the dominant. The difference, the syntonic comma [81/80], is, however, musically irrelevant. "Our musical practice is ignorant of this twofold **d** in C major" [Unsere musikalische Praxis weiß von diesem zweierlei d in C-dur nichts].[5] As a conceptualized tone, the acoustically cleft **d** is an undivided unity. "This enharmonic identification of acoustical data differing by a syntonic comma is simply indispensable for our perception of music" [Diese enharmonische Identifikation der um das syntonische Komma verschiedenen akustischen Werte is für unser Musikhören schlechterdings unentbehrlich].[6]

Through his insight that the conceptualization of tone allowed him to disregard acoustical differences, Riemann touched, of course, on only part of the situation that he analyzed.

1. The expression "enharmonic identification" is equivocal. What Riemann has in mind is taking things acoustically different to be musically the same. But an "enharmonic identification" is also just the reverse: taking things musically different to be acoustically the same, as for example the identical tuning of **a♭** and **g♯** in equal temperament.

And finally, even taking things musically different to be musically the same—for example, the reinterpretation of the dominant seventh a♭ as the augmented sixth g♯—can be designated an "enharmonic identification."

2. Riemann, engrossed in his own system, misunderstood the theory of Moritz Hauptmann (against which he engaged in a polemic). For Hauptmann, the syntonic comma was relevant not *per se* but as the acoustical manifestation of a musical difference—a bifurcation in the conceptualization of tone. The assertion that the tone a fifth below the third of the subdominant is different than that a fifth above the root of the dominant means that in C major, the d-minor triad is "internally divided" [*in sich entzweit*]: on the one hand, it should be the subdominant parallel, on the other, a dominant of the dominant.

3. Not only Riemann's but also Hauptmann's system of tonal conceptualizations is independent of the acoustical substrate. The double determination of **d** can be acoustically presented without being musically conceptualized, and conversely, musically conceptualized without being acoustically presented.

4. The fact that a musical conceptualization is independent of the given acoustical data means either that its acoustical correlate can be distorted, or else that such an acoustical correlate does not exist. There is an acoustical equivalent to the musically conceptualized "fifth." And a tempered fifth, heard "as it ought to be" [*zurechtgehört*], is nothing more than a distorted pure fifth. But the conceptualization of the tone **d** as at one and the same time the lower fifth of the third of the subdominant, and the upper fifth of the dominant, is a musical idea with no acoustical correlate.

. . .

Hugo Riemann's theory of functions is an attempt to explain the tonal connection between chords. Underlying his complicated system is the simple axiom that chords representing a key can be reduced to three functions—tonic, dominant, and subdominant—and that one should seek the reason for the relationships between chords as chords (and not as mere results of voice leading) in the functions that the chords represent. "Our doctrine of the tonal functions of harmonies is nothing but the further development of the Fétisian concept of tonality. The tenacious relationship of all harmonies to the tonic has found its most pregnant expression imaginable in the designation of all chords as more or less strongly modified manifestations of the three main pillars of logical harmonic structure: the tonic itself and its two dominants" [Unsere Lehre von den tonalen Funktionen der Harmonien ist nichts anderes als der Ausbau des Fétis'schen Begriffes der Tonalität. Die festgehaltene Beziehung aller Harmonien auf eine Tonika hat ihren denkbar prägnantesten Ausdruck gefunden in der Bezeichnung aller Akkorde als mehr oder minder stark modifizierte Erscheinungsform der drei Hauptsäulen des harmonisch-logischen Aufbaues: der Tonika selbst und ihrer beiden Dominanten].[7]

The metaphor "main pillar" [*Hauptsäule*], of which it is uncertain whether it implies "function" or "chord," conceals an irresolvable difficulty in Riemann's formulation of the theory of functions. Riemann leaves undecided the question of whether "tonic," "dominant," and "subdominant" are terms for chordal scale degrees or for functions. The difference between appearance and significance, between what is presented and what is represented, is left up in the air.

The ambiguity is, however, no accidental terminological shortcoming, but the expression of a problem that goes to the heart of the matter. On the one hand, there is a fundamental distinction between what something signifies and the form through which it is represented. In C major, the chords **f–a–c'** and **d–f–a**, as subdominant (S) and subdominant parallel (Sp), fulfill the same function—that of a subdominant. In the abbreviations "S" and "Sp," the letter "S" is thus to be understood as a special sign for the function "subdominant" that **d–f–a** shares with **f–a–c'**. And the addition of "p" in "Sp" indicates a modification of the chord, not the function.

On the other hand, according to Riemann the basic form of the subdominant in C major is **f–a–c'** = S, while **d–f–a** = Sp is a variant. The tone **d** in **d–f–a** is to be considered a "nonharmonic" substitute for the fifth **c'**. The functional identity of S and Sp, and the distinction between basic form and variant, are, however, two mutually independent factors.

Functional identity is conceivable without a reduction of Sp to S, or of S to Sp. For example, the proportions 2/1 and 3/2 both satisfy the conditions of the function $(n+1)/n$ without the concept of function implying a need to understand one of the proportions as a variant of the other.

On the other hand, it is possible to comprehend the term "subdominant" as only the designation of a chordal scale degree—not a function—and to formulate the theory of functions without the concept of function. Judging from Riemann's thesis that **f–a–c'** = S in C major is the basic form of a group of chords that result from (1) chromatic alteration of the third (**f–a♭–c'**), (2) substitution of a sixth for the fifth (**f–a–d'** and **f–a♭–d♭'**), or (3) substitution of a lower second for the root (**e–a–c'** and **e♭–a♭–c'**), one might conclude that the theory of harmonic functions is a rigorous theory of fundamental progressions in which the number of degrees shrinks to just three (I, IV, V). Even

according to the theory of fundamental progressions, different chords—
B–d–f, **B–d–f–a**, **B♭–d–f**—represent the same chordal scale degree: the
supertonic in A minor. And the theory of functions differs from the
theory of fundamental progressions only in that it allows, as valid means
for modifying a chordal scale degree, not only added dissonances and
chromatic alterations, but also the substitution of the sixth for the fifth,
or the lower second for the root. Yet if the proposition that Sp fulfills
the same function as S proves nothing but that Sp, as an "apparent
consonance," is a variant of S, then the concept of functions becomes
superfluous.

. . .

According to the definition that Riemann gave in his *Lexikon*,[8] functional symbols express the significance of chords "for the logic of
musical composition" [für die Logik des Tonsatzes]. "Logic" is a
fundamental concept in the theory of functions. Yet only once, in an
1872 essay entitled "Musical Logic,"[9] did Riemann explicitly define it.
As it turns out, the logic that Riemann had in mind was dialectics.

"My explicitly set forth and clearly avowed goal was henceforth the
practical realization and the furthest possible amalgamation of the ideas
of Hauptmann, Helmholtz, and von Oettingen" [Mein deutlich vorg-
estelltes und klar ausgesprochenes Ziel war nun die praktische Verwertung und tunlichste Verschmelzung der Ideen Hauptmann's, Helmholtz's und v. Oettingen's].[10] The idea of combining Helmholtzian
empiricism—the deduction of musical laws from the harmonic series—
with the dialectics of Hauptmann served as the basis for Riemann's
interpretation of the cadence in the essay on "musical logic."

As the tonic at the beginning of the I–IV–I–V–I cadence, degree I
is, according to Moritz Hauptmann,[11] an "unreconciled assertion"
[*unvermittelte Setzung*]. Then, in relation to IV and V, I is "internally
divided" [*in sich entzweit*]—torn apart into the opposing definitions of
being both dominant to IV (I–V = D–T) and subdominant to V
(I–V = S–T). But at the end of the cadence, the "being-a-dominant"—
the "negation" of degree I as the tonic—changes into a "having-a-
dominant." Instead of being dominant to IV and subdominant to V,
I now has IV and V for its own subdominant and dominant. Out of
the "negation of negation," out of the "internal division" [*Entzweiung*],
degree I arises as a "self-reconciled" [*mit sich vermittelte*], restored
tonic.

Riemann reinterpreted Hauptmann's dialectical interpretation of the
cadence so that it could be combined with the Helmholtzian theory
of chordal relationships. "The first tonic is thesis, the subdominant

together with the tonic six-four chord is antithesis, and the dominant together with the concluding root-position tonic triad is synthesis; the tonic is thetic, the subdominant antithetic, and the dominant synthetic" [These ist die erste Tonika, Antithese die Unterdominante mit dem Quartsextakkord der Tonika, Synthese die Oberdominante mit dem schließenden Grundakkord der Tonika; thetisch ist die Tonika, antithetisch die Unter-, synthetisch die Oberdominante].[12] The dominant chord is considered "synthetic" because—according to Helmholtz—it is contained in the harmonic series of the tonic chord. "If I should progress from C–e–G to G–b–D,[13] then I would turn toward a chord that had already been heard in the first chord" [Wenn ich von C–e–G fortschreite zu G–h–D, so wende ich mich zu einem Klange hin, welcher schon in dem ersten Accorde mitgehört (worden ist)].[14] The subdominant chord, on the other hand, is "antithetical" because its root falls outside of the harmonic series of the tonic chord. "It is just the reverse with the progression from C–e–G to F–a–C. The sound of F is not prepared by the first chord; it must be newly discovered and instituted" [Umgekehrt ist es mit dem Schritte von C–e–G nach F–a–C. Der F-Klang ist in dem ersten Accorde nicht vorbereitet, er muß neu gefunden und eingesetzt werden].[15]

In Riemann's interpretation of the cadence, the relationship between I and V appears as a simple, nondialectical statement of the key. The changeover from "being-a-dominant" to "having-a-dominant," the dialectical "internal division" and "restoration," is restricted to the relationship between I and IV. Instead of becoming a subdominant directly, through a plagal cadence, IV becomes a subdominant indirectly, through an identification of the dominant I in I–IV with the tonic I in V–I.

Implicit within the interpretation of degree IV (and the progression IV–I) as "antithetic" and degree V (and the progression V–I) as "synthetic" is the notion that the I–IV–V–I cadence cannot appear in the retrograde form I–V–IV–I. For it would be absurd to let "synthesis" precede "antithesis." The determination of chordal meanings, of "harmonic logic," is thus connected with a rule for the proper sequence of chordal scale degrees.

The major-mode cadence was the model on which, in his "Musical Logic," Riemann developed the dialectic of chords. Only in his "Musical Syntax" of 1877, dedicated to Arthur von Oettingen, the founder of "dualism" in harmonic theory, did Riemann analyze not only the major-mode, but also the minor-mode cadence. The cadences are analyzed, in fact, in a rigorously "dualistic" sense. The major mode is based on the overtone series, the minor mode on the undertone series.

A portion of the tonic chord's harmonic series (its overtone or undertone series) forms, in major, degree V but not IV, and in minor, degree iv but not v. Thus in major, IV is "antithetic" or "antilog" and V is "synthetic" or "homolog." By constrast, in minor, v is "antithetic" and iv is "synthetic." And so in major, I–IV–V–I should be considered the "natural" cadence, in minor, i–v–iv–i.[16] Riemann attributes opposite meanings to analogous degrees: in relation to the first degree, the fourth degree is "antilog" in major and "homolog" in minor, while the fifth degree is "homolog" in major and "antilog" in minor.

The Roman numerals that represent chordal scale degrees are simple ordinal numbers. The number "IV" does not signify anything about the meaning of the chord that it labels. The chord can be "homolog" or "antilog." But the letters "T," "D," and "S," used by Riemann since 1893[17] as abbreviations for "tonic," "dominant," and "subdominant," should be seen as special signs for harmonic functions, for the meanings of chords. Functional designations explain the "logic of musical composition" [*Logik des Tonsatzes*].

The signs for the harmonic functions are, nevertheless, inconsistent with the dialectical interpretation of the cadence, with the "logic" that Riemann had developed in his "Musical Syntax" of 1877. If the subdominant is "antilog" and "antithetic" in major, but conversely "homolog" and "synthetic" in minor, then "subdominant" is a designation not of a single meaning, but of contrary meanings that cancel each other out. The function "S" and the "logos" [here *Logos* = "meaning"] hinted at by the expressions "homolog" and "antilog" are completely at odds.

The divergence could have been avoided had Riemann abandoned the "dualism" that forced the interpretation of i–v–iv–i = T–D–S–T as the "natural" cadence in minor. If, in both the major and minor modes, the subdominant represents "antithesis" and the dominant "synthesis," then "function" and "logos" are identical. But Riemann resolutely clung to "dualism." And the result of his remaining steadfast to the goal of the "furthest possible amalgamation of the ideas of Hauptmann, Helmholtz, and von Oettingen" was the undermining of the concept of functions.

· · ·

The contradiction between the concepts of function and "musical logic"—irresolvable under the assumptions of the "dual" system—suggests that the content of the categories "dominant" and "subdominant" should be defined in a way other than by the dialectical schema "antithesis-synthesis." One might, for example, try looking for the meaning of the term "subdominant" in those features or relationships common to all chords having a subdominant function.

The expectation is quickly disappointed, of course, that a recurring tone might form the *vinculum substantiale* [material link] between all chords that fulfill or could fulfill the subdominant function in a certain key. Both the *Leittonwechselklang* of the major subdominant [in C major, **e–a–c′** from **f–a–c′**] and the *Leittonwechselklang* of the minor subdominant [**f–a♭–d♭′** from **f–a♭–c′**] are subdominant chords in a major key. But **e–a–c′** and **f–a♭–d♭′** have no tone in common.

Even an attempt to explain the association between chords of the same function by reference to recurring relationships—instead of to common features—would run into irresolvable difficulties. Chords of the same function are, to be sure, often interchangeable, but not always. Between the tonic and the dominant one can have, in place of the subdominant, its parallel [**d–f–a** in C major] or *Leittonwechselklang* [**e–a–c′**]. But the experiment of replacing dominants with their *Leittonwechselklänge* in the progression (D)–D–T results in the tonally incomprehensible chord progression a♯-minor/b-minor/C-major [the G-maj. dominant becomes b-min., and then its secondary dominant, F♯-maj., becomes an a♯-min. chord]. Defining the concepts of harmonic function by relationships in which chords of the same function may or may not appear is thus not a possibility, if absurd consequences are to be avoided.

To define the content of functional concepts, and to explain the connection between chords of the same function, Riemann alternately relied on both chordal relationships and chordal features. Functions are based on the "orientation toward the current tonic" [Stellung zur jeweiligen Tonika].[18] And by the "orientation" of the dominant and subdominant he must have had in mind the fifth-relation that connects them with the tonic. Thus the fifth-relation is the phenomenon that lays the foundation for the concept of functions.

A subdominant parallel or dominant parallel is not, however, in a fifth-relation with the tonic. Thus secondary chords, though they fulfill the same functions as primary chords, apparently do not participate in the relationships that determine the content of the concepts of dominant and subdominant. The problem was never articulated by Riemann. Yet his hypothesis that secondary chords are mere "apparent consonances" can be understood as an attempt to cling to the functional identity of degrees I and vi, or ii and IV, without abandoning the role of the fifth-relation in establishing harmonic functions.

The roots of parallel chords in major and *Leittonwechselklänge* in minor, and the fifths of *Leittonwechselklänge* in major and parallel chords in minor, are to be taken as "apparent consonances" or "conceptual dissonances" [*Auffassungsdissonanzen*]—as surrogate tones to which there still clings the memory of the true harmonic tones they replace. And so the fifth-relation with the tonic can shine through a *Leittonwechselklang* of the major dominant or subdominant, even though a tone a half step below substitutes for the root. But the arguments on which Riemann supports his theses are fatally flawed.

1. Riemann describes "apparently consonant" secondary chords as "chords whose use in composition is determined by the derivation from the primary chords that they replace" [Akkorde, für deren Setzweise die Ableitung von den durch sie vertretenen Hauptklängen maßgebend ist].[19] The appeal to the chords' "use in composition" [*Setzweise*] can only mean that "conceptual dissonances" fall under the prohibition against doubling dissonant tones. But the rule against doubling the root of the subdominant parallel in major, which Riemann defines as a dissonant *sixte ajoutée*, is erroneous if it is intended as an assertion about musical reality and not as an arbitrarily imposed norm. And only as an empirical rule would it provide support for the theory of "apparent consonance."

2. According to the theory of functions, the parallelism of major and minor, the correlation between C major and A minor, is based on the phenomenon of "apparent consonance": the fifth of a major chord is interchangeable with the sixth, the root of a minor chord with the lower second. The a-minor chord is an "apparent consonance" in the key of C major, and the C-major chord is one in the key of A minor. Thus the interpretation of a chord as an "apparent consonance" presumes that the key is well established to which the chord should relate. Yet in the sequences a–d–C–F and F–C–d–a, the parallelism of the a-minor and C-major, or d-minor and F-major, chords is a phenomenon that directly asserts itself without one having first to determine whether A minor or C major should be the tonic. And if the major-minor parallelism is independent of the establishment of a key, it evades explanation by the theory of "apparent consonance."

3. The concept of "apparent consonance" embraces phenomena so diverse that one may question whether it makes sense to subsume them under the same category. From the major-minor parallelism of the a-minor and C-major, or d-minor and F-major, chords one must distinguish a major-minor analogy that, under the assumptions of the theory of functions, can be explained only by doing violence to the theory itself. The ii°–V–I cadence in minor is analogous to the ii–V–I cadence in major, and the i–V–VI deceptive cadence in minor is analogous to the I–V–vi deceptive cadence in major. Yet in the minor mode, according to the symbolization of the theory of functions, degree

ii is not a subdominant parallel nor is degree VI a tonic parallel. Riemann explains degree VI in minor as the *Leittonwechselklang* of the tonic, and degree ii in minor as a fragment of a subdominant seventh chord (A minor: **B–d–f–a**), a chord which—read from the top down—is to be viewed as corresponding to the dominant seventh chord in major (C major: **g–b–d′–f′**). But the notion that **B** is the "characteristic dissonance" of the subdominant seventh chord **B–d–f–a** is frustrated by musical reality, in which it is evident that **a** is the chord's actual dissonance.[20] For the theory of functions, the phenomenon of the major-minor analogy is a "blind spot" [*blinder Fleck*].

4. While it would be wrong to dismiss the term "apparent consonance" as merely a terminological phantom, the range of phenomena to which the term applies is quite narrow. The e-minor chord in the progressions C–e–G and G–e–C is undeniably a dependent, intermediate type of sonority. On a strong beat it appears as a chord caused by a suspension, on a weak beat, by an anticipation. As a chord caused by a suspension it shares the function of the succeeding harmony (C|e–g = T|Dp–D and G|e–C = D|Tl[21]–T), when caused by an anticipation it shares the function of the preceding harmony (C–e|G = T–Tl|D and G–e|C = D–Dp|T).

First, however, the phenomenon of "apparent consonance" resists generalization into a fixed principle. Second, one can derive, as "apparent consonances," not only secondary chords from primary chords, but also primary chords from secondary chords. And third, "apparent consonance" is not a fundamental phenomenon, but one based on other factors.

a) In the major-mode cadence T–Sp–D–T, conceiving of the root of the subdominant parallel as a "dissonance" seems, if not impossible, then at least forced. An interpretation of the root of the parallel chord as an anticipation of the dominant's fifth would presume that the subdominant parallel falls on a weak beat. But in general, it falls on a strong beat.

b) In the major-mode cadence S–Sp–D–T, the root of the subdominant parallel is a neighbor note to the fifth of the subdominant. Thus the subdominant parallel is an "apparent consonance." But S–Sp can be reversed, as Sp–S, without compromising the tonal sense of the cadence. And in the progression Sp–S–D–T, the fifth of the subdominant is a passing tone between the root of the subdominant parallel and the third of the dominant.[22] The basic form S appears as a variant, the variant Sp as a basic form. The phenomenon of "apparent consonance" thwarts rather than supports the basic principles of the theory of functions.

c) As a passing chord in the cadence Sp–S–D–T, the subdominant is an "apparent consonance" without an inherent tonal function distinct from that of the subdominant parallel. But the six-four chord in the progression $T–D_4^6–T^6$ is also a passing chord; and yet it still has an undeniably dominant function. Thus the mere fact that a chord, or part of a chord, is treated as the result of a passing tone, a suspension, or an anticipation is insufficient to make it operate as an "apparent consonance." A second requirement that must be met is for the chords to be in a third-relation: S following Sp is a "apparent consonance," but D_4^6 following T is not. And the fact that "apparent consonance" is tied to two prerequisites—the third-relation of the chords and the treatment of part of the chord as a passing tone, suspension, or anticipation—means that it is a dependent phenomenon based on other factors, that it thus cannot be the founding principle of a system of chordal functions.

. . .

Riemann asserts that tonal functions are based on two complementary factors—the fifth-relation of the primary chords and the "apparent consonance" of the secondary chords. His thesis is seriously flawed. Yet it would be wrong to view the theory of harmonic functions as a theory of harmonic fictions. After all, it is undeniable that the subdominant and subdominant parallel fulfill the same function in the cadence.

The idea that a function is a meaning capable of being represented by various chords without one of the chords having to be interpreted as the basic form and the others as mere variants—an idea hidden by Riemann's theory of "apparent consonance"—does justice to the parallelism of major and minor, and to the circumstance that while Sp can be dependent on S, the reverse is also possible (S–Sp–D–T and Sp–S–D–T). Functional identity must be distinguished from material dependency.

On the other hand, attention should be drawn to the dialectical schema that Riemann expounded in 1872 as "musical logic." Since "musical logic," functional designations, and the "dualistic" system are incompatible to the extent that any combination of two of the factors excludes the third, Riemann later discarded "musical logic." But it is "dualism," rather than the dialectical schema, that can be sacrificed.

The characterization of the subdominant as "antithetic," and of the dominant as "synthetic," implies that the progression S–D is the norm and its retrograde D–S a deviation. And undeniably the chord progression D–S (Dp–S, D–Sp, Dp–Sp) is a rare exception. In Beethoven's Op. 2 sonatas—disregarding subdominant sixth chords that form a passing chord between the root position and first inversion of the dominant,[23] and sequences in which Sp follows D (C major: C–G–d–a) or S follows Dp (G major: G–D–e–b–C–G)[24]—only in a single passage is the T–S–D–T cadence reversed to T–D–S–T.[25]

In Riemann's "musical logic"—the dialectic of the cadence—it is assumed, without being proved, that the number of functions is limited to three. And an attempt to explain this limitation may rely less on the theory of functions than on its apparent opposite, the theory of fundamental progressions or chordal scale degrees. That is, the empirical knowledge underlying the theory of functions can be expressed most simply by the proposition that chords at the interval of a fifth or second are functionally different, while chords at the interval of a third are functionally similar [indifferent].

The basic principle of the theory of fundamental progressions is that the fifth-progression is the establishing factor of tonal relationships. Riemann, of course, failed to recognize that what is crucial is not the relationship between chords a fifth apart, but their functional difference, and that a second-relation establishes a difference analogous to that of a fifth-relation. (Rameau's method of reducing second-progressions of the basse fondamentale to fifth-progressions by supposing a "suppressed root" expresses this same circumstance in a somewhat distorted manner.)

Only through the hypothesis that chords a fifth or a second apart are functionally different while chords a third apart are functionally similar is it possible to understand the fundamental tenet of the theory of functions—that the number of functions is limited to three. If three chords are all a fifth or a second apart from each other (C–d–G, C–F–G), then a fourth chord would either be a repetition or a parallel of one of the preceding chords. The subdominant and subdominant parallel are functionally equivalent because both, owing to functional differences, contrast with not only the tonic but also the dominant, and therefore represent a third function.

One could object that the connection between harmonic functions and chordal root relationships ought to be understood as a chance coincidence, not as a founding of functions on the difference or similarity in root relationships. Just because two factors coincide does not prove that the one depends on the other. But an analysis of the I–IV–vii°–iii–vi–ii–V–I sequence of fifth-progressions shows that it is, in fact, a question of dependence, because this sequence not only cannot be completely defined in terms of functions, but it also appears as an exception to the rule of different and similar root relationships.

Riemann mentions that sequences of fifth-progessions (more precisely, their medial degrees) evade attempts at a functional interpretation. "But, as Fétis was the first to correctly recognize, as long as the sequence continues, the proper harmonic motion—the cadencing— is at a standstill" [Wie zuerst Fétis richtig erkannte, steht aber die eigentliche Harmoniebewegung, die Kadenzierung, so lange still, als die Sequenz währt].[26] And one should not dismiss as accidental the fact that what entangles the theory of different and similar root relationships in a contradiction is precisely the sequence of fifths. The uncertainty of the subject matter itself corresponds to a dilemma for the theory. On the one hand, a rigid functional interpretation would have to attribute a tonic function to degrees iii and vi of the sequence in major, and a subdominant function to degrees VI and ii° of the sequence in minor. On the other hand, the functionally equivalent degrees iii and vi in major and VI and ii° in minor are separated from each other by the interval of a fifth. Thus they are at the same time both "similar" [indifferent] and "different." Yet one may consider as adequate a theory that fails exactly where even the phenomenon it is supposed to explain becomes vague and uncertain.

SYSTEM AND HISTORY

In 1912, Hugo Riemann wrote in the preface to his *Musikgeschichte in Beispielen* that "surely the proper goal of historical research is to reveal the ultimate natural laws, common to all periods, that control all perception and artistic forms" [Ist doch der eigentliche Zweck der historischen Forschung, das allen Zeiten gemeinsame Urgesetzliche, das alles Empfinden und künstlerische Gestalten beherrscht, erkennbar zu machen]. And it was as the discovery of such "ultimate natural laws" that Riemann viewed the "dual system of harmony," which he had developed through the "practical realization and the furthest possible amalgamation of the ideas of Hauptmann, Helmholtz, and von Oettingen" [praktische Verwertung und tunlichste Verschmelzung der Ideen Hauptmann's, Helmholtz's und v. Oettingen's].[1]

Helmholtz, on whom Riemann relied, was more cautious. While Riemann the historian believed that the basic principle of the system of harmony could be found in nature, Helmholtz the natural scientist looked to history. "Hence follows the principle, still not sufficiently current with our music theorists and historians, that the system of scales, keys, and their harmonic fabric is not based on immutable natural laws, but is the consequence of aesthetic principles which, in company with the progressive development of mankind, have already been subject to change and will yet be subject to change in the future" [Daraus folgt der Satz, der unseren musikalischen Theoretikern und Historikern noch immer nicht genügend gegenwärtig ist, daß das System der Tonleitern, der Tonarten und deren Harmoniegewebe nicht auf unveränderlichen Naturgesetzen beruht, sondern daß es die Consequenz ästhetischer Principien ist, die mit fortschreitender Entwickelung der Menschheit einem Wechsel unterworfen gewesen sind und ferner noch sein werden].[2] But if the "harmonic fabric" of major-minor tonality is the "consequence of aesthetic principles," then Riemann's theory must be understood as dogma: as an attempt to explicate the harmony of one epoch—the 17th through the 19th century—in terms of systematically coherent concepts.

It would be a mistake to perceive an indictment in the character-ization of Riemann's system as dogma.[3] Reinterpreting a "natural system" as a dogma does not mean that the theory is unsupported or flawed, but only that the range of phenomena that it encompasses is limited. At the same time, of course, it alters the theoretical status of the principles on which the system is based. In a dogma understood as such, there is nothing of "ultimate natural laws" in the proposition that the perfect fifth and major third are the only "directly intelligible"[4] intervals. Rather, it is an axiom that enables one to present the manifestations of 17th- through 19th-century tonal harmony in a sys-tematic context.

According to Helmholtz, major-minor tonality is based on the notion of establishing musical coherence through relationships between chords.[5] It is an "aesthetic principle," a "stylistic principle"[6] that is historically motivated, not something found in nature. The realization of a "stylistic principle," however, depends on rules and means that are "conditioned by the nature of things" [durch die Natur der Sache bedingt].[7] "If the goal is correctly established toward which the artists of a certain genre strive, and the main direction of the course on which, for that purpose, they have entered, then one can demonstrate, with more or less certainty, why they were compelled to observe this or that rule, why they were forced to make use of these or those technical means" [Wenn der Zweck richtig festgestellt ist, dem die Künstler einer gewissen Stilart nachstreben, und die Hauptrichtung des Weges, den sie dazu eingeschlagen haben, so läßt sich übrigens mehr oder weniger bestimmt nachweisen, warum sie gezwungen waren, diese oder jene Regel zu befolgen, dieses oder jenes technische Mittel zu ergreifen].[8] Thus according to Helmholtz, the "nature of things" (in which Riemann tried to find "ultimate natural laws") dictates the "means," but not the "goal."

As a result, there is yet a second distinction between Riemann's and Helmholtz's principles (in addition to the distinction that the doctrine of harmony viewed by Riemann as a "natural system" would have been characterized by Helmholtz as dogma). The two factors of the harmonic system that Helmholtz termed the "nature of things" and the "stylistic principle" were interpreted differently by Riemann and Helmholtz. With Riemann they appear as postulate and result, or as substructure and superstructure. With Helmholtz they are the means and the goal. While Riemann accentuates the "nature of things" as the true foundation of the theory of harmony, Helmholtz emphasizes a "stylistic principle" as the goal realized through the various means of tonal harmony.

The difference seems irresolvable. An attempt, however, to define the "nature of things" and the "stylistic principle" more precisely indicates that the categories of "postulate," "result," "means," and "goal" are inadequate. As a result, the difference between Riemann's and Helmholtz's interpretations loses something of its significance. On the one hand, the "nature of things," taken by Riemann as the basis of the system of harmony, must be understood as the sum total of possibilities—not the sum total of clearly outlined, readily given facts. And on the other hand, the "stylistic principle" of which Helmholtz spoke consists of nothing more than that the individual features of tonal harmony—the restriction of the modes to major and minor, the fundamental bass, the emancipation of the seventh chord, and the distinction between a function and a chordal scale degree—are linked together and appear as the cofactors of a system. And it is doubtful whether it makes sense to designate the correlation as the "goal" and its cofactors as the "means."

An analysis of the different meanings of "major third" [große Terz = "large third"] may suffice to make clear both the significance of the definition of the "nature of things" as the sum total of possibilities, and the characterization of the "stylistic principle" of tonal harmony as a correlation of cofactors. A major third can be conceived as: first, a directly intelligible, irreducible consonance, [a Durterz = a "major-mode third"]; second, a ditone—the combination of two identical whole tones; and third, a distance whose unit of measure is the half step. The first meaning is realized, or intended, in tonal harmony, the second in the intervallic compositional technique of the 14th and 15th centuries, and the third in "composition with twelve tones related only to each other" [Kompositionen mit zwölf nur aufeinander bezogenen Tönen (Schoenberg)].

The Durterz corresponds to the proportion 4:5, the ditone to the ratio 64:81, and the third measured as a distance conforms to the logarithms of equal temperament. But to see modifications in tuning and temperament as the basis or precondition for a change in the meaning of intervals would be a mistake stemming from a "naturalistic" bias. A major third [große Terz] need not be tuned in "just intonation" to appear as a major third [*Durterz*] in a tonal context. It can be tempered without compromising its meaning. The meaning of "major third" is, to echo Carl Stumpf, an "object of conceptualization and the mind's proclivity for seeking relationships" [Sache der Auffassung und des beziehenden Denkens], a categorical factor that can surely be supported by tuning, but is neither tied to it nor dependent on it.

This analysis admits of two inferences that complement each other.

1. If the interpretations of the major third are independent of tuning and temperament, then they must be based on the contexts of a system, contexts in which the third forms a cofactor. The major third [*große Terz*] becomes the "major" third [*Durterz*] in tonal harmony, that is, in correlation with the interpretation of the triad as a direct unity and of the lower tone of the fifth and major third [*große Terz*] as a root. The relation of the cofactors, both reciprocally and to the whole, cannot be reduced to a cause and effect. An effort to determine whether the unity of the triad is based on the definition of the third as "major" third [*Durterz*], or vice versa, would be as futile as it would be superfluous. To lay the foundation for a historical investigation, the fact suffices that while in tonal harmony the three features are mutually interconnected [(1) the third as *Durterz*; (2) the lower tone of the fifth and major third as root; (3) the triad as a direct unity], they do not apply at all to the polyphonic practice of the 14th and 15th centuries. According to the contrapuntal rules of the late Middle Ages, the major third tends toward the perfect fifth or . And in this 3–5 progression: (1) the third is a ditone; (2) a differentiation between root and secondary tone is not possible; and (3) the minor third, which ought to progress to the unison or , forms with the major third a complex that should be understood not as a primary unity—a chord—but as a secondary combination.

2. The number of meaningful interpretations of the major third is quite small. It is unlikely that in addition to its interpretations as "major" third, ditone, and distance, there would be still other interpretations in which the third appears as a cofactor in a system. The sum total of possible meaningful interpretations is, however, the "nature of things." One could reply that the expression "major third" [*große Terz*] is equivocal and feigns a unity of subject that does not exist—that the "major" third [*Durterz*], ditone, and third measured as a distance are three different intervals, not changing meanings of the same interval. The objection could hardly be refuted were the meaning of an interval dependent on the tuning or temperament in which it is intoned. The fact, however, that the interpretation is independent of

the intonation, that the different explanations can thus refer to the same substrate, proves that a unity of subject does stand apart from the changes in meaning.

. . .

Both the theory of fundamental progressions and the theory of functions were conceived as "natural systems," not as dogmas. Hence the search for criteria on which to base a historical determination of the origin of tonal harmony violates the very intentions at the root of these theories. In his *Traité de l'harmonie* (1722), Rameau cites an "example of Zarlino, to which we add the fundamental bass" [Exemple de Zarlin, auquel nous ajoûtons la Basse fondamentale].[9]

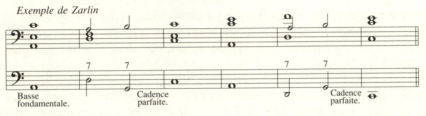

Example 6

The addition of a supplementary voice is intended as a clarification, not as an alteration. Rameau is convinced that Zarlino's 6–8 clausula

would have been perceived as a fragmentary *cadence parfaite*.

But if one understands Rameau's "natural system" as a dogma with restricted historical validity, then out of this reinterpretation one can derive a historical criterion. That is, if the 6–8 clausula is to be considered a dominant cadence and thus an analog to V–I, then its penultimate sonority must be interpreted as a fragment of the dominant seventh chord. The dominant character of the vii[6]–I cadence presupposes the emancipation of the dissonant seventh.

To avoid floundering in vague uncertainties, this study must proceed from the determinable criteria of compositional technique. The number of such criteria, however, is small.

1. In tonal harmony, a triad is a directly given unity. But whether what appears to us as a V–I cadence was, in the late 15th century, intended as a chord progression or as a combination of interval progressions cannot be directly determined from the surviving musical sources. In the formula , the contratenor bassus [**g–c′**] rep-

resents not the root movement of a chord progression, but a supplementary voice added to a discant-tenor framework. On the other hand, the lowest voice can appear as a harmonic bass if the tenor substitutes e', the third, for c'. Of course as long as the dominant character of the cadence ♩ is not an established fact (and, as mentioned, it assumes the emancipation of the dissonant seventh), it is doubtful, even in the V–I cadence, whether the bass was to be understood as a *basse fondamentale* and the succession of sonorities as a chord progression.

2. The precise period in which the conception became widespread that the root position and first inversion of a chord are "harmonically identical" is something that cannot be deduced from the surviving musical sources. It must instead be inferred from the evidence left by theorists.

3. The emancipation of the dissonant seventh comes to light in the seventh chord on degree V, not degree ii. The seventh chord on degree ii results from a suspension within the discant-tenor clausula ♩. And as long as the suspension was regularly prepared and resolved, it is impossible to determine whether this dissonance was conceived as a cofactor in a chord or as a relation between a dissonant tone and a reference tone—whether it was "harmonically" or "contrapuntally" motivated. The seventh chord on degree V is the first to evade the rules of counterpoint. In general, it cannot be explained as a suspension, or even as a passing tone: not as a suspension because it falls on a weak beat, and not as a passing tone because degree IV or ii precedes it [so that there is no consonant tone to pass *from*].

4. Riemann brought the differentiation between primary and secondary degrees to the center of the theory of functions, but this differentiation is not tied to that theory's hypotheses. One can question the explanation of secondary chords as "apparent consonances" without having to deny the fact that ii, iii, and vi are subordinate to IV, V, and I. One can determine whether degrees ii, iii, and vi were or were not conceived as secondary degrees from two features of compositional technique: from the chords' metric placement and from their root progressions. If degrees ii, iii, and vi regularly or predominantly occur on weak beats and result from a third-progression of the chordal roots, then they are intended as secondary degrees. An example is degree iii in the progressions I–iii–IV and I–iii–V. It is an unaccented chord resulting from a passing tone or anticipation, and can be interpreted as the *Leittonwechselklang* of the tonic—as a secondary form of I—because it is connected to I by a third-progression of chordal roots.

5. One of the distinctive features of tonal harmony is the fact that

it excludes the "minor dominant" in major and the "major subdominant" in minor. And just as with the distinction between primary and secondary degrees, one can grant this fact without having to accept the speculative explanation of the theory of functions—the recourse to the axiom that the perfect fifth and major third are the only "directly intelligible" intervals. Hermann Erpf, in contrast to Riemann, does admit the Mixolydian degree v as a tonal dominant and the Dorian degree IV as a tonal subdominant.[10] But this is a mistaken idea apparently based on a misunderstanding of "modal reminiscences" in 19th-century harmony. In the 19th century, the Mixolydian degree v should be understood as an altered dominant with a chromatic—not diatonic—third, as a deviation from the tonal norm that did not, however, endanger the chordal context. This was possible because tonal harmony was so firmly established that it was capable of tolerating exceptions to the rule. In the 19th century, the "modal" character of the chord is a mere illusion, though—as a historical reminiscence—an aesthetically relevant illusion. But the fact that 19th-century harmonic tonality allowed pseudo-modal chordal degrees as cross-modal borrowings is no basis for then subsuming the original Mixolydian degree v and Dorian degree IV (whose thirds were diatonic in the 16th century) under the concept of tonal harmony.

6. It is, as mentioned, one of the criteria of harmonic tonality that the T–S–D–T cadence is not reversed to become T–D–S–T. And not only are degrees IV and V affected by the rule that the functional progression S–D is irreversible, but so are degrees ii and iii, which according to the theory of functions must be understood as secondary forms of IV and V. The progressions V–ii (D–Sp), iii–IV (with the meaning Dp–S and not Tl–S), and iii–ii (Dp–Sp)—just like V–IV (D–S)—are all avoided. It is difficult to give sufficient reasons for the rule. For instance, the mere fact that the cadential effect of plagal progressions (I–V, IV–I) is weaker than that of authentic ones (I–IV, V–I) is not sufficient to exclude from tonal harmony the doubling of the plagal cadence—I–V–IV–I [= IV/V–V—IV–I]. But the validity of the rule can scarcely be doubted. Compliance with it is a historical criterion whose relevance becomes evident in conjunction with the other defining features of tonal harmony.

CHAPTER II

INTERVALLIC AND CHORDAL COMPOSITION

TERMINOLOGY

It would be futile to attempt the separate definition of such basic concepts of tonal harmony as "chord" or "*basse fondamentale*," or to name specific criteria by which one could determine whether a sonority is or is not a chord. For terms like "chord" and "*basse fondamentale*" do not designate objective facts that one can point to in a musical score. Rather, these terms denote cofactors in a particular mode of musical perception, factors that receive their full meaning only in relation to other factors.

1. "Chord" was originally termed the mere sounding together of different tones.[1] But in the theory of tonal harmony, (1) only sonorities of three or more tones are labeled as chords, (2) sonorities of two tones are interpreted as fragments of three- or four-tone sonorities, (3) chords are understood not as resultants—as combinations of tones and intervals—but as directly perceived unities, and (4) the intervals between the roots or reference tones of chords are viewed as the criterion of chordal relationship. This more precise definition has not always been considered a narrowing of the concept of chord, for Rameau and even Riemann were sufficiently uncritical to impute if not the theoretical conceptualization then at least the musical perception of earlier centuries to their own concept of chord.[2] Yet if one does understand the new concept as a limitation, then, since tonal harmony is the subject of the following studies, the older concept must be dropped.

2. Rameau's theory of the *basse fondamentale* assumes both the concept of chordal inversion and the distinction between chordal dissonances and nonharmonic tones. And conversely, both the hypothesis that chords can be reduced to basic forms consisting of superimposed thirds and the assertion that a suspended seventh is a chordal dissonance, while a suspended fourth is a nonharmonic tone, are questionable and devoid of meaning without the category of the *basse fondamentale*. To conceive of the sixth chord **f–a–d'** as an inversion of the root-position chord **d–f–a** only makes sense if the root **d** is understood as part of a *basse fondamentale*. If one compares **d–f–a** and **f–a–d'** as separate sonorities, then one can argue against Rameau that **f**, as intervallic root of the major third **f–a**, rivals **d** as root of the fifth **d–a**. This argument, however, can be set aside for two reasons. First, the category "*basse fondamentale*" is not based on the concept

of chordal inversion. On the contrary, the *"basse fondamentale"* can be understood only in a reciprocal relationship with chordal inversion. And second, a psychological proof of chordal inversion is as superfluous as it is questionable. The theory of tonal harmony does not assert that we are constrained to hear the tone **d'** as the root of a sixth chord owing to acoustical or perceptual laws, but only that the concept of inversion makes possible a theoretical representation of the chordal relationships within the system of tonal harmony. In the chord progression ♮ , the *basse fondamentale* is the fifth-progression **d–G** because the sixth chord is an inversion. But at the same time, the sixth chord is interpreted as an inversion in order to result in a fifth-progression as the *basse fondamentale*. Without the thesis of the primacy of root progressions by fifth over progressions by second, Rameau's theory would be nothing but an "empty scheme of thirds" [*Terzenschematismus*], as it was misconstrued by Riemann.[3]

A precise understanding of the theory of tonal harmony—an understanding that takes into account the reciprocal relationships of musical categories and does not fix on a particular one taken out of context—is at the same time the necessary condition for a historical differentiation of tonal harmony from what preceded it. In considering, for example, a chain of sixth chords where second-progressions are the norm and fifth-progressions are a rarity restricted to the "descending-fourth" clausula[4] , deciding whether or not to interpret a sixth chord as an inversion is not only difficult but superfluous. A series of second-progressions ought not to be understood as having a *basse fondamentale*, and without the reciprocal concept of the *basse fondamentale*, the concept of inversion loses its meaning. To be sure, even in the 15th century the sixth chord was perceived as a sonority less stable than the five-three chord. And likewise, a consciousness of the octave identity of the tones **d** and **d'** in the chords **d–f–a** and **f–a–d'** can be taken for granted. But these facts alone are an insufficient basis on which to found the concept of inversion. The interval progressions and represent the same cadence—the "mi clausula."

But it would be arbitrary to designate the one as the inversion of the other, because the category "chordal root" is irrelevant to the cadential effect of the 3–1 and 6–8 interval progressions.

3. The separation of harmony and counterpoint makes sense only under the assumptions of tonal harmony. A root progression such as IV–V–I or a functional progression such as S–D–T leaves open the

matter of voice leading, which can be absurd without invalidating the "harmonic logic." But the correlate of a harmony thought to be independent of voice leading is a voice leading thought to be independent of harmony. Ernst Kurth's thesis[5] that "chord" in Bach's "linear counterpoint" is a result of voice leading, not a prerequisite to it, still does not exclude the possibility that the degree or function a chord represents is predetermined by a harmonic plan. The individual chord may appear as the pure result of voice leading precisely because the general schema of a degree or functional progression can leave the particular form of a chord undecided—its voicing and any dissonances or chromatic alterations. Thus, instead of being mutually exclusive opposites, the concepts of linear and harmonic counterpoint complement each other.

Successfully interpreting the contrapuntally motivated "independence of the voice parts" requires that one either (1) presuppose a harmony thought to be independent of voice leading, or (2) downgrade sonorities to the status of incidental occurrences of indifferent type, or finally (3) reduce their significance to an aspect of "intervallic compatibility" [*Intervallverträglichkeit*].[6] The first interpretation purports that harmonic considerations do appear to be of secondary importance, not, however, because they are a matter of indifference, but because they are self-evident. The second interpretation is a misunderstanding of Kurth's thesis of linear counterpoint, one against which, with some consternation, he attempted to defend himself.[7] Finally, the third interpretation (which Kurth allows along with the first) fails to recognize the significance of the older type of counterpoint not yet separated from harmony.

The relationships among, and differences between, tonal harmony, linear counterpoint, and the older concept of counterpoint (which embraced both voice leading and the progression of sonorities) can be demonstrated through three possible interpretations of simple interval progressions.

Example 7

According to the theory of tonal harmony, these interval progressions are fragments of chord progressions that must be filled in by one's musical imagination. They represent the *basse fondamentale* iv–V in A minor [ex. 7a–c] or vii–I in F major [ex. 7d–f]. And according to the dogma of the primacy of fifth-progressions over second-progressions, degrees iv and vii should be explained as seventh chords with "suppressed roots" (ii[7] and V[7] respectively). The interpretation does some violence to the material:[8] it presumes not only the reinterpretation of the Phrygian cadence as a half cadence in minor, but also the "emancipation of the seventh chord."

Kurth's theory permits only the voice leading—thus in ex. 7 only the contrary motion—to be considered as a "contrapuntal" factor. But his concept of "intervallic compatability"—the complement of "voice leading"—is questionable. On the one hand, it implies that it does not matter in these interval progressions whether imperfect consonance precedes perfect consonance, or vice versa. And on the other hand, it implies that the individual sonorities stand on their own and are connected to previous and subsequent sonorities only owing to the stimulus of the voice leading. So if an interval progression represents no functional or degree progression, then according to Kurth it is nothing but a juxtaposition of consonances. The progression breaks down into isolated sonorities.

By contrast, under the concepts of the older theory of counterpoint, the interval progressions 6–8, 3–5, and 3–1 would be defined as progressions from an imperfect to a perfect consonance through contrary motion by half and whole step. The change of interval quality, the particular voice leading, and the pitch successions should be understood as individual factors in a larger concept of counterpoint— factors that may of course be differentiated, but not divorced from each other and subjected to separate rules. The prohibition of parallel fifths and octaves is directed against identical pitch progressions in different voices, but it is also raised against consecutive simultaneities having identical sonorous characters. And the rule that a dissonant suspension must be resolved by a descending second is not only a precept of voice leading, but it also means that the dissonance has to be followed by an imperfect consonance and not—in abrupt contrast—by a perfect consonance.

These interval progressions represent neither functional nor degree progressions, nor are they purely a result of voice leading and intervallic compatability. "Interval progression" is a concept contrary to the categories of both linear counterpoint and tonal harmony.

. . .

These systems are not, of course, mutually exclusive in a rigid way. Vestiges of interval progressions without chordal roots survive in tonal harmony and pose difficulties for its theory.

Example 8

According to the theory of the *basse fondamentale*, the sixth chord [ex. 8a] and the seventh chords [exs. 8b and 8c] should be interpreted as a seventh chord and as ninth chords, all with "suppressed roots." One can hardly deny the implicit assumption of the hypothesis: that the impression of a relationship between the chords is not based on the second-progression of the *basse fondamentale* (IV–V) and thus must be explained in some other way. But the conclusion that a third must be supposed under the first chord, that the roots' second-progression is thus "properly" a fifth-progression (ii⁷–V), is questionable. In ex. 8a it forces the contrapuntal license of a seventh progressing in direct motion to a fifth[9] . And in exs. 8b and 8c, the progression of the fifths of the seventh chords to the thirds of the triads is essential in order to avoid parallel fifths [so supposition of a suppressed root is superfluous as a motivation for the voice leading]. If, however, one puts aside the hypothesis of a suppressed root, then the impression of a relationship between the chords is explicable only if one allows as a chord-connecting factor not only the *basse fondamentale*, but also interval progressions without chordal roots—contrary motion from the sixth to the octave and from the seventh to the fifth.

THE PRINCIPLE OF CONTRASTING SONORITIES

Joseph Smits van Waesberghe described the "principle of contrasting sonorities" in 12th- through 14th-century polyphony as a preliminary stage of tonal harmony.[1] The functions of sonorities are based on melodic functions, not vice versa. "The evolution of harmony in Europe . . . proceeds at first via the vertical expression in chords of the horizontal melodic functions of unisonal song."[2]

The system of melodic functions outlined by Smits van Waesberghe is based on the "chain of thirds" **d–f–a–c'–e'–g'–b'**. A "fundamental note" forms a "functional unit" with two or three thirds above it (e.g., **d** with **f–a** or **f–a–c'**). This expression does not mean that the tones merge into a chord in the sense of tonal harmony, or that they form a type of stationary melody. It means only that the fundamental note **d** has a closer relationship with **f** and **a** than with **c** or **e**. A mode's second chain of thirds (in the d-mode, **c–e–g–b**) operates as a "functional contrast." The fundamental note **d** and the "principal third" **d–f** are elucidated and functionally fixed by the "counter-notes" **c** and **e** or by the "contrasting thirds" **c–e** and **e–g**. The role of the fourth is problematical. Smits van Waesberghe distinguishes three types. The first, a "*quarta consonans*," would be, for example, an upbeat **d** to a fundamental note **g**. The second, a "transitional fourth," mediates the transition from one functional unity to another: for example, from a fundamental note **d** to a contrasting-fifth **g** [**g** as fifth of **c–e–g**]. And the third, a "deviation fourth," should be understood as an expanded third: the contrasting third **e–g** of the finalis **f** is replaced by the contrasting fourth **d–g** owing to an aversion toward the half-step progression (of course **d** then also forms a functional unity with **f**, resulting in a "double function").[3]

The principle of contrasting sonorities, in contrast to tonal harmony, does not presume that a five-three or six-three sonority is a chord, that is, a directly perceived unity. Instead, it makes the functions of sonorities originate in melodic functions. The principle is justified by the fact that in the 12th through the 14th century a simultaneity was the result of successively conceived voices. One could object that the system of thirds was abstracted from polyphonic clausulas like

$$ \text{and} $$

, and then transferred to monophonic contexts. The thesis that the functions of sonorities originated in melodic functions would thus be based on circular reasoning. Yet first, concerning the functions of sonorities in a polyphony that follows the principle of successively conceived voices, legitimate inferences can indeed be drawn from melodic functions. And second, the system of thirds is justified if not by Gregorian chant, then at least by later medieval sacred and secular melodies.[4]

"The Gregorian cadences are based on the contrasting third or thirds of the fundamental note, namely (in the Dorian mode) on **e–c** against **d**, **g–e–c** against **f–d** or **a–d**.

"The result of this in polyphony is obvious: the two-note 'chord' on **c** (**c–e**) will in the cadence contrast with **d** in Dorian, **e–g** on **e** with **f** and **d**, and the triad on **c** (**c–e–g**), as well as that on **e** (**e–g–b**) with **d–a** (the third being avoided in the final chord in the Middle Ages). In this way in the polyphonic development we get in the cadence chords which, expressed in terms of degrees of the scale, can be represented by VII–i and ii–i. These can also occur in the same way in the Phrygian and Mixolydian modes.

"The same rule can be followed in the Lydian mode, except that here we may also have the euphonic deviation of the Lydian mode, which has already been discussed, the result becoming more graceful if, instead of **g–e** as the contrasting third of **f**, the interval **g–d** is used or the following progression [musical notation] = vii–II–I. Here we have two different functions before the tonic is reached."[5]

Of course Smits van Waesberghe's sketch of a theory of chordal functions leaves many questions unresolved.

1. Degree symbols like VII and ii presume the concept of inversion. But whether the lower tone of a third or the upper tone of a sixth can always be considered the fundamental tone is questionable, even implausible. In the first place, the idea of a *basse fondamentale* in the 14th century is not only anachronistic, but superfluous to the explanation of the cadential effect of interval progressions such as [musical notation] , [musical notation] , or [musical notation] . The cadential effect is based on the contrast in sonority between imperfect and perfect consonance, and on contrary motion by half and whole step. Second, in the interpretation of the Lydian cadence [musical notation] as vii–I, Smits van Waesberghe is forced to impute to the half-step progression a precedence over the whole-step progression that contradicts the medieval classification of intervals.[6] And third, the vii–i Phrygian cadence is only an apparent analogue of the vii–I Lydian cadence: [musical notation] (vii–I) arose from [musical notation] (ii–I); [musical notation] (vii–i), on the contrary, from [musical notation] (III–i). One could object that the distinctions between the hypotheses are canceled out in the final product. But it is simpler, in conformity with the medieval characterization of intervals, to acknowledge a precedence of the whole-step progression at the cadence (Lydian **g–f** or Phrygian **d–e**), to explain the half-step progression (**e–f** or **f–e**) in the other voice as a supplementary, secondary progression, and to renounce the use of degree symbols that imply the concept of inversion.

2. The distinction between the "contrasting third" in the Dorian and Mixolydian clausulas and the "deviation fourth" in the Lydian and Phrygian clausulas is due not only to the difference in the modes, but also to historical developments. The 4–1 [musical notation] and 5–8 [musical notation] clausulas are characteristic of the 12th and early 13th centuries, the 3–1 and 6–8 clausulas of the later 13th and the 14th centuries.

3. The principle of connection by half step, first formulated by

Marchettus of Padua,[7] should not be traced back to the Phrygian and Lydian clausulas. Instead, the reverse is true: the substitution of

and for the clausulas and is,

along with the alteration of the Dorian and Mixolydian *subtonus* to a *subsemitonium* ["lower semitone," i.e., leading tone], a consequence of the principle of connection by half step.

4. Smits van Waesberghe's attempt to interpret the upper and lower contrast chords as proto-forms of the subdominant and dominant is dubious. In tonal harmony, the dominant and subdominant form a contrast that requires a mediating tonic to restore a balance. But in the chordal technique of the 14th century, the upper and lower contrasting sonorities (e.g., g–b–e′ and g–b–d′) merge into one another. They contrast only with the fundamental sonority, not with each other.

For that reason the interval progression can, without changing

its meaning, be combined not only with but also with

.

5. In the 13th and 14th centuries, the harmonic interval of a third was still perceived as an unstable, dependent consonance supported by an adjoining fifth or unison. "Every imperfect dissonance [e.g., a third] sounds quite consonant immediately prior to a [perfect] consonance" [Omnis imperfecta discordantia immediate ante concordantiam bene concordat].[8] The fact that two tones at the interval of a third form a functional unity thus does not presuppose an emancipation of the third to the status of an independent simultaneity. On the contrary, the consonant character of the simultaneity appears as the result of the functional unity of the melodic tones.

. . .

The compositional technique of the Latin double motet *Desolata mater ecclesia—Quae nutritos filios—Filios enutrivi* (transmitted anonymously in the *Roman de Fauvel* and dating from between 1310 and 1314) is defined by the alternation of perfect and imperfect consonances.

Example 9

The thirds and sixths are not dissonances, nor are they the chance result of voice leading—a result permitted only on weak beats so as to remain inconspicuous. Rather, they are imperfect consonances whose contrast to perfect consonances stands out as the principle for connecting sonorities. The fact that perfect consonance appears on strong beats and imperfect consonance on weak beats can be discerned as a norm. Yet the reverse arrangement is not excluded (mm. 2, 11, 24). The alternation of sonorities of different character became a principle of compositional technique as a simple result of the Franconian rule.[9]

The motet concludes on f–c′–f′. Yet the Lydian mode is negated by the Mixolydian mode. Except for in mm. 20–21 and 27–28, it is **g–b(♭)–d** that appears as the fundamental sonority, **f–a–c′** as the lower contrasting sonority, and **a–c′–e′** as the upper contrasting sonority. If one grants **g–b(♭)–d** as the "functional unity" and **f(♯)–a–c(♯)–e** as the "functional contrast," then the successions of sonorities composed of an imperfect and a perfect consonance are almost all intelligible as functions of the g-mode. The simultaneities represent functional sonorities, provided that they consist of tones with the same melodic function. Exceptions are the successions (mm. 13–14), (mm. 20–21), (m. 25), and (mm. 27–28). In mm. 13, 20, and 27 the deviations from the G-sonority can be interpreted as passing tones. In m. 25, however, the functional unity is conspicuously disturbed. Anyone who has adopted the principle of contrasting sonorities as a category of musical perception expects **c′**, the contrasting fifth, to be placed over the contrasting tone **f** , and would not expect **d′**, the fundamental fifth.

The principle of contrasting sonorities is an analogue of modal rhythm. (The tenor of the motet *Desolata mater ecclesia* represents the second rhythmic mode.) A rhythmic mode is based on an alternation or opposition of longs and shorts that lacks the "inner dynamic" of metric rhythm. While it is not improbable that an accent fell on the beginning of a perfection, this does not imply that there was an upbeat character to the even-numbered time values—the breve of the first, "trochaic" mode and the long of the second, "iambic" mode.

The multi-measure metric period [*Taktperiode*] of the 17th through the 19th century, the rhythmic analogue of the tonal cadence, is based on the principle of subordination—on the gradation of metric accent. Of course two factors need to be distinguished within the concept of stress. On the one hand, the beginning of a measure carries an accent; on the other, it seems like the goal of the upbeat. The fact that the last measure in a period can act as the "heaviest" is, on the contrary, not based on the system of accents. It only means that the last measure, the outcome as it were of the period, sums up all the preceding measures.

Modal *ordines* [groups of rhythmic feet], in contrast to a multi-measure rhythmic period, result from simple addition. A *"tertius ordo"* [in mode 1, long short, long short, long short, long] differs from a *"secundus ordo"* [long short, long short, long] not in the greater weight of its ending, but only in its number of units.

In an analogy to modal rhythm, one can characterize the principle of contrasting sonorities as being both antithetic and additive. The tonic of a tonal cadence appears as a goal and result; to describe the cadence, Hauptmann and Riemann made use of the terminology of Hegelian dialectic. But the fundamental and contrasting sonorities form an antithesis that demands no continuation. Instead, the antithesis is self-contained and, as it were, without further effect. Moreover, as with the rhythmic *ordines*, the disposition of simultaneities is formed by the simple addition of individual contrasts. The true principle of 14th-century chordal technique would be missed if, in *Desolata mater ecclesia*, one attempted to interpret the successions 𝄢 (mm. 4–5) and 𝄢 (mm. 13–14) as "modulations" and tried to conceive of the G-sonority in mm. 6 and 15 as a "reinstatement of the mode."

From the simple fact of a conception of successively composed voices, one ought not to infer a precedence of voice leading over the succession of sonorities. A rule like the prohibition of parallels, which in the 14th century was chiefly formulated for the octave and unison (later also for the fifth),[10] is much more doubly based: parallel fifths signify not only an offense against the demand that the voices should be diverse and dissimilar,[11] but also against the principle of the alternation of sonorities of different character. They were allowed in three-voice composition if they coincided with the interval progression 3–1 or 3–5: 𝄢 (*Desolata mater ecclesia*, mm. 13–14) or 𝄢 (mm. 22–23). The explanation that the parallel fifths are "hidden," and thus to be understood as "dead" intervals between voices not directly related, is certainly not unambiguous. Though it immediately makes clear the parallel fifths between upper voices [e.g., m. 1],[12] it is insufficient to justify the parallel fifths between tenor and triplum.[13] If one considers only voice leading, the contention that parallel fifths are "hidden" by the simultaneous interval progressions 3–1 and 3–5 is a flawed hypothesis. Parallel fifths between the outer voices are, after all, quite conspicuous. Thus the concept of a "dead" interval succession, if one allows it, can be confirmed only with regard to the succession of sonorities. It is less that the parallel motion is hidden by contrary motion than that the similarity of the fifths is hidden by the difference between the five-three sonority and the open fifth.

. . .

In the 14th century, the primary interval progression was taken to be the movement from an imperfect to a perfect consonance through contrary motion by half and whole step[14] (3–1, 3–5, 6–8, and their octave duplications):

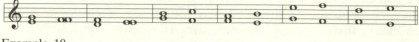

Example 10

Anonymous 13 writes, "The third composed of a whole tone and a semitone requires a unison after it, and that of two whole tones requires a fifth after it. The sixth composed of a semitone with a fifth requires a fifth after it, and that of a whole tone with a fifth requires an octave after it" [La tierce de ton et demiton requiert unisson après li et celle de deux tons quinte après li. La sixte de demi ton avuec quinte requiert après li quinte et celle d'un ton avuec quinte requiert double après li].[15] Other theorists do not count the oblique motion of the minor sixth to the fifth as one of the primary interval progressions. "Concerning consonances, three are consonant *per se* and perfect, namely the unison, octave, and fifth; three are consonant *per accidens* [i.e., dependent on the context], namely the minor third preceding the unison, the major third preceding the fifth, and the major sixth preceding the octave" [Consonantiarum sunt tres per se et perfectae scilicet unisonus diapason et diapente; tres sunt per accidens scilicet semiditonus, ditonus in ordine ad diapente vel unisonum, tonus cum diapente in ordine ad diapason].[16] The fact that the minor sixth lacks either the half step or whole step connection to a perfect consonance (6–8 or 6–5, respectively) was sufficient to exclude it even from the concept of imperfect consonance. "And other species, namely the minor third, major third, and major sixth, produce imperfect consonance because they tend to ascend or descend toward the aforesaid types of perfect consonance, that is, the minor third toward the unison, the major third toward the fifth, and the major sixth toward the octave, ascending or descending in turn" [Et aliae species videlicet semiditonus et ditonus, tonus cum diapente faciunt consonantiam imperfectam, quia tendunt ascendere vel descendere in speciebus praedictis perfectis scilicet semiditonus in unisono, ditonus in diapente, tonus cum diapente in diapason ascendendo vel descendendo seriatim].[17]

In the 13th century, the progressions 3–1, 3–5, and 6–8 were the result of passing tones (4–3–1 and 5–6–8) or "neighbor-note sonorities" (5–3–5).[18] For example, in the *Discantus positio vulgaris* the sixth is described as a passing dissonance between the fifth and octave, a dissonance analogous to the seventh, the passing dissonance between the octave and fifth.[19] But Anonymous 4 already admits the major sixth, by itself a *"vilis discordantia"* [vile dissonance], as an *"optima con-cordantia"* [best consonance] when immediately preceding the octave.[20]

Marchettus of Padua designates the third, sixth, and tenth as dissonances, but differentiates them, as tolerable, from the intolerable dissonances, the second, seventh, and ninth. "But of these diaphonies or dissonances, some are suffered in accordance with hearing and reason, and others not. Of those that are suffered, however, there are principally three, namely the third, sixth, and tenth" [Harum autem dyaphoniarum seu dissonantiarum alie compatiuntur secundum auditum et rationem et alie non. Que vero compatiuntur sunt tres principaliter, scilicet 3, 6, 10].[21] The fact that up until the 15th century thirds and sixths were classified by some theorists as imperfect dissonances, and by others as imperfect consonances, does not signify a distinction in the type of musical perception or in its stage of development. Rather, it must be traced back to a problem in the theory itself.

In the Middle Ages, the determination of whether thirds and sixths were consonances or dissonances was a problem that did not admit of an unequivocal solution. This was because the conditions of consonance—simple numerical proportion, a direct relationship between the tones, the fusing of the pitches, and the autonomy of the sonority—were partially, but not entirely, satisfied. One could either classify thirds as dissonances, though they were permissible as simultaneities, because they did not represent any superparticular numerical proportions; or one could express the euphony of thirds by the word "consonance," but their mathematical imperfection and the lack of autonomy of their sonority by the additional word "imperfect." Marchettus describes the third and sixth as contrary-motion dissonances that—in contrast to oblique-motion, passing, and suspension dissonances—cannot be divided into a dissonant tone and a reference tone, but must instead be resolved by the progression of both voices. "Therefore these dissonances and ones similar are suffered by the ear because they are nearer to a consonance when they move in contrary motion. Thus when two voices are in a dissonance suffered by the ear, each of them, feeling need of consonance, should move in the following manner: namely, that if one tends upward, the other tends downward, always being situated the smallest distance from the consonance to which they tend" [Hee autem dissonantiae et hiis similes ideo compatiuntur ab auditu, quia sunt magis propinque consonantiis cum moventur sursum et deorsum. Oportet enim, quod quando due voces sunt in dissonantia que compatitur ab auditu quod ipsarum quaelibet requirens consonantiam moveatur ita: videlicet, ut si una in sursum tendit, reliqua in deorsum, semper distando per minorem distantiam a consonantia, ad quam tendunt]. In order to be endured as simultaneities, the dissonances must progress to a perfect consonance through contrary motion by half and whole step.[22] "But other dissonances or diaphonies are therefore not suffered by the ear, because even if they move in contrary motion, they nevertheless are not situated the smallest distance from a consonance" [Alie vero dissonantiae, sive dyaphonie, ideo non compatiuntur ab auditu, quia etsi moveantur sursum et deorsum, non tamen ante consonantiam per minorem distantiam sunt distantes].

This description leaves one question open. Should the whole tone and the minor seventh, as long as they progress through contrary motion by half and whole step to a fourth (a perfect consonance according to Marchettus) and to a fifth, respectively, also be considered tolerable dissonances along with the third and the sixth? The possibility should not be excluded, for if one assumes it as a hypothesis, then 13th-century classifications of intervals become explicable that would otherwise be incomprehensible.

Johannes de Garlandia distinguishes three types of dissonances: (1) the minor second, tritone, and major seventh as perfect, intolerable dissonances; (2) the major sixth and minor seventh as imperfect, tolerable dissonances; and (3) the minor sixth and whole tone as medial dissonances.[23] His classification would be absurd as a judgment of the sonorous characters of the intervals (and it also cannot be blamed on a compulsion for systematization, since the analogy with the classification of consonances merely requires the formation of three groups, not the inclusion of the major sixth with the minor seventh, or the minor sixth with the whole tone). Yet it becomes comprehensible if one considers the resolutions of the dissonances to perfect consonances.

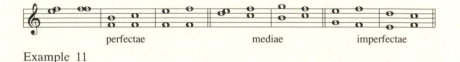

perfectae   mediae   imperfectae

Example 11

The "*discordantiae perfectae*" [perfect dissonances] are oblique-motion dissonances with a half-step connection to the unison, fifth, and octave. On the other hand, the "*discordantiae imperfectae*" and "*mediae*" [imperfect and medial dissonances] are contrary-motion dissonances with half- and whole-step connections to the fourth, fifth, or octave. And the distinction between the "*imperfectae*" and the "*mediae*" is based on the precedence of the octave (6–8) and fifth (7–5) over the fourth (2–4 and 6–4).[24]

. . .

In the 14th century there existed a different, albeit peripheral, technique of composition quite unlike the method of adding contrasting sonorities. It should be distinguished from the "principle of alternation," the regular alternation of perfect and imperfect consonances, as the "principle of distinctions" ["distinctions" are segments of chant]. The expression is meant to signify that a chant's articulated structure, neglected and interfered with by the addition of contrasting sonorities, becomes the defining factor of chordal technique. Chains of thirds or sixths with fifth or octave endings correspond to the segments of the cantus firmus. Imperfect consonances, interpreted in the 14th century as "sonorities of tension or motion," appear as a representation and expansion of the melodic "motion" contained in a chant neume or distinction.

Anonymous 13 describes the relationship between melodic and chordal technique in a terminology that is not easily understood. "For there are three types of notes, namely *appendans* [lit. "appending"], *non appendans*, and *désirans appendans* ["desiring to be appending"]. *Notes appendans* are as follows: (example is missing), on which one should sing thirds-fifths or sixth-octave, both at the beginning of the discant as well as in the middle; likewise: (example is missing), on which one should sing fifth-octave or third-fifth. *Notes non appendans:* (example is missing), on which one should sing octave-fifth or fifth-third; likewise: (example is missing), on which one should sing octave-third, etc. *Notes désirans appendans* are when the tenor ascends one, two, or three notes scalewise and the last one is *appendans*; all those prior are *désirans appendans*, as we see here: (example is missing)" [Car il sont III manières de notes, c'est ascavoir appendans, non appendans et désirans appendans. Notes appendans sont comme ici: (example is missing) sur lesquelles on doilt dire tierces quintes ou sixte double tant en commencement de déchant comme en moyen, item: (example is missing) sur lesquelles on doit dire quinte double ou tierce quinte. Notes non appendans: (example is missing) sur lesquelles on doit dire double quinte ou quinte tierce. Item: (example is missing) sur lesquelles on doit dire double tierce etc. Notes désirans appendans sont quand la teneur monte une note ou II, ou III en droit degré et en la fin soit une appendant, toutes celles par devant sont désirans appendans; si comme yci: (example is missing)].[25]

The term *notes* signifies the tones of the cantus firmus, not an interval formed by the cantus firmus and discant.[26] The antithesis between *notes non appendans* and *notes appendans* is connected with a reversal of the intervallic progressions: *notes appendans* require progressions from a more imperfect to a more perfect consonance (3–5, 6–8, and 5–8[27]); *notes non appendans*, by contrast, from a more perfect to a more imperfect consonance (8–5, 5–3, and 8–3). Since Anonymous 13 prohibits parallel perfect consonances, *notes désirans appendans* must correspond to the connecting of imperfect consonances.

It is unlikely that stepwise progressions of the cantus firmus are intended by the expression *notes appendans*.[28] In the first place, if *appendans* and *en droit degré* are taken to be synonyms, then the designation *notes désirans appendans* for a tenor *en droit degré* is superfluous and incomprehensible. And second, Anonymous 13 numbers among the progressions *sur notes appendans* even the interval progression 5–8 above a descending third in the cantus firmus.[29] Hence the classification of the tones in the cantus firmus cannot be based on the chant's melodic progression, but must be founded on some other criterion.

Anonymous 13 segments the chant into sections—neumata or distinctions—that the discantor is obliged to accompany with chains of thirds or sixths ending in a fifth or octave respectively. The middle sections begin with imperfect consonances, and only the very first begins with a perfect consonance. "When at the beginning of the chant, the first and last [tones of the discant] should be an octave and those in between sixths, or the first and last a fifth and those in between thirds. When in the middle of the chant, the first [tones] are sixths and the last is an octave, or the first [tones] are thirds and the last is a fifth" [Se c'est en commencement de chant la première et la darrenière doilt etre double et les moiennes sixtes, ou la première et la darrenière quinte et les moiennes tierces. Se c'est en moyen chant, les premières son sixtes et la darrenière double, ous les premières sont tierces et la darrenière quinte].

The terminology of Anonymous 13 becomes comprehensible if one relates the interval progressions required over *notes appendans*, *non appendans*, and *désirans appendans* to the just-cited description of the principle of distinctions (the latter follows immediately upon the former in the text). The progressions of *notes désirans appendans* appear in the middle or even at the beginning of sections, those of *notes appendans* at the end of sections, and those of *notes non appendans* between distinctions. Thus *notes appendans* are the next-to-last and last tones of a chant segment [*Tongruppe*]; *notes non appendans* are tones separated by a caesura; and *notes désirans appendans* are the initial or middle tones of a distinction that strive toward its ending. Therefore the effects of the sequence of sonorities—the "connecting" character of the progression from an imperfect consonance to a perfect consonance, the "disconnecting" character of the reverse progressions, and the "tension-producing" character of the concatenation of imperfect consonances—were conceived by Anonymous 13 as means for the representation of melodic "motion."

Toward an Understanding of 15th-Century Harmony

The thesis that tonal harmony originated in the early 15th century, though certainly not undisputed,[1] appears to have solidified as the common opinion of historians.[2] Werner Korte writes that with the discovery of chordal relationships, "One happened upon a completely unknown domain, since the perception of chords, as opposed to the perception of a polyphonic flow, represented something completely new" [Man begab sich auf ein vollkommen unbekanntes Gebiet, da das Hören von Klängen gegenüber dem Hören von mehrlinearem Ablauf etwas vollkommen Neues darstellte].[3] The antithesis is questionable—tonal harmony and linear counterpoint are not mutually exclusive. "Without a doubt functional relationships are present that, when marked exclusively as tonic, dominant, or subdominant, are characterized incomparably more clearly than by a Roman-numeral symbolization of degrees, which fails to point out the degrees' interrelationships" [Ohne Zweifel liegen Funktionsbeziehungen vor, die mit ausschließlicher Bezeichnung durch Tonika und Dominante unvergleichlich deutlicher charakterisiert sind als durch die Stufenbezeichnung, die keine Beziehungen untereinander anzeigt].[4] Korte is nevertheless forced to renounce a functional interpretation of chords in a second-relation with the tonic. And thus he has to concede that sonorities a second apart relate to each other not according to the principle of dominant and subdominant relationships, but according to the principle of contrasting sonorities. "Both the signs D^{D+} and $^D D+$ [V/V and IV/IV][5] must be excluded because their frequent presence in close connection with the tonic should not be interpreted in our sense of a dominant-of-a-dominant or a subdominant-of-a-subdominant" [Auszunehmen sind die beiden D^{D+} und $^D D+$ Bezeichnungen, deren häufiges Vorkommen in enger Beziehung zur Tonika nicht in unserem Sinne einer Dominant zur Dominant zu deuten ist].

In his analysis of Leonel's motet *Ave maris stella*,[6] Korte limits himself to a tonal interpretation of the "established" sonorities

.[7] First, he thus appears to doubt whether six-three sonorities can be taken as chords of the sixth—as inversions of root-position chords. Yet without the presumption that the triad and its inversions are "functionally identical," the system of functions loses its meaning. And second, Korte is forced to postulate remote functions even in his analysis of the "structural sonorities" [*Gerüstklänge*]:

d	g	d	F	d	B♭	C	a	d	g	F	C	g	C	g
D°	T°	D°	Dp⁺	D°	Tp⁺	S⁺	Sp°	D°	T°	SS⁺	S⁺	T°	S⁺	T°

.

The notion of a major subdominant in a minor mode contradicts the theory of functions, if one grants the validity of Riemann's formulation.[8]

According to Riemann, a direct harmonic relationship is established between two chords only when their reference tones are a perfect fifth or a major third apart [or are identical]. The reference tone of the major chord **c–e–g** is **c**, and the reference tone of the minor chord **c–e♭–g** is **g**. It follows from Riemann's assumptions that there is the possibility of a minor subdominant in the major mode (the minor chord **f–a♭–c** has the same reference tone, **c**, as the major chord **c–e–g**) or a major dominant in the minor mode (the major chord **g–b–d′** has the same reference tone, **g**, as the minor chord **c–e♭–g**). On the other hand, these very assumptions exclude the possibility of a major subdominant in the minor mode (the reference tone **f** of the major chord **f–a–c′** is not connected by a perfect fifth or major third to the reference tone **g** of the minor chord **c–e♭–g**) or a minor dominant in the major mode (the reference tone **d** of the minor chord **g–b♭–d′** is not connected by a perfect fifth or major third to the reference tone **c** of the major chord **c–e–g**). Riemann's thesis is based on a principle—harmonic "dualism"— that may well be flawed. Yet the musical reality it tries to substantiate is undeniable. The major subdominant in the minor mode and the minor dominant in the major mode are questionable "functions," and not just because they fall outside of Riemann's system. On the contrary, to justify his theory, Riemann could appeal to the fact that the theory made it possible to explain the already questionable status of the major subdominant in the minor mode and the minor dominant in the major mode.

· · ·

Dufay's three-voice chanson *Helas, ma dame par amours*[9] serves as a paradigm of tonal harmony in the early 15th century. According to Heinrich Besseler, it furnishes "the proof that in the 15th century, it was possible to have music composed strictly voice by voice on a chordal-harmonic foundation" [den Beweis, daß im 15. Jahrhundert streng stimmig komponierte Musik auf akkordlich-harmonischer Grundlage möglich war].[10] The number of fifth-progressions—to use the terminology of the theory of fundamental progressions—is twice as large as that of second-progressions. Six-three sonorities and unsupported sixths are rare (mm. 9, 13, 19, 21). The tones **c**, **g**, and **d** appear as the primary degrees, with the seven segments of the chanson ending on **c**, **d**, **g**, **d**, **g**, **d**, and **c**. The sonorities on secondary degrees, since they are exceptional occurrences, present no obstacles to a reduction by the theory of functions. The B♭ sonority (mm. 13 and 24) and the E♭ sonority (m. 21), which occur only as incomplete triads (**b♭–d** and **e♭–g**), can be explained in G minor as either Tp and Sp, or as fragmentary T and S. The tone **a** under the octave **c′–c″** (m. 3) and the tone **b** under the third **d′–f♯′** (m. 27) appear as "supposed thirds," and thus as exemplary realizations of the concept of a secondary degree (i.e., a degree dependent on a primary degree). And the F sonority **f–c′–a′** (m. 19) is a simple "passing chord" between **g–b♭–b♭′** and **e♭–c′–g′**.

For all that, the thesis is questionable that *Helas, ma dame* expresses "the new unity of tonality." Besseler's characterization of the counter-tenor as the "bearer of the harmony" [*Harmonieträger*] lays itself open to the objection that it is an added, not a fundamental, voice.[11] The discant and tenor form a compositional framework that can stand on its own as two-voice counterpoint. And irregular dissonances reveal that the countertenor—the last voice to be composed—is related in m. 4 only to the discant and not to the tenor, and conversely in m. 9 only to the tenor and not to the discant.

One could object that tonal harmony and a conception of successively composed voices are not mutually exclusive—that the plan of a chord progression, as a compositional framework, could allow for a "linear" elaboration through voices composed one after the other. A "music composed strictly voice by voice on a chordal-harmonic foundation" is indeed possible. But it presupposes that the notion of chords has become a foregone conclusion. Only when tonal chord combinations have stabilized as conventional formulas can they constitute the basis or guide for the successive composition of voice parts. The evolution from manifestly "chordal-harmonic" composition to works based on a latent "foundation" cannot be reversed.

Of course, the theory of functions—in contrast to the theory of fundamental progressions—can waive the requirement that the triad be understood as a chord (i.e., as a directly perceived sonorous unity) and still make sense as a theory.[12] It need only require that the tones form a system that (1) is based on the tonal relationships of the perfect fifth and major third, and (2) is related to a central point. The C-major system consists of the fifths **f–c**, **c–g**, and **g–d**, and the thirds **f–a** (or **a♭–c**), **c–e**, and **g–b**. The A-minor system consists of the fifths **d–a**, **a–e**, and **e–b**, and the thirds **f–a**, **c–e**, and **g–b** (or **e–g♯**). Besseler, however, characterizes Dufay's chordal technique in *Helas, ma dame* as "functional tonality with the free alteration of thirds" [dominantische To-nalität mit Terzfreiheit];[13] and the concept of "the free alteration of thirds," the switching between major and minor thirds on **c**, **g**, and **d**,[14] is incompatible with functional harmony.

The system of functions is conceivable without the concept of a chord, but not with "the free alteration of thirds." Conversely, a chordal technique in which the determination of thirds is left open would have to presume the concept of a chord in order to be considered tonal harmony. And inasmuch as neither the concept of a chord nor the system of functions is realized in *Helas, ma dame*, the thesis that Dufay established tonal harmony must be set aside.

The technique of the *cantilena* style—the method of supplementing a discant-tenor framework with a lower-voice countertenor—is described in the *Ars discantus per Johannem de Muris*.[15] And in the same treatise (which in spite of the reference to Johannes de Muris probably dates from no earlier than 1400, since it permits the countertenor to descend up to a tenth below the tenor) there is developed a theory of interval progressions that seems useful in elucidating the compositional technique of Dufay's *Helas, ma dame*.

The rules of the *Ars discantus* on the "perfecting" of minor thirds or sixths and the "imperfecting" of major thirds or sixths[16] can be combined into the single principle that if an imperfect consonance progresses to a perfect consonance without a half-step connection, then a whole step should be changed to a half step:

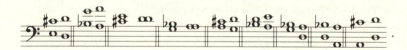

The universal validity of this rigorous precept might be called into question. Certainly an attempt to use it to stylize entire pieces from the period around 1400 would miss the mark.[17] Still, it does permit inferences to be drawn about the way music was heard in the early 15th century. It means that the progression from an imperfect to a perfect consonance through a half-step connection was perceived as an especially compelling and convincing interval sequence—as a "primary" progression determining and motivating the music's forward progress.

The concept of the half-step connection is inseparable from that of the interval progression. It must not, in the 14th and 15th centuries, be mistaken for an independent factor and turned into a "leading-tone principle" (in certain monophonic repertories the concept appears to have been a carry-over from polyphony). As late as the 13th century, the half step was still experienced as a problematic interval not easily understood, as the irrational remainder between the perfect fourth and the ditone $[4/3 \div (9/8)^2 = 256/243\,!]$. In a melodic half step, no "tendency" was perceived of the lower tone toward the upper, or of the upper toward the lower. The second tone was not taken to be the "goal" of the first. Instead, the half step was avoided in clausulas because it lacked clarity as an interval. The tendency of the leading tone, elevated by Ernst Kurth to a "primal phenomenon" of music,[18] is a "second nature" that gradually accrues to half-step scale degrees through participation in the interval progressions 3–1, 3–5, and 6–8.[19] The tendency of imperfect consonance toward perfect consonance and the tendency of a leading tone toward its goal are two sides of the same coin.

In contrast to the function of chords in tonal harmony, the structural significance of interval progressions—those progressing from imperfect to perfect consonance with a half-step connection in one of the voices—is independent of the underlying scale. The functional principles of tonal harmony both establish a connection between chords and confirm the underlying scale: the scale is conceived as resulting from the dismantling of the three primary chords [and the arranging of their constituent tones in a series]. In the 14th and 15th centuries, however, the underlying scale and the principle of connecting sonorities by interval progressions with a half-step connection stand disconnectedly side by side—the "perfecting" of the third and sixth in the progression has no effect on the Dorian character of the clausula. Hence for chromatic alterations, the term "accidentals" is warranted if it expresses the fact that the mode—marked by melodic features and the disposition of cadential degrees—takes on a different hue but is not transformed into something else; is not a "Lydian" cadence.

. . .

Riemann's attempt to reduce 15th-century works to the major, minor, or Phrygian modes through the rigorous application of musica ficta[20] suffers not only from a distorted interpretation of some terms used by Adam von Fulda[21] but also from a mistake in his assumptions. The idea was foreign to him that a principle for connecting sonorities could be independent of the underlying scale. So in considering the fact that 14th- and 15th-century rules of interval progression derange the modes, he felt compelled to conclude that musica ficta signified a revision of the modes according to the yet to be formulated but already operative norms of the "natural" major-minor system. First, however, Riemann's explanation denies the relationship between the half-step connection and the progression from an imperfect to a perfect consonance. A raised tone is understood as a major third, a lowered tone as a minor third, in a sequence of chords, not intervals. Second, the perfecting of a third preceding a fifth, which results in the irregular sequence of functions D–S (the reverse of the regular progression S–D), contradicts the norms of tonal harmony. And third, were Riemann's interpretation correct, one could hardly explain the undeniable decline of musica ficta in the second half of the 15th century. But if one takes the correlation of the half-step connection with the progression from an imperfect to a perfect consonance to be one of the basic assumptions of musica ficta (along with the proscription of tritones), then the abandonment of the wealth of chromatic alterations becomes understandable. That is, in the later 15th century the effect produced by the interval progression imperfect-to-perfect—the correlate of chromatic alteration—was destroyed by the tendency to avoid the "empty sonority" of a perfect consonance.[22]

. . .

The context into which an interval progression was inserted had no effect on the progression's meaning. For example, the interval progression can be combined with , but also with

or without altering the meaning of the initial sixth

g–e♭'. [If the third voice substitues c for b♭ or g,] the sixth is not transformed from the third and root of VI to the fifth and third of iv—it remains the same as before. The successions of sonorities in three-voice composition are combined interval progressions, not chord relationships represented by a *basse fondamentale*.

. . .

The feasibility of inserting an interval progression into various successions of sonorities without altering its meaning must not be confused with the way the theory of functions identifies the iv and VI chords in minor as representives of the same subdominant function. In the theory of functions, taking different chords to be the same thing is an expedient meant to render feasible the reduction of chord progressions to the cadential model of tonal harmony. The progression is interpreted as Sp and D if a G-minor chord follows, but as S-*Leittonwechselklang* and T if it stands on its own. The idea that in the first case **c′** replaces **b♭**, and in the second **d′** replaces **e♭′**, is a hypothesis intended to explain the impression of a tonal relationship between the chords. The appearance of a similarity between the method of including the chords **g–b♭–e♭′** and **c–g–e♭′** under one functional category and the feasibility of combining the interval progression , without changing its meaning, with either **b♭–a** or **c–d** as a third voice is thus misleading. To say that an interval progression always remains the same is only to say that its meaning is self-contained. The distinction between what a sonority sounds like and what it represents is, in the 15th century, meaningless.

· · ·

An interval progression is self-contained. Its meaning is independent of a reference from individual intervals to a tonic. In tonal harmony, the relationship between the subdominant and the dominant is mediated by the tonic. The connection of chords on **c** and **d**, for example, requires a continuation and legitimization by a chord on **g**. In *Helas, ma dame*, on the other hand, the next-to-last and last sonorities of the Phrygian clausula relate to each other directly (mm. 9–10, 19–20, and 26–27). In lines 2, 4, and 6 of the chanson they form not half cadences, but endings that stand with equal right alongside those on **g** of lines 3 and 5, and those on **c** of lines 1 and 7. The clausulas on **c**, **g**, and **d** form an association without a central focus: an association in which the difference between the g-mode of the vocal middle section and the c-mode of the instrumental opening and closing sections—perplexing to a tonal way of hearing—implies no contradiction.

· · ·

The development from the "parallel cadence" (ex. 12a) to the "octave-leap cadence" (ex. 12b) and then to the "fourth-leap cadence" (ex. 12c) is taken as a sure sign that a consciousness of harmonic tonality was arising.[23]

Example 12

First, however, the octave-leap and fourth-leap cadences can be explained as the mere result of transferring the countertenor below the tenor. The fifth below the penultima in the tenor [**g** in ex. 12] is quite simply the only consonance possible if one is to avoid not only parallel octaves between countertenor and discant, or countertenor and tenor, but also a leap of a sixth or seventh in the countertenor.

Second, if meant to account for how the fourth-leap cadence was heard, the hypothesis of a change in harmonic consciousness turns out to be superfluous. Using the categories of the *Ars discantus per Johannem de Muris,* the fourth-leap cadence can be interpreted as an analog of the parallel cadence. The parallel cadence is composed of the interval progressions 6–8 and 3–5, the fourth-leap cadence of the progressions 6–8 and 10–8.

Third, the parallel cadence, though without the leading tone to the fifth, persisted alongside the fourth-leap cadence. And it is difficult to imagine that the one type of cadence was heard as a combined interval progression while the other was heard as a chord progression. To be sure, the parallel cadence was still in use in the late 17th and 18th centuries, though viewed as a weaker cadence.[24] So it seems that even in the 15th and 16th centuries its presence is no argument against the possibility of interpreting the fourth-leap cadence as an expression of functional harmony. Yet the insertion of the parallel cadence into the system of tonal harmony involved a change in meaning: the penultimate chord, vii^6, was perceived as a dominant chord with "suppressed root." Thus the tonal interpretation of the parallel cadence assumes that independence is granted to the seventh chord, something foreign to the 15th and 16th centuries. If in the 15th century the fourth-leap cadence was understood as an analog of the parallel cadence, then conversely, in the 18th century the parallel cadence appears as a fragment of a fourth-leap cadence with a dissonant seventh.[25]

And fourth, in the 15th and still in the 16th centuries, the leap of a fourth in the bass was considered a subsidiary cadential motive when compared to the descending second in the tenor. In the description of the fourth-leap cadence given by Guilelmus Monachus, the bass and discant relate to the tenor, not the tenor and discant to the bass.[26] Of course Guilelmus characterizes the fourth-leap cadence as the norm and the parallel cadence as the exception. But the exceptional character of the parallel cadence is based not on its lack of a proper "root progression" but on the mix-up of the melodic clausulas among the voices—the discant formula appears in the tenor, the tenor formula in the bass.[27] In 1523, Pietro Aaron classified the cadence ⟨music example⟩ as a mi-clausula [i.e., on **e**], not as a la-clausula [on **A**].[28] He thus demotes the bass's lower-fifth **A** to the status of a supplementary tone, and the descending leap of a fourth to that of a secondary factor in relation to the 6–8 discant-tenor clausula. And in 1558, Zarlino would not allow the discant-bass clausula as the cadence of a two-voice composition—it is a reduction that lacks the basic framework, the tenor formula.[29]

One might think that theorists failed to deal with the novelty of the early stages of tonal harmony not because they failed to perceive it, but because the concepts were lacking to describe it.[30] Nevertheless, many features in the compositional technique of the 15th and even the 16th centuries also give evidence that the penultimate sonority of the fourth-leap or octave-leap cadences was not understood as a chord. The first text-line of Palestrina's motet *Surge, propera amica mea, et veni*,[31] published in 1563, concludes in mm. 25–26 with a cadence that reveals how Palestrina attempted to satisfy the demand for *ricchezza dell'-harmonia* [harmonic richness] without sacrificing the tenor formula:

A 6–8 mi-clausula (alto and bass [*8va* ]) is interlocked with

a 6–8 *subsemitonium* clausula (discant and tenor [*8va* , c♯″

is the *subsemitonium*]). An analogous cadence is found in mm. 26–27 of Verdelot's madrigal *Madonna qual certezza*,[32] published in 1537.

The voice crossing—superfluous or even absurd by modern standards—and the obsolete octave leap in the bass (not an archaism based on the text) can only be understood if one grants that **A** and **d** are not related to each other as roots of a V–I chord progression in D minor, but are separated from each other as the finals of different, though interlocked, clausulas.

On the other hand, it is undeniable that the primary interval progressions, to the extent they presuppose both the contrast between imperfect and perfect consonance and the dependent status of imperfect consonance, suffer a drastic loss of effect through the tendency toward *ricchezza dell'harmonia*.

The 15th-century emancipation of imperfect consonance comes to light both in the definition of thirds as superparticular proportions (5:4 and 6:5)[33] and in the unrestricted allowance of parallel imperfect consonances. The mere fact that larger numbers of imperfect consonances were permitted in direct succession—two or three by Anon-ymous 13 (14th century), three or four by the *Optima introductio*, four or five by Anonymous 11 (15th century)[34]—is still not a sure sign of their consolidation as a stable consonance. Even a longer chain of imperfect consonances can be understood as "motion" that tends toward the "rest" of a perfect consonance. But Adam von Fulda's polemic against limiting such parallel motion reveals that by the end of the 15th century, imperfect consonance was no longer perceived as a "tension sonority," as a dependent interval related to a perfect consonance. Instead, it had become an independent, self-sufficient sonority. "Although older scholars once would forbid all sequences of more than three or four imperfect consonances, we who are more modern allow them, especially tenths if they yield ornament, there being, of course, a middle voice present" [Licet olim veteres ultra tres aut quatuor imperfectas se sequi omnes prohiberent, nos tamen mod-erniores non prohibemus, praesertim decimas, cum ornatum reddant, voce tamen intermedia].[35]

The granting of independence to imperfect consonance and the tendency toward *ricchezza dell'harmonia* did not, however, completely invalidate the concept of interval progression as a category of musical perception. On the one hand, in 1558 Zarlino does declare the presence of complete triads to be a condition of *compositione perfetta* : "Because in perfect composition, as I will explain elsewhere, the third and fifth (or their octave duplications) must in fact be present at all times"[36] [Conciosiache é necessario (come dirò altrove) che nella Compositione perfetta se ritrovino sempre in atto la Quinta et la Terza over le sue Replicate]. But on the other hand, he carries on the tradition of requiring a half-step connection when passing from an imperfect to a perfect consonance: "So that this rule is easily obeyed, whenever one wishes to proceed from an imperfect to a perfect consonance, make sure that at least one of the parts moves by a major semitone, whether implied or expressed. And in following this rule, the use of chromatic and enharmonic tones will be of great benefit" [Acciocche con facilità se osservi questa Regola che qualunque volte se vorra procedere dalla Consonanza imperfetta alla perfetta di fare che almeno una delle parti se muove con un movimento nel quale sia il Semituono maggiore tacito overo espresso. Et per conseguire tal cosa giovera molto l'uso delle Chorde chromatiche et dell'enharmoniche].[37] The "structural" [*kon-struktive*] linkage of sonorities depends on interval progressions. The sound of complete triads is a merely a "coloristic," inessential attribute. And the triad is still not a "chord," because root progression—the relationship between chordal roots—is still not the governing principle for combining sonorities.

In the psychology of perception there is no primary category known as "sonorous unity" [*Klangeinheit*]. Rather, a sonority's perceived unity is an "object of conceptualization and the mind's proclivity for seeking relationships" (Carl Stumpf) [*Sache der Auffassung und des beziehenden Denkens*]. The fact that a chord is immediately conceived as a unity does not mean that its individual tones and intervals "fuse," that is, blend together so completely that a listener can barely distinguish them.[38] Instead, it means that the chord relates to the preceding and succeeding chords as a whole and not through individual interval progressions standing out from the sonorities. The criterion for the chordal character of sonorities is the principle of connecting the sonorities by root progressions. What contradicts the concept of chord is not the independence of the voices, but the method of linking sonorities through interval progressions. The categories "chord" and "root progression" are in a reciprocally dependent relationship. The tones of a chord form a unity in relation to a chordal root. And it only makes sense to speak of a root when the succession of roots establishes a recognized musical context.

The changeover from interval progression to *basse fondamentale* implies that sonorities in a fifth-relationship take precedence over those a second apart. According to the concepts of 15th- and 16th-century counterpoint, the progressions and are complete unto themselves. They do not call for a completion or justification by a preceding or following progression. The factor linking these sonorities together is the interval progression of the outer voices, 10–12 and 10–8. If, on the other hand, one comprehends these sonorities as chords, and takes the measure of chordal relationship to be progressions of the *basse fondamentale*, then the chords are not directly, but only indirectly, related and require the mediation of a third chord: as D–S in C major and S–D in D minor they "tend" toward a tonic. The whole step between their chordal roots is interpreted as two fifths [**g'**–(**c'**)–**f** and **G**–(**d**)–**a**]. Unlike the theory of functions, which explains the whole-step interval between the g-minor and A-major chords as an indirect fifth-relationship, the theory of fundamental progressions interprets the g-minor chord as a ii[7] chord with "suppressed root"—the whole step **g–a** thus being reduced to a fifth–progression (**e–A**). But this distinction is secondary to the common assumption of both theories that the fifth-relation is the basic principle for linking chords.

The cadential character of a succession of sonorities is based on the collaboration of factors that both connect and disconnect the various entities involved. That is, a cadence must be marked both by comprehensible relationships and by clear distinctions. In the parallel cadence of the 14th and 15th centuries, the connecting factors were the half- and whole-step linkages and the "tendency" of dependent, imperfect consonance to move toward perfect consonance. The disconnecting factors, on the other hand, were the sonorities' contrasting characters, the lack of a common tone between the penultimate and final sonorities, and the "inner distance" between tones a whole step or half step apart. The V–I cadence is relatively poor in terms of such properties. The wide "external distance" between the roots has a differentiating effect, while in addition to a common tone, the fifth-relation and the leading tone establish coherence. The contrary motion of the dominant's third and fifth to the tonic's root—as the discant-tenor clausula, the prerequisite to, and origin of, the V–I cadence—becomes superfluous and a matter of indifference in tonal harmony. The major sixth or minor third relates not to the octave or unison as an interval, but to the root of the dominant as the third or fifth of a chord.

COMPOSITIONAL TYPES AND FORMULAS IN THE 15TH AND 16TH CENTURIES

There is a habit, based on the pedagogical separation of the disciplines of counterpoint and harmony, of combining the concepts of "modal counterpoint," "intervallic composition," "reference to the tenor," and a "successive conception of the voices" into a collective idea, and of placing it in rigid opposition to the concepts of "tonal harmony," "chordal composition," "reference to the bass," and a "simultaneous conception of the voices." This unfortunately leads to the fallacy of speaking of chordal composition and tonal harmony where only a precedence of the bass over the tenor, or a simultaneous conception of the voices, can be discerned. But a simultaneous conception of the voices does not imply reference to the bass, reference to the bass does not imply chordal composition, and chordal composition does not imply tonal harmony.

In 1523 Pietro Aaron rejects the successive conception of the voices, not, however, because he perceived a chordal context to be the true basis and framework of composition, but because of the flaws and shortcomings in the voices that were composed last: "In writing first the cantilena or soprano and then the tenor, a place is often lacking for the contrabass when this tenor is finished, and when the contrabass is finished many notes of the contralto can find no place . . . " [facendo prima il canto over soprano di poi il tenore, quando e fatto detto tenore, manca alcuna volta il luogo al controbasso, et fatto controbasso assai note del controalto non hanno luogo . . .]. Only simultaneously planned voices work together on an equal or nearly equal melodic footing. "Hence modern composers are thought to be better at this, as is evident in compositions written for four, five, six, and more voices in which each voice has a comfortable, easy, and pleasant place because modern composers consider all the voice parts together and not one after the other as mentioned above" [Onde gli moderni in questo meglio hanno considerato come e manifesto per le compositioni da essi a quattro a cinque a sei et a più voci fatte, dele quali ciascuna tiene luogo commodo facile et grato, perche considerano insieme tutte le parti et non secondo come di sopra e detto]. On the other hand, Aaron leaves open the possibility that, besides the tenor or discant, the bass or even the alto could be the voice composed first. "And if you wish to compose the cantilena, the tenor, or the contrabass first, the choice is yours, as one sees with some of the present day, who many times begin with the contrabass, sometimes with the tenor, and sometimes with the contralto" [Et se te piace componere prima il canto, tenore o controbasso, tal modo et regola te resti arbitraria come de alcuni al presente se osserva, che molte fiate danno principio al controbasso alcuna volta al tenore et alcuna volta al controalto].[1]

1. In the 15th and 16th centuries, composition with a cantus-firmus tenor was considered the representative type. In the *Ars discantus per Johannem de Muris* (circa 1400), the tenor is described as the structural voice, the discant as the first counterpoint, and the countertenor as the second counterpoint.[2] And in 1613, by way of Zarlino, the same treatment of the successive conception of the voices was still being handed down by Johannes Nucius.[3] "The tenor is like a thematic thread and is the first voice composed. Almost all of the other voices depend on it and are arranged according to its lead. It seems to be called 'tenor' from 'tenendo' [Latin: "holding"]" [Thenor velut thematis filum, et primum vocum inventum, quem ferè aliae respiciunt voces, et ad cuius nutum formantur, à tenendo dictus videtur].[4]

The fact that the tenor is a cantus firmus or *cantus prius factus* [preexistent voice] does not necessarily mean that interval progressions are related primarily to the tenor. The characterization of the tenor as the "*fundamentum totius relationis*" [the basis of the whole relationship] means only that if the individual voices differ in mode, the tenor represents the mode of the entire composition.[5] One must, however, differentiate "tenor" as the reference voice of compositional technique from "tenor" as the representative of the mode. "And know that the contratenor, insofar as it is lower than the tenor, is called the tenor" [Et est sciendum, quod contratenor in quantum est gravior tenore dicitur tenor].[6] The fact that Anonymus 11 designates a lower-voice contratenor as a "tenor" is not a terminological absurdity. It means, rather, that the two functions of the tenor—to be a *cantus prius factus* and a reference voice—are separated from each other and divided between different voices. In the 16th century, the differentiation of functions was consolidated into the distinction between the bass as a contrapuntal reference voice and the tenor as a representative of the mode. This distinction is at the root of Zarlino's metaphorical description of the individual characters of the voices,[7] and in 1612 was prepared as a formula by Johann Lippius: "For the bass melody is the foundation, the tenor and discant (between which there is tasteful interchange) form the principle or ruling voices, and finally the alto is used for filling in" [Melodia namque Bassi est fundamentalis: Tenoris et Discantus (quorum elegans vicissitudo) est Principalis sive Regalis: Alti denique est explementalis].[8] In 1597 Thomas Morley[9] drew the obvious pedagogical consequences. While he borrowed Zarlino's table of intervals,[10] which has the discant as the first, the bass as the second, and the alto as the third counterpoint to the tenor, he supplemented it with the advice that, given a tenor, one should first compose the bass, and then an upper voice.[11]

2. Several 15th-century theorists—Anonymous 11[12] and Anonymous Coussemaker IV[13]—seem to have in mind a discant-tenor framework that can stand on its own as two-voice counterpoint, since the fourth is missing from the intervals they list between discant and tenor.

A paradigmatic form of discant-tenor composition is the framework consisting of parallel sixths with beginning and ending octaves. The addition of a contratenor altus results in fauxbourdon. But the result of a four-voice elaboration is a type of phrase that, were the nature of its origin unknown, would have to be interpreted as a root-position chord progression.[14]

Example 13

In ex. 13a, the chords seem to represent the D-minor functions Tp–Dp–Tp–Dp–T–D–T, and in ex. 13b, the G-minor functions D–Tp––Sp–D–T–D–T. Yet according to Guilelmus Monachus the phrases are based on a tenor cantus firmus. In relation to the tenor, the discant forms parallel sixths with beginning and ending octaves, the bass forms fifths and thirds, and the alto forms fourths and thirds. "And note that with respect to four-voice composition, or with four voices based on whatever cantus firmus or ornamented cantus is at hand, you should see to it that the contratenor bassus has the fifth below the tenor in penultimate concords. Likewise see to it that the antepenult is a third below the tenor, the ante-antepenult a fifth below, and that the beginning or first note is a unison. But the discant has its penultimate consonance a sixth above the tenor, so that in a final consonance it will always be an octave above the tenor. And in like fashion the first note should be an octave; the rest of the notes, however, are always sixths. The altus, on the other hand, should always make its penultimate consonance a fourth above the tenor so that the antepenult will be a third above, and that which is the ante-antepenult will be a fourth, and the preceding note will always be a third, so that the last is always (a fifth above or) a third above or a unison, and likewise with the first note." [Et nota quod circa compositionem quatuor vocum sive cum quatuor vocibus supra quemlibet cantum firmum, sive supra quemlibet cantum figuratum facias quod contratenor bassus semper teneat quintam bassam in penultima concordii. Item quod antepenultima sit tertia bassa, et illa que est (ante) antepenultima(m) sit quinta, ita quod principium sive prima nota sit unisonus. Supranus vero semper teneat suam penultimam sextam altam supra tenorem, ita quod finis concordii sit semper octava alta supra tenorem. Et prima nota pariter etiam sit octava, relique autem notule sint semper sexte. Contravero altus semper faciat suam penultimam quartam supra tenorem, ita quod antepenultima sit semper tertia alta, et illa que est (ante) antepenultima(m) sit quarta, et antecedens sit semper tertia, ita quod ultima sit semper (quinta alta vel) tertia alta vel unisonus vel octava bassa ("vel octava bassa" should be deleted) et prima notula pariter].[15]

The description appears to set forth the contratenor bassus, instead of the soprano, as the second voice in order of conception. But in terms of compositional technique the bass is a consequence of the discant-tenor framework, not a prerequisite for the soprano. If one has to avoid parallel perfect consonances and leaps of a sixth or seventh in the bass, then the alternation of fifths and thirds below the tenor is the only possible addition to parallel sixths that a lower voice can make. According to Guilelmus, the contratenor altus is also invariable. The alternation of fourths and thirds above the tenor can, however, be replaced with parallel fourths.

3. In his "Regula ad componendum cum tribus vocibus non mutatis" ["The Rule for Composing with Three Unaltered Voices"][16] Guilelmus Monachus describes a type of three-voice composition with a soprano as *cantus prius factus*, a *"secundus supranus"* [second soprano] that forms parallel thirds with a unison beginning and ending, and a contratenor as a supplementary voice. The parallel thirds below a discant cantus firmus are nothing but an inversion of the parallel sixths above a tenor cantus firmus.[17] And the contratenor—analogous to the bass in four-voice composition with a discant-tenor framework—is limited to the alternation of fifths and thirds below the cantus firmus. Through the agency of the discant-tenor framework, composition with

a discant cantus firmus was thus, in the 15th century, closely connected
with composition with a tenor cantus firmus. In his listing of four-voice
interval combinations, Anonymous Coussemaker IV carries on the
method of the *Ars discantus per Johannem de Muris*, that is, taking
the tenor for granted and describing the discant as the first
counterpoint.[18] But in the examples of "Discantus in unisono" [discant
at the unison],[19] it is the continually recurring discant and not the
varying tenor that appears as the preexistent voice.

4. Composition with a discant-bass framework is already clearly
marked in many frottolas from the early 16th century,[20] but only at
the end of the century was it conceived as a special type by Thomas
Morley. The "harmony text" in the *Arte de tañer fantasia* (1565) by
Tomás de Santa Maria[21] is still tied to traditional musical schemata.

Example 14

Following Guilelmus Monachus, the alternation between the 10–8–5
and 8–6–3 sonorities would be explained as an elaboration of the parallel
sixths of a discant-tenor framework, an elaboration resulting in a
four-voice composition. But according to Tomás de Santa Maria, one
only counts the intervals between bass and soprano—the outer voices
serve as the compositional framework, the inner voices as filler. "One
should know that even in any sort of consonance—whether of three
or four voices, or more—for all that, consonance is understood and
reckoned from the contrabass to the soprano, which are the outer
voices, because the inner voices, which are the tenor and the contralto,
only serve as accompanying consonances and to fill in the void existing
between the outer voices" [Es de saber que aunque qualquiera consonancia se de a tres, o a quatro voces, o a mas, con todo eso siempre
la consonancia se entiende y se quenta deste el contrabaxo al tiple,
que son las vozes extremas, porque las vozes intermedias, que son tenor
y contraalto, solamente sirven en las consonancias de acompanamiento
y de hinchir el vazio que ay entre las extremas].[22] The reinterpretation
of the discant-tenor framework as a discant-bass framework presumes
that the interval combinations have stabilized as formulas conceived
or "grasped" directly in four voices. The origin in successively composed voices is canceled out by the result—the sequential schema. On

the other hand, the comment that one counts only the intervals between the outer voices suggests that the 8–6–3 chords could have been replaced by 8–5–3 chords—thus that these simultaneities are not chords and representatives of chordal scale degrees, but mere fillings in of the octave with consonances.

In Thomas Morley's description, discant-bass composition is not tied to a particular schema. "Maister: Then (to go to the matter roundly without circumstances) here be two parts make in two middle parts to them and make them foure, and of all other cordes leave not out the fifth, the eight and the tenth, and looke which of those two (that is the eight or the tenth) commeth next to the treble to set uppermost."

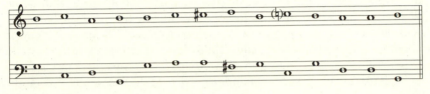

Example 15

The determining principle is the demand for complete triads. The sixth, however, is still understood as an alternative to the fifth, not as the root of an inverted chord. "But when you put in a sixt then of force must the fifth bee left out, except at a Cadence or close where a discorde is taken thus, which is the best a manner of closing, and the onelie waie of taking the fifth and sixth together."[23]

Example 16

The vertical lines in Morley's example are not bar lines. They do not exclude the possibility of interpreting the 6–5 sonority as a dissonant suspension. On the other hand, the sonority's consolidation to the status of "chordal dissonance" is clearly prefigured. But the 6–5 sonority evades the interpretive methods of both the theories of fundamental progressions and of functions: the sixth is neither the root of an inversion of a ii[7] chord nor a *sixte ajoutée* to the subdominant triad. Rather, the 6–5 sonority is nothing but "the fifth and sixth together." The distinction between chordal root and bass is still meaningless.

5. The reference of voices to the bass becomes the norm of compositional technique in the 16th century. This does not, however, imply that the simultaneities were understood as chords, as directly given unities. The "harmonic identity" of root-position and sixth chords was actually concealed by the accentuation of the real bass.

In 1606, Joachim Burmeister constructed four-voice compositions from the bottom up. "If it should please the tenor's tone to join the bass tone **c** at the octave, the diagrams will show it to be on middle **c′**. If it wishes to be within this octave above **c**, then with equal facility **e**, **g**, or **a** is taken up. Then a tone is found for the alto voice through the same process, a tone which is aptly combined in its interval and movement and easily produced, and which goes with the two previously arranged voices, namely bass and tenor. Lastly, combining, with equal dexterity and fitness, the melody's tone in the discant in a harmony with the other voices will draw welcome attention" [Si libuerit Tenoris sonum in Octavae spaciò cum Baßi sonò C conjungere, schemata exhibebunt c ordinis meson. Si intra diapason arctius, eàdem facilitate offendetur E vel G vel a. Deinde in Alto Melodiae sonus invenietur eòdem negotio, quem intervalli aptitudo et motus ejusdem compositus pronuntiationique conveniens, quò priorum duarum vocum Baßi videlicet et Tenoris peractà syntaxi factum est, admittet. Ultimò locò Melodiae sonum in Discantu pari dexteritate et commoditate cum reliquis vocibus in harmoniam devincere notitiam hauserit].[24]

Burmeister's terminology, however, betrays the fact that three-voice simultaneities are not conceived as chords, but are pieced together from intervals above a reference voice, the bass. According to a medieval tradition of characterizing the intervals,[25] the major third and sixth, among the imperfect consonances, are considered *"plenae de tonis"* [full of tone], the minor third and sixth as *"non plenae de tonis"* [not full of tone]. And Burmeister's designations *"perfectus cum semiimperfecto"* (**A–c–e**=perfect fifth and minor third), *"perfectus cum plene imperfecto"* (**c–e–g**=perfect fifth and major third), *"puri semiimperfecti"* (**A–c–f**=minor sixth and minor third), and *"puri plene imperfecti"* (**c–e–a**=major sixth and major third)[26] mean that for him, the character of a sonority depends on the characters of its intervals in relation to the bass. Thus the bass is the reference tone not only of the "root-position triad," but also of the "sixth chord." Moreover, in his listings of four-voice sonorities,[27] Burmeister always doubles the tone in the bass. He thus understands it as the principal tone, even if—according to the theory of the *basse fondamentale*—it is the third of a chord.

Even more decisively than in Burmeister's *Musica poetica*, the reference of the voices to the bass is made the basic principle of compositional analysis in the *Rules how to compose* by Giovanni

Coperario (circa 1610). "What chords parts are to use in Contrapoint. If the Bass rise a 2, Canto demands a 10, next an 8, Alto first an 8, next a 5, Tenor first a 5, next a 3."[28] Yet in compositional technique from around 1600, reference of the voices to the bass is but one point of view among others. As the exclusive principle of compositional analysis it is not justified in every case. In his presentation of $^6_5$ sonorities, Coperario fails to recognize that the upper voices are not primarily related to the bass, but form 2–3 or 7–6 suspensions.

Example 17

"How to use a 5, and 6 together. If the Bass rise a 2 then the 6, or 13 must hold, and then use the 11, or 4 then holding the sam[e] you must use the 10, or 3, the other 6 must rise a 2, and next the 5 . . . In the last two scores you must note the Bass holding of his first note, and the next 15 a minim. In the first (of the two last examples) the Bass rises a 2, and then falls a 5. In the last the Bass rises a 4, and in these two the 6, and 5 are used both together in severall parts, and cleane contrarie to the other three first examples."[29] The fact that the bass is not the primary voice shows itself in the *"quarta consonans"* [consonant fourth] (exs. 17a-c), which contradicts the rule that the fourth, as a dissonant suspension, should be prepared by a consonance, either a third or fifth. But the consonant fourth is justified to the extent that the upper voices form a regular 2–3 or 7–6 suspension, alongside of which pales the simultaneous, irregular suspension of the fourth.[30]

. . .

The characteristic schemata of tonal harmony—the "complete" cadence [*vollständige Kadenz*] (I–IV–V–I or I–IV–I–V–I, also I–ii–V–I), the "circle-of-fifths progression" (I–IV–vii–iii–vi–ii–V–I), and the "major-minor parallelism" (minor: v–i–VII–III = major: iii–vi–V–I, or minor: III–VII–i–v = major: I–V–vi–iii)—are typified in the compositional formulas of the 16th and early 17th centuries. This outward correspondence is not, however, a sufficient justification for a tonal interpretation. First of all, the formulas are not based on a system of chords. Instead, the reverse is true: the system of chords arose from a coalescing of formulas. The principle of tonality, which in a theoretical presentation appears as the first step, is historically the last to be reached.

1. The "major-minor parallelism" is prefigured in the discant-bass framework of the *Passamezzo antico* and the *Folia*.

Example 18

Nevertheless, interpreting them as chordal compositions and as expressions of tonal harmony would be questionable. First, the discant-bass framework ⟨♦⟩ allowed not only the alto line **f′–f′–d′–d′** but also **g′–f′–e♭′–d′**. Consequently the bass is not the foundation of a root-position chord progression, but simply part of an interval progression of the outer voices that is filled in with consonances.

Second, **g**, not **b♭**, is the original first pitch in the bass of the passamezzo antico.[31] The F-major sonority must thus be directly related to the g-minor sonority, and an interpretation of the F-major sonority as the dominant of the relative major is out of the question. One need not deny that composers of the 16th century were cognizant of the "parallelism" of the g-minor and Bb-major sonorities, and of the "dominant effect" of the progression F–B♭. But the direct relationship between the g-minor and F-major sonorities was not perceived as being reconciled by a B♭-major chord, as in g–B♭ = T–Tp and B♭–F = Tp–Dp.

"Parallelism" and "dominant effect" were indeed perceived as phenomena, but they were not understood to be the principles around which a system was formed.

Third, when the folia is heard as a tonal composition, there is forced on it an "inner dynamic" that was foreign to the 16th century. The modern listener, for whom the categories of functional harmony and meter have become second nature, understands the tonic as a goal of the dominant (a full cadence) or the dominant as an appendage of the tonic (a half cadence). In particular, for the modern listener an "upbeat" scansion (connected with an "inner crescendo") and the chord progression D–T appear as the norm, while a "downbeat" scansion and the chord progression T–D appear as the exception. The schema of the folia is thereby subjected to a change of phrasing that disorders and confuses the symmetry: T D │ T (D) │ Tp (D) │ T D. The 16th century was acquainted with neither the absolute metrical opposition between upbeat and downbeat phrasing nor the analogous harmonic differentiation between "goal-directed" and "appended" chords. The sonorities in the folia were joined together without there having been sensed a "compulsion to progress" between the second and third sonorities, or a "harmonic caesura" between the third and fourth.

Fourth, in the canzonettas and madrigals of the late 16th century, the succession of sonorites D–g–F–B♭ does stabilize into a compositional topos that was conceived directly in four voices.[32] Yet the formula permits modifications that exclude a tonal interpretation. In Monteverdi's madrigal *Ch'io no t'ami* (mm. 12–14),[33] the pattern breaks off after the third sonority and is immediately repeated in a reduced setting. The fact that the "Tp" [B♭-major] can be lacking means that it does not mediate the relationship between the "T" and the "Dp" [i.e., between the g-minor and F-major sonorities]. In the madrigal *Vivrò fra i miei* (mm. 4–7),[34] Monteverdi replaces the g-minor sonority of the D–g–F–B♭ schema with a G-major variant. The B♭-sonority is thus not a "Tp." While D and G, as well as F and B♭, are linked together by a "dominant effect," G and F are linked by the 3–5 interval progression in the outer voices .

2. The diatonic "circle-of-fifths progression" (I–IV–vii–iii–vi–ii–V–I) is one of the basic formulas of tonal harmony in the late 17th and early 18th centuries. Indeed Rameau used it as a model in developing his theory of the *basse fondamentale*. Yet in the early 17th century, it was a tonally ambiguous compositional schema.

First, the prototypes of the diatonic circle-of-fifths progression lacked the definiteness of a fixed beginning and ending; they were aimless. The cadence, instead of following from the progression as an expected outcome, was externally attached to it. In mm. 22–35 of *Ninfa che scalza il piede*[35] (a tenor solo with basso continuo), Monteverdi employs a sequential schema in which one can detect a canonic model.

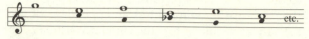

Example 19

The first sequence spans thirteen progressions, the second ten. The first sequence breaks off on the schema's accented third (as the dominant of G-major), the second on the schema's unaccented sixth (as the dominant of C-major). The listener's knowledge of a canon at the lower fifth hinders a consolidation of the sonorities into chords. And an attempt to subject the succession of sonorities C–F⁶–Bb–e⁶–a to a tonal interpretation as T–S–(S)–Dp–Tp would, because of the harsh harmonic caesura between (S) and Dp [Bb-major and e-minor], upset the uniformity of the sequence.

Second, it was possible to chromatically alter the canonic sequential schemata of the 16th and early 17th centuries without altering their meaning. In the madrigal *Mentre io miravo fiso*,[36] Monteverdi sets out the prototype of the circle-of-fifths progression in two versions. The second, with the same text, follows the first at the lower fifth, and should thus be understood as an imitation. But a transposition to the same pitch level dramatically points out the harmonic contrast between the two versions: (1) D G⁶ C F⁶ b e⁶ a d⁶ g (2) D G⁶ c F⁶ Bb Eb⁶ Ab d⁶ g . The second version, rather than being a chromatic variant of a diatonic original, is but one of the possible ways of presenting, through specific tonal degrees, an abstract, tonally neutral interval schema. A tonal analysis would miss the meaning of the schema because it presumes a "logical" precedence of the chordal system over the details of compositional elaboration. But with Monteverdi just the reverse is true. The intervallic schemata assert an independent existence and significance irrespective of the differences between diatonic and chromatic writing, or between tonal closure and open-ended modulation.

Third, the prototypes of the diatonic circle-of-fifths progression were metrically ambiguous. Toward 1700, the strong beats in the progression I–IV–vii–iii–vi–ii–V–I fall on degrees IV, iii, ii, and I. Degree IV appears as the goal of degree I; the downbeat appears as the goal of the upbeat. The diatonic circle-of-fifths progression is the harmonic analogue of the four-measure period. Metric inversion—beginning on a strong beat—forces a modulation.

Example 20

But in ex. 20 from Tarquinio Merulas's canzona *La Strada*[37] (mm. 11–13) published in 1637, the metric inversion and the C-major ending of the G-major sequence should still not be understood as deviations from a norm, but as an indication of the schema's earlier metric and harmonic ambiguity.

Example 21

The diatonic circle-of-fifths progression composed of seventh chords (ex. 21a) owes its origin to the 16th-century suspension clausulas on the degrees mi, ut, and la (ex. 21b). On the other hand, a chain of seventh chords implies assumptions that were foreign to the 16th century. The diminished fifth was avoided as a melodic interval, and only allowed as a harmonic interval when followed by a third

( ), not by a unison ( ). Furthermore, the lower voice leaping up a fourth to initiate the dissonance of the upper voice's suspension was, in the 16th century, a rare exception.[38] And finally, "tied" dissonance was carried over from strong beats to weak beats only in the 17th century, and at first still hesitantly.

3. In tonal harmony, the I–IV–V–I cadence is, in spite of its name, less a cadential formula than a model of harmony. It appears as the simplest expression of the principle that lies at the root of tonal harmony: the idea that the tonic is the reconciliation and outcome of the opposition between the subdominant and the dominant. The cadence is the representation of a key through chords, and it is no mere metaphor when complicated chordal relationships, as long as they remain within the boundaries of one key, are explained as "extended cadences."

The actual I–IV–V–I pattern must thus be distinguished from the function that the pattern fulfills as a model in tonal harmony. And the question about the origin of the cadence is itself equivocal. The fact that isolated instances of the chord progression can be detected around 1500 does not directly prove that it already had the meaning it receives in tonal harmony.

Edward E. Lowinsky described the development of tonal harmony as the growth of a seed: "The seeds of tonality began to sprout in the cadence; the cadence grew to a phrase and evolved into an ostinato pattern; frottole and villancicos were at times composed over free variants of standard bass melodies."[39] The concept of growth carries with it the notion that the earliest emergence of the I–IV–V–I progression was already a sign and an expression of a new "feeling of tonality," which then gradually brought entire forms, instead of isolated sections, under its dominion. It seems, however, that the transition from the sporadic use of the I–IV–V–I pattern to a consciousness of its function as a model ought to be understood more as a "qualitative leap."

Hugo Riemann's conviction that tonal harmony is the only "natural" harmony prompted the conjecture that the I–IV–V–I cadence originated in a more "natural," unwritten folk or *Gebrauchsmusik* [utilitarian music] that existed alongside the learned art of the Netherlanders. And one could, in searching for corroboration, refer to Josquin's motet *Ave Maria*.[40] There the I–IV–V–I progression (mm. 94–101) leaps so dramatically from the surrounding context that the hypothesis that this harmonic schema I–IV–V–I forced its way into Netherlandish counterpoint from the outside, from *Gebrauchsmusik*, seems downright inescapable. On closer analysis, however, doubts arise. The basic structure of mm. 94 to 110—a canon at the lower fifth between superius and tenor—can be reduced to a simple schema:

Example 22

The question thus becomes whether the harmonic schema was compositionally realized in the guise of a canon, or whether the canon was supplemented by a bass. A preexistence of the harmonic schema is not out of the question, but it is unlikely. In the first place, in neither the superius nor the tenor is the canon's melody directly related to the harmony. The G-major tonality of the superius stands at odds with the C-major tonality of the tenor, and even the tenor line c'–d'–e'–c' is merely adapted to the harmonic schema instead of containing it within itself as "immanent harmony." And in the second place, if the canon is assumed to be primary in terms of compositional technique, then the bass can be deduced from it. If contrapuntal errors are to be avoided, then the scale steps in the bass, which appear to be I–IV–V–I, are the only ones possible.

On the other hand, it is undeniable that around the year 1500—thus at the same time as Josquin's *Ave Maria*, published in 1502 by Petrucci—the I–IV–V–I schema appears as a chord progression in a ricercar for lute by Joanambrosio Dalza.[41]

Example 23

Since the time of Dufay, the V–I progression had a preliminary contrapuntal represention in the "*clausula formalis*" [see ex. 24, upper voices], without of course being intended as a chord progression. What is new is the IV chord as the antepenult on a strong beat.

The fourth degree in the bass occurs in conjunction with the six-five dissonance.

Example 24

The discant and tenor formulas served as the clausula's framework, while the bass formed a supplemental voice. In comparison, the five-three sonority as antepenult on the fourth degree signifies an "emancipation," a stepping forward of the bass formula to become the fundamental voice. But on the other hand, the dependency on the six-five sonority is not entirely at an end. The "complete" I–IV–V–I cadence is still a secondary form of the *clausula formalis*.

According to the theory of tonal harmony, the cadential function of the subdominant is based on its fifth-relation with the tonic and its contrasting second-relation with the dominant. And the six-five sonority is considered a variant of the subdominant—the "appearances" of compositional technique are based on the "logic" of the chordal system. But historically the reverse is true. The six-five sonority is the prototype and prerequisite for the subdominant as antepenult of the cadence.

In tonal harmony, three factors need to be distinguished concerning the subdominant: (1) the fifth-relation with the tonic; (2) the contrast ("dialectical," not "complementary") of the second-relation with the dominant, a contrast that demands a resolution by the tonic; and (3) the interchangeability of IV and ii. The relation of the ii chord to the tonic, rather than being direct, is indirect—as a substitution for the subdominant (in the theory of functions) or as a dominant of the dominant (in the theory of fundamental progressions).

In the *clausula formalis*, the "IV" often appears on a weak beat as the preparatory consonance of the suspension.

Example 25

Yet it would be a mistake to perceive it as being in a contrasting second-relation to "V." The bass's **f** is only one of the possible consonances below the discant's **c″**. It has a contrapuntal, not harmonic-tonal, basis.

The dependence on the model of the *clausula formalis* can still be detected in the "subdominants" of Dalza's ricercar:[42]

Example 26

Such a lute composition is more a loosened form of strict counterpoint than the expression of an original impulse independent of the art of the Netherlanders.

Lowinsky[43] cites a *Pavanna alla ferrarese* by Dalza that is based exclusively on I, ii, IV, and V chords. The sonority on the second degree is to be understood as the subdominant parallel: "Even the chord of the second degree is handled in a modern manner as a substitute for the subdominant."[44] Yet a comparison of a variant (mm. 57–60 [ex. 27]) of the phrase that Lowinsky seems to have in mind [mm. 1–4] is sufficient to show that ii–V–I is not a substitute for the IV–V–I formula, which does not occur in the *Pavanna alla ferrarese*.

Example 27

In m. 59, degree ii relates directly to degree I as a complementary second-contrast, not indirectly as a subdominant parallel. It would be anachronistic to interpret what was normal around 1500 in terms of something that is more obvious to us—the IV–V–I cadence—but was then abnormal.

On the other hand, the I–IV, IV–I, and V–I fifth-relations in the

Pavanna alla ferrarese are so strikingly marked that Lowinsky was unquestionably right to see in them something quite new.

The fact that a five-three sonority can stand on its own and need not be resolved in spite of the factor of unrest and instability perceived in the third, was a part of early 15th-century musical experience. But compositional technique remained bound to the categories of intervallic composition. Although the effect of the triad was desired, chords did not form the material of composition. Antoine Brumel's motet *Sicut lilium*, according to Lowinsky a paradigm of tonal harmony,[45] is characteristic of this situation. Brumel's concern for the effects of sonorities is unmistakable. But the five-three sonorities, no matter how crucial in determining the overall impression, represent not a compositional premise, but a compositional result—the "aesthetic" surface of the work. The compositional technique is based on the norms and methods of intervallic composition. In the first phrase, the series of sonorities that Lowinsky interprets as F: I–vi–IV results from imitations on a falling-third motive. Measures 11–15 are based on fauxbourdon. Measures 16–19 depend on the complementary second-contrast of F–g–F. The 3–5 interval progression—the progression from the major third to the perfect fifth—establishes the connection between the C-major and B♭-major chords in mm. 20–23. And a discant-tenor framework underlies the final cadence. The impression that there is a question of chordal composition is an illusion, even if an aesthetically relevant illusion.

Compared with Brumel's technique, Dalza's method is "modern," though at the same time primitive. In the *Pavanna alla ferrarese*, the fifth-progressions in the bass seem like the roots of fundamental progressions. Nevertheless, the potential for tonal harmony that is indicated in Dalza remained largely undeveloped. First, around 1500, composers lacked the prerequisite techniques with which to develop, from a fundamental progression of chordal roots, musical forms that stretch beyond the simplicity of dance forms. And second, while the fifth-progression was certainly recognized as a convincing progression, it was not understood as the founding principle of a chordal system. Since it was merely one formula among many, its coexistence with the whole-tone contrast—conceived as a self-contained progression—did not imply a contradiction.

A saltarello by Paolo Borrono, cited by Lowinsky,[46] is characteristic.

Example 28

At first it seems that the IV–V–I chord progression should be understood as a "dialectical" contrast between subdominant and dominant that resolves itself in the tonic. The fact that in the second full measure IV and V are separated from I by a phrase ending could be interpreted as an artful displacement of harmonic and formal articulations. But mm. 6–8 point out that for Borrono, IV–V is a formula that can exist even when separated from I. It is a self-contained whole-tone contrast to which a second whole-tone contrast, ii–I, is joined.

To speak of tonal harmony would thus be an exaggeration. In the 16th century, the "complete" I–IV–V–I cadence appears in direct proximity to compositional formulas that do not admit a tonal interpretation. And the supposition that a listener, in the course of a work or even one passage, switched between a tonal and nontonal mode of musical cognition would be problematical. To be sure, relics of an earlier stage of development can be carried forward, as petrified formulas, into a newer system of composition and of listening. But the converse, that mere fragments and scattered anticipations of what is to come comprise a consciousness of a system, be it ever so rudimentary, is unlikely. The "complete" cadence existed as a compositional topos without being conceived as the founding principle of a chordal system.

THE DEVELOPMENT OF CHORDAL THEORY

In tonal harmony, the concept of a chord is based on assumptions that in tonal theory are nearly inseparable because of their close mutual association within a closed system. Yet if the prehistory of the concept is to be presented, then these assumptions must be differentiated: (1) complementary intervals (two intervals that add up to an octave—fifth and fourth, third and sixth) are considered "harmonically identical"; and the lower tone of the fifth and third—thus the upper tone of the fourth and sixth—is understood as the "root" of the interval; (2) a major or minor chord is composed of a root (as *"centre harmonique"*), a third, and a fifth; the chord position with the root in the bass is taken as the norm, the transfer of the third or fifth to the bass is viewed as the exception ("chordal inversion"); (3) in a major chord the characteristic interval is the major third or minor sixth, in a minor chord it is the minor third or major sixth; (4) the six-four sonority is considered a consonance if it is understood as an inversion; (5) chordal relationship—according to theory of fundamental progressions—is represented by the succession of chordal roots ("root progressions"); and (6) the chordal system of a particular key is divided into primary and secondary degrees.

1. In the older theory of intervals, thirds and sixths were understood as compound intervals, not as directly given phenomena. The major third, the *"tertia perfecta,"* is composed of two whole tones, the minor third, the *"tertia imperfecta,"* of a whole tone and a semitone. The major sixth, the *"sexta perfecta,"* is composed of a perfect fifth and a whole tone, the minor sixth, the *"sexta imperfecta,"* of a perfect fifth and a semitone. The terms "perfect" and "imperfect"[1] signify that the contrast between the "perfect," firmly outlined whole tone and the "imperfect," vague semitone was perceived as the distinguishing feature of the major and minor third or sixth.

In the 16th century, the characterization of thirds and sixths is not combined with a theory of intervallic roots. But it is not out of the question that this characterization was tacitly based on a conception of intervallic roots that contradicts the tonal chord system. If one assumes that, in an interval proportion, the tone represented by the smaller number is the interval's root, then one can interpret the "perfection" of the major third and sixth as the coincidence of root and bass, and the "imperfection" of the minor third and sixth as the divergence of root and bass. The representative of the smaller number is the lower tone in the major third (4:5), the upper tone in the minor sixth (5:8, 8 = 4), the lower tone in the major sixth (3:5), and the upper tone in the minor third (5:6, 6 = 3).

2. Hugo Riemann[2] referred to a passage by Walter Odington to demonstrate that by around 1300, the third and fifth of the major or minor chord were already related to the *centre harmonique* of the root.

"Therefore taken together, the major or minor third, fifth, octave, major or minor tenth, twelfth, and double octave, would, if compared to the same lower voice, appear in the proportions of the following formula: 64:81:96:128:162:192:256 [e.g., calculated from **c**: **c–e–g–c′–e′–g′–c″**]" [Compatientur ergo se simul, si eidem voci gravi comparentur, ditonus vel semiditonus, diapente, diapason, diapason cum ditono vel semiditono, diapason cum diapente, bis diapason ut in his numeris patet sub hac formula: 64. 81. 96. 128. 162. 192. 256.].[3] But to understand Odington one must bear in mind that while the third was considered a consonance, the sixth was still considered a dissonance. Anonymous 4 allows sixths if they originate as the intervallic remainder between the third and the octave, or the fifth and the tenth.[4] And under the assumptions of the 13th century, even Odington's passage has theoretical import only if one assumes that it was meant to justify the sixth as a hidden dissonance. The fact that the lowest voice is characterized as a reference voice ("si eidem voci gravi comparentur") does not mean that it was conceived as the *centre harmonique* of a major or minor triad. It only means that it is the common tone of the primary intervals—third and octave, fifth and tenth, tenth and double octave—from which a sixth can arise as a secondary interval.

Gafurius and Zarlino construct the triad empirically by combining intervals, and mathematically by dividing them. According to Gafurius, the major triad is not based on a *centre harmonique*—on the relation of a third and a fifth to a root. Rather, it is composed of two thirds and represents the "harmonic proportion" 15:12:10—the division of the fifth according to the formula where the ratio between the first and third numbers [15:10 = 3:2] is equal to the ratio between the differences of the first and second pairs of numbers [(15–12):(12–10) = 3:2]. "The fifth is composed of two of the first simple intervals, namely the minor and major third, maintaining the [same] mean tone; hence the outer consonance [i.e., the fifth] is brought into greater smoothness almost as if in a certain imitation it partakes of the harmonic mean" [(Quinta) componitur ex duobus primis simplicibus scilicet tertia minore atque maiore concordi medietate servata. Inde suaviorem ducit extremitatum concordiam quasi quae certa imitatione harmonicae adhaereat medietati].[5] The six-three sonority is constructed from a third and a fourth, not derived as a "sixth chord" from the five-three sonority—the "root-position triad." "Now when the smaller consonance, namely the fourth ["consonances" are here the fourth and fifth], is superimposed on a major third, then the outer tones unite in a major sixth mediated by a common tone harmonizing most aptly" [Quod cum minor consonantia videlicet diatessaron superposita fuerit tertiae maiori tunc

extremi invicem termini sextam ipsam maiorem communi chorda me-
diatam atque concinnitati aptissimam conducent].[6]

Hugo Riemann's thesis that Zarlino was the discoverer of the "dual
nature of harmony"[7] can be considered refuted.[8] The arguments against
it should be supplemented by a presentation of the system of sonorities
as outlined by Zarlino. Zarlino does not regard the "sixth chord" and
the "six-four chord" as inversions of a "root-position chord." Rather,
he compares sonorities consisting of the same intervals in different
arrangements:

fifth and fourth:	c g c'	and	C c g
	6 : 4 : 3		4 : 3 : 2
major and minor third:	c e g	and	A c e
	15 : 12 : 10		6 : 5 : 4
fourth and major third:	G c e	and	c e a
	20 : 15 : 12		5 : 4 : 3
fourth and minor third:	e g c'	and	B e g
	24 : 20 : 15		8 : 6 : 5

The first group, on the left, represents the "*ordine naturale*" [natural
order], the second group, on the right, the "*ordine accidentale*"
[incidental order].[9] The series of superparticular proportions (2:1, 3:2,
4:3, 5:4, 6:5), supplemented by 8:6,[10] defines the "*luogo naturale*"
[natural placement] of the intervals: the interval which is "earlier" and
"closer to the beginning" is meant to precede, not follow, the "later"
interval. The arrangement given by nature thus has the fifth (3:2) below
the fourth (4:3), the fourth below the major third (5:4), the major third
below the minor third (6:5), and the minor third below the fourth (8:6),
not vice versa.[11]

Disregarding the last row, the sonorities in the "*ordine naturale*"
represent "harmonic proportion" (6:4:3, 15:12:10, and 20:15:12), and
the sonorities of the "*ordine accidentale*" represent "arithmetic proportion" (4:3:2, 5:4:3, and 6:5:4). Zarlino's "discovery" was not the
"dual nature of harmony," but the correspondence of the consequences
stemming from two biases: first, that "harmonic proportion" should
take precedence over "arithmetic proportion," and second, that the
lower position ought to serve as the "*luogo naturale*" of the intervals
that are "earlier" in the series of superparticular proportions.

The founder of the modern theory of chords is neither Zarlino nor
Rameau, but Johann Lippius. Lippius conceived of the triad directly
as a unity—as a chord. "The simple and direct harmonic triad is the
true and triune root of all the fullest and most perfect harmonies" [Trias
harmonica simplex et recta radix vera est unitrisona omnis harmoniae

perfectissimae plenissimaeque].[12] The triadic root appears as a *centre harmonique* out of which Lippius, like Rameau later, permits the fifth to "issue." "Of the monads or three root voices, which also constitute three root dyads, the first two are the outer voices, namely the first, or lowest, and the last, or highest voice, begotten of the lowest" [Soni monades, seu voces radicales tres constituentes etiam tres dyades radicales sunt primo duae extremae, scilicet prima, ima basis, et ultima seu summa ab illa genita]. The third is understood as resulting from a division of the fifth. "Then the two outer voices, ringing together with a perfect masculine sound, are conjoined by the gentler sweetness of a medial voice proceeding from them . . ." [Deinde est una media duas illas extremas perfecto masculoque tinnitu conspirantes leniori sua dulcedine coniungens, ex iisdem procedens . . .].[13] Through the terms "*basis*," "*media*," and "*ultima*," the tones are defined as parts of a triad. Even when the "*basis*" and the "*ultima*" form a fourth (**G–c**) instead of a fifth (**c–g**), they remain what they were. "Hence sometimes, although it is rare, even the *ultima* and the *media* of the triune root monads may be used in the bass" [Unde basso interdum, quamquam rarius, etiam ultima, et media unitrisonae radicis monade licet uti].[14] The combinations of the third and fourth, the six-three and six-four sonorities, are interpreted as chords with the third or the fifth in the bass, in other words as true six and six-four chords.

Chordal inversion was understood as a special case of the octave transfer of chord tones. "A diffuse harmonic triad is one whose parts or root voices are dispersed less close to each other and spread out in different octaves, either just one voice or all or them" [(Trias harmonica) Diffusa est, cuius partes seu voces radicales minus sibi invicem vicinae dispersae sunt atque diffusae in diversas octavas: et vel quaedam tantum, vel omnes]. But Lippius stresses the distinction between the transfer of the "*media*" or "*ultima*" to the bass and the simple exchange of chord tones in the upper voices. "And a harmonic triad is always better whose *basis* maintains the lowest position, with the rest of the voices being above it" [Ac semper melior est trias harmonica, cuius basis imo substat loco, caeterae superiore].[15] By contrast, in the chordal system of Heinrich Baryphonus[16] the sixth chord **e–g–c′**, in relation to the octave expansion of the root position triad to **C–e–g**, appears as an inversion of the root; the sixth chord **E–c–g**, in relation to the octave expansion **c–g–e′**, appears as an inversion of the third; and the six-four chord **G–c–e**, in relation to the octave expansion **c–e–g′**, as an inversion of the fifth.

Contemporaneously with Lippius, Thomas Campion recognized around 1613 that the proper root of a sixth chord is not the tone in the bass, but the third below it. "Such Bases are not true Bases, for where a sixt is to be taken, either in F. sharpe, or in E. sharpe, or in B. or in A. The true Base is a third lower, F. sharpe in D., E. in C., B. in G., A. in F."[17]

Andreas Werckmeister[18] distinguishes four groups of chords: (1) "common settings" [*Ordinar-Sätze*] with the three upper voices in close position (**C–c–e–g**); (2) "dispersed common settings" [*zerstreuete Ordinar-Sätze*] with the three upper voices in open position (**C–c–g–e′**); (3) "uncommon settings" [*Extraordinar-Sätze*] with the fifth doubled instead of the root; and (4) "special settings" [*sonderbahre Sätze*] "above which, in a thoroughbass, stand the accidentals and figures" [über welchen im General-Basse die Signaturen und Zahlen überstehen]. Inverted chords, as deviations from the thoroughbass norm of the five-three chord, are included with the dissonances in the group of "special settings." It is the real bass of thoroughbass practice, not the abstract root of chordal theory, that governs musical conceptions.

3. In Zarlino's description of the intervals' characters,[19] the major third is likened not to the minor third, but to the major sixth. Major thirds and sixths are taken to be lively, happy, and sonorous ("vive et allegre, accompagnate da molta sonorità"), the minor thirds and sixths as sweet and tender, though at the same time a little sad and languid ("quantunque siano dolci et soavi, declinano alquanto al mesto, over languido").

This characterization of intervals agrees with Zarlino's principle of relating to each other, as different combinations of the same intervals, the sonorities **G–c–e** and **c–e–a** (or **B–e–g** and **e–g–c′**). On the other hand, the idea that the minor sixth-three chord and the major six-four chord (or the major sixth-three chord and the minor six-four chord) express the same affect contradicts the modern concept of a major or minor character that remains unchanged by chordal inversion. Zarlino's interval characterizations were taken over by Lippius, even though they seem opposed to the theory of chordal inversion. "The ditone or major third sounds, in its sweet imperfection, more animated, vigorous, and lively: further, the semiditone or minor third sounds, also in tender imperfection, softer, milder, and sadder: then the major sixth resounds, in its imperfection, as if higher and brighter: finally, the minor sixth resounds still more dispirited, softer, and languid" [Ditonus seu tertia maior dulci imperfectione concinnere alacrius, vegetius, vivacius: porro semiditonus seu tertia minor suavi quoque imperfectione concinnere mollius, remissius, tristius: deinde sexta maior sua imperfectione circumsonare quasi altius et laetius: sexta denique minor sic etiam circumsonare demissius, mollius, languidius].[20] The contradiction is nullified if one allows that the "harmonic identity" of the sixth-three and five-three chords does not exclude an opposition in their characters. From the concept of chordal inversion, the inference of a "harmonic" foundation for aesthetic judgments of sonorities, judgments based on chordal theory, is possible but not necessary.

4. In 16th-century counterpoint, the six-four sonority was divided into a dissonant-sounding fourth and a consonant-sounding sixth.[21] According to the theory of tonal harmony, however, either the fourth is a dissonance and so is the sixth, or the sixth is a consonance and so is the fourth. In the theory of functions, the expression "dissonance" denotes not an interval, but a tone: one that is neither the third nor the fifth of the *centre harmonique*. With the fourth as the root, the six-four sonority is a consonance—a six-four "chord." Conversely, with the tone in the bass as the root, the six-four sonority is a dissonance—a double suspension.

In the theory of degrees, the chord progression admits of two interpretations. To construe a fundamental bass composed of fifth-progressions, one must either make the six-four sonority represent I (between IV and V) or explain first the F-major chord as ii[7] with a "suppressed root" and then the six-four sonority as a double suspension resolving to V. Hence in the theory of fundamental progressions, the consonant or dissonant character of the fourth above the bass is bound up in a reciprocal relationship both with the principle of chordal inversion and with the construction of the *basse fondamentale*.

But the theory of chordal inversion is not a necessary condition for being able to conceive the fourth above the bass as a consonance. In 1581, Andreas Papius—with an archaizing tendency—defines the fourth as a perfect interval without considering its position in a sonority. Instead of reducing the fourth to a fifth, he employs it analogously to the fifth as a support and structural interval for combinations of imperfect consonances.[22]

On the other hand, the fourth can pass for a dissonance even when it is understood as the octave complement of the fifth. Andreas Werckmeister has the six-four sonority originate in the transfer of the alto clausula to the bass. "The discant, alto, and tenor formulas can also be placed in the bass" [Die Discantisirende, Altisirende und Tenorisirende können auch loco fundamenti gesetzet werden]:[23]

Example 29

The identity of the formulas is not invalidated by the exchange of the voices. Thus **e–c′–g′** and **g–c′–e′** are "inversions" of **c–e′–g′**. Yet Werckmeister raises a polemic against the opinion that the fourth above the bass is a consonance. "But when it [the fourth] is alone or put in place of the bass it forfeits its position and must be resolved as a dissonance. Now although some would allow this progression indiscriminately, then this very harmony will not always attain its effect" [Wenn sie aber bloß / oder anstatt deß fundaments gesetzet wird / verlieret sie ihren Sitz / und muß alß eine dissonanz resolviret werden. Ob nun wol einige diesen progressum ohn unterschied zulassen wollen / so wird doch dieselbe harmonie nicht allemal ihren effectum erreichen].[24]

5. The categories "chord" and "root progression" are complementary concepts. In relation to a root, a chord is an immediate unity and not a mere combination of intervals. And a "root" is a compositional category—and not merely a category in the "psychology of music"— only when chordal relationship is based on root progressions and not on interval progressions.

The "*Tabula naturalis*" [roughly: "A Listing of Natural Progressions"] may serve as a sufficient though not a sure sign that in the 17th century a root propression was understood as the representative of a chord progression, and that interval progression—as a category of musical cognition—was replaced by, or paled alongside of, chord progression.

Ascendendo   Descendendo

Example 30

In the "*Tabula naturalis*," the root progression of the bass forms the organizing principle for combinations of root-position chords. It should not be misunderstood as a mere vehicle of thoroughbass practice with little or no significance for the categories of musical cognition. The *Tabula naturalis* is not primarily a presentation of chords that can be struck to a given sequence of notes in a thoroughbass. Rather, it means that chord combinations represented by the root progression of the bass were conceived as the basis and material of composition. "This table is indispensable and forms the foundation of all music, a foundation close to which, wherever possible, everyone should and usually does compose; nor should one willingly depart from it" [Haec tabula maxime est necessaria, totiusque musicae fundamentum: iuxta quam, ubicunque potest, omnia componi solent ac debent: nec facile ab ea recedendum].[25]

One could object that the interpretation of the bass progressions as root progressions is questionable to the extent that, since the six-three chord is missing from the *Tabula naturalis*, there is no way to determine whether the chord progression I[6]-V would have been classified as a third-progression of the bass or as a fifth-progression of the chordal roots. Yet it is likely that the *Tabula naturalis* and the deduction of the chordal inversions were mutually related. Johann Crüger adopted not only Johann Lippius's theory of chords but also, in the second edition of his *Synopsis musica*, the *Tabula naturalis* of Wolfgang Schönsleder or Johann Andreas Herbst.[26]

The consolidation of combined interval progressions into chord progressions is connected with a reinterpretation of the rules of "musica ficta" into prescriptions for forming chords over bass progressions. The progression with a chromatically lowered minor third becomes a plagal cadence with a minor subdominant. The progression with a chromatically raised major third becomes an authentic cadence with a major dominant.

Example 31

Francesco Bianciardi[27] and Lorenzo Penna call for a minor third above the first tone of a descending fourth or ascending fifth in the bass, and a major third above the first tone of a descending fifth or an ascending fourth—the reverse is considered the exception.[28] The same rule is presented by Franz Xaver Murschhauser as an expression of the cadential principle. "Concerning the major third, it is built on the same such bass note or key from which one, by a cadence or in the manner and likeness of a cadence, leaps either a fourth above or a fifth below" [Die Tertiam majorem betreffend / wird selbige demjenigen Fundamental-Clavi, oder Schlüssel aufgesetzt / von welchem man durch eine Cadenz, oder auf die Weis / und Gleichnus einer Cadenz, entweders in die Quart hinauf / oder in die Quint hinab springt].[29] "Concerning the minor third, this interval is especially required above such bass notes that form a cadence either at the fifth above or the fourth below, provided that the tone on which the composition is organized naturally permits this third and carries such a cadence, or allows it *per accidens*, that is, as chance would have it" [Von der Tertia minori. Diese wird absonderlich auf diejenige Fundamental-Claves erfordert / welche eine Cadenz entweders in die Quint hinauf / oder in die Quart hinab formiren / wenn anderst derjenige Ton, auf welchen die Composition eingerichtet / eine solche Tertiam ex natura sua, und eine solche Cadenz mit sich führet / oder per accidens, das ist / zufälliger Weis zulässet].[30] Out of the principle of a half-step connection in progressions from an imperfect to a perfect consonance there thus arises in the 17th century one of the defining features of a functional mode of perception: the affinity between dominant function and the major mode, subdominant function and the minor mode.[31]

6. The first attempt at a division of the chordal system into primary and secondary degrees is the thoroughbass rule requiring a six-three chord over a mi-degree in the bass. In the untransposed system, the sixth chord over a **B** in the bass is necessary to avoid a diminished fifth. But according to Galeazzo Sabbatini,[32] not only **B** and any sharped notes, but also an **e** in the bass should "be accompanied by the third and sixth." And in 1679, Lorenzo Penna demands the sixth chord even on the la-degree. "Second rule: That each note in the bass is accompanied by thirds and fifths or their octave equivalents, except the mi-degrees, which ordinarily use thirds and sixths or their octave equivalents . . . Be advised that the mi-degrees in keys with B natural are **b♭** (fa), **b♮** (mi), and **e** (la mi); and in keys with B flat they are **a** (la mi re) and **d′** (sol la re)" [Seconda Regola. Che ogni nota di fondo se accompagni di terze, e quinte, ò loro replicate, eccetto li mi, quali per ordinario usano le terze, e seste, ò loro replicate . . . Sia avertito, che le note del mi nelle chiave per h quadro sono b fa h mi et e la mi; e nelle chiave di b molle sono a la mi re et d sol la re].[33] Penna counts the la-degree "**d′** (sol la re)" among the "mi-degrees."

The requirement that six-three chords be formed above the mi and la tones in the bass results in a reduction of the major-mode chord system to four primary degrees:

c	d	e	f	g	a	b
I	ii	I^6	IV	V	IV^6	V^6 ·

The rule for sixth chords—formulated by Penna in the abstract without regard to a specific mode—was applied to the major mode by Matthew Locke in 1673. "If G be the Tone, F sharp, B, and E, are proper notes to play Sixes on. If A be the Tone, then G sharp, C sharp, and F sharp, are proper for Sixes."[34]

Through the rule for sixth chords, the triads on iii, vi, and vii were demoted to the status of exceptions. The rule thus implies a division of the the major-mode chordal system into primary and secondary degrees. The fact that ii was considered a primary degree along with I, IV, and V should not be misunderstood as a defect and inconsistencey in the theory. Even compositional practice in the late 17th century compels a recognition of an independent ii, and consequently a modification of the theory of functions. And in Rameau's first outline of a theory of harmony, ii, instead of IV, is still taken as the third primary degree alongside I and V.[35]

The notion of a reduction of the secondary degrees to the primary degrees was foreign to the 17th century. Yet the evidence that the perception of chord progressions was based on a division of the chordal system into primary and secondary degrees is sufficient to justify the use of the term "tonal harmony." For Riemann's thesis that iii in major should be understood as Dp or as the *"Leittonwechselklang"* of the tonic, and that vi should be understood as Tp or as the *"Leittonwechselklang"* of the subdominant, is not a simple description of fact. Instead, it is a speculative interpretation of a phenomenon fundamental to tonal harmony as a way of perceiving music—the dependent status of iii and vi.

DISSONANCE TREATMENT IN THE EARLY 17TH CENTURY

Dissonance, along with root progression, is one of the constituent factors of chordal relationship. In the thoroughbass theory of the early 18th century (the basis for Rameau's theory of harmony), dissonance and root progression were interrelated: the ascending fourth or descending fifth in the bass is matched with the seventh chord, the ascending fifth or descending fourth with the six-five chord.[1]

The transition from the categories of the older style of counterpoint to the concept of dissonance in tonal harmony was mediated by the more modern counterpoint of the early 17th century—the counterpoint of madrigals and monody. The terms "counterpoint" and "monody" seem to be mutually exclusive. Yet Giulio Caccini's polemic against traditional counterpoint only points out that in monody, counterpoint is a means, not an end: counterpoint was demoted but not invalidated. Caccini understood the relationship between the voice part and the bass as counterpoint, as an interval progression: "For my own part, I attend to this (i.e., counterpoint) in order only to make the two parts agree with each other, to avoid certain notable errors, and to bind some harsh effects more for the accompaniment of the affect than for the employment of artifice" [. . . essendomi io servito di esso (scilicet contrappunto) per accordar solo le due parti insieme e sfuggire certi errori notabili, e legare alcune durezze più per accompagnamento dello affetto che per usar arte].[2] The retention of the concept of counterpoint should not be misunderstood as a terminological embarrassment, as a lack of appropriate categories. For in monody, the conditions that must be present to make a harmonic analysis seem an adequate description of compositional technique—that the bass represents triads or seventh chords, and that the voice part is based on chords and can thus be divided into chord tones and "nonharmonic tones"—are partially, but not entirely, fulfilled. The seventh still has not merged with the triad to form a seventh chord. And the remaining dissonances cannot always be interpreted as tones appended to chords, but must often be viewed as parts of intervallic progressions. The categories "chord" and "nonharmonic tone" are not inappropriate to describe the compositional technique of the early 17th century.[3] But then neither are they are fully adequate.

Adriano Banchieri justifies deviations from strict counterpoint as a means of representing the text. "Other dissonances are used in various contested ways, which modern composers call 'harsh effects' [*durezze*]. 'Harsh effects' are composed of notes usually not permitted; nevertheless they are permitted when occasioned by the text. But those wishing to employ them need to consider them carefully" [Usansi altre dissonanze in variati modi conteste, dalli Compositori moderni chiamate Durezze, le quali componendole in note, non vengono permesse, nulla dimeno in occasione di parole vengono permesse, ma bisogna volendole praticare considerarle bene].[4] Modern, "licentious" counterpoint does not signify a fundamental change in the technique of composition. Instead, viewed as an exception to the rule, it presupposes strict counterpoint. "Thus I say that the novice writer of counterpoint should first learn the rules and precepts of traditional counterpoint, and then avail himself of this studious invention; that is to say, place in score one singable voice so composed that it would be beautiful and polite to sing, then weave above it a new counterpoint in imitation of those affects and inventions that studiously present themselves" [Dico per ciò che il novello contrapuntista deve prima apprendere le regole e precetti nell' Osservato Contrapunto, poi servirsi di questa studiosa inventione cioè à dire, ponere in partitura una voce cantabile di compositione che habbia vago e polito cantare, sopra quella tessere un nuovo Contrapunto e imitare quelli affetti e inventioni, che studiosamente produvirsi].[5]

To be able to describe the modern counterpoint of the 17th century, one must separate out the individual features of traditional dissonance treatment.[6] (1) In the 16th-century, a dissonance was not primarily related to the following consonance, but formed a transition between consonances. It signified less a tension resolved by consonance, than a charming or even annoying interruption—a negative factor in contrast to the positive factor of consonance. (2) In the dissonance treatment of the 16th century, voice leading was closely correlated with the distinction between accented and unaccented beats. Dissonance arose through a second-progression in one of the voices and had to be resolved, if it was unaccented, by a second-progression in the same voice (passing and neighboring tones). Conversely, if it was accented, the dissonance had to be resolved by a second-progression in the other voice (suspensions). (3) Dissonances were set up and resolved exclusively by second-progressions. (4) Dissonances arose through the oblique motion of one of the voices. "Note against note" dissonance was prohibited.[7] (5) A dissonance—as an interval—could be divided into a dissonant tone, which had to be followed by a second-progression, and a reference tone, which was under no compulsion to move. The dissonant tone was dissonant in relation to another voice, not to a chord. (6) The distinction between a "chordal dissonance" (a seventh) and a "nonharmonic tone" (a fourth) was foreign to the 16th century. The 4–3 and 7–6 suspensions were considered dissonances of the same category.

1. In the 15th and 16th centuries, dissonance was conceived not in contrast and opposition to consonance, but as a scarcely noticeable interruption in the sequence of consonances. Prosdocimo de' Beldomandi and Anonymous 11 allow dissonance provided that it be inconspicuous.[8] And Gafurius characterizes not only the passing tone, but also the suspension as "concealed" dissonance. "But that dissonance which is concealed by syncopation and by swift passage is allowed in counterpoint" [Quae vero per sincopam et ipso rursus celeri transitu latet discordantia admittitur in contrapunctu].[9] The fact that Guilelmus Monachus[10] and Nicola Vicentino[11] perceive a suspension as a charming rather than annoying incident, does not change the significance of dissonance as a mere transition between two consonances. Even Zarlino remarks, as did Guilelmus and Vicentino, that a suspension heightens and illuminates the beauty of the following consonance: "Not only is such a dissonance not displeasing, but it is highly satisfying because it makes such [i.e., the following] consonance be heard with more sweetness and smoothness" [. . .che non solamente tal Dissonanza non li dispiace ma grandemente in lei se compiace, perchè con maggior dolcezza e maggior soavità fa udire tal Consonanza]. Nevertheless, he interprets the initiation of the suspension by an oblique-motion second-progression in another voice as a means of keeping the dissonance half hidden. It implies no tension, no crescendo, but a relaxation, a decrescendo. "Hence the voice held in the suspension then loses that liveliness which it had when first struck. So that being enfeebled, and being struck by a more vigorous movement in another strong voice (a voice moving from one degree to the next with a more vigorous movement), the dissonance is hidden above its second part so that it

is scarely heard, especially since it passes quickly by" [La onde la voce allora nel perseverar della Sincopa perde quella vivacità che havea nella prima percussione di modo che fatta debole; et essendo percossa da un movimento più gagliardo d'un altra voce forte che se muove da un luogo all'altro con più gagliardo movimento nella quale è nascosta la Dissonanza sopra la sua seconda parte, tal Dissonanza à pena se ode; essendo anco che prestamente se ne passa].[12]

Knud Jeppesen's[13] thesis that the suspension was conceived as a "primary" phenomenon, while the passing tone was conceived as "secondary," is one-sided. For in the first place, not only the passing tone but also the suspension was interpreted as a "hidden" dissonance. And in the second place, if one recognizes the suspension as a "primary" phenomenon and a contrast to consonance, then one would have to grant the same status to a passing tone the length of a minim.

Example 32

The 2–3 suspension in the upper voices[14] is prepared by a third whose upper tone [e′] is at the same time a passing tone in relation to the bass. And if the dissonant suspension is meant to be conceived as a "primary" phenomenon, then one can hardly deny the same standing to its preparatory consonance, and thus also to the passing tone.

To be able to explain counterpoint as a "harmony"—as an agreement of disparate or contrasted elements—Zarlino cites, along with other factors, the differences between the consonances. "The fourth condition that one seeks to satisfy is this: that the melodies and the conjoining of voices be varied, because harmony arises only from the diversity of melodies and from the diversity of consonances set together with variety" [La quarta conditione, che se ricerca, è: che le Modulationi, e il concento sia variato, percioche da altro non nasce l'Harmonia, che dalla diversità delle Modulationi e dalla diversità delle Consonanze messe insieme con varietà].[15] He does not mention dissonances. They only became conceived as a "primary" phenomenon of counterpoint in the late 16th and in the 17th centuries. Around 1590, Vincenzo Galilei let the theory of counterpoint shrink to a description of how to form dissonances.[16] According to Giovanni Maria Bononcini, counterpoint is based on the antithesis between consonance and dissonance. "Counterpoint is an artful disposition of both consonances and dissonances"

[Il Contrapunto è una artificiosa disposizione di consonanze, e dissonanze insieme].[17] And Christoph Bernhard defines the *"Con- und Dissonantien"* as the *"Materia"* [material] of counterpoint. A *"harmonischer Contrapunct"* [harmonious counterpoint] should consist of "con- and dissonances well placed against each other" [wohl gegeneinander gesetzten Con- und Dissonantiis].[18]

2. In the modern counterpoint of the 17th century, the correlation breaks down between, on the one hand, a dissonant tone and its reference tone, and on the other, strong and weak beats.

e al do- lor in pre - da   sel - ve   ha   so - spi - ra - to

Example 33

By the norms of the Palestrina style, the accented ninth in ex. 33a[19] [G–a'] should have been resolved to a tenth by a descending second in the bass (as a 2–3 suspension), not by an ascending second in the upper voice (as a passing tone). The accented passing tone, the *"transitus inversus,"*[20] is one of the distinctive features of modern counterpoint. Conversely, the ninth on the weak beat in ex. 33b[21] is initiated as a passing tone in the upper voice, but resolves as a suspension of the lower voice. The unaccented suspension, the *"syncopatio inversa,"*[22] is the counterpart to the accented passing tone. Of course this deviation from 16th-century norms has the effect of making the distinction between a dissonant tone and its reference tone questionable, and the terminology uncertain. Thus one can scarcely determine whether the first dissonance in ex. 33b was conceived as an analogue of a lower-voice suspension, but on a weak beat, or as an anticipation in the upper voice—thus whether the upper or the lower tone is meant as the dissonance.

The dissonant figures of modern counterpoint call to mind archaisms from the period around 1500.

Example 34

Knud Jeppesen[23] interprets this citation from Josquin's mass *Faysant regres* (Gloria, mm. 23-24) as an anticipation in the upper voice [alto bb]. Yet one could also speak of an irregular suspension in the bass. The strong beat is switched with the weak beat, or more to the point, the distinction between strong and weak is suspended.

3. A second feature of dissonance treatment in the modern counterpoint of the 17th century—along with the interchange of strong and weak beats—is the elision of the regular consonance of preparation or resolution.

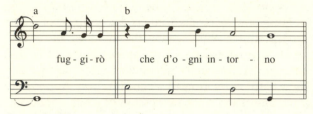

Example 35

Missing in ex. 35a is the preparatory consonance before an accented passing tone,[24] and in ex. 35b, the preparatory consonance before an unaccented passing tone.[25] Yet in neither case is the dissonance's interpretation as a passing tone at risk. To be able to speak of passing tones, it is thus not a necessary condition that they be approached by step, but only that they be initiated over a held tone in another voice[26] and be resolved by step. Christoph Bernhard classifies the unprepared passing tone as a special case of "*heterolepsis*," of the "taking up of another voice" [Ergreiffung einer anderen Stimme].[27] The missing preparatory consonance is meant to be filled in, if not by the thoroughbass, then at least by the musical imagination.

It is doubtful whether, in the early 17th century, an unaccented, unprepared seventh that progresses in contrary motion to a fifth[28] (less often to a third[29]) can be considered a chordal dissonance [like, for example, the seventh of V^7].

Example 36

The elision of the preparatory consonance is not a sufficient criterion of a dissonance being consolidated into chordal dissonance.

The counterpart of unprepared passing tones are suspensions resolved by leap, or by an ascending instead of a descending second.[30] Bernhard classifies them as a second special case of "*heterolepsis*," of the "taking up of another voice."[31]

Example 37

The irregular resolution of a suspension—of a fourth to the fifth (ex. 37a),[32] of a seventh to the octave (ex. 37b)[33] or to the third (ex. 37c),[34] of a ninth to the sixth (ex. 37d)[35] or to the fifth (ex. 37e)[36]—thus means, if one accepts Bernhard's explanation, that the two-voice counterpoint of monody should be understood as the reduction of a three-voice counterpoint, not as the reduction of a chordal composition.

Suspended sevenths that leap down to the fifth, sevenths whose resolution is thus contrapuntally incompatible with the sixth—the normal resolution—seem to force the interpretation that they are chordal dissonances, inasmuch as an interpretation as "*heterolepsis*" is out of the question.

ma tu gen - til   can - tor   s'a   tuoi   la - men - ti

Example 38

Yet beneath the suspended minim that leaps down to the fifth (ex. 38a[37]) one can construe a regularly resolved suspended semibreve in a latent voice—thus in the thoroughbass (ex. 38b). In consequence, even the downward leap of a suspended seventh—like the lack of a preparatory consonance before a passing seventh—is not a sufficient criterion of an emancipation from counterpoint and a consolidation of chordal dissonance.

4. A third feature of the dissonance treatment in modern counterpoint is the admission of "note-against-note" dissonance, something forbidden in the 16th century.[38]

mi - ra   deh mi - ra   ri - de il pra - to

Example 39

The seventh is initiated on either a strong (ex. 39a)[39] or a weak beat (ex. 39b)[40] in contrary or similar motion, and is resolved by contrary motion. The distinction between the dissonant tone and its reference tone is invalidated. And instead of forming a transition between two consonances, the dissonance is entirely related to the consonance that follows it.

Example 40

In the face of "note-against-note" dissonance, the method of contrapuntal reduction, if it does not completely break down, appears as arbitrary speculation. In the trio *Non partir ritrosetta* from Monteverdi's eighth book of madrigals[41] (ex. 40), the "note-against-note" seventh is set forth in three forms that permit a contrapuntal reduction. Underlying mm. 1–5 (ex. 40a), a suspended breve (ex. 40b [**f'**]) could be construed as a latent compositional framework. In m. 6 (ex. 40c) the "note-against-note" dissonance probably ought to be explained as an *"anticipatio transitus"*[42] — as the anticipation of a passing tone [i.e., **g** from **f–g–a**]. And in mm. 21–25 (ex. 40d), the parallel sevenths in the outer voices result from a crossing of traditional dissonance figures. The first such model pattern is the resolution of a suspended seventh to a six-four sonority with *"quarta consonans"* [a consonant fourth] (ex. 40e). The second is the preparation of a 2-3 suspension in the upper voices by a third whose upper tone [**c'**] is at the same time a passing tone in relation to the bass [cf. ex. 32] (ex. 40f).[43] Yet the variety of the possible preconditions for "note-against-note" dissonance is canceled by the similarity of the result.

It is uncertain whether the "note-against-note" seventh can be considered a seventh chord or must be understood as an intervallic dissonance. In Monteverdi's *L'Orfeo,* it is exclusively resolved to a fifth. In *L'Incoronazione di Poppea*, it is also resolved, though rarely,[44] to a third through an ascending leap of a fourth in the bass. In the succession of sonorities ![sonorities], the connecting factor is the interval progression 7–5, not the second-progression of the bass as foundation of a chord progression. Only in relation to an ascending leap of a fourth in the bass does the seventh appear as as chordal dissonance. "Note-against-note" dissonance thus facilitates the transition from voice-leading dissonance to the seventh chord.

5. At a second stage in the development of modern counterpoint, which though not strongly marked is nevertheless clearly indicated in the works of Monteverdi, the category of interval progression is replaced by that of chord progression. Individual voices remain directly related to each other only through their melodic and rhythmic characters. The conception of the intervals between the voices is mediated by the tones' chordal reference—by their classification into harmonic and nonharmonic tones.

As an indication that voices were no longer related to each other directly through intervals, but indirectly through a conception of chords, there appears a type of dissonant anticipation that contradicts 16th-century norms.

fa- ma   ec - cel - si pre - gi   ne   giun - ge al ver

Example 41

The traditional portamento dissonance signified that on a weak beat, a tone that would become a consonance on the following strong beat could be anticipated as a dissonance. But in the citation from Monteverdi's *Orfeo*[45] [ex. 41, see the starred notes], the upper voice substitutes the third for the anticipated root, or the fifth for the anticipated third. Thus the conception of a chord underlies these anticipations.

According to the thoroughbass rules of the early 17th century, the two excerpts from *Vorrei baciarti*[46]—a duet from Monteverdi's seventh book of madrigals [ex. 42]—present cases where all the unstressed quarter notes in the bass, not to mention both the eighth notes in mm. 46 and 71, must be understood as passing tones.[47]

Example 42

Hence the thoroughbass represents the chord progression d–a–F–d–A(a). And an attempt to characterize the octaves or tenths **e–e′**, **e–g′**, and **g–g′** in mm. 46, 70, and 71 as consonant resolutions of relatively accented passing tones in the upper voices would be misplaced. The resulting consonance is a simple accident of coinciding "nonharmonic tones." The voices do not form an interval progression meant to be perceived as such, but are independently related to chords.

The transition from the older to the more modern conception of dissonance was facilitated by a technique that admits of contrary interpretations.

Example 43

In the collision of seconds in ex. 43,[48] one can scarcely decide whether the tones **e′** and **a′** should be understood as dissonances added to G- and C-major chords (thus as "nonharmonic tones"), or whether the tones **d′** and **g′** are meant as suspensions whose reference tones leap down from the upper voice to the bass (e′–e and a′–A). The difference between these interpretations—a difference which may not be dismissed as a mere terminological difficulty or embarrassment—touches on the foundations of compositional technique and of musical cognition. According to the second interpretation, the excerpt is based on an intervallic framework of the outer voices, a framework filled in with consonances and suspensions. But according to the first interpretation, the passage is based on a root progression (V–I–IV–V–I) elaborated into an actual chord progression, against which are highlighted the individual "nonharmonic tones."

. . .

A rigid contrasting of intervallic and chordal composition would be a gross simplification of musical reality. In modern counterpoint, the category of interval progression was not entirely abandoned, but only demoted to the status of a secondary factor.

Example 44

If one considers ex. 44 apart from its thoroughbass,[49] then it appears that the e in the vocal bass is a relatively accented neighboring-tone and that the f is an unaccented passing tone. Yet the concept of a regular three-voice counterpoint is thwarted by the thoroughbass. The succession of a ninth and a seventh between the upper voice and the instrumental bass (which the vocal bass paraphrases) is not intended as an interval progression. Rather, the voices are related, independently of each other, to the d-minor and F-major chords.[50] A dissonant passing tone in the bass (e) coincides with a chord tone in the upper voice (f′), and a chord tone in the bass [f] coincides with a dissonant passing tone in the upper voice [e′]. But on the other hand, it can hardly be denied that the seventh is perceived not as a mere accident, but as the "tension sonority" of the 7–5 interval progression. The basic category of the older type of counterpoint, that of the interval progression, is preserved in modern counterpoint as a secondary factor.

One could object that the 9–7 interval progression is a result of a crossing of dissonances, something not out of the question even in the style of Palestrina. That is, the first dissonance coincides with the preparatory consonance of the second dissonance, and the second dissonance coincides with the consonance that resolves the first dissonance. In this way the interval progression would not disprove the possibility of a contrapuntal interpretation.

Example 45

Knud Jeppesen[51] cites a measure from Palestrina's motet *Fuit homo* in which an unaccented passing tone in the soprano [**b′**] forms a "note-against-note" dissonance with the resolution of a relatively accented passing tone in the alto [**f′**]. Yet in order to be conceived as being independent of each other, the colliding tones must be related, in Palestrina, to a third voice—the bass. In Monteverdi, by contrast, they must be related to a chord.

6. Chordal dissonance—the autonomous seventh-chord—is not a simple "fact" residing in the notes themselves, nor is it a "basic phenomenon" of musical perception that can be psychologically explained as the "fusion" of the dissonant tone through the agency of mediating thirds.[52] Instead, it is an "object of conceptualization and the mind's proclivity for seeking relationships" (C. Stumpf) [Sache der Auffassung und des beziehenden Denkens]. Understood as a category of musical cognition, chordal dissonance is based on a reciprocal relationship between root progression and the resolution of dissonance. Thus it presupposes that root progression is conceived as the representative of chordal relationship.

Example 46

The seventh is perceived as chordal dissonance in those cases where the root changes in conjunction with the resolution of the dissonance (exs. 46a and 46b), but as a "nonharmonic tone" in those cases where the root remains unchanged (exs. 46c and 46d).[53]

The character not only of root progression but also of the resolution of dissonance is altered by this reciprocal relationship (a relationship that cannot simply be divided into a cause and an effect). On the one hand, root progressions that can be combined with the seventh's resolution to the tone a second below[54] appear as primary progressions of the *basse fondamentale*,[55] namely, the descending fifth and the ascending second, as opposed to their mirror inversions, the ascending fifth and descending second. On the other hand, the suspended seventh is no longer perceived as an "appendage" of, or "something held over" from,[56] the preceding consonance, but as a "tension dissonance" that strives toward the following consonance as its goal. The "dynamic" conceptions of root progression and the resolution of dissonance are two sides of the same coin.

Paul Hamburger described the evolution from the 16th to the 17th century as the transition from a primacy of the less conspicuous "nonharmonic" tone to a precedence of the more conspicuous chordal dissonance. Yet Hamburger wrongly understands the concepts of "intervallic dissonance" and "nonharmonic tone" to be synonymous. The criterion of a "nonharmonic" tone—as opposed to a chordal dissonance—is the lack of a "change of harmony" during the resolution of the dissonance. In contrast, the concept of intervallic dissonance denotes a principle of interpreting dissonance that historically precedes—and excludes—the difference between chordal dissonance and "nonharmonic" tones. The fact that a seventh in the soprano resolving to a sixth over the tenor is understood as an intervallic dissonance means that the progressions of the remaining voices, with or without a "change of harmony," have no effect on the significance of the dissonance. In the 16th century, the differentiation between chordal dissonance and "nonharmonic" tones is meaningless.

The error in his original assumptions has consequences that can be pursued even down to technical details.

Example 47

According to Hamburger,[57] "the ii^7–V formula" (ex. 47a) is a rare exception in the 16th century because composers avoided "changing the harmony concurrently with the resolution of the seventh" [gleichzeitig mit der Septauflösung die Harmonie zu wechseln]. To be able to explain why the "ii$^6_5$–V formula" (ex. 47b) was a fixed topos in spite of the analogous "change of harmony," Hamburger is forced to interpret a seventh between upper voices—voices whose separate tones form consonances with the bass—as a hidden dissonance, as though the seventh were "something midway between consonance and dissonance" [Mitte zwischen Kon- und Dissonanz].[58]

But in the first place, even "the ii^7–V formula" was used in the 16th century, though only when the "root of V" entered after a pause in the lower voice (ex. 47c).[59] The distinguishing feature of the irregular formula of ex. 47a, as opposed to the regular formulas of exs. 47b and 47c, is not the "change of harmony," but the upward leap of the suspension's reference tone in conjunction with the resolution of the dissonance. In the 16th century, oblique motion was considered the norm not only for the initiation of a suspension, but also for its resolution.

And in the second place, Hamburger's presumption that the resolution of dissonance is made more striking by a "change of harmony" is based on an erroneous generalization that makes one category of tonally oriented listening into a "basic phenomenon" of musical perception. The resolution of dissonance is not "naturally" emphasized by a "change of harmony," but becomes conspicuous in tonally oriented listening because it appears, in reciprocal relationship with the root progression, as a defining feature of harmonic progression. Conversely, a "nonharmonic" tone is, by itself, neither more nor less conspicuous than a chordal dissonance. The point is that in major-minor tonality, a "nonharmonic" tone is of no consequence for harmonic progression.[60] The degree of conspicuousness of a resolution of dissonance connected with a "change of harmony" is "an object of conceptualization and the mind's proclivity for seeking relationships" [eine Sache der Auffassung und des beziehenden Denkens (C. Stumpf)].

THOROUGHBASS HARMONY

The term "thoroughbass harmony" is questionable, since thoroughbass in the 17th century is less a foundation for compositional technique than a tool of performance practice. At some times the figures appear as a fragmentary notation of counterpoint, at other times as a rudimentary notation of chords.

The figures for dissonance should be understood as an abbreviation of a contrapuntal notation. It would be a mistake to suppose that becoming accustomed to figures like 7, $\frac{4}{2}$, and $\frac{6}{5}$ aided in giving independence to the seventh chord.

Example 48

A figure like $\frac{4}{2}$ could mean an accented suspension of the upper voices (ex. 48a) or of the bass (ex. 48b), or an unaccented passing tone of the upper voices (ex. 48c) or of the bass (ex. 48d). The figure thus presupposes that the correlation between (1) strong or weak beats and (2) a second-progression or a held tone had become "second nature" to the thoroughbass player.[1] Being forced to read three intervals from one abbreviation—the preparatory consonance, the dissonance, and the consonance of resolution—did not give rise to a consciousness of the "$\frac{4}{2}$ chord" having an independent existence and meaning. Instead, it had the result of consolidating the categories of traditional counterpoint.

The repertory of chord names derived from the figuration of the thoroughbass constitutes a historically chance nomenclature without theoretical content. It does seem that the chord name indicates the interval from the bass tone to either the root or the dissonance. Yet if this supposition were correct, then the name "four chord" would have sufficed in place of "six-four chord." And the fact that $\frac{4}{2}$ was abbreviated as 2 (a "2 chord"), while $\frac{6}{4}$ was not similarly abbreviated as 4, must be explained historically, not theoretically. Originally, the figure "2" was of no use since it could signify not only $\frac{4}{2}$ but also $\frac{5}{2}$. Likewise, the figure "4" could signify not only $\frac{6}{4}$ but also $\frac{5}{4}$. But the $\frac{5}{2}$ chord became rare earlier than did the $\frac{5}{4}$ chord,[2] and so while the abbreviation of $\frac{4}{2}$ to 2 was possible, that of $\frac{6}{4}$ to 4 was not.

The figures of thoroughbass, as signs of exceptions or "*sonderbahren Sätzen*" [special settings] (Werckmeister), take for granted the norm of the root-position triad, and over bass notes with a diminished fifth above them, the six-three chord. On the one hand, the assumed equivalence of the $\frac{5}{3}$, $\frac{10}{5}$, and $\frac{12}{10}$ sonorities does seem to approach the concept of chordal inversion as formulated by Lippius, Campion, and Baryphonus. "Thus the conception that chords formed from tones with the same note names have the same harmonic significance to a certain extent already underlies the figures of thoroughbass as they initially took shape. This conception was, however, still veiled by the inviolable bass. It is only with Rameau's innovation that the figures of thoroughbass first arrive, as it were, at a realization of their true nature" [Die Auffassung der aus gleichnamigen Tönen gebildeten Akkorde als harmonisch gleichbedeutender liegt also gewissermaßen schon der Generalbaßbezifferung, wie sie von Anfang an sich gestaltete, zu Grunde, aber noch verhüllt durch den unantastbaren Baß; durch Rameaus Neuerung kommt gleichsam die Generalbaßbezifferung erst zur Erkenntnis ihres eigentlichen Wesens].[3] The obligatory, unfigured six-three chord above bass notes with a diminished fifth above them was probably—according to the rule formulated by Thomas Campion— understood as an inverted chord.

But on the other hand, insight into the significance of the abstract *basse fondamentale* was obstructed by the pre-eminence of the real bass of thoroughbass practice. (The figure "6," instead of indicating the interval from the bass to the root, meant that the sixth should be substituted for the fifth.)

The six-three chord admitted of three interpretations. First, it could be understood as an inverted chord. Second, as a $\frac{6}{3}$ sonority it could be juxtaposed—with equal claim—to the $\frac{5}{3}$ sonority. And third, it could be explained as a subsidiary form of the triad above the same bass—thus as a secondary chord, but with the bass as the "root."

The thoroughbass of Ludovico Viadana's *Cento Concerti ecclesiastici* (1602) is unfigured and was printed as a partbook. Thoroughbass improvisation was possible because the "root-position" chord was presumed as the norm, and the "sixth chord" was taken as an exception that, analogous to the various dissonances, was restricted to specific compositional formulas that could be gathered from the bass. Viadana's compositional technique is "motetlike."[4] And a reconstruction of the rules on which the accompaniment of a solo motet like *Exaudi me, Domine*[5] was based indicates that the opinion that a thoroughbass presumes a consolidation of sonorities into chords is a dubious hypothesis.

1. The sixth must substitute for the fifth above bass notes with diminished fifths. The sixth-chord rule of the later 17th century suggests, as was pointed out, a division of the chordal system into primary and secondary degrees. Viadana, however, provides a $\frac{6}{3}$ sonority not over the bass tones **b**, **e**, and **a** of the untransposed system [i.e., all three secondary chords], but only over **b**. His compositional practice can be formulated by a traditional rule of counterpoint—the prohibition of *"mi contra fa."*

2. The bass clausula (exs. 49a and 49b) can be supplemented by the discant clausula—the 4–3 suspension.

Example 49

It would be a mistake to interpret the initial sixth as an inverted chord and representative of degree I. In the early 17th century, the first tone of the bass formula **B♭–c–d–G** was generally set as a $\frac{5}{3}$ sonority. The $\frac{6}{3}$ sonority was used only in cases where the sixth was necessary as the preparatory consonance to a 4–3 suspension. The choice of sonorities depended on the presence or absence of the discant clausula. "Counterpoint," not "harmony," appears as the deciding factor.

3. Above passages of descending seconds in the bass the upper voice forms parallel tenths. The middle voice alternates between fifths and sixths, or fifths and octaves. Thus the $\frac{6}{3}$ sonority is not an inversion of a root-position triad. Rather, the sixth—alongside the fifth and the octave—is but one of the possible consonances used to fill in the tenth.

The thoroughbass of early 17th-century monody is based on fragments of 16th-century compositional technique: (1) the complete triad and (2) the dissonance figure composed of three intervals—the preparatory consonance, the dissonance, and the consonance of resolution.

In monody, the single chord can stand on its own. It has its significance not as part of a chord progression and as a function in a key, but directly through its pure existence. Moreover, it is a given unity, not a combination of intervals.

Unlike the newer conception of chord, dissonance must still be conceived as an interval and as a transition between two consonances. The categories of "chordal dissonance" and "nonharmonic tones," which reconcile the relationship between chord and dissonance, were missing from the technique of early monody.

Example 50

In the first excerpt from Giulio Caccini's monody *Dovro dunque morire*[6] (ex. 50a), the thoroughbass figures appear as an abbreviation in three voices of a five-voice composition. The overlapping of dissonance figures—a half-note suspension (8–7–6) [music] a whole–note suspension (3–4–3) [music] and a quarter-note passing tone (8–7–3) [music] —is reminiscent of madrigal techniques. The preparatory consonance for the seventh [**d** in the bass] is a passing tone in relation to the upper voice [an implied **g′**], and the consonance of resolution [**c♯′**] coincides with an anticipation in the voice part [**a′**].

Yet in contrast to the compositional technique of the 16th century, dissonance is not an incidental feature of voice leading. Rather, it is for the sake of dissonance that the contrapuntal fragments are employed. In the preface to *Le Nuove musiche*, Caccini characterizes the remnants of counterpoint as a means of expressing the text and as exceptions to the norm of the sustained-tone style [*Halteton-Manier*]: ". . . but holding firm the tone in the bass—except that when I wish to adopt the common usage I play the instrument with the inner voices in order to express a certain affect, voices which otherwise are not fitting" [. . . tenendo però la corda del basso ferma, eccetto che quando io mene volea servire all' uso commune, con le parti di mezzo tocche dall'istrumento per esprimere qualche affetto, non essendo buone per altro].[7]

In the second example from *Dovro dunque morire* (ex. 50b), an unprepared fourth on a strong beat is required by the figures.[8] Yet the elision of the preparatory consonance is not a sufficient criterion for reinterpreting this intervallic dissonance as a "nonharmonic tone." The "unprepared suspension" must be understood as the abbreviation of a 4–3 suspension and referred back, as an artistic license, to the norm of the regular suspension. As the discant clausula, the 4–3 suspension had turned into a stereotyped formula that one could abridge without changing its meaning. Even in the fragmentary discant clausula, the antepenult (the "suspension" [**g′**]) is not related to the dominant chord in G minor as a "nonharmonic" tone. It relates to the other voices—the bass clausula in the thoroughbass and the tenor clausula in the voice part—as an intervallic fourth and a second.

. . .

The stereotyped bass formulas of the early 17th century ought not to be misunderstood as "representatives" of chord progressions. The real bass still maintains a precedence over the abstract *basse fondamentale* and asserts an autonomous significance in relation to the chords. The dilemma of modern editors with regard to many thoroughbasses of the early 17th century—the uncertainty in choosing between root-position and six-three chords—cannot be charged to mere ignorance of "things once self-evident but now lost to the past" [*verloren gegangene Selbstverständlichkeiten*] [Riemann]. In fact, the dilemma is intrinsic to the style. For if the thoroughbass chords did no more than to fill out the intervals between the notated voices with consonances, then deciding between the fifth or sixth above the bass is of secondary, or even of no, importance.

On the one hand, it can hardly be denied that the bass formulas of the early 17th century prefigure the typical chord progressions of tonal harmony. But on the other hand, upon closer inspection it is the differences from tonal harmony that come to the fore.

First, the constantly recurring feature is a series of tones, not a chord progression. The ascending "Lydian" fifth-progression of the bass, with the tritone as the fourth tone (**c–d–e–f♯–g**), permits four interpretations: (1) as IV–IV^6–V^6–I [in G major] with the bass **d** as a passing tone;[9] (2) as IV–V–vi–V^6–I;[10] (3) as IV–ii/IV–IV^6–V^6–I with ii as a simple "passing chord";[11] and (4) as IV–V–IV^6–V^6–I with the "harmonic caesura" between V and IV^6 justified by the repetition of the IV–V progression.[12] All these interpretations are formulas of tonal harmony—the chord progression C–d–e–D^6–G, which contradicts a tonal interpretation, is avoided by Monteverdi in his seventh book of madrigals. Nevertheless, the bass formula is not "based" on the "harmonic logic" of the chord progressions. Rather, the chord progressions are "presentations" of the bass formula. The bass formula is the establishing and founding factor, not something that is established by, and founded on, something else.

Second, the $\frac{5}{3}$ and $\frac{6}{3}$ sonorities are often interchangeable. In the duet *Non è di gentil core* from Monteverdi's seventh book of madrigals[13] (mm. 4–13), the bass formula **e–f–g–c** is first presented in C and then repeated in d, F, a, and d. In mm. 4 and 7, where the bass is on the "mi-degrees" **e** and **A** (in C major and F major), the interpretation of the first bass tone as I^6 is required by the sixth-chord rule. By contrast, the six-three chord is excluded from m. 11 because of the upper voices, and is doubtful or unlikely in mm. 5 and 9.

Third, the "dynamic" factor of tonal harmony, the reciprocal relationship between the whole and its parts, was still foreign to the bass formulas of the early 17th century. In a tonal mode of listening to the progression C–a–D–G–G^7–C, the meaning of the chords changes as they are presented. At the beginning, after the second chord, the presumption is T–Tp; then, after the fourth chord, S–Sp–D–T; and finally, T–Tp–(D)–D–D^7–T [I–vi–V/V–V–V^7–I]. One need not be consciously aware of the revisions and confirmations of earlier interpretations by later ones for the reinterpretations to be effective. In contrast, bass formulas are based on the principle of "coordination" [as opposed to subordination]. An individual scale degree of the bass formula is inserted into the whole by custom, not by the mind's proclivity for seeking relationships.

Fourth, bass formulas lack the "tendency" toward a tonal "center of gravity." It is often uncertain whether the chord progression over the descending fourth-progression **c–B–A–G** should be understood as I–V^6–vii^6/V–V in C major or as IV–I^6–vii^6–I in G major. And it seems that the question neither can nor should be resolved, since it is of no consequence and perhaps even meaningless. The stability of a chord progression founded on a bass formula should not be confused with tonal integrity. Tonal harmony depends on the mediation between a given, particular chord progression and the abstract system of fundamental progressions or functions. A tonal chord progression owes its integrity to the relation of the parts to the whole. But a bass formula represents nothing but itself. It is not legitimized by a system and has a direct effect only as a concrete Gestalt.

COORDINATE AND SUBORDINATE STRUCTURE

If a term is sought to characterize the harmonic language of the late 16th and early 17th centuries, then in contrast to the "principle of subordinate structure" in tonal harmony one can set forth a "principle of coordinate structure." The term is meant to signify that sonorities are linked one after the other without giving rise to the impression of a goal-directed development. A first chord forms a "progression" with a second chord, and a second with a third. But the earlier chord progression is independent of the later one and vice versa.

The "dynamic" factor of tonal harmony (the reciprocal relationship between the part and the whole, and the "tendency" toward a goal) and the distinction between what is given and what it means (the combining of different chords under the same functional concept) are two aspects of the same thing, something whose characteristic feature is subordination. C-major and a-minor chords are directly connected only by two common tones. Yet in a tonal context, one expects the subordination of one of the chords by the other. And if it must be decided whether a C-major chord is the parallel of an a-minor chord, or an a-minor chord the parallel of a C-major chord, then the chord progression C–a is subject to a compulsion to continue on to other chords. The tendency toward a goal is the correlate of a determination of function.

The transition to tonal harmony is based both on reinterpretation and on selection.

1. In the tonal cadence S–D–T in A minor, the tonic seems to resolve the antithesis between the subdominant and the dominant. By contrast, in the 16th century the "chord progressions" d–E and E–a, as a mi-clausula and a *subsemitonium* clausula respectively, were joined together without forming a "logical" connection. In coordinate harmony, the d-minor and E-major chords are related to each other directly. But in subordinate harmony they are related indirectly through the mediation of the a-minor tonic.

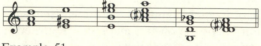

Example 51

Andrea Gabrieli's chordal technique in the madrigal *O beltà rara*[1] (published in 1566) seems to offer hardly any resistance to an interpretation as harmonic tonality—a = T, E = D, d = S, A = (D) S [V/iv], and g = (S) S [iv/iv]. Slight deviations, however, reveal that the chords follow the principle not of subordinate but of coordinate structure. First, the chromatic B♭ is not tonally motivated. In m. 8, the third above **g′** is altered to **b♭′** because the g-minor and A-major chords should be linked by a half-step connection, not because the g-minor chord was understood as iv of iv. The **b♭′** is related not to a d-minor tonic but to the two A-major chords between which it is inserted. Second, the a–E cadence of the first and last lines is not meant as a half cadence in A minor. Rather it signifies that the e-degree should be taken as the final. The madrigal is in E Phrygian, not A minor. The means of chordal technique necessary for tonal harmony are already formed but not yet brought to bear on major-minor tonality.

2. In the theory of tonal harmony, the dominant and subdominant relationships appear as the starting points of the chordal system.[2] But historically they were not something simple and uncompounded that was "spontaneously discovered."[3] Rather, they were the result of a "coalescing" or unifying of different factors: chordal relationship as well as chordal position.

In the E–A–D–G–C "chain of dominants"—one of the compositional formulas of the late 16th and early 17th centuries—the sonorities are indeed connected to each other by leading tones and fifth-progressions of the roots. But the second chord is still not the "tonic" of a "dominant." An effort at constant reinterpretations (D–T=D–T= D–T=D–T) would be a distortion. In the sequence, the dominant relationship is only prefigured. It is still merely a means of connecting sonorities, not the principle of a chordal system based on subordination.

The subdominant and dominant share their positions in the cadence with sonorities that, in the theory of tonal harmony, can be reduced to primary chords, but which do not yet permit such a reduction in the 16th and early 17th centuries.

Example 52

As antepenults in the cadence, the $\frac{5}{3}$ sonority (ex. 52a) and the $\frac{6}{5}$ sonorities (exs. 52b and 52c) are "similar" to each other—not, however, because the $\frac{6}{5}$ sonorities could be derived from the $\frac{5}{3}$ sonority as subdominants with *sixtes ajoutées*,[4] but because they appear in the same position. In the theory of tonal harmony, the $\frac{6}{3}$ sonority as the penultimate chord in the cadence (vii[6]–I) is considered a fragment of the dominant seventh chord. The interpretation is an attempt to explain the fact that the chords have the same position by the hypothesis that they represent the same function. It is, however, an interpretation that presumes the autonomous seventh chord—a category foreign to the 16th and early 17th centuries. Historically, the interchangeability of sonorities is not based on tonal functions. On the contrary, the possibility of equating functions is first indicated in the correspondence of chordal positions.

The separate factors in the concept of "dominant"—chordal relationship and cadential position—are still differentiated in Rameau's terminology. On the one hand, the name "*dominante*" designates not a fixed tonal function, but a seventh chord over the first tone of a descending fifth in the *basse fondamentale*. That this chord be in the position preceding the tonic is an added stipulation expressed by the term "*dominante tonique*." On the other hand, Rameau's doubts about whether ii depends on IV, or vice versa,[5] reveal a consciousness of the rivalry between the precedence of ii in the traditional cadence and the precedence of IV in the system of chords.

3. A third feature of the transition toward tonal harmony—besides the reinterpretation of direct chordal relationships as indirect relationships, and the interpretation of chordal positions as chordal functions—is the characterization of the difference between tonally

closed and tonally modulating sequences. Both types are distinguished from the aimlessness of the "open" sequences of the 16th and early 17th centuries. In the later 17th century, the tonal circle-of-fifths progression has two functions. First, as a "closed" sequence (I–IV–vii–iii–vi–ii–V–I), it represents a key. Second, as a "modulating" sequence, it facilitates the transitions between a composition's key centers. The significance of the modulating sequence is thus defined through its antithesis to the closed sequence. By contrast, the concept of an "open" sequence designates a compositional method that is historically antecedent to the difference between tonally closed and modulating sequences.

Example 53

In the excerpt from Monteverdi's eighth book of madrigals [ex. 53],[6] the sequences (mm. 116–22) appear at least to permit, if not to require, a tonal interpretation: in D minor, VII–III–VI–ii–V–I; and in A minor, VII–III–VI–ii–V–I. Yet the tonal interpretation is thwarted by a "chain of dominants"—A, D, G, C, F (mm. 122–24)—based on the principle of coordinate structure. The D-major chord in m. 122, perplexing to a tonal way of listening, is neither a chromatic variant (a subsidiary deviation from the tonal schema supposedly conceived as the norm) nor a "dominant of the dominant of the relative major" (a term that would be just an empty expression with no basis in musical experience). Instead, the D-major chord is a sign that the chords are linked together without characterizing, or modulating to, a key. The cadence in mm. 125–26 is an external ending, not the "goal" of the sequence.

4. One of the features characterizing the process of founding a pitch structure on bass formulas is—stated rather baldly—that the difference between $\frac{5}{3}$ and $\frac{6}{3}$ sonorities over the same bass has little or no importance. Chordal relationship depends on the real bass, not on the abstract *basse fondamentale*. Yet the technique of treating the difference between the fifth and the sixth as a secondary factor is—in a paradoxical reversal of the archaic into the modern—one of the assumptions of a mode of listening that subsumes different chords (a "primary chord" and a "parallel chord" or "*Leittonwechselklang*") under the same functional concept.

Example 54

In the excerpt from Monteverdi's seventh book of madrigals (ex. 54),[7] the upper voice forces a $\frac{5}{3}$ instead of a $\frac{6}{3}$ sonority above the **e** in the bass. This is in contradiction to the sixth-chord rule [of $\frac{6}{3}$ sonorities above mi-degrees]. Provided that the sixth-chord rule expressed a norm both of accompaniment and of musical cognition, it suggests that the $\frac{5}{3}$ sonority was perceived as a deviation from the $\frac{6}{3}$ sonority—thus that iii in C major was perceived as a secondary chord in relation to I[6]. In a tonal way of listening, the e-minor chord is reinterpreted from vi in G major to iii in C major. And in conformity with Hugo Riemann's derivation of secondary chords, the **e** in the bass (in the context of vi in G major) appears as part of a C chord in the G chord, and the **b'** in the upper voice (in the context of iii in C major) appears as part of a G chord in the C chord.

Example 55

In the 15th century, the bass formula **e–f–g–c** originated as a voice added to the discant-tenor clausula (ex. 55a). The fact that in the 16th century it was sometimes placed below the discant-tenor clausula in doubled note values (ex. 55b) can be taken as a sign of its growing autonomy. In Monteverdi's cadence [ex. 54], representing a third stage of development, the bass formula has become the foundation of the pitch structure. On the resolution of the suspension in the first soprano [**c''–b'**], the reference tone **d''** in the second soprano is not held but moves to the dissonant neighbor-note **e''** [a dissonant fourth from the second soprano's **b'** if these voices are viewed as the traditionally self-sufficient discant-tenor framework]. The primary counterpoint of the discant clausula in the first soprano is thus the bass, not the splintered tenor clausula in the second soprano.

. . .

Hans Zingerle[8] described the origin of tonal harmony "around 1630" as the result of a selection: the chord progressions G–F, G–d, e⁶–F, e–d, and F–e, "stylistically" manifestations of Monteverdi's "Renaissance harmony," were excluded from the "classical harmony" of Cavalli, Carissimi, and Luigi Rossi because they contradict the "principle of dominant relationships."

Example 56

1. Zingerle defines neither the "principle of dominant relationships" nor the principle of "Renaissance harmony" in greater detail. And the underlying assumption of this classificatory style criticism—that distinguishing features are necessarily the essential and characteristic features—is questionable. It leads to the formulation of Monteverdi's principle of harmony as the "renunciation of dominant relationships," and thus to interpreting his harmony as the negation of a norm that, according to Zingerle, originated only in the later 17th century.

The rule that the T–S–D–T cadence, the model of tonal chord progression, does not allow the reversal of S–D to D–S, is sufficient to establish the obsolescence of the G–F, G–d, e^6–F, and e–d progressions. This cadence rule, rather than being taken as dogma (it would be too narrow to define the boundaries of 19th-century tonal harmony), is taken as a hypothesis that, on the one hand, can be derived from the theory of tonal harmony and, on the other hand, can make it possible to explain the obsolescence around 1630 of the chord progressions G–F, G–d, e^6–F, and e–d. Conversely, if the exclusion of the cited progressions can be based on a rule deducible from the theory of tonal harmony, then this exclusion can be considered a criterion of the transition to tonal harmony.

The chord progressions G–F and G–d (D–S and D–Sp) are directly affected by the cadence rule. The progressions e^6–F and e–d contradict it only if one excludes interpreting iii as a secondary chord of the tonic. In the "parallel cadence" e^6–F, which should be understood as a combined interval progression (3–5 and 6–8), a tonal way of listening emphasizing **g** as the bass compels an interpretation of the e^6 chord as a dominant parallel, and thus as a contradiction of the cadence rule. But in the chord progression C–e–F, iii (on a weak beat) is not Dp but a "passing chord," which Hugo Riemann would relate to I as a secondary chord ("*Leittonwechselklang*").

2. In Zingerle's description of the transition to tonal harmony, the attempt to explain not only the chord progressions G–F, G–d, e^6–F, and e–d but also d–C and d–e as criteria of "Renaissance harmony" appears as a dubious hypothesis.

Example 57

In the excerpt from Monteverdi's seventh book of madrigals (ex. 57),[9] the chords d and C undoubtedly represent the functions Sp and T in C major.

3. In a tonal way of listening, the direct succession of G and F chords, or G and d chords, is perceived as a break in the progress of the harmony. Yet the chords can follow each other provided, first, that the "harmonic caesura"[10] is justified by a formal caesura (a motivic or phrase boundary), and second, that both chords can be related, independently of each other, to a third, mediating chord. Indirect chordal relationships forced by harmonic caesuras are one of the distinguishing features of subordinate, as opposed to coordinate, harmonic structure.

Example 58

The descending bass line in the excerpt from Monteverdi's seventh book of madrigals (ex. 58)[11] should not be mistaken for an undifferentiated scale. In conformity with the way the lines of text are apportioned to the voice parts, the bass line breaks down into the fourth-progressions **g–d** and **c–G**. Thus the harmonic caesura between the D-major and C-major chords corresponds with a formal caesura. And the chords relate to each other not directly, but indirectly—through the mediation of the G-major chord. The fact that the fourth-progression is tonally ambiguous and scarcely allows for a judgment between IV–I^6–vii^6–I and I–V^6–vii^6/V–V in no way alters the indirect chordal relationship. In tonal harmony, the concept of a tonic presumes indirect chordal relationships, but the converse is not true. The individual factors of tonal harmony, which have a strong connection in a closed system, arose independently of each other.

Example 59

In the above excerpt by Monteverdi (ex. 59),[12] Francesco Malipiero interpreted the bass **f** as calling for a V_2^4 chord in C major. Malipiero's realization of the thoroughbass is erroneous. Yet it reveals—as a false reconciliation of opposing concepts—an inherent difficulty. One can either divide the bass into two fourth-progressions (**c–g** and **f–c**) or interpret it is as a uniform octave-progression. In the first case, the G-major and F-major chords are separated from each other by a harmonic caesura. But in the second case, according to the principle of coordinate structure, they are directly related—the connecting factor

is the interval progression  (3–5). Malipeiro's interpretation

evades either alternative. It is an attempt to maintain the uniformity of the progression in a way that denies the harmonic caesura between the G and F chords, and it accomplishes this by reinterpreting the triad above **f** as a $\frac{4}{2}$ chord.

Example 60

In a tonal hearing of ex. 60,[13] the break between the G and F chords forces a reconciliation through indirect chordal relationships, so that the mediating C-major chord appears as the goal and result of the chord progression. One could object that the harmonic caesura does not correspond with a formal caesura, and that a tonal interpretation is thus in doubt. Yet on the other hand, one can hardly deny that a tonal interpretation of the chord progression G–F as a contradiction that must be resolved lends a pathos to the portrayal of the text that is lost in a coordinate interpretation [as a normative 3–5 interval progression].

In ex. 61, by Monteverdi,[14] the norms of tonal harmony require an e^6 chord above the **G** so that the sequence can be understood as T–D–Tp–Dp–S–T in C major with an "appended" dominant and dominant parallel that are related to the preceding, not to the following, chord. Monteverdi, however, leaves the choice between the G and e^6 chords—between an accented (**d″**) and an unaccented (**e″**) passing tone—unresolved as a secondary factor.

ov' io già spar - si

spar - si di - let - to - so

Example 61

o vaghe her - bet -te o fio -ri o ver-di mir-ti o ver - di mir - ti

mir - ti o ver - di mir - ti o ver - di mir - ti

Example 62

In a tonal way of listening to ex. 62,[15] the F chord acts as a troubling interpolation that shatters the harmonic continuity. And the impression of a juxtaposition of unconnected sonorities is reinforced by the downbeat fifths in the outer voices. This is in accord with Moritz Hauptmann's observation[16] that the second of two parallel fifths is not comprehensible as a result of the first, but instead forms a new beginning. Nevertheless, the appearance of a lack of cohesion vanishes—the downbeat fifths become inconspicuous—if one understands the measures not as a I–♭VII–vi–V chord progression but as an example of intervallic composition. And one can perceive the interval progressions and as the factor that connects the sonorities. On the other hand, parallel triads with downbeat fifths are a compositional schema of the late 16th and early 17th centuries that stabilized as a set topos.[17] And in Monteverdi's seventh book of madrigals one can interpret the chord progression G–F–e as the petrified remnant of an earlier stage of development.

ei roz - zi ac - cen -ti in - deg - na mu - sa

Example 63

In *Tempro la cetra* (ex. 63), a variations cycle on a strophic bass, the chord progression G–F–e—"beyond the pale" in tonal harmony— coincides with a text which it subtly characterizes through its musical status as an archaism[18] ["ei rozzi accenti indegna musa" translates as "in rude accents, unworthy muse . . ."]. The association is no accident, for in the three other strophes the bass is changed from f to f♯.

A chord progression excluded from the repertoire of commonplace formulas, which thus stands out from the context as an unusual and noteworthy occurrence, can become a means of expression: musical expression clings to the exceptional, to that which differs from the schema. Yet not only that which is novel, but also that which is antiquated can represent a departure from the norm. And provided that the pathos of the exceptional in the passage from *Tempro la cetra*—a pathos that takes tonal harmony as the norm—did not become attached to it only through later history, but already underlay it at its conception, then it would not be the least testimonial of Monteverdi's sagacity, celebrated by Schütz, that he discovered the expressive force in the obsolescence of formulas which he himself had first caused to become archaic.

CHAPTER III

MODE AND SYSTEM

Key and Scale

The word "key" [*Tonart*] is equivocal. In the early 18th century, it signified both "mode" and "*proprietas vocis.*"

According to a theory that goes back to the Middle Ages,[1] the "*proprietas vocis,*" a tone's individual character, depends on the lower adjoining interval. A scale degree is "*dural*" if it has a "hard" whole tone or a "hard" major third below it, but "*mollar*" if a "soft" semitone or a "soft" minor third. In his 1691 treatise *Musicalische Temperatur*,[2] Andreas Werckmeister still intends the expression "*e-moll*" [E minor] to mean not the minor key with E as its root, but the scale degree E♭. And by "*e-dur*" [E major] he means not the major key with E as its root, but the scale degree E♮. "*E-moll,*" characterized by the "soft" semitone **d–e♭** and the "soft" minor third **c–e♭**, is the lowered chromatic alteration of the "hard" scale degree E♮.

Johann Mattheson turns the relation between scale degree and interval on its head. In his terminology, "*e-moll*" is still a *proprietas vocis*, the individual character of a tone. Yet what is intended is not the tone E♭, which rests on a "soft" third (**c–e♭**), but the tone E♮, on which a "soft" third rests (**e–g**). The basis for the reinterpretation is the crossing of the terms "*proprietas vocis*" and "mode" in the concept of "*Ton-Art*" ["key," but literally "tone-type" or "tone-character"]. If the "*Ton-Art*"—the character—of the mode is to coincide with the "*Ton-Art*" of its root, then the lower instead of the upper tone of the "soft" third must be defined as "*mollar.*" "In the seven diatonic scale degrees (Mattheson is counting from **d** to **c′**) there are first two soft keys, then two hard keys, third two soft keys again, and finally a hard key . . . No one will dispute the fact that it is both natural and proper for D and E to take the minor third, F and G the major third, A and B again the minor third, and C the major third" [In den sieben diatonischen Klang-Stuffen sind erstlich zwo weiche Tonarten, hernach zwo harte, drittens wieder zwo weiche, und endlich eine harte . . . Kein Mensch wird streiten, das D und E nicht die kleine Tertz, F und G die große, A und H wieder die kleine; C aber die große, ursprünglich und eigentlich zu sich nehmen].[3] The idea that "soft" F♯ minor is a variant of "hard" F major by virtue of the raised chromatic alteration of its root demonstrates how closely connected the notion of "*proprietas vocis*" still is with that of "mode" in the concept of

"Ton-Art": "Hence if the otherwise large third of a 'hard' key must become accidentally small owing to the raising of its root, then in consequence there necessarily results a 'soft' mode, because the interval is drawn closer together" [Wenn hergegen bey einer harten Tonart, durch Erhöhung ihres Grundklanges, die sonst große Tertz, zufälliger Weise, klein werden muß, so entstehet daraus nothwendig ein weicher Modus, weil das Intervall enger zusammen gezogen wird].[4]

The fact that Mattheson, though he is thinking in terms not of modes but of major and minor keys, explains the keys with "diatonically" notated roots and thirds as primary forms and those with "chromatically" notated roots and thirds as variants, is a sign of how difficult 18th-century theorists still found it, even the "enlightened" ones, to adequately describe the modern system of keys. The distinction between diatonic and chromatic keys to which Mattheson clings had been obsolete for a century. The fact that this distinction completely misses the meaning of the modern key system is evident in the absurd consequence that B minor—but not D major—is counted among the primary, "diatonic" keys.

. . .

In major-minor tonality, unlike in the system of modes, the relation between key and scale is essential and not merely accidental.

1. Along with the final and the *repercussa*, the ambitus forms one of the determining factors of a mode. A mode is limited in its tonal compass. It is based on the filling out of an octave by tones, or more precisely, the filling out of a fourth-fifth-octave framework by whole tones.[5] By contrast, it would be nonsensical to speak of the fixed ambitus of a major or minor key. Their tonal compass, even if occasionally restricted, is nonetheless in principle infinite, because the set of tones is determined not by the disposition of scale degrees within an octave, but only by the relation of tones to the root. The interval c–c′ limits the c-Ionian mode, but not the C-major scale. And the external coincidence, the fact that it is the same set of tones which fill out the octave from c to c′ in c-Ionian but relate to the root as prime, third, or fifth of the tonic, dominant, or subdominant in C major, should not conceal the difference: the Ionian mode is an octave species but C major is a system of functions. A C-major scale, even though it highlights the tones C, c, c′ . . . as *"points d'attraction,"* is not "composed of octaves," while a second or third c-Ionian octave is in fact understood as a return of the first in a different register.

2. In the case of major-minor tonality, the distinction between "transposed" and "untransposed" scales misses the mark. As a relative

distinction it is meaningless; as an absolute distinction it fails entirely. If F major is a composition's basic key, then the C-major scale can be classified as "transposed," the d-minor scale as "untransposed." But the distinction between the divergence and coincidence of key signatures has little or no significance for the difference between a "fifth-relation" (F major and C major) and a "third-relation" (F major and D minor). The absolute distinction—the alternative to the relative distinction—lies in the idea that the expression "untransposed" characterizes the position and significance of C major and A minor in the system of keys. Yet this is an illusion generated by the notation. F major and D minor relate to C major and A minor not as transpositions of basic forms, thus as copies of models, but as different, equally valid localizations or realizations of the major and minor systems of functions. The cycle of keys has no fixed starting point. The notation which in major-minor tonality distorts the very situation it expresses, was perfectly adequate for the system of the modes. For up until the 16th century, transposition—"*cantus mollis*" or "*cantus fictus*"—was considered a deviation from the norm, from the "proper" diatonic scale. The transposed scale—the copy—represented the diatonic to a lesser degree than did the untransposed scale—the model. And the boundary between a key signature indicating a transposition and an accidental indicating a chromatic variant was often fluid.[6]

3. In major-minor tonality, the diatonic scale—understood as a specific arrangement of five whole steps and two half steps—can be conceived as a feature common to both major and minor. Yet that which unites them, the diatonic scale, is less strongly marked than that which divides them, the antithesis between major and minor. The correspondence in the disposition of whole and half steps is hidden by the disparity in the relationships to the root. The change in character to which **a** and **c′** are subject when conceived first as tonic root and third in A minor and then as the subdominant third and tonic root in C major is so compelling that the diatonic scale, the uniting factor, pales as an abstraction. In modality, on the other hand, the diatonic scale—the uniting factor—appears not merely implicitly as a hidden common feature, but explicitly as the "embodiment" of the modes. Major and minor operate as antitheses against the background of the diatonic scale that includes them both, while the modes form a series whose individual members, the modal scales, differ from the preceding or following scale by only a single scale degree: the Aeolian mode differs from the Phrygian in its second scale degree, and from the Dorian in its sixth scale degree. A series, however, throws into bold relief the factor connecting the members, thus the diatonic scale, rather than an antithesis. Of course the fact that the series appears as such presumes

that the modes do not have a separate, independent existence but are sequentially interrelated. This condition is satisfied rarely in monophony but frequently in polyphony. Indeed, the reciprocal relationship of the modes is one of the features by which modal polyphony differs from modal monophony.[7] And so the conjecture presents itself that it is precisely in polyphony that the diatonic scale, the "embodiment" of the modes, attains an independent existence and effect. Thus diatonicism, not a mere joint implication of the modes, comes to the fore as an explicit phenomenon alongside that of mode. The "emancipation" of the diatonic scale is, however, one of the factors that facilitated the transition from the system of modes to major-minor tonality.

. . .

A mode has a different relationship to the diatonic scale than does a major or minor key. Whether it makes sense to formulate the difference as a simple antithesis is certainly open to question, though Hugo Riemann's theories on major-minor tonality and Jacques Handschin's on modality suggest it. According to Riemann,[8] in a major or minor key the functions tonic, dominant, and subdominant—or the chords that represent them—are the primary factor, and the scale that results from dismantling the chords is the secondary factor. If the scale in major-minor tonality is therefore based on the functional and chordal relationships of the key, then according to Handschin[9] the opposite holds true in modality. The diatonic scale, writes Handschin, forms the "substructure," the mode the "superstructure." Thus it seems that the change undergone by the relation between key and scale can be understood as a simple reversal: the original founding factor, the scale, comes to be founded on the key. And that which was founded on the scale—the key—becomes in turn the founding factor. But neither Riemann's nor Handschin's thesis is so firmly established that an attempt to describe the development from modality to major-minor tonality could be based on it. The antithesis must, in spite of its seductive simplicity, be abandoned. An analysis, which must be temporarily deferred because the statement of its hypotheses would be too involved, will show that the relation between diatonic scale and mode should not be understood as that of "substructure" and "superstructure." Furthermore, the relation between key and scale in major-minor tonality is not as unambiguous as it appears in Riemann's presentation.

The relation must be historically differentiated. If in modality, as mentioned, one can observe an "emancipation" of the diatonic scale that leads to its having an individual and not merely implicit effect, then conversely, in major-minor tonality one can observe a gradual diminishing in the importance of the scale. And the historical differences between the earlier and later stages in the development of major-minor tonality can be detected in the divergent expositions of the relation between key and scale in the theories of degrees and of functions.

One of the principles of the theory of fundamental progressions is the idea that the chords on the seven diatonic scale degrees form—to use Handschin's term—a "closed society" [*geschlossene Sozietät*] and that the tonal integrity [*Geschlossenheit*] of a harmonic key is based on the diatonic scale. The Roman numerals do not represent mere ordinal numbers, or a quantity that could even be greater or lesser without altering its true nature. Rather, they express the fact that exactly seven—and not six or eight—degrees appear as a cycle. If, according to the theory of fundamental progressions, the closure of a key is thus based on the scale, then the establishment of the tonic chord rests on another principle which, along with that of the cycle of scale degrees, establishes the harmonic key: the dominant effect of the seventh chord with major third and minor seventh. The tonic of the untransposed diatonic scale is C because G is the only degree above which there appears a dominant seventh chord. Of course in the minor mode the second principle of degree theory runs into a contradiction with the first principle. On the one hand, the raised chromatic alteration of the seventh degree is "essential" [*konstitutiv*] because it is the prerequisite for a dominant seventh chord on the fifth degree. On the other hand, it is "chromatic-accidental" because the diatonic scale ought to guarantee the closure of the key.

The theory of functions avoids the contradiction from which the theory of fundamental progressions suffers, in that it conceives the scale not as the prerequisite and supporting basis for the key, but as the result of a dismantling of the functional chords.

The deduction of the scale is attractive by virtue of its simplicity. But the appearance of clarity is deceptive, since the central category— the concept of a function—is equivocal. And from this ambiguity there results confusion in the description of the relation between key and scale.

That the concept of a function is a "dual concept" becomes evident if one asks whether "Tp" designates the same function as, or a different function than, "T." The answer of a functions theorist would undoubtedly be: "p" means "parallel." And the fact that the a-minor chord is considered a "parallel" in C major means that it can "substitute" for the C-major chord and fulfill the function of the tonic. If "T" consequently expresses the function of the tonic parallel, then "p" is a chord designation. But if the combined abbreviation "Tp" expresses both a function "T" and a chord "p," then the same applies for the seemingly single sign "T." It marks a function that the C-major chord shares with the a-minor chord, but it also designates the C-major chord in contrast to the a-minor chord. It combines a formal factor, a "chordal function," with a material factor, a "functional chord."

The scale is a material factor. Thus, if it is to appear as a "result," it must be deduced from the functional chords—not from the chordal functions. But functional chords are not just the primary chords—the tonic, dominant, and subdominant. They also include the secondary chords—the "parallel" chords and "*Leittonwechselklänge.*" The thesis that the closure of the scale and the set of chords fashioned from it is "functionally" based can thus only mean that the system of nine functional chords is convergent with the scale. The correspondence is, however, not complete.

1. The symmetry of the system of functional chords requires, as an analog to the *Leittonwechselklänge* of the tonic and subdominant, a *Leittonwechselklang* of the dominant. Yet the b-minor chord in C major—the *Leittonwechselklang* of the dominant—falls outside of the diatonic scale and suggests, provided that F♯ is not a fleeting neighbor-note, the idea of a change of key, of a modulation to G major. The notion that the *Leittonwechselklang* of the dominant is a component of the key is a fiction resulting from the forced constraints of the system.

2. According to the theory of functions, iii (in C major, the e-minor chord) acts either as the *Leittonwechselklang* of the tonic or as the dominant parallel: as *Leittonwechselklang* in the progression C–e–F, as dominant parallel (Dp) in the progressions C–G–e–C and C–G–a–e. But the concept of "Dp" is questionable. In the chord progressions meant to justify it, iii appears either as a neighboring-chord (G–e–G) [i.e., a change of chord due to the movement of a neighbor-note] or as part of a sequence (C–G/a–e). The decisive criterion, the legitimization by the cadence, is lacking. To be sure, T in the cadence can be replaced by Tp (a deceptive cadence), and S by Sp (I–ii–V–I). But D cannot be replaced by Dp. Dp is not an analog of Tp and Sp.

On the one hand, the system of functional chords thus exceeds the key. It postulates a functional chord—the *Leittonwechselklang* of the dominant—that falls outside the key. On the other hand, this system is inadequate to substantiate the key's set of chords. It explains iii by a concept—that of the "dominant parallel"—that is poorly motivated. The key, as a closed set of chords, must therefore be based not only on a functional principle, but also on a "material" principle—one that explains why the b-minor chord falls outside the key even though functions theory postulates it, and why iii, whose significance is inadequately expressed by the concept of "Dp," is an element in the key's set of chords. And the "material" principle can be nothing other than the scale—the diatonic scale. So to be able to explain the closure of the set of chords, even the theory of functions is compelled to hypothesize the scale.

At the same time it bears asking whether a key, to be what it is, must appear as a "closed" set of chords. The definition of the key as a system of functions purports, if narrowly interpreted, that the material representation of the functions—thus even the scale—is variable and of secondary importance to the concept of the key. (For example, the function "S" is, as a function, independent of its alternative representations—in C major, either **f–a–c** or **f–a♭–d♭**.) Yet for the idea of "C major," if it is of little importance which chords fulfill the functions S and D, then no fixed limits are drawn for the set of chords. And therefore functions theory matches a stage in the development of harmonic tonality at which the "closed" key becomes an "open" one that presents itself not as a closed cycle of scale degrees but as, in principle, an infinitely extendable embodiment of relationships directed to one center—the tonic.

. . .

It is in the nature of the tonal system that the finals of the modes—the hexachord degrees **c–d–e–f–g–a**—and the roots of the "primary" major and minor keys—the scales with the signatures ♮, ♭, ♯—correspond one to the other. But it would be a dubious simplification to conclude from this coincidence that without exception the keys of D minor, E minor, F major, and G major arose from the d, e, f, and g modes by means of a "transformation"—by changing their scales. To negate the hypothesis of a uniform transformation of all the modes, it is enough to recall the fact that in the 15th and 16th centuries ♭ but not ♯ was used for transposing the scale. However regular the transformation from f-Lydian to f-Ionian or from d-Dorian to d-Aeolian might have seemed, the effect of a transformation from e-Phrygian to e-Aeolian or from g-Mixolydian to g-Ionian would have been just as disturbingly irregular. It would also be wrong to see the transformation of mode as being the primary significance of the ♭-accidental, which had stabilized as a general signature. F-Ionian, the "major" variant of f-Lydian, is a common mode, but d-Aeolian, the "minor" variant of d-Dorian, is rare. The idea that the use of the Ionian and Aeolian modes—traditionally "beyond the pale"—came about surreptitiously through the transformation of the Lydian and Dorian modes is thus only partially substantiated. And even in the case of the Ionian mode, doubts are not out of the question. It could have been that the lowered chromatic alteration of the fourth degree (the Lydian tritone) was based less on a sense of key tending toward major than on a technical problem of composition: the ♭ was forced by the cadence type

Discant   **g' – f' – e'– f'**

Tenor   **b♭ – a – g – f**

If the idea of a transformation of the modes—the notion that without exception the keys of D minor, E minor, F major, and G major arose through the alteration of the modal scales—is consequently exposed to many doubts, then on the other hand, the opposite thesis—that the modes were transformed into the major and minor keys through a change in their keynotes—rests on hypotheses no less vague. The thesis would imply that **a** in the Dorian mode and **c'** in the Lydian mode (the *confinales*), and **a** in the Phrygian mode and **c'** in the Mixolydian mode (the plagal *repercussae*) gradually succeeded as keynotes in place of the finals. The hypothesis can indeed be partially supported by examinations of Phrygian and Mixolydian compositions. But to formulate it as a general principle would be a gross simplification.

"Transformation" and "change in keynote" are categories about which next to nothing can be settled in a theoretical exposition—in a "*Gedankenexperiment.*" The determination of their significance has as its prerequisite the analysis of representative works.

. . .

In major-minor tonality, "change of key" or "modulation" is so simple a concept that a definition of it might seem a superfluous triviality or pedantry. Yet if one does insist on a precise definition, it turns out to be rather complicated. The detailed formulation stating that one speaks of a modulation when there is a change of tonic or of key signature, or of both tonic and key signature, is unavoidable. For example, the transitions from A minor to C major or A major are both modulations, though A minor shares a key signature with C major and a tonic with A major.

A transfer of this definition to the interrelationships of the modes would be a distortion of the facts. It would presume as a matter of course that which is itself questionable: that even in modality it is legitimate to subsume changes of keynote or signature under the same concept—that of "modulation." In the theory of the 16th and still of the 17th centuries, "change of mode"—"*mutatio*" or "*alteratio toni*"— and "change of system"—substituting the "*cantus mollis*" (the ♭-system) or "*cantus fictus*" (the ♭♭-system) for the "*cantus durus*" (the

♮-system)—are separate circumstances. "Modulation," as a comprehensive embodiment of both factors, is a category of major-minor
tonality.

. . .

The fact that the change of mode was differentiated from the change
of system in 16th- and 17th-century theory suggests that even in
major-minor tonality the concept of modulation is not as self-evident
as it seems when one is engrossed in the customary terminology of
harmony textbooks. It could hardly be denied that there is a difference
between a transition to the parallel—from A minor to C major—and
a modulation to the dominant—from A minor to E minor—and that
it cannot be determined *a priori* whether the difference is fundamental
or one of degree. And one could surmise that this difference is also
determined by the opposition between a change of mode and a change
of system, and thus that the separation of these categories still has a
residual effect on major-minor tonality.

The relation between C major and A minor should accordingly be
understood as corresponding to a change of mode, while the relation
between A minor and E minor comprises a change of system. Yet the
relationship of parallel keys includes not only a "material" factor, the
correspondence of the set of tones, but also a "functional" factor, the
analogy of chordal meanings. The chords of a key appear with the
equivalent function in the key of its parallel, but with divergent function
in the key of its dominant or subdominant. (For example, the a-minor
chord still has tonic significance in C major, but subdominant significance in E minor.)

The objection that the analogy or heterology of the functions is based
on the conformity or diversity of the set of tones is misplaced, since
the similarity of the sets of tones is masked by the dissimilarity in the
tones' characters: **c** is a "different" tone in A minor than in C major.
But if the correspondence of the set of tones is reduced to a latent
implication by the divergence in the tones' characters without thereby
affecting the analogy of the chordal functions, then that analogy cannot
be attributed to the correspondence of the sets of tones. And provided
that the similarity or dissimilarity of the sets of tones—thus also of the
key signatures—is a secondary, hidden factor, then the concept of
"modulation," which embraces the change of signature along with the
change of keynote, recovers its legitimacy.

THE DEVELOPMENT OF THE TONAL SYSTEM

On the one hand, the expression "tonal system" denotes a "material scale," the set of tones at the disposal of a musical praxis. On the other hand, it designates a form of musical perception that turns tonal material into a complex of tonal relationships. The ambiguity may be confusing, but it is due not to terminological caprice but to a difficulty in the subject itself. A tone taken by itself is an acoustical datum, not a musical phenomenon. It becomes a musical phenomenon only in association with other tones. A tonal system as a material scale, if it is to pass for musical reality, is thus unthinkable without a tonal system as a complex of tonal relationships.

Therefore it is of material and not merely terminological significance that in the older musicological literature the transition from "modality" to tonal harmony around 1600 was frequently described as a change between two "tonal systems." Underlying the notion of characterizing the change as one of "tonal system" is the idea that the diatonic scale, the system of the modes, and Pythagorean tuning on the one side, and the set of diatonic-chromatic-enharmonic tones, major-minor tonality, and just intonation on the other side form two mutually opposed complexes—thus that the cofactors of the one not only are inseparably connected to each other, but also stand in exclusive contrast to those of the other. The term "tonal system" is then a comprehensive expression for a set of tones, a tuning, and a conception of key or mode.

By contrast, in newer expositions—motivated by a skepticism toward oversimplified "coordinations" [*Zuordnungen*] and an aversion to subjecting history to systematization—the concept of a tonal system is separated from a conception of key or mode, and restricted to tunings and sets of tones. The narrower demarcation of the concept is undoubtedly clearer and less ambiguous than the wider one. But it includes the danger of ascribing to the set of tones an autonomous existence and significance independent of the conception of key or mode, something it never had, provided it is to be understood musicologically and historically.

However hazy it may seem, the wider, equivocal concept of the tonal system thus has the advantage of leaving open the problem of the relation between the set of tones, the form of musical perception, and the conception of key or mode. By being split into separate, unrelated investigations—on mode and key, or on tuning and temperament—the problem, instead of being solved, is brought to the point of disappearing. For that reason one could allow the notion out of which derived the idea of a change in the "tonal system" around 1600 to be assumed, if not as firm knowledge, then at least as a hypothesis—the notion that "tendencies" toward major-minor tonality are concealed within those theories and practices of the 15th and 16th centuries that allude to the alteration or suspension of the diatonic scale and the system of the modes. The "tendencies" are: in the three-hexachord system, an intimation or proto-form of the tonic, dominant, and subdominant harmonic functions; in the 12-tone system of musica ficta, a modification of the modal scales into the major and minor scales; in the 17- or 19-tone system of speculative theory, an anticipation of, or preparation for, the modern method of transposition; in just intonation, a basing of tonal relationships on chords and chordal relationships; and in the chromaticism of madrigals, a start toward functional chromatic harmony.

The interpretation of a "tendency" includes the idea that the nature of a thing shows itself most clearly in the consequences that proceed from it. Phenomena that fit together into a system in the tonal harmony of the 17th and 18th centuries appear in the 15th and 16th centuries as scattered single factors that can relate to each other not directly, but only from the viewpoint of the later development in which they "coalesce."

The opposite thesis would be that one must go back to the origin of a thing in order to know what it is. And a historian reluctant to characterize two centuries as a self-contradictory state of transition having its meaning outside of itself and being realized by mere "tendencies" would attempt to determine, along with the indirect significance detectable in later effects, the immediate and primary meaning of the three-hexachord arrangement or the 12-tone system.

But whether a phenomenon still has its earlier, or already has its later, significance comes to light in the contexts in which it appears. What is crucial is not the isolated presence of cofactors of tonal harmony, but the relationship that they have to each other.

. . .

Sixteenth-century chromaticism is considered a radical alteration of the tonal system, an alteration that marks, or even brought about, the transition from the modal system to major-minor tonality. "Our modern tonal system resulting from the reduction of the old church modes to major and minor, equal temperament, harmony, even that most recent achievement of modern times, the concept of tonality established by Fétis, they really possess within themselves a flash point. For it was they that, as it were, gave the signal for the revolution against the diatonic system, disordered and broke up the church modes, and finally gave rise to a total transformation of the perception of art" [Unser modernes Tonsystem, hervorgegangen aus der Reduktion der alten

Kirchenmodi auf Dur und Moll, die gleichschwebende Temperatur, die Harmonik, selbst die jüngste Errungenschaft der Neuzeit, jener von Fétis statuierte Begriff der Tonalität, sie haben den Strahlpunkt eigentlich in ihr. Denn sie war es, die gleichsam das Signal zur Revolution gegen die Diatonik gab, die Kirchenmodi verwirrte und auflöste und endlich eine gänzliche Umwandlung der Kunstanschauung herbeiführte].[1]

In the above citation, the antithesis that Theodor Kroyer constructs between "major-minor tonality" and the "diatonic system" may be confusing and provoke the objection that even a major or minor key, just like a mode, is based on the diatonic scale. And it seems that Kroyer must have fallen victim to the fallacy that chromaticism, because it destroyed the modal system, had to be the foundation of major-minor tonality, and thus to the error that the negation of an earlier situation is necessarily the basic premise of a later one.

Kroyer's conception of a change of the tonal system around 1600 is, however, not as unsupported as it appears to be when taken at face value. First, by the term "diatonic"—more precisely "older diatonic"— not only the scale as such could be intended, but also the scale as the embodiment of the modes. But since, as will yet be demonstrated, the diatonic system can be adequately understood only in its relation to the modal system, and not by itself in the abstract, then Kroyer's apparent error—the opposing of major-minor tonality and the diatonic scale—contains an insight that need only be made more precise to permit far-reaching conclusions.

Second, behind Kroyer's antithesis could be the idea that while the diatonic scale has a fundamental significance even in major-minor tonality, only in the modal system does it have significance as a limitation. Or formulated the other way around, chromaticism, destructive to the modal system, can have a constructive effect in tonal harmony. It is one of the factors on which depends the dynamic character of tonality, the "tendency" of chords toward one another and toward the tonic. Thus for Kroyer's antithesis to prove meaningful, it suffices to stress the exclusionary sense of the diatonicism of the modes and the constructive sense of the chromaticism of major-minor tonality.

Third, modulation—the change of key and thus also the disposition of "chromatic" tones—belongs among the fundamental features of major-minor tonality. The notion that from a single mode there arose a single major or minor key would be an ahistorical fiction. In musical reality, the modes, and analogously the major and minor keys, exist in their relationships to each other. And the system of mutually related keys originated in the system of mutually related modes. But the system of the modes is diatonic, while that of the major and minor keys is diatonic-chromatic.

. . .

The concept of the "older," modal diatonic system was meant to support, through greater precision, the attempt to justify Kroyer's antithesis of "major-minor tonality" and the "diatonic system." The concept includes the assumption that the diatonic system is not a constant, but a historically variable phenomenon. The idea of variability in the diatonic scale may provoke disagreement, since the set of seven diatonic scale degrees appears as a given, as a constant which one can submit to, or avoid, but not alter. Yet the concept of the diatonic system embraces not only the set of scale degrees but also their relationship. And relationship is subject to a change of principles.

Up to the middle of the 16th century, the diatonic scale was constucted as a system of direct and indirect fifth-relations: a circle of fifths from **f** to **b** (**f–c–g–d–a–e–b**), placed together within an octave, results in the diatonic scale. On the other hand, according to the theory of major-minor tonality, the diatonic scale is based on a framework of three fifths filled in with thirds: in C major, F–a–C–e–G–b–D; in A minor, D–f–A–c–E–g–B.[2]

The external token of the difference in these structures is the acoustical definition of the major third. In the fifth-structure the major third appears as a combination of two equal whole tones, as a ditone, as a double whole tone with the proportion 64:81 [8/9 × 8/9]. But on the other hand, in the fifth-third-structure it appears as a harmonic third with the proportion 4:5 (= 64:80) — the difference, 80:81, is the syntonic comma. Yet the difference in intonation is a mere accident. One can conceive a harmonically tuned third as a ditone and, conversely, a Pythagorean tuned ditone as a harmonic third. The intonation is nothing but the acoustic exterior of a difference between two structures of the diatonic system.

Various means have been sought to deny this variability and to preserve a constant, "natural" diatonic system. The first is the attempt to conceive the fifth-structure as the enduring substructure, even in major-minor tonality, and to allow the fifth-third-structure as a mere superstructure.[3] The ditone composed of two equal whole tones is of course modified, but not invalidated, by the harmonic third, which in contrast to the ditone is not a derived but a self-substantiated interval immediately manifested as a consonance. But the hypothesis of substructure and superstructure suffers from the arbitrary decision to explain what stands in the foreground as a matter of secondary importance, and what stays hidden as a matter of primary importance.

A second means would be the opposite thesis, that the fifth-third-structure is the nature-given norm of musical cognition and the fifth-structure is a mere speculation without significance for musical practice.[4] Yet a historian, to be able to concur with this thesis, would have to deny what exists in the preserved texts and allow mere conjecture to take precedence over the documents which until the middle of the 16th century testify unmistakably to the fifth-structure of the diatonic system.

A third means also leads one astray. The assertion[5] that the fifth-structure and the fifth-third-structure are not mutually exclusive but cooperate, that in major-minor tonality the fifth-structure comes into play in the Pythagorean tuning of the dominant's third and the fifth-third-structure in the just tuning of the tonic's third, is based on a misunderstanding. The habit of many violinists of raising the leading tone, thus the third of the dominant, has only its musically insignificant acoustic exterior in common with the Pythagorean third of the Middle Ages. This acoustic similarity is of no importance because even the trivially augmented dominant third is conceived as a self-substantiated consonance and not as the combining of two equal whole tones into a ditone.

Thus one cannot avoid the fact that the diatonic system, unchanging as a set of tones, was, as a relationship between tones, subject to a change of structure, to a transition from the fifth-structure of modal diatonicism to the fifth-third-structure of major-minor tonality.

It might seem superfluous to describe the relationship of the tones in major-minor tonality. The fact that the tonic of a major or minor key forms the point of departure and focus of a network of tonal relations, that starting from **c**, first the fifths **F** and **g** are defined as subdominant and dominant and then the remaining tones as thirds and fifths of the tonic, subdominant, and dominant, has been impressed upon even listeners who know nothing of the theory of major-minor tonality as a fixed schema in the perception of tonal relationships.

In the older, modal diatonic system, in contrast to major-minor tonality, it would be a distortion to relate the tones exclusively or even just primarily to a modal keynote viewed as a point of departure and focus. It is obvious that in C major, **b** is connected to the root **c** as the third of the fifth. On the other hand, it might be difficult or even impossible to imagine **c** and **f** in the e-mode as the fourth and fifth fifths below the keynote **e** [e–a–d–g–c–f]. And so in descriptions of the system of the modes it has become the musicological custom to narrow the significance of the keynote, to represent the modes as octave species of the diatonic scale, and to attribute the diatonic scale to the circle of fifths from **f** to **b**.[6]

The method of basing the modes on the scale and the scale on the circle of fifths, if intended as a norm of musical cognition, leads to two consequences. First, it implies the thesis that a tone, independent of a mode, always has the same character—thus that **e** is primarily understood as the sixth tone in the circle of fifths from **f** to **b** and only secondarily as the first degree in an e-mode or the second degree in a d-mode. And second, it entails the assertion that the character of an interval is defined by the number of fifths between its two tones— thus that the major third implies an "inner distance" of four fifths between its tones (**f–c–g–d–a**) and the diatonic half step an "inner distance" of five fifths (**f–c–g–d–a–e**).

These consequences, as norms of musical cognition, are not without problems. It could hardly be denied that **e** changes its meaning when it is introduced as the first degree of an e-mode and then continued as the second degree of a d-mode. And the thesis that the character of **e** is still primarily marked by its position in the circle of fifths can only be salvaged by adding that a tone's character is concealed and modified by the mode, but not invalidated by it. Yet it must be objected that in a music theory that seeks to describe phenomena, a modification that conceals a tone's character is indistinguishable from an actual change of character.

On the other hand, it ought not to be denied that the changes produced in the individual degrees by a change of keynote appear less important in the system of the modes than in major-minor tonality. In tonal harmony, the tones **c** and **e** lose their musical identity when transferred from a C-major to an A-minor context, thus when heard first as root and third and then as third and fifth. (The fact that the observation of a radical change in the tones' characters is denied in Hugo Riemann's "dualistic" system says nothing against the observation, but only speaks against Riemann's system). But in the system of the modes, it would be an exaggeration if one also described the change in significance which, for example, the third **e–g** experiences in a transition from an e-mode to a d-mode as a radical change of tonal character.

The second of the consequences stemming from the appeal to the circle of fifths, the assertion that in the fifth-structure of the diatonic system the minor third comprises three fifths, the major third four fifths, and the half step five fifths, is, if not erroneous, then at least insufficient. The fact that the whole tone is defined as the difference between a fourth and a fifth, the major third as a combination of two whole tones, and the semitone as the difference between a major third and a fourth, does not imply that the fifth-relation on which the system is based is actually present in the ramifications of a derivation of intervals as three, four, or five fifths. One can mentally reconstruct the intervening stages at the end of which stands the semitone. Musical perception, however, is limited. For it, the premises vanish in the actual outcome. Upon hearing an interval, one can make oneself aware of the last stage in its derivation, but not the earlier stages. Thus one can think at the same time of the fourth and fifth in reference to the whole tone, or of the doubling of the whole tone in reference to the major third, but not of four fifths in reference to the major third.

Therefore the circle-of-fifths schema is insufficient as a description of the diatonic system. But if one describes it under the hypothesis that in hearing an interval, only the last stage of its derivation is present, then it turns out that the diatonic system appears more and more modally cast.

The simple, "perfect" consonances are given directly: octave, fifth, and fourth. They form the framework of an octave scale (d–g–a–d' or e–a–b–e'). On the other hand, the basic melodic interval is the whole tone — as the difference between the fifth and the fourth, it is a derived interval of the first rank, but one consolidated to an independent significance and comprehensibility. The major and minor thirds result from the agency of the whole tone: as the sum of two whole tones and as the difference between a whole tone and a fourth.

In consequence, the principle which one must take as the basis for the concrete nature of the diatonic scale is the filling out by whole tones of a fourth-fifth-octave framework. Yet the result of this filling out is a mode. Or formulated another way, the diatonic scale, if one constructs it by filling out a fourth-fifth-octave framework, appears in modal form. In the fourths of this framework, the whole tones are inserted at the bottom (c–d–e–f), at the top (e–f–g–a), or the one whole tone at the bottom and the other at the top (d–e–f–g).

The construction of the older, modal diatonic scale from tetrachords is historically the earliest and objectively the most firmly established method. In the first place, it takes into account the fact that the conception of remote fifth-relations is in need of support. The semitone, whose definition as the fifth fifth is a flimsy abstraction, becomes intelligible if one understands it within the terms of a tetrachord as the intervallic remainder between a fourth and two whole tones.

In the second place, the problematic hypothesis that the mode is a mere superstructure and only trivially modifies the meaning of the tones becomes superfluous. The appeal to tetrachordal structure is an alternative or a point of reconciliation between two dubious extremes—

between the assertion that the meaning of **e** and **g** changes little or not at all in a transition from an e-mode to a d-mode, and the opposite thesis that **e** changes from a root to a second upper-fifth and **g** changes from a third lower-fifth to a first lower-fifth. If one relates the third **e–g** to tetrachords, then in the d-mode it appears as the difference between the fourth **d–g** and the whole tone **d–e**, while in the e-mode it appears as the difference between the fourth **e–a** and the whole tone **g–a**. Thus on the one hand, tetrachordal theory does justice to the tones' change of significance in a change of mode. And on the other hand, if one attributes the changes in significance to different relationships with modal keynotes, then one avoids getting lost in intangible abstraction.

Since a whole tone implies two intervals of a fifth, the result of the filling out of a fourth-fifth-octave framework with whole tones is always a diatonic scale which in the abstract can be attributed to the chain of fifths from **f** to **b**. (The objection that the tetrachord principle is insufficient to substantiate the diatonic scale, since even a scale like **e–f–g–a–b–c♯′–d♯′–e′** could be understood as a filling out of a fourth-fifth-octave framework, comes to naught. The whole tones **b–c♯′** and **c♯′–d♯′** presume the intervening tones **f♯** and **g♯** [whole tone = double fifth, i.e., **b–c♯ = b–(f♯)–c♯′**], and are thus out of the question when the lower tetrachord appears as the Phrygian or ancient Dorian **e–f–g–a**.)

The modal and abstract representations of the diatonic system are two sides of the same coin, and it would be prejudiced to think that one has to decide which takes precedence over the other. Hidden behind the notion that there must always be a first and founding phenomenon from which a second phenomenon is then derived lies a false expectation of reality.

The problem was viewed most clearly at its origin in the ancient world. The ancient "modes" are given in two mutually related manifestations: as *harmoniai*, as octave segments of the diatonic scale, and as *tropoi*, as presentations or realizations of all the modes in the same octave (Dorian **e′–d′–c′–b–a–g–f–e**, Phrygian **e′–d′–c♯′–b–a–g–f♯–e**, Lydian **e′–d♯′–c♯′–b–a–g♯–f♯–e**). With the tropoi, the method of constructing the modes by filling out a fourth-fifth-octave framework is made manifest. The three fundamental tropoi, Dorian, Phrygian, and Lydian, originated through various insertions of whole tones into the unchanging framework **e′–b–a–e**.[7] The custom of interpreting the tropoi as "transposition scales" is thus misleading. Whoever conceives of the relation between harmonia and tropos as one of "transposition," reducing the tropos to a derived form of the original harmonia, thus fails to recognize that the tropos was based on the filling out of a framework of perfect consonances, and that the modal diatonic scale represented by the tropos and the abstract diatonic scale from which one can cut out octave species form a correlation that cannot be reduced to primary and secondary factors.

. . .

The idea of differentiating three of four tone characters corresponds to the tetrachord principle, to the procedure of filling out a fourth-fifth-octave framework with whole tones. In antiquity, the idea was developed into a solmization, in the Middle Ages into a variant of hexachord solmization.

In the ancient solmization passed down by Aristides [Quintilianus],[8] the scale degrees are classified according to immediately adjacent intervals and divided into three groups:

A	B	c	d	e	f	g	a	b	c'	d'	e'	f'	g'	a'
τε	τα	τη	τω	τα	τη	τω	τε	τα	τη	τω	τα	τη	τω	τε

The τω-degrees **d** and **g** are surrounded by two whole tones, the τα-degrees by a whole tone below and a semitone above, and the τη-degrees by a semitone below and a whole tone above. A special case is **a** = τε, which appears as a fourth tone character notwithstanding the fact that, like **d** and **g**, it is surrounded by two whole tones. It could be motivated by the constraint that a solmization must avoid employing the same syllable on two consecutive degrees.

The schema of three tone characters that directly defined the solmization in antiquity appears, in the later Middle Ages, in the form of an adjunct theory of hexachordal solmization. In 1490, Adam of Fulda mentions the widely disseminated opinion that for each of the three hexachords there were two characteristic solmization syllables or degrees: ut and fa for the "soft" hexachord (**f** to **d'**), re and sol for the natural hexachord (**c** to **a**), and mi and la for the "hard" hexachord (**g** to **e'**). "Yet there are some who assign to each [hexachord] two degrees which seem to go together; for these authors give to the soft b (hexachord) ut and fa, to the natural (hexachord) re and sol, and to the hard b (hexachord) mi and la" [Sunt tamen nonnulli, qui unicuique duas quasi sibi convenientes attribuunt voces; nam donant b mollari ut et fa, naturali re et sol, h durali mi et la].[9] The tones **b**♮ and **b**♭, "hard" b and "soft" b, were considered the characteristic tones (*principes soni*) of the hexachords. But b and b♭ owe their character, their *proprietas*, to the "hard" whole tone **a–b** and the "soft" semitone

a–b♭.[10] The opinion cited by Adam of Fulda thus purports that the
"*mollar*" degrees ut and fa are similar to "soft" b [b♭], and the "*dural*"
degrees mi and la are similar to "hard" b [b♮]. Yet the similarity cannot
be based solely on the lower adjacent interval, on the "soft" semitone
under the "*mollar*" degrees b♭, **f**, and **c**, and on the "hard" whole tone
under the "*dural*" degrees b♮ and **e**. After all, the "*natural*" degrees
also have whole tones under them. Rather, in order to understand
Adam von Fulda one must refer to the *Quatuor principalia* of the
pseudo-Tunstede in which each hexachord is analyzed as three pairs

of similar degrees: ut　re　mi　fa　sol　la . Pseudo-Tunstede char-

acterizes the degrees according to the adjoining intervals on both sides.
The low degrees (*voces graves*) ut and fa have a whole tone above them
and a semitone below; conversely, the high degrees (*voces acutae*) mi
and la have a semitone above them and a whole tone below; and the
middle degrees (*voces circumflexae*) are surrounded by two whole
tones.[11]

.　.　.

In the later Middle Ages, the three-hexachord system, the overlapping
of the "hard" (**G–e, g–e′**), "natural" (**c–a, c′–a′**), and "soft" hexachords
(**f–d′, f′–d″**), was the presentational and conceptual form of the tonal
system. But on account of b♭, which forms an autonomous degree in
the three-hexachord system, not a chromatic variant of b♮, the integrity
of the modal diatonic system seems to become disordered or even
invalidated.

The supplementing of the diatonic scale by b♭ admits of three
interpretations. First, it can be viewed as the splitting of a degree.
Although b♭ is subordinate to b♮, it is not subordinated to it as a
chromatic variant—both tones represent the same degree.[12] Second,
it can be viewed as a "system enlargement," as an extension of the
diatonic heptatonic scale to an octatonic scale. And third, it can be
viewed as a "change of system,"[13] as a conversion from the original
register of the diatonic scale to a transposition down a fifth.

.　.　.

It is no accident that the interpretations of the b♭ as a splitting of a
degree, as a system enlargement, and as a change of system, however
diverse they may be, all reduce the idea of the hexachord to a mere

means of representation. The hexachord—more precisely, the individual hexachord—is not, in contrast to the heptatonic and pentatonic scales, a self-significant system of tones.

In the anhemitonic ("without half steps") pentatonic scale (**c–d–f–g–a–c′**), the minor third appears as a "step," not as a "leap," because an intermediate degree is missing between **d** and **f** as well as between **a** and **c′**. The expression "third," which presumes the idea of a middle tone, of a "second," is inadequate. The "scale steps" in the heptatonic scale—the half step and the whole step—correspond to the whole step and minor third in the pentatonic scale. And in the pentatonic scale there exists the same difference between the minor third as a simple interval and the major third as a compound interval as exists in the heptatonic scale between the whole step and the minor third.

The pentatonic and heptatonic scales are systems. In comparison, the hexachord is a mere auxiliary construction. As a system it would be self-contradictory. The procedure of filling in the **d–f** but not the **a–c′** third with an intermediate degree would, if conceived as a principle of the system, lead to the absurd consequence that the listener would have to alternate between the interval conceptions of the pentatonic and heptatonic scales—thus between the idea of the minor third as a "step" and as a "leap."

To recognize the hexachord as a meaningful construction instead of a contradictory system, one must both double it—only when there are two hexachords is a system formed—and understand it as a means of presentation. The two-hexachord system of Guido of Arezzo, which still excluded the **b♭**, was a method for demonstrating the relationship and similarity of tones a fifth apart—the "*finales*" **d–e–f–g** and the "*confinales*" **a–b–c′–d′**.[14] According to Guido, **d** and **a**, or **e** and **b**, were perceived as being similar to each other because they are surrounded by the same intervals. But the lower limit at which the similarity of the intervals turns into dissimilarity is marked by **c** or **g**, and the upper limit by **a** or **e′**. The hexachords **c–a** and **g–e′** thus have the function of representing the range within which coincide the surrounding intervals of fifth-related tones.

. . .

Under the hypothesis that not six, but only three tone characters were distinguished, the difference between the apparently antithetical interpretations of **b♭**—between the explanations of a change of system and of an expansion of the system to the octatonic scale—loses the trenchancy of a dichotomy. The effect of a **b♭** is often too slight for one to be able to speak of a "change of system," a transposition. And on the other hand, it would be an understatement to speak of a mere chromatic "coloration." The influence of b♭ on the characters of the adjacent degrees is unmistakable. Yet the influence is "localized." And a "localized" effect corresponds to the idea that a trichord is the frame within which tones, through their reciprocal relationships, appear as having clearly contrasting characters. By substituting b♭ for b♮, the characters of the directly adjacent degrees a and c′ are indeed changed: a becomes "*dural*" instead of "*natural*," c′ "*natural*" instead of "*mollar*." But the more remote tones are not affected, or affected only weakly.

. . .

Adherence to a rigid dichotomy between the significance of chromatic alterations as accidentals and as transpositions—the denial of a middle ground between the extremes—would not be justified by musical reality. Neither would it be justified by a 14th-century theory of chromaticism that would seem self-contradictory and confused if one analyzed it according to the hypothesis abstracted from major-minor tonality that a chromatic alteration is either a "coloration" or the sign of a "change of system."

As defined in the *Introductio secundum Johannem de Garlandia*, "False music is when they make a semitone out of a whole tone and vice versa. Every whole tone is divisible into two semitones, and as a consequence, the sign designating the semitone can be applied to all whole tones" [Musica falsa est, quando de tono faciunt semitonium, et e converso. Omnis tonus divisibilis est in duo semitonia et per consequens signa semitonia designantia in omnibus tonis possunt applicari (Coussemaker: amplificari)].[15] In the divisibility of the whole tone—"omnis tonus divisibilis est in duo semitonia"—Rudolf von Ficker saw the principle by which to explain chromaticism. And he conjectured that a relationship had existed between, on the one side, the name "*musica falsa*," the explanatory principle of whole-tone division, and the character of chromatic alterations as accidentals, and, on the other side, the name "*musica ficta*," the explanatory principle of hexachord exchange, and the character of chromatic alterations as transpositions. "Chromatic tones produce musica falsa through the division of the whole tone, musica ficta through the transposition of a hexachord to a suitable degree. In the former case, the tones receive significance as accidentals, in the latter case, as proper scale degrees" [Die musica falsa gewinnt die chromatischen Töne durch Teilung des Ganztons, die musica ficta durch Transposition eines Hexachords auf

eine beliebige Stufe. Dort erhalten die Töne akzidentelle, hier leiter-
eigene Bedeutung].[16] His interpretation may be attractive by virtue of
its simplicity. It is, however, wrong.

The *Ars contrapunctus secundum Philippum de Vitriaco* adopts the
definition from the *Introductio secundum Johannem de Garlandia*. But
it substitutes the term "musica ficta" for "musica falsa" and supplements the definition of chromaticism by adding that a chromatically
lowered degree should be sol-fa'd as "fa" and a chromatically raised
degree as "mi." "Therefore, where we find a round b [=♭] we
pronounce this syllable fa, and where we find a square b [=♮] we
pronounce that syllable mi" [Ubi igitur invenimus ♭ rotundum, dicimus
istam vocem fa, et ubi invenimus ♮ quadratum, dicimus illam vocem
mi].[17] Thus one is forced either to lay aside the text of the *Ars
contrapunctus secundum Philippum de Vitriaco* as self-contradictory, or
to abandon or at least modify the interpretation that the division of
the whole tone as the principle of "musica falsa" and the change of
hexachord as the principle of "musica ficta" are mutually exclusive.

1. In the *Introductio secundum Johannem de Garlandia*, the principle
for deducing chromatic tones is not the division of the whole tone—
splitting **f–g** into the chromatic semitone **f–f♯** and the diatonic semitone
f♯–g. Rather, it is the substitution of semitones for whole tones and
vice versa. "Musica falsa is when they make a semitone from a whole
tone and vice versa" [Musica falsa est, quando de tono faciunt semitonium, et e converso]. (The mention of the division of the whole tone
["omnis tonus divisibilis est"] is nothing but an argument against the
objection that accidentals are irrational. The *Introductio* counters this
objection by alluding to the fact that the undeniable ability to divide
the whole tone **a–b** by **b♭**, or the whole tone **b♭–c'** by **b♮**, can be
transferred to all whole tones.) The forms of alteration are enumerated
in the *Ars nova* of Philipp de Vitry (or pseudo-Vitry). "And they have
such a property, namely that in descending, the round b [=♭] causes
a semitone to be made into a whole tone, and in ascending causes a
whole tone to be made into a semitone. And the reverse happens with
this other figure ♮, namely that it causes an ascending semitone to be
made into a whole tone and a descending whole tone to be made into
a semitone" [Et talem proprietatem habent, videlicet quod ♭ rotundum
habet facere de semitonio tonum, tamen in descendendo, et de tono
in ascendendo habet facere semitonium. Et e converso fit de alia figura
ista ♮, scilicet quod (Hugo Riemann's completion:[18] de semitonio
ascendente habet facere tonum et) de tono descendente habet facere
semitonium].[19]

Along with the augmentation of the semitone **c'–b** to the whole tone
c'–b♭ described by Vitry (or pseudo-Vitry), one must keep in mind

the diminution of the whole tone **b–a** to the semitone **b♭–a**. In the first place, the altered degrees have a leading-tone significance. And in the second place, as mentioned, according to Simon Tunstede (or pseudo-Tunstede) a scale degree is sufficiently characterized only by two intervals, those adjoining above and below. Thus **b♭** is characterized not by **a–b♭** or **b♭–c'** alone, but only by the semitone and the whole tone together. "Whence hard ♮ is said to have a whole tone below and a semitone above itself; but soft ♭ is said to have a semitone below and a whole tone above itself" [Unde ♮ durum dicitur habere tonum sub se et semitonium supra se; sed ♭ molle dicitur habere semitonium sub se, et tonum supra se].[20] Hence chromatic alterations signify that interval progressions switch places—the progression semitone-to-whole-tone (**c'–b–a**) becomes the progression whole-tone-to-semitone (**c'–b♭–a**). And the principle of attributing the origin of chromatic degrees to the reversal of the whole-tone-to-semitone progression accords well with a tonal system in which the diatonic semitone forms a mere remainder between two whole tones and a perfect fourth. The fourth scale degree necessary for the determination of the semitone in the interval progressions **c'–b–a** and **c'–b♭–a** is not mentioned by Tunstede (or pseudo-Tunstede). It can be either **g** or **d'** [i.e., **c'–b♭–a–g**, **c'–b–a–g**, **d'–c'–b♭–a**, or **d'–c'–b–a**].

2. If von Ficker's interpretation of "musica falsa" and "musica ficta" were correct, then the fact that the *Ars contrapunctus secundum Philippum de Vitriaco* mentions the division of the whole tone while at the same time defining chromatic alteration as a change of hexachord would be nothing but the thoughtless caprice of a compiler. But the appearance of a contradiction, of a mixing of mutually exclusive theorems, vanishes if one allows two points. First, the principle by which to explain chromatic tones is not the division of the whole tone but the reversal of interval progressions, the interchange of the progressions whole-tone-to-semitone and semitione-to-whole-tone. And second, a change of hexachord need not be understood as a transposition. When a chromatic alteration is sol-fa'd as "fa" or "mi," the change brought about in a tone's significance is "localized." A theory intimated by Simon Tunstede (or pseudo-Tunstede) and handed down by Adam of Fulda in a more precise formulation distinguishes within the hexachord not six but three tone characters that were designated *"dural," "mollar,"* and *"natural."*[21] Thus the rule that a chromatically lowered degree is understood as fa does not imply a transposition of the scale to the lower fifth. Instead, it means that the neighboring degrees of the *"mollar"* fa should be defined as a *"dural"* mi and a *"natural"* re or sol. The confining of scale degrees to a "local characterization"—the reduction of the six hexachordal degrees to three tone characters—and

the method of attributing chromatic alterations to interchanges of trichordal intervals mutually support and complement each other. According to the theory of the *Ars contrapunctus secundum Philippum de Vitriaco*, a chromatic tone has the significance of neither an accidental nor a transposition. The effect of the "coloration" is not confined to a single tone nor does it embrace the entire system—only the adjacent degrees are affected.

3. Inasmuch as raised chromatic alterations are a feature of the cadence, it is even less likely that hexachordal terminology implies a conception of chromatic tones as tokens of a "change of system," as a transposition of the scale. In the polyphonic clausula of the g-mode—the "double leading-tone cadence"—it is impossible for **f♯'** and **c♯'**, notwithstanding their solmization as "mi," to be understood as transpositions, as proxies for the **e'** and **b** characters of the untransposed scale. The fact that the "Lydian" clausula [ ] is transferred from the degree on **f** to that on **g** does not mean that the clausula must be taken as the basis for the scale **g–a–b–c♯'–d'–e'–f♯'–g'**. After all, the consequence would be absurd that the g-mode was invalidated and replaced by the transposed f-mode in the very cadence that is supposed to consolidate the g-mode.

4. There is a dichotomous establishment of chromaticism in the treatises of the 14th, 15th, and even 16th centuries. On the one hand, as mentioned, chromatic alterations were explained as a change of hexachord—more precisely, as an interchange of the whole-tone-to-semitone progression. But on the other hand, chromatic alterations were motivated by the "*regola delle terze e seste*" [rule of thirds and sixths], by the norm that an imperfect consonance should resolve to a perfect consonance through a half-step progression in one voice and a whole-step progression in the other voice (or).

In consequence, chromaticism appears as leading-tone chromaticism, as a means of forcing sonorities to progress and thereby bring about musical coherence.

But in contrast to the leading-tone chromaticism of the 17th and 18th centuries, that of the 14th and 15th centuries lacks a tonal or modal function. The key of A minor is characterized as a harmonic key by the leading tones **f** and **g♯** [**f** is the descending leading tone of dualistic harmony, i.e., the third of the *sub*-dominant], in which the "pull" of the subdominant and dominant toward the tonic is pointedly expressed. By contrast, in the a-mode of the 14th and 15th centuries, the leading tones **b♭**, **d♯**, and **g♯** are modally irrelevant. The chromatic alterations resulting from the *regola delle terze e seste* "color" the mode without, whether in a constructive or destructive sense, being important to it. Thus 𝄢 is a Dorian, not a transposed Lydian, cadence. Leading-tone chromaticism, essential in major-minor tonality, is incidental in the system of the modes.

. . .

If an attempt is made to interpret any of the diatonic-chromatic systems or sets of tones described in the treatises of the 13th to the 16th centuries, then the "localized" significance of chromatic alterations, their motivation by the *regola delle terze e seste*, and their lack of modal function must be taken into account. (One can hardly rely on musical documents because only in rare exceptions were chromatic alterations notated. In fact as exceptions, they permit no reliable conclusions to be drawn about the norm.)

A chromatic or chromatic-enharmonic system can be analyzed according to various criteria which must be kept separate if confusion is to be avoided. One could term them "material" and "functional" criteria. With regard to "material," a system appears constructed symmetrically or asymmetrically, regularly or irregularly. But "functionally," chromatic degrees should be understood either as leading tones or as transpositions.

If one assumes that the nature of a tonal system can be read from the notation in which it appears, then the tonal system of major-minor tonality comprises 35 degrees within the octave. They are the result of the procedure of setting out each of the seven diatonic degrees in a basic form and four variants (single and double sharps and flats), thus converting c, for example, into c♯ and c𝄪, c♭ and c♭♭. Yet the notation owes the appearance of being self-evident and logical to mere custom, since it is questionable according to both material and functional criteria. (Of course the problems of a material and functional definition of chromatic alterations should not be confused with the difficulties based on what is in principle the unbounded nature of chromatic-enharmonic systems. Tones such as B triple sharp and B triple flat, though not part of the notational system, are musically real when arrived at through modulations. And speculations about a limit to modulation, which is nonexistent, are irrelevant to the attempt to determine the significance of the 35-degree notation.)

According to material criteria, from the point of view of symmetry and regularity, both the 21-degree system resulting from simple sharping and flatting, and the 35-degree system resulting from double sharping and flatting, are absurd. It is an unmotivated schematism that subjects degrees a semitone apart to the same method of alteration applied to degrees a whole tone apart—thus that in the 21-degree system not only the whole tone **f–g** but also the semitone **e–f** is doubly divided (notated in just intonation: **e–f♭–e♯–f** and **f–f♯–g♭–g**).

Yet even functionally, as the sum total of leading tones and transpositions, the 21- and 35-degree systems can hardly be justified. An unbroken transposition scheme—one whose limits are formed by the tritone transposition of the diatonic scale, **g♭** or **f♯** becoming the tonic of the major scale and **a♭** or **g♯** the Dorian final—leads to a 19-tone, not a 21-tone, system (in just intonation **c–c♯–d♭–d–d♯–e♭–e–e♯–f–f♯– g♭–g–g♯–a♭–a–a♯–b♭–b–c♭**, or as a circle of fifths **c♭–g♭–d♭–a♭– e♭–b♭–f–c–g–d–a–e–b–f♯–c♯–g♯–d♯–a♯–e♯**). On the other hand, leading-tone chromaticism tends toward a 17-degree system. If one creates the upper and lower leading tones to all the degrees of the untransposed diatonic scale, then in Pythagorean tuning there results the scale **c–d♭–c♯–d–e♭–d♯–e–f–g♭–f♯–g–a♭–g♯–a–b♭–a♯–b**. (In the modal system, **g♭** is the bass tone of the penultima in the Phrygian f-clausula, and in C major, it is the upper leading tone of the subdominant. In the modal system, **a♯** is the third of the penultima in the Lydian e-clausula, and in C major, it is the leading tone of the dominant parallel [Dp = E minor, whose reference tone is **b**].) And finally, even the transfer of the 17-degree leading-tone chromatic scale to the 19-degree transposition scheme results not in a 21- or a 35-degree system, but in a 27-degree system whose limits are marked by **d♭♭**, the upper leading tone of the subdominant in G♭ major, and by **d♯**, the leading tone of the dominant parallel in F♯ major [Dp = A♯ minor, whose reference tone is **e♯**]. The 21- and 35-degree systems are not musically motivated. Their only motivation stems from the workings of the notation.

The diatonic-chromatic systems presented in the treatises of the 13th to the 15th centuries vary between having 12, 14, or 17 degrees. Across these systems one can neither recognize nor reconstruct an unequivocal and continual development from a lesser to a greater set of tones. Rather, it appears that one must view the 12- and 17-degree systems as the lower and upper limits of the contemporary possibilities. The attempt to stipulate norms and to dismiss what oversteps them as speculative would be a distortion of a chromaticism whose character is incidental and whose range could therefore be undefined.

1. Hieronymus of Moravia, in his *Tractatus de musica* originating from perhaps the second half of the 13th century, describes a tonal system with the lowered chromatic alterations **b♭**, **e♭**, **a♭**, **d♭**, and **g♭**. "Secundum optimos practicos" [according to the best practitioners], the chromatic tones are deduced by transposing the mi-fa-sol-la tetrachord

to all the diatonic degrees. "The four syllables or elements of music, in character as before, namely these: mi-fa-sol-la, are taken up, and the first synnemenic tetrachord [i.e., one with a lowered degree] is placed over the one from **G** to **c**, so that in this first tetrachord and all others a semitone precedes the two whole tones. The second tetrachord is from **A** to **d**, the third from **c** to **f**, the fourth from **d** to **g** (which are called the low tetrachords), the fifth from **f** to **b♭** . . .]" [Sumantur voces sive elementa musicae IIII virtute qua prius, haec scilicet mi fa sol la, et ponatur primum tetrachordum synemmenon in unum a Γ in C, ita tamen, quod in primo tetrachordo et in aliis omnibus, semitonium duos tonos antecedat. Secundum tetrachordum est ab A in D, tertium a C in F, quartum a D in G, quae dicuntur gravia, quintum ab F in b fa . . .].[22] Raised chromatic alterations are not mentioned. One could deduce the chromatic tones **f♯**, **c♯**, **g♯**, and **d♯** by analogy to the derivation of the lowered alterations, thus through a transposition of the Lydian tetrachord ut-re-mi-fa to all the diatonic degrees. Of course the extended analogy is questionable. In the first place, it is philologically unsupported. And in the second place, even this ex-panded system would be asymmetrical: **a♯** is missing, so that five flats stand opposed to four sharps.

2. To be capable of consistent realization, the "*regola delle terze e seste*" [rule of sixths and thirds]—the norm that an imperfect conso-nance should resolve to a perfect consonance by a half-step progression in one voice and a whole-step progression in the other voice—presumes a system in which each minor third or sixth can be changed to major and each major third or sixth can be changed to minor. The d-clausula requires **e♭** or **g♯** and **c♯** (or), the g-clausula **a♭** or **c♯** and **f♯** (or), and the a-clausula **b♭** or **d♯** and **g♯** (or).

. . .

According to Hugo Riemann,[23] an example in the *Ars contrapunctus secundum Philippum de Vitriaco* should be understood as representing a 14-tone system with **b♭**, **e♭**, **a♭**, **f♯**, **c♯**, **g♯**, and **d♯**. The example illustrates the rule: "Musica ficta is when we make a semitone out of a whole tone and conversely, a whole tone out of a semitone. For every whole tone is divisible into two semitones . . . Therefore, where we find a round b [= ♭] we pronounce this syllable fa, and where we find a square b [= ♮] we pronounce that syllable mi" [Est ficta musica quando de tono facimus semitonium et e converso de semitonio tonum. Omnis enim tonus est divisibilis in duo semitonia . . . Ubi igitur invenimus ♭ rotundum, dicimus istam vocem fa, et ubi invenimus ♮ quadratum, dicimus illam vocem mi].[24]

Example 64

An interpretation of ex. 64 as a 21-tone system with c♭ and f♭, b♯ and e♯, though the uniform distribution of the accidentals across all degrees may initially make it seem plausible, can nevertheless be excluded. This is because only the diatonic whole tones could be intended as the ones to be split ("omnis enim tonus est divisibilis in duo semitonia"), not the e–f♯ and e♭–f that would be necessary for the deduction of e♯ and f♭. If the scale is interpreted as a 14-tone system (**c–c♯–d–d♯–e♭–e–f–f♯–g–g♯–a♭–a–b♭–b**), then the symbol ♭♮ in front of **e**, **a**, and **b** implies a lowered alteration, and in front of **c**, **d**, **f**, and **g** the canceling of a raised alteration. Conversely, the symbol ♮♭ in front of **c**, **d**, **f**, and **g** implies a raised alteration, and in front of **e**, **a**, and **b** the canceling of a lowered alteration.

The asymmetry is disturbing, in that the whole tones **c–d**, **f–g**, and **a–b** are split only once while **d–e** and **g–a** are split twice. One could do away with the asymmetry by interpretating ex. 64 as a 12-tone scale with a simple division of all the whole tones (**c–c♯–d–e♭–e–f–f♯–g–a♭–a–b♭–b**). But this interpretation suffers in turn from the defect that the signs ♭♮ and ♮♭ in front of **d** and **g** could be explained only by a forced reading. One would have to argue that the sign ♮♭ marks a mi-degree and the sign ♭♮ a fa-degree, and that ♮♭ in front of **g** signifies not g♯ but g as mi in relation to **a♭**, and that ♭♮ in front of **g** signifies not the cancellation of g♯ but g as fa in relation to f♯. The only sensible alternative to Riemann's explanation would be an interpretation as a 17-tone symmetrical system with double division of all the whole tones (**c–c♯–d♭–d–d♯–e♭–e–f–f♯–g♭–g–g♯–a♭–a–a♯–b♭–b**). This is possible with two provisos: first, that in the example from the *Ars contrapunctus secundum Philippum de Vitriaco* the coexistence of the descending and ascending series of accidentals signifies an essential difference and not a mere duplication; and second, that according to Philipp de Vitry,[25] in ascending, a ♮ signifies the expansion of a semitone to a whole tone and a ♭ the contraction of a whole tone to a semitone, and in descending, a ♮ signifies the contraction of a whole tone to a semitone and a ♭ the expansion of a semitone to a whole tone. Consequently, in the descending ♮♭ scale, **a**, **g**, **f**, **d**, and **c** are sharped and the flatting of **b** and **e** is canceled; in the ascending ♮♭ scale, **c** and **f** are sharped and the flatting of **d**, **e**, **g**, **a**, and **b** is canceled; in the descending ♭♮ scale, the **b** and **e** are flatted and the sharping of **a**, **g**, **f**, **d**, and **c** is canceled; and in the ascending ♭♮ scale, **d**, **e**, **g**, **a**, and **b** are flatted and the sharping of **c** and **f** is canceled.

. . .

3. The 17-tone system with the chromatic degrees **b**♭, **e**♭, **a**♭, **d**♭, **g**♭, **f**♯, **c**♯, **g**♯, **d**♯, and **a**♯, which could be hypothetically inferred from the example in the *Ars contrapunctus secundum Philippum de Vitriaco*, was explicitly presented by Prosdocimo de' Beldomandi in his *Libellus monochordi* of 1413. Prosdocimo constructs it by the double division of all the whole tones in the diatonic scale: "And in this way, over the entire monochord, you will be able to have two semitones between any two consecutive letters of the musical hand sounding a whole tone" [Et isto modo per totum monochordum habere poteris bina semitonia inter quaslibet duas litteras immediatas in manu musicali tonum resonantes].[26] The 17-tone scale is irregular as a material scale. The alternation between diatonic semitone (**c–d**♭ and **d–e**♭) and diesis (**d**♭–**c**♯ and **e**♭–**d**♯) is interrupted by the semitones **e–f** and **b–c**. But functionally, it forms a closed system of leading-tone chromaticism. Each diatonic degree is surrounded by two leading tones, an upper and a lower.

The same 17-degree system developed by Prosdocimo through the double division of the diatonic whole tones was constructed by John Hothby in his *Calliopea leghale* through the transpositions of hexachords extending from **d**♭ = ut (thus **g**♭ = fa) to **f**♯ = ut (thus **a**♯ = mi).[27] (Hothby's peculiar, confusing terminology—he labels **d**♭ as "*c del secondo ordine*" and **c**♯ as "*c del terzo ordine*," **e**♭ as "*d del secondo ordine*," and **d**♯ as "*d del terzo ordine*"—loses the appearance of paradox if one allows for the fact that in Pythagorean tuning, **d**♭ is lower than **c**♯.) In spite of its hexachordal terminology, Hothby's deduction is a theory of leading-tone chromaticism, not of chromaticism through transposition. Provided that the influence of a chromatic alteration on a tone's character was, as mentioned, "localized," then the exchange of hexachords, even the extremes of **d**♭ = ut and **f**♯ = ut, should be understood not as a transposition but as a means and a roundabout way of forming an upper leading tone to **f** and a lower leading tone to **b**. Or expressed in hexachordal terminology: in the 17-tone system, all the diatonic degrees appear both as mi (with a semitone above them) and as fa (with a semitone below them). Even the paradigmatic fa-degree **f** is reinterpreted as mi by **g**♭ = fa, and the paradigmatic mi-degree **b** is reinterpreted as fa by **a**♯ = mi. The 17-tone scale is the embodiment of a consistent leading-tone chromaticism based on the untransposed diatonic scale.

4. The 14-degree system necessary to satisfy the *"regola delle terze e seste"* included **b**♭, **e**♭, **a**♭, **f**♯, **c**♯, **g**♯, and **d**♯. In the 15th century, the transition from the double leading-tone cadence (𝄢) to the cadence with a tritone between discant and countertenor (𝄢) brought about a reduction in chromaticism, a restriction to just **b**♭, **f**♯, **c**♯, and **g**♯. The *"fa fictum"* **e**♭, analogous to **b**♭ in the transposition of a scale down a fifth, restored the system to 12 tones; **d**♯ and **a**♭ were omitted. Of course in the treatises, **g**♯ was often displaced by **a**♭. Anonymous 11 counts the tones **b**♭, **e**♭, **a**♭, **f**♯, and **c**♯ as *"coniunctae"*; **g**♯ is missing.[28] And Ramos de Pareia notes: "Therefore this soft b will be placed in five locations as follows, namely **B**, **e**, **a**, **e**′, and **a**′" [Locabitur igitur istud b molle in quinque locis secundum eos scilicet in b mi et in e la mi, in a la mi re primo, in e la mi acuto et in a la mi re secondo].[29] One can seek the basis for this divergence between theory and practice in the fact that the three-hexachord system suggested a construction of the 12-tone scale with **a**♭ instead of **g**♯. If it is assumed that a raised alteration transforms a fa-degree into a mi-degree, and a lowered alteration transforms a mi-degree into a fa-degree, then the scale **c–c**♯**–d–e**♭**–e–f–f**♯**–g–a**♭**–a–b**♭**–b** results from the sharping of the three fa-degrees **c**, **f**, and **b**♭ and from flatting of the three mi-degrees **b**, **e**, and **a**. The text of the Anonymous 1 of Lefage—in spite of Rudolf von Ficker's divergent interpretation—is also a description of a 12-tone system with **a**♭, not **g**♯. "Note that there are four letters on which musica ficta always commences, namely A, B♭, D, and E(♭), and it is called feigned music [*musica ficta*] because where there is mi we sing fa and where there is fa we sing mi" [Nota quod quatuor sunt litterae, in quibus semper incipitur musica ficta, videlicet A, B, D, E, et dicitur ficta musica, quod ubi est mi dicimus fa, ubi est fa dicimus mi].[30] "E" should be understood as "soft E" or *"E fictum"*—as **e**♭—because it is not the hexachord on **e** with **g**♯ but the hexachord on **e**♭ with **a**♭ that conforms to the rule that chromatic alterations signify an exchange of mi for fa or vice versa [i.e., **a** la *mi* re becomes **a** *fa*].

5. The 17-tone scale with **b**♭, **e**♭, **a**♭, **d**♭, **g**♭, **f**♯, **c**♯, **g**♯, **d**♯, and **a**♯, a consistent material scale in the Pythagorean tuning of the 15th century, had to be supplemented in the just intonation of the 16th century in order to be complete. While in Pythagorean tuning **f**♭ and

e♯ as well as c♭ and b♯, all missing from the 17-tone scale, are localized outside of the intervals e–f and b–c' (f♭–e–f–e♯ or c♭'–b–c'–b♯), in just intonation they are localized within them (e–f♭–e♯–f or b–c♭'–b♯–c'). As the Pythagorean "*semitonium minus*" [small semitone], the diatonic semitone does not admit of division, but as the "*semitonium maius*" [large semitone] in just intonation it requires it. If the scale is to be consistent, then the semitones e–f and b–c' must be divided analogously to the way that c♯–d and d–e♭ are split by d♭ and d♯ respectively. It seems the problem was first recognized by Francesco Salinas. Salinas formed the 12-tone chromatic scale with g♯, not a♭: c–c♯–d–e♭–e–f–f♯–g–g♯–a–b♭–b. Diatonic degrees with a diatonic semitone below them (f and c) receive a chromatic semitone above them (f♯ and c♯), while diatonic degrees with a diatonic semitone above them (e and b) receive a chromatic semitone below them (e♭ and b♭). "For e and b have a lesser semitone below them, since in the diatonic genus they have a greater semitone above them" [Nam e et h habent Semitonium minus inferne; quoniam in genere Diatonico habent maius superne].[31] The fact that Salinas chose g♯ and not a♭ as the fifth chromatic tone has no theoretical basis. It should rather be understood as a concession to musical practice. From the division of the diatonic semitones in the 12-tone chromatic scale—the "*semitonia maiora*" c♯–d, d–e♭, e–f, f♯–g, g♯–a, a–b♭, and b–c—Salinas developed the 19-degree chromatic-enharmonic scale c–c♯–d♭–d–d♯–e♭–e–e♯–f–f♯–g♭–g–g♯–a♭–a–a♯–b♭–b–b♯. "And thus all the greater semitones are to be divided" [Et dividenda sunt ita omnia Semitonia maiora].[32] Salinas named the degrees resulting from the division of the diatonic semitones "enharmonic"—d♭, d♯, e♯, g♭, a♭, a♯, and b♯: his "*d enharmonium molle*" is d♭, his "*d enharmonium sustentum*" is d♯. The 19-tone scale with e♯ and b♯, but without f♭ and c♭, is a consistent, though asymmetrical, system abbreviated on the "flat" side.

. . .

The hypothesis behind the analysis of the 12-, 14-, 17-, and 19-degree systems—the idea that chromatic alterations function as leading tones—is not as self-evident as it seems. And if errors are to be avoided, the concept of leading-tone chromaticism must be historically differentiated. The leading-tone chromaticism of the 14th and 15th centuries, which independent of the particular mode emphasizes the tendency of imperfect consonances to resolve to perfect consonances, differs from the tonal leading-tone chromaticism of the 17th and 18th centuries not only in its different relation to the key but also in its very character as leading-tone chromaticism.

The theory of tonal harmony ascribes a dominant effect to a sharp and a subdominant effect to a flat. The dominant third in minor is a fundamental raised alteration, the subdominant third in major an incidental lowered alteration. And a major tonic with lowered third acts as a subdominant of the dominant while a minor tonic with raised third acts as a dominant of the subdominant.

It is undeniable that a correlation or affinity exists between the leading-tone character of chromaticism and the functions of tonal harmony. But what is uncertain is which factor ought to be considered the founding factor and which ought to be considered the derivative. Is the effect of the leading tone an irreducible phenomenon, something logically prior to the tonal functions, or, just the reverse, is the significance of a half step functioning as a leading tone based on the chordal relationships of tonal harmony?

According to Ernst Kurth,[33] there is a latent tendency in the major third to progress to the fourth, thus to the subdominant, and a latent tendency in the minor third to progress to the second, thus to the dominant. Therefore the effect of the leading tone, as an expression of "melodic energy," is a primary factor that establishes the tonal functions.

The opposite thesis would be, first, that an individual major or minor chord is, by itself, motionless and not, as Kurth supposes, imbued with a "tendency," and second, that the leading-tone effect of a half step that brings two chords together must be understood not as a primary, but as a secondary phenomenon that arises only if one of the chords is conceived as the tonic and the other as a subdominant or dominant related to it. If, in the absence of a preceding context, a C-major chord alternates with an f-minor chord, then according to this thesis, only the establishment of a tonic determines whether the C chord is heard as the dominant of the f chord, thus with **e** as the leading tone to **f**, or the f chord is heard as the subdominant of the C chord, thus with **a♭** as the [upper] leading tone to **g**. In a case where the sense of key is still uncertain, one does not perceive, for example, both **e** and **a♭** as leading tones. On the contrary, the consciousness of a tonic is a necessary condition for establishing the leading-tone effect of the one tone, and for excluding that of the other.

A second objection against Kurth's interpretation of the leading tone would be that the striving of the leading tone cannot be separated from the fourth- or fifth-progression of the fundamental bass. The root progression and the leading tone jointly determine the effect of the dominant or subdominant (or). A degree that borders on a half step is not *per se* a leading tone. It becomes one only *per accidens*, through the coincidence of a half-step progression in one voice with a "root progression" in the other, be it a fifth-progression or a whole-step progression. In the V–I cadence of harmonic tonality, the correlate to the half step is formed by the fifth-progression; in the modal clausula ♩ , it is formed by the whole-tone progression. The half step receives its "sense of direction" only through its relationship to the other voice. Thus the leading-tone effect is not a primary phenomenon that establishes the function of the cadence. Instead, it is a secondary phenomenon that is either dependent upon the function of the cadence or joined with it in a close correlation. It is unsuited to be the founding principle of a system.

Of course a leading-tone tendency can accrue to the half-step progression not only through another voice but also through the melodic context. Whether **b** should be understood as the leading tone to **c'**, or on the contrary, **c'** as the [upper] leading tone to **b**, depends on the mode. In the c-mode, **b** appears as the lower leading tone to the final, while in the e-mode, **c'** appears as the upper leading tone to the *confinalis*.

The fact that the same leading-tone effect can arise from different assumptions is presumably the motive that induced Kurth to isolate it as a phenomenon. Yet although it can be established in various ways, the leading-tone effect still remains a phenomenon directed by some other founding factor.

In the intervallic composition of the 14th and 15th centuries, leading-tone effects are, as mentioned, tied to progressions from imperfect to perfect consonances. The tendency of a leading tone toward its goal tone and that of imperfect consonance toward perfect consonance reciprocally support each other in interval progressions such as ♩ or ♩ . On the one hand, the resolution toward which an imperfect consonance is impelled is subject to the rule that one of the voices should progress to a perfect consonance by a half-step progression: the major third tends to expand to the fifth, the minor third tends to contract to the unison. And on the other hand, to operate as a leading tone, a tone must be part of an imperfect consonance: **b** is a leading tone in the third **g–b** or in the sixth **d–b**, but not in the fifth **e–b**.

The leading-tone character of a scale degree is independent of the modal context—the "*Ton-Art*." In the tonal chord progression C–f–C, the leading-tone effect of **e** or **a♭** is manifested only if either C major or F minor is established as the chords' key of reference. But in the interval progression 𝄢 ♭8 oo , the leading-tone character of a♭ is unaffected by the context in which it is located, thus unaffected even by the mode. The tendency of imperfect consonance toward perfect consonance is sufficient to make the diatonic half step appear as a leading tone.

The older and newer leading-tone chromaticisms hence differ from each other not merely in isolated features of the relationships between leading-tone effect and key or mode, but fundamentally, in their independence from or dependence on key or mode. The basis for the difference, however, is the change forced on the significance of thirds and sixths.

As an imperfect consonance which tends toward resolution in a perfect consonance, a third or sixth is both a necessary and a sufficient condition to cause a diatonic semitone to become a leading tone. But as an autonomous interval it loses the fundamental significance for the leading-tone effect that it had in the older counterpoint. It lacks the factor of instability that as an imperfect consonance it imparted to the leading tone and from which it drew its effect. This does not mean that in tonal, chordal composition there is no dynamic force outside of dissonance—no "chordal life force" [*Triebleben der Klänge*], to use Schönberg's phrase. But it is contained less in the individual chord progression than in the chords' functional relationship. The establishment of the leading-tone effect is passed from imperfect consonance to tonal functions. The character of a leading tone changes from a phenomenon based on a type of sonority to one based on tonal functions.

However clearly the main features of its development stand out, it is still difficult to define with historical precision the transition from the older to the newer understanding of thirds and sixths. Little can be gleaned from the terminology of theorists since even in the 17th and 18th centuries they had not renounced the term "imperfect consonance," though it had long since been debased from an expression that denoted the essence of the thing to a mere classificatory concept. (They needed it to formulate the proscription of hidden parallels.)

Even the results of studies of compositional technique are not unequivocal. To demonstrate that the third changed from a dependent interval to an independent interval—thus that the concept of imperfect consonance lost its meaning—it is not enough to cite final chords in which the fifth is filled in by the third. In the 16th century, it was not felt to be a contradiction if a composition consisted of complete triads, but the musical continuity was based on interval progressions from imperfect to perfect consonances with a half-step progression in one of the voices. Instead of being mutually exclusive, *"armonia piena"* [full harmony] as a principle of sonority and the interval progression fromimperfect to perfect consonance as a principle of musical progression complemented each other.

If the consolidation of the third as an autonomous interval is to be described, then a third factor that should be considered—in addition to terminology and compositional technique—is tuning, the transition from Pythagorean to harmonically determined interval proportions. Just intonation generally prevailed from the middle of the 16th century on, above all due to the authority of Zarlino.

Thirds were considered consonances, though "imperfect" ones, in the 14th and 15th centuries. And even without having to be immediately resolved they still retained a tendency toward perfect consonances—a factor of instability. This is expressed acoustically in the Pythagorean interval proportions: the complicated Pythagorean proportions 64:81 and 27:32 [major and minor third] approach the simple harmonic proportions 4:5 and 5:6 but deviate from them by a slight difference, the syntonic comma 80:81. In viewing the circumstance that while thirds were based on "inharmonic" proportions they were still counted among the consonances, it would be wrong to see a contradiction or the mark of an "asynchronism" between compositional practice and the speculative theory of the tonal system. Rather, the Pythagorean proportions are the precise correlate of the concept of *"consonantia imperfecta."* The dependent third conforms to the Pythagorean, the independent third to the harmonic tuning of intervals.

. . .

Debates on the tonal system and tuning, even the musicologically well founded among them, often suffer from a confusion of terminology that may be attributed to a lack of knowledge of the problem. The circumstance is ignored that differences between tunings are not the same as structural differences between tonal systems. The result is a confusion of concepts that comes dramatically to light in the habit of speaking of "tonal systems" and meaning instead "tunings."

The equation of tonal system with tuning is unsupported: a tonal system can appear in several tunings and, conversely, a tuning in several tonal systems. In the tonal harmony of the 17th to 19th centuries, the 12-tone, equal-tempered tuning is not an acoustically adequate representation of the diatonic-chromatic-enharmonic system. Instead, it is a simple compromise that conceals the conflicts between mutually divergent tendencies in the tonal system. In dodecaphonic music, however, equal temperament proves to be the complete image of the system. The difference between the musical structure and its acoustical exterior is abolished.

Thus on the one hand, if different tonal systems—the harmonically tonal and the dodecaphonic—can present themselves in the same tuning, 12-tone equal temperament, then on the other hand, the same tonal system—the harmonically tonal—can appear in different tunings—"just," mean-tone, or equal-tempered. And it may not always be possible to make an unequivocal determination of which tuning comes closest to the intention of the system.

The fact that a tonal system's range of validity does not always coincide with that of a tuning is the simplest reason, though not the only one, why the concepts must be kept separate. Even the principles underlying the relationship between tonal system and tuning can differ. And it is one of the essential though scarcely noticed distinctions between the modal and harmonically tonal systems that there was a categorical modification of the relationship between tonal system and tuning in connection with the material modifications made to both the tonal system and tuning.

The Pythagorean tuning of the Middle Ages, which maintained its undisputed validity until the 15th century, has an exact correspondence with the tonal system for which it forms the acoustical exterior. For no musical phenomenon is an acoustical correlate lacking, and for no acoustical phenomenon is a musical correlate lacking. Even the factors that, from modern perspectives, seem like deficiencies in the tuning—the Pythagorean comma and the "inharmonic" proportions of thirds and sixths—are, in the Middle Ages, musically motivated so that nowhere is there a gap between the tonal system and the tuning.

As the difference between the diatonic and chromatic semitones, the comma is a musical, and not merely an acoustical, reality. Even conceptions in which the musical difference between **g♯** and **a♭** is abolished so as to change the acoustical comma into a merely troublesome disturbance—enharmonic shifts or cyclical modulations through all the transposition scales—were foreign to the Middle Ages. In fact, they were foreign on specifically musical grounds, and not from external considerations of acoustical obstacles. Before the 16th century, nowhere is there evident a disposition toward far-reaching transpositions or toward a chromaticism that would make it possible to imagine an enharmonic shift.

Like the comma, the ditone—the "inharmonic" third—should also be understood as a musical phenomenon rather than as a mathematically motivated acoustical defect. As mentioned, it corresponds to the concept of "*consonantia imperfecta*." And the hypothesis is unnecessary that in musical practice, as opposed to mathematical theory, the third was intoned as the 4:5 natural third. Even in the Middle Ages it is not out the the question that the harmonic third [4:5] was perceived as a musical fact of nature. This natural third is nevertheless denied by the content of that which was composed. The compositional technique calls attention to the factor of the pitches spreading apart, not of their fusing.

If the relationship between tonal system and tuning in the Middle Ages therefore appears to be one of flawless unity, then, since the 16th century, it has been characterized by contradictions that admit of compromises but not of solutions. One can say without exaggeration that the tonal system of tonal harmony is acoustically a fiction, since there is no conceivable tuning that would do complete justice to it. The postulates that, on the one hand, whole tones must always be defined as 8:9 and, on the other hand, all major thirds must be defined as 4:5, are irreconcilable. Yet the acoustical fiction is the musical reality. All whole tones are musically the same. The distinction between the two sizes, 8:9 and 9:10, is an incidental factor of the tuning, not an essential factor of composition and musical cognition.

If the dissociation of the major and minor whole tones is an acoustical difference without a musical correlate, then conversely, in the tonal system of tonal harmony there are musical differences whose acoustical correlate is uncertain or even unimportant. The contrast between diatonic and chromatic semitones is musically real without there necessarily being an acoustical presentation of it. The contrast is unmistakable even when an acoustical differentiation is either lacking or opposite to what it should be. Nowhere does the fact that the tuning is irrelevant show itself more clearly than in the habit of emphasizing leading tones, thus in the phrase c′–g♯–a raising the g♯ as though it were a♭, and in the phrase c′–a♭–g lowering the a♭ as though it were g♯. Notwithstanding the fact that the intonation interchanges g♯ and a♭, the musical meaning, the conception of g♯ as the third above e and of a♭ as the third below c′, is never at risk. (It would be a mistake to interpret the emphasizing of leading tones as a remnant of Pythagorean tuning. The incidental deviation of the raised g♯ and lowered a♭ from the proportion 4:5 in no way alters the meaning of the intervals: in tonal harmony, e–g♯ and a♭–c′ are harmonic thirds independent of their particular intonation.)

The indifference of listeners to the acoustical differentiations between major and minor semitones is the basis for justifying 12-tone equal temperament, while the musical irrelevance of the distinction between major and minor whole tones is the basis for justifying methods of mean-tone tuning. On the other hand, the proportion of the perfect fifth is distorted by both mean-tone tuning and equal temperament. Yet however insignificant the deviation may be, it is nonetheless unavoidable. And the fact that when the defect clinging to the acoustical representation of the harmonic tonal system is smoothed over in one place it will always spring up in another is proof of an irreconcilable divergence between tonal system and tuning. There is no "just" intonation—the tuning known by that name suffers from having an acoustical difference between two sizes of whole tones, a difference to which nothing corresponds musically.

The quarrel among theorists of the early 16th century was finally settled in favor of just intonation (against the opposition of Gafurius,[34] who held fast to the Pythagorean interval proportions). But the problems involved in the relationship between tonal system and tuning were left untouched. And it is no accident that they went unnoticed. As long as it was a dogma untainted by skepticism that the mathematical determinations of intervals were not measurements extrinsic to music but direct expressions of its essence, the thought of an irreconcilable divergence between musical meaning and acoustical representation could never arise. Rather, the fact that the distinction between two sizes of whole tone was mathematically unavoidable in "just" intonation was sufficient to exclude any doubt of its musical reality.

Only Ramos de Pareia, the first Renaissance theorist to define the thirds as 4:5 and 5:6, gives evidence—to be sure negative evidence in the form of a hesitation to pursue the consequences of his interval measurements—that if he did not clearly recognize the circumstance of a divergence between tonal system and tuning, then at least he had an inkling of it. On the monochord, he constructed a fragmentary two-octave scale of interval proportions:[35]

A	d	e	f	a	d'	e'	a'
24	18	16	15	12	9	8	6

The major third is established as a consonance by the *proportio sesquiquarta* [4:5 or 12:15], the minor third by the *proportio sesquiquinta* [5:6 or 15:18]. "And the major or minor third becomes a consonance through this comparison" [Et ex ista comparatione ditonus sive bitonus consonantia fit].[36] On the other hand, Ramos emphasizes that his measurement of the monochord results in the same 8:9 proportion of the whole tone as that of the Guidonian monochord. "So through our division of the monochord, just as through his [Guido's], the whole tone is efficaciously found so that the interval **d–e** matches the numbers 18 and 16" [Et per nostram divisionem sicut et per suam tonus efficaciter reperitur ut **d e** quam 18 et 16 numeri implent . . .].[37] The minor 9:10 whole tone is neither contained in the fragmentary two-octave scale nor mentioned in the text. Yet it is improbable, if not out of the question, that a mathematician like Ramos could have overlooked the impossibility of combining two 8:9 whole tones into a 4:5 third. And so the supposition presents itself that what appeared unavoidable to the mathematician—the distinction between two sizes of whole tone—was repugnant to the musician. Ramos of course suppressed the problem because he could not have solved it without sacrificing the conviction that the nature of things is expressed in the mathematical definition of intervals—a conviction that sustained his very existence as a theorist.

The fact that the theorists misunderstood and indeed *had* to misunderstand the difference between tonal system and tuning resulted in the mathematical determinations of the intervals being unceasingly investigated while the structure of the tonal system, whose difference from its acoustical exterior went unnoticed, was never examined.

If one bases the diatonic scale on the harmonic interval proportions, then one is forced to choose between two variant tunings. In the third **c–e**, either **c–d** is a major whole tone and **d–e** is a minor whole tone, or **c–d** is minor and **d–e** is major. In the first scale

c	d	e	f	g	a	b	c'
	8:9	9:10	15:16	8:9	9:10	8:9	15:16

the third **d–f** and the fifth **d–a** are diminished by a syntonic comma (80:81), in the second scale

c	d	e	f	g	a	b	c'
	9:10	8:9	15:16	8:9	9:10	8:9	15:16

the third **b–d'** and the fifth **g–d'**.

In the 19th century, from the circumstance that in "just" intonation either the d-minor or the G-major chord is distorted, Moritz Hauptmann[38] drew the conclusion that the contrast between major and minor is preformed in the dichotomous tuning variants, that the nature of tonal harmony is preformed in the nature of the *"Tonsystem."* In the first tuning the three major chords are unaffected, in the second the three minor chords. Thus the first is a major tuning, the second a minor tuning.

On the other hand, Hauptmann must deny the second degree in major the function of subdominant parallel: according to Hauptmann, the fifth **d–a** in major is a dissonance. Hence his deduction of major-minor tonality from harmonic tuning is both rudimentary and frag-

mentary, since the parallelism between major and minor, which Hauptmann fails to appreciate, is undeniably one of the basic factors of tonal
harmony.

. . .

The analysis of the development to which the tonal system, as a system
of tone relationships and functions, was subject between the 15th and
17th centuries should have demonstrated that the consolidation of the
third from a dependent to an independent sonority, the transition from
basing the leading-tone effect on types of sonorities to basing it on tonal
functions, and the substitution of just intonation for Pythagorean tuning
were mutually connected through their reciprocal effects.

The attempt to date these changes with greater historical precision,
thus to move beyond the vague conclusion that they occur in the 16th
century, was abandoned since it appears to be a hopeless enterprise.

MODAL POLYPHONY

An attempt to describe the differences between a monophonic and a
polyphonic presentation of the modes, if it is to avoid the unfathomable,
must be able to rely on the assumption that an unambiguous, firmly
outlined concept of the modes can be gleaned from the chant repertory
and the musical treatises of the Middle Ages. Yet anyone holding this
expectation will be disappointed—not in fact because there were
inadequate historical interpretations, but because the subject itself is
ambiguous. A simple enumeration of modal features—perhaps the
assertion that a mode is defined by its *finalis* and *repercussa*, its ambitus
and division of the octave, its melodic archetypes and formulas—would
be an oversimplification. That is, it would conceal the circumstance that
the separate defining features represent different stages of historical
development. "Mode" is a historical concept that resists definition as
a fixed cluster of features. To understand what the modes are, one has
to know their history.

Of special significance for the description of modal polyphony are
three factors that form the respective starting points for the modal
theories of Aurelian of Réôme, Hermannus Contractus, and Guido of
Arezzo: (1) the relation of modal formulas to the comprehensive system
of tonal relationships embodied in the diatonic scale; (2) the partitioning
of the octave into a modal framework; and (3) the function of the modal
final as a relational center.

1. The *Musica disciplina* of Aurelian of Réôme is the oldest medieval
treatise on the modes (the ascription of the Codex Vindobonensis 109

to Alcuin is erroneous[1]). According to Aurelian, the attempt to characterize or define the mode of a chant can be based on the *finalis*, but also on the *initialis*,[2] on particular melodic formulas (*litteraturae*), but also on the melodic development (*modulatio*). "Note well that in offertories, responsories, and invitatories the modes need be sought nowhere else than where the verse endings are introduced and where the sense of the *litteratura* rather than the *modulatio* is especially to be preserved. But in introits, antiphons, as well as in communions, always let the modes be sought at the beginning" [Notandum sane, quia in offertoriis et responsoriis atque invitatoriis non aliubi requirendi sunt toni, nisi ubi fines versuum intromittuntur, maximeque servandus est sensus litterature quam modulationis. In introitis vero, antiphonis, nec non communionibus semper in capite requirantur].[3] Aurelian reconciles the praxis of the *cantores* with the theory of the *musices*.[4]

One *litteratura*—a modal formula such as "*noeane*" or "*noeacis*"—can express itself in various melodic forms. To explain the connection between these forms, Aurelian refers to the system of direct and indirect consonant relationships: "But he who would know the fullness of this science we refer to [the study of] music; and if he wishes to be well versed in it he should turn his attention to the consonance of proportions and the speculation concerning intervals, as well as to the certitude of numbers; and then he will be able to understand the reason why one and the same *litteratura* results in different arrangements of sound" [Caeterum qui plenitudinem huiusce vult nosse scientiae, ad musicam eum mittimus, et si in ipsa voluerit versari, ad consonantiam proportionum ac speculationem intervallorum, nec non ad certitudinem oculos vertat numerorum, et tunc nosse poterit, quamobrem in una et eadem litteratura diversus efficiatur sonoritas concentus].[5] As the object of a mathematical theory, the diatonic scale—the embodiment of consonant relationships—constitutes the basis of the commonly formed modes.

2. The modes were first defined as partitionings of the octave by Hermannus Contractus in the early 11th century. His explanations are, of course, far from unambiguous. The characterization of the modes as octave types or "species" is a relic from the music theory of antiquity—a relic, however, that becomes distorted and, even in its reinterpreted form, complicates and interferes with the idea of the modes held by Hermannus Contractus. Hermannus bases his theory on circular reasoning. That is, to be able to deduce the *octoechos* (the system of eight modes) from the diatonic scale, he partitions the scale according to a principle that takes the *octoechos* for granted. He joins together four alternately conjunct and disjunct Dorian tetrachords (the ancient Phrygian), calling their degrees "*prima vox*," "*seconda vox*," "*tertia vox*," and "*quarta vox*." In this way **d** appears as both *quarta vox* and *prima vox*.

Graves							*Superiores*						
1	2	3	4				1	2	3	4			
A	B	c	d	e	f	g	a	b	c'	d'	e'	f'	g' (a')
			1	2	3	4				1	2	3	4
			Finales							*Excellentes*			

The principle of partitioning the octave is ancient, but here it is given a new meaning. Hermannus intends his disposition of tetrachords not as a description of a particular mode—the ancient Phrygian or the medieval Dorian—but as a representation of the scale that precedes and underlies all the modes. In fact its true meaning lies in making it possible to claim that Dorian fourths, fifths, and octaves extend from a *prima vox* to a *prima vox*, Phrygian from a *seconda vox* to a *seconda vox*, Lydian from a *tertia vox* to a *tertia vox*, and Mixolydian from a *quarta vox* to a *quarta vox*.

The plagal and authentic octaves are viewed as being equivalent. "The first final and its adjunct tone, which are primes, necessarily require all which are primes: namely, the first letters of each tetrachord, which are **A d a d'**, the first species of octave, which are **A–a, d–d'**, . . . " [Protus cum suo subiugali, quia primi sunt, necessario omnia quae prima sunt, requirunt; primas videlicet in omnibus quadrichordis literas, quae sunt A D a d, primas species diapason, quae sunt A a D d . . .].[6] The Hypodorian octave differs from the Dorian octave in its arrangement of whole tones and semitones—its *species*. But this is to be considered irrelevant because only the framework tones, not the tones in between them, determine the essence of a fourth, fifth, or octave. "In which description it should be noted that the principle and propriety of a species are contained in its first and last tones, for the tones interposed between them are subservient on account of their deficiency" [In qua descriptione illud est notandum, quod principio et fine principalitas vel proprietas specierum continetur: nam interpositae voces ex caritate subserviunt].[7] As a result, even though the partitioning of the scale into the four groups of *primae, secundae, tertiae,* and *quartae voces* forms the foundation of the system that he constructed, Hermannus engages in a polemic against the doctrine of the four tone qualities given in the *Musica enchiriadis*[8] and clings to the idea of *septem descrimina vocum*, the seven tone characters. He understands the differences between tetrachordal degrees to be differences in the "*positio vocis*" [the position of a tone], not differences in the "*qualitas vocis*" [the quality of a tone]. "But according to the type of number found in the fourth or fifth position, the prime agrees with the prime, the second with the second, the third with the third, and the fourth with the fourth. Of course I am speaking according to position, not according to the tone itself." [At vero secundum troporum (numerum) in quarto vel quinto loco reditum concordat prima cum prima, secuda cum secunda, tertia cum tertia, quarta cum quarta: secundum positionem dico, non secundum vocem].[9] In speaking of the significance of a tone "*secundum positionem*" [according to its position] Hermannus can only have in mind the function of a scale degree as a modal framework tone—in every other respect **d** as a *quarta vox* and **d** as a *prima vox* are identical. This schema of framework tones forms the real substance of Hermannus's theory of the modes. The remainder is rife with misunderstanding and the trappings of a misguided emulation of antiquity.

3. According to Guido of Arezzo, a mode is an embodiment of tone relationships whose focal point is a keynote. "Even though a certain chant produces all the tones and intervals, the tone that ends the chant is the principal one" [Cum autem quilibet cantus omnibus vocibus et modis (=intervallis)[10] fiat, vox tamen quae cantum terminat, obtinet principatum].[11] The tones owe their coloration to their relationship with the keynote. "The preceding tones . . . thus adapt to the keynote so that in some extraordinary way they seem to draw their apparent color from it" [Et praemissae voces . . . ita ad eam aptantur, ut mirum in modum quamdam ab ea coloris faciem ducere videantur].[12] On the other hand, Guido bases the rule that the keynote should function as a final, or that the final should be considered the keynote, on the argument that only at the end of a chant does the character—the *modus*—of a keynote become unmistakable. "But at the end of a chant we clearly know from the preceding tones the character of the last tone" [Finito vero cantu ultimae vocis modum ex praeteritis aperte agnoscimus].[13] So even though the tones adjoining the keynote may be colored by it, the character of the keynote itself depends on its relationships with the remaining tones. The fundamental category of the Guidonian theory of the modes is the notion of a reciprocal relationship. The notion, of course, is not openly formulated but lies concealed in an equivocation, in the ambiguity of the word *modus*. Under the title "Quod sex modis sibi invicem voces iungantur"[14] ["That Tones Be Joined to One Another in Six Ways"] Guido enumerates the intervals—the relationships between tones—that to him appear melodically serviceable: the semitone and whole tone, the minor third and major third, the perfect fourth and perfect fifth. Yet the term *modus* designates not only intervals but also tones' characters, and the second meaning is not unconnected with the first. The character, the *modus*, of a tone is nothing else but the aggregate of relationships, the *modi*, by which one tone is connected to the others. Only as part of a context is a pitch transformed from an acoustical datum to a musically defined tone. "The first *modus* of a tone is when a tone descends by a whole tone and ascends by a whole tone, a semitone, and then two whole

tones, as with **A** and **d**." [Primus modus vocum est, cum vox tono deponitur et tono et semitonio duobusque tonis intenditur, ut .A. et .D.].[15] The tone **A** is analogous to **d** because **A** is surrounded by the same intervals in the **G–e** hexachord as is **d** in the **c–a** hexachord. (The Guidonian description of the tone characters—the *positiones*, to use Hermannus's terminology—avoids the double definition of **d** as "*prima vox*" and "*quarta vox*"; **g** appears as the only "*quarta vox*.")

Finally, the fact that Guido calls even the modal scales *modi*—"Here are four *modi* or tropes which by custom they call tonoi [modal scales]" [hi sunt quattuor modi vel tropi, quos abusive tonos nominant][16]— means that he understood modal scales as explications of the characters of their keynotes. The relationships that a tone implies and that define its character are turned outward and displayed by the modal scale whose keynote it forms. The ambiguity of the word *modus* is thus not a sign of terminological carelessness but an expression of an essential correlation. Relationships between tones, "*modi, quibus voces iungantur*," establish the character, the "*modus*," of a tone, and the "*modus*" of a tone becomes evident in the modal scale, the "*modus*," in which it functions as the final.

. . .

The features by which a polyphonic presentation of the modes differs from a monophonic one are generally explained as results of either a clash or a collaboration of modal melody and rudimentary harmony. Without there being any qualification of what exactly should be meant by the term "harmony," it is put forward as an antithesis to "modality." This "harmony" lies in the nature of polyphony and urges an evolution of compositional practice toward a course whose goal and end is the transformation of the modes into the major and minor keys.

The assertion that "harmony" is the essence of polyphony is either tautological or false: tautolglical if "harmony" is to mean nothing but "chordal technique"; false if the concept of harmony presupposes major-minor tonality. Likewise, the notion that the "essence" of polyphony needed seven centuries first to prevail against opposition from the principle of modal melody and then to reach its consummate manifestation in major-minor tonality is certainly questionable from the view of the philosophy of history.

Knud Jeppesen believes that "harmony" constitutes an "opposing point of view"[17] in relation to modality. And he supports his view with the argument that the leading tone, the *subsemitonium modi*, "is the essential change made to the ecclesiastical modes in the transition to polyphony" [die wesentliche Änderung (sei), die sich beim Übergang zur Mehrstimmigkeit an den Kirchentönen vollzieht].[18] "By this time it was felt that cadential structures like the following one, for example, no longer had a convincing effect" [Man empfand nunmehr, daß Schlußbildungen, wie z. B. die folgende, nicht überzeugend wirkten]:[19]

Example 65

First, however, the development of the leading tone was based not on a notion of chords but on the rule that the movement from an imperfect to a perfect consonance should be facilitated by a half-step progression in one of the voices. Second, it is doubtful whether chromatic alterations at the cadence bring about "changes in the ecclesiastical modes." If one interprets as a "Lydian" cadence and ＿ as "Phrygian," then one is forced to the absurd conclusion that the Dorian mode is invalidated and replaced by the Lydian or Phrygian mode in the very cadence that is supposed to unambiguously characterize it as Dorian. To avoid this conclusion one has to concede that in modality—in contrast to major-minor tonality—chordal technique and the notion of key are separate categories. Chromatic alterations are contrapuntal means that have no effect on the mode.

The chromatic alterations that Jeppesen interprets as "changes in the ecclesiastical modes" under the influence of "harmonic considerations" are thus neither "changes in the ecclesiastical modes" nor the result of "harmonic considerations" in the sense of major-minor tonality.

A more cautious opinion is held by Georg Reichert, who observes a crossing of "tonal" and "modal" features in the polyphonically presented ecclesiastical modes of the 15th and 16th centuries. On the one hand, a hierarchy of cadence degrees—an "underlining of the formal structure" that assumes a "system of functionally graded sonorities"[20]—is clearly marked in the chansons of Dufay and Lasso. Yet on the other hand, it would be wrong not to appreciate the "modal nature" of the ecclesiastical scales. The modal basis of Dufay's works "does not exhaust itself in the regulation of a composition's harmonic development. Rather, as a clear after-effect of the original melodic mode, the polyphonic mode represents a form of development—even if a very loose type—of notable expressive power" [Sie erschöpft sich nicht in der Regelung des harmonischen Verlaufs der Komposition, sondern stellt in deutlicher Nachwirkung des ursprünglich melodischen Modus eine (wenn auch sehr lose) Verlaufsform von bemerklicher Prägekraft dar].[21]

Reichert's terminology is as ambiguous as the phenomenon it is intended to describe.

1. His expression "functional gradation" leaves open the question of whether he means tonal functions in Hugo Riemann's sense—tonic, dominant, and subdominant—or the formal functions within a chant—*finalis* and *repercussa*. After all, even the role of the *repercussa* is a "function." Thus one can interpret the positions of the "*clausulae secondariae*" [secondary clausulas]—**a** in the d-mode, **a** in the e-mode, **c′** in the f-mode, **c′** in the g-mode—as (authentic or plagal) *repercussae*[22] and still speak of "functional gradation" without bringing to mind Riemann's theory of functions.

2. An expression such as "degree IV or V," however neutral it may seem, implies a hypothesis that may or may not do justice to the musical reality of the 16th century. Whoever labels **a** as degree V in the d-mode and degree IV in the e-mode tacitly assumes that the crucial point for the significance of the "a"-degree is the disparity between its positions in the d- and e-modes, not the identity of its position in the diatonic scale. In major-minor tonality, the "material" identity of the a-minor chord in D- and E-minor contexts is secondary, if not insignificant, in relation to the "functional" difference between the roles of dominant and subdominant. But in a modal context, it is questionable and indeed improbable that the "a"-degree also has a dramatic reversal of character when it is related to **e** instead of **d**.[23]

3. The description of polyphonically presented modes as "forms of development" [*Verlaufsformen*] is ambiguous. On the one hand, it could mean that the modal characters of the individual voices, instead of thwarting and neutralizing each other, mutually support and complement one another. On the other hand, it could be meant that an attempt was made in the 15th and 16th centuries to differentiate the modes by means of stereotyped progressions of sonorities—by means of harmonic analogues to the melodic formulas of the early Middle Ages. But first, the situation where all the voices cooperate in expressing the mode is not a fixed norm. It is but one possibility that tolerates its opposite—the modal contrast between voices—alongside of it. And second, attempts to analytically refine the vague impression that a mode is characterized by "harmonic formulas" quickly enter the realm of the intangible.

While Jeppesen is of the opinion that the polyphonic presentation of the ecclesiastical modes is based on a type of harmony that formed a rudimentary prototype of major-minor tonality, Bernhard Meier is convinced that modal, intervallic composition should be understood as the exact opposite of tonal, chordal composition. "That monophonic music and the rules for its melodic organization are dealt with in the first part of treatises, while polyphonic music and the rules for the sonorities formed by its voices are dealt with only in the final part, should not be regarded as just a set arrangement dragged along by tradition. Rather, it matches the musical consciousness of the period, a consciousness that had no knowledge of modern tonality based on triads and their combinations but knew only of the modality of monophonic melodies largely predetermined by variable archetypes. This consciousness viewed a polyphonic composition—in the literal sense of the name 'cantus compositus' [composite song]—as a combination of modally designed voices regulated by intervallic counterpoint" [Daß die einstimmige Musik mit den Regeln ihrer Melodiebildung im ersten, die mehrstimmige mit den Regeln des Zusammenklanges ihrer Stimmen erst im abschließenden Teil der Lehrbücher behandelt wird, ist nicht nur als traditionell mitgeschleppte Anordnung zu betrachten, sondern entspricht dem Bewußtsein der Zeit, die keine auf Dreiklänge und ihre Verknüpfung begründete moderne Tonalität, sondern nur die durch variierbare Modelle weitgehend vorbestimmte Modalität einstimmiger Melodien kennt und ein mehrstimmiges Stück—im Wortverstand der Bezeichnung "cantus compositus"—als intervallkontrapunktisch geordnete Zusammenfügung modal erfundener Stimmen ansieht].[24] His formulation is so precise that even the questionable aspects of the idea that it expresses stand out clearly.

1. Meier seems to understand "intervallic counterpoint" only as a limitation, as the basis for the compatibility of different voices. He fails to recognize that an interval progression such as 6–7–6–8 is not merely a restriction on the combination of the discant and tenor clausulas. Rather, as a progression, it constitutes the substance of the cadence: only in conjunction with the tenor formula does the discant formula turn into a cadence. But if interval progression—the relation between the voices and not their mere compatibility—is recognized as the determining factor of counterpoint, then the idea of a coexistence of modally characterized, separate voices incurs the suspicion of being a hypothesis that, while attractive due to its simplicity, is nonetheless flawed.

2. Those who conceive of 15th- and 16th-century polyphony as cantus compositus, as the combining of autonomous and mutually independent voices, will prevent themselves from seeing that the defining features of a mode—finalis and repercussa, ambitus and octave partitioning—change their meanings in a polyphonic context. There the finalis appears as the ultima of a 6–8 clausula, the repercussa as a degree for the clausula secundaria, the ambitus as the sum total of the separate voice ranges [Lagenstimmen], and the partitioning of the octave as the framework for "tonal" imitation. The passing down of an unchanging set of terms does not guarantee the identity of their meanings.

3. If one interprets the compositional technique of the 16th century

as the complete opposite of that of the 17th, then it becomes impossible to explain the transition from modality to major-minor tonality (unless one elevates the precipitous volte-face to a developmental principle of history). Meier's hypothesis is "historical" to the extent that it stresses the distance that separates the past from what is present and familiar. But it is also "ahistorical" because it closes off the possibility of conceiving historical changes in terms of an evolution.

The restriction of the analysis to individual voices is lifted in the studies of Siegfried Hermelink. Hermelink considers Palestrina's modal use of chords from the point of view of the "keynote-ambitus relationship."[25] In the notation of vocal polyphony, ledger lines are generally avoided. Thus the ambitus of a soprano voice extends from **d'** to **g″** if the treble clef is indicated, and from **b** to **e″** if the soprano clef is indicated. The fact that a fixed limit of an eleventh is set for the notated soprano voice—the absolute pitch level and thus the dispute over the *chiavette* [transposing clefs] are irrelevant to the analysis of the "keynote-ambitus relationship"—is not without influence on the chordal character of a mode. In the soprano's ambitus, if the middle range is favored, then when the treble clef is indicated, a C-major chord is likely to be in octave position, an F-major chord in fifth or third position. Thus, provided the soprano is notated in the treble clef, the c-mode differs from the f-mode by virtue of a precedence of the octave position of the tonic chord. (If the soprano clef is indicated, then in the c-mode the fifth position of the tonic chord comes to the fore, in the f-mode the octave or third position.)

Hermelink's deduction—one can hardly speak of it as the result of empirical investigations since the statistical verification the topic suggests is still lacking—should be supplemented by the observation that in Palestrina's soprano voices the upper range of the eleven-tone ambitus is more frequently utilized than the lower range. Hence the third position of the d-minor chord with **f″** in the soprano is not as rare as it ought to be, given Hermelink's schema. And when the treble clef is indicated, **d″** appears as a middle-range tone and **g'** as a lower-range tone, even though both are equidistant from the middle of the five-line system.

. . .

Judgments concerning which modes are represented by polyphonic compositions are fraught with difficulties, and not just for the 20th-century historians who must take into account *"verloren gegangene Selbstverständlichkeiten"* [from a title by Hugo Riemann meaning roughly "things once self-evident but now lost to the past"]. Such judgments were already difficult for the theorists of the 16th century.

In the descriptions of the modes given by Pietro Aaron and Gioseffo Zarlino, relics of the old and observations of the new entwine to form a complex that must be disentangled and explicated.

Musicologists have become accustomed to viewing the tenor principle of the 15th century—the rule that the tenor represents the mode of a polyphonic composition—and the ambitus schema of the 16th century—the norm that the authentic octave in the tenor and soprano should be matched by the plagal octave in the alto and bass, the plagal octave in the tenor and soprano by the authentic octave in alto and bass—as two features of the same compositional technique.[26] The tenor principle was formulated by Tinctoris,[27] Aaron,[28] and Zarlino,[29] while the ambitus schema was described by Martin Agricola,[30] Zarlino,[31] Gallus Dressler,[32] and Michael Praetorius.[33] Cyriacus Schneegaß, who relies on Zarlino's *Istitutioni harmoniche*, unites both principles into a single proposition: "In composite songs [=polyphony], a certain authentic is mixed together with its plagal, and conversely a plagal with its authentic in such a way that one of them is dominant and the other is subservient. The former, that is, the strongest, is in the discant and tenor; the latter is in the alto and bass" [In compositis cantionibus quilibet Authenta cum suo Plagio, et vice versa Plagius cum Authenta . . . commiscentur, ita tamen, ut alter illorum dominetur, et alter subserviat: Ille scilicet potissimum in Discantu et Tenore, hic in Alto et Basso].[34] Yet it is doubtful whether Schneegaß does justice to Zarlino's intentions.

In the 16th century, the precedence of the tenor was not self-evident. For Pietro Aaron,[35] it is not a dogma unconditionally established as a fact. Rather, it is an empirically based rule that loses its validity when the conditions on which it depends go unfulfilled. The tenor determines the mode as long as it remains the voice with the cantus firmus. If the cantus firmus is taken over by the bass, then the bass represents the collective mode of the composition. Of course from time to time the mode can be gathered from the tenor of compositions even without a cantus firmus, whether because the tenor was the first voice to be composed or because it is the only voice in which the complete octave species of the mode appears (Aaron mentions the Mixolydian octave, which cannot be completed by the soprano).

If Aaron's explanations can be taken literally, the norm that the mode of a polyphonic composition depends on the mode of the tenor is thus tied to specific conditions: either to cantus-firmus composition, or to the method of composing the voices in succession, or to a restriction of the total ambitus that prevents the soprano from duplicating the tenor octave. And the rule no longer applies when its preconditions are invalidated: thus, for example, when a composition for which there is no underlying cantus firmus is based on a simultaneous conception of the voices and has a total ambitus in which the soprano matches the tenor and the alto matches the bass. But pervasive imitation in the absence of a cantus firmus, a simultaneous drafting of the voices, and a total ambitus that spans eighteen or nineteen degrees are the very foundations of 16th-century composition.

To be able to interpret the tenor as the representative of the mode, even Zarlino describes it as the first voice to be composed. "First consider the material, that is, the words of your subject. Then decide on a mode that is appropriate to their character. That done, take care that your tenor proceeds in a regulated modulation through the tones of that mode . . . " [Considerata prima la materia, cioè le Parole soggette; debbe dipoi eleggere il Modo conveniente alla loro natura. Il che fatto osservarà, che'l suo Tenore procedi regolatamente modulando per le chorde di quel Modo . . .].[36]

It is true that for Zarlino, the primacy of the tenor is tied to a condition that in the 16th century represents more the exception than the rule. Yet one ought not overlook the fact that in Zarlino's descriptions of the modes the accent falls not on the role of the tenor but on the ambitus schema—the rule that the authentic octave in the tenor and soprano should be matched by the plagal octave in the bass and alto, and the plagal octave in tenor and soprano by the authentic octave in bass and alto. In Zarlino's theory, the ambitus schema and the primacy of the tenor are more antithetical than complementary. The thesis that the determining factor in the coordination of the authentic tenor with the plagal bass or the plagal tenor with the authentic bass is the difference between a mode's authentic and plagal forms as displayed in the tenor[37] mistakes Zarlino's intention. Zarlino emphasizes the features common to authentic and plagal, not those that differentiate them. It is of secondary or even of no importance whether the species of fifth that establishes a mode is supplemented by a fourth above, resulting in the authentic octave, or by a fourth below, resulting in the plagal octave. "Therefore modern musicians take the lowest tone of each mode's species of fifth as the final of that mode; it does not make any difference whether the fourth is placed above or below [the fifth]" [Imperoche i Musici moderni pigliano per chorda finale di ciascun Modo la chorda più grave di ciascun Diapente; sia poi la Diatessaron posta nell' acuto, overo nel grave, che non fà cosa alcuna di vario].[38] In addition to the species of fifth, a mode's authentic form shares with its plagal form the keynote and the degrees used for cadences. "And they not only have their finals in common, but they also share the places for their cadences" [Et non solamente hanno le chorde finali communi: ma hanno etiandio i luoghi delle Cadenze].[39] The authentic and plagal variants form an inseparable unity that establishes the modal relationship between the voices of a polyphonic composition. "Hence by such a bond and kinship (so to speak) that is found between them, they are united in such a fashion that even if someone wished to separate the one from the other they would be unable to do it—so strong is their union. This will be seen when we discuss what one must do in adapting to each other the separate voices of a composition" [La onde per tal legamento, e parantella (dirò cosi) che se trova tra loro, sono in tal maniera uniti, che quando bene alcuno volesse separarli l'uno dall' altro non potrebbe: tanta è loro unione; come vederemo, quando se ragionarà di quello, che se hà da fare nell'accomodar le parti nelle cantilene].[40] In Zarlino's theory, the ambitus schema is therefore a consequence of the idea that the authentic and plagal modes are inseparable.

There is a contradiction between the tenor principle and the idea expressed in the ambitus schema of a collective mode encompassing both authentic and plagal forms. And the dilemma forces a decision: one has to give up the reconciling and inclusive notion that the ambitus schema and the primacy of the tenor are two features of the same modal circumstance. The tenor principle and the indivisible unity of the authentic and plagal forms of the mode are mutually exclusive. The choice between them, however, is not hard to make. In the 16th century, the compositional requirements for the primacy of the tenor wither to trivial vestiges of what they were and pale to archaisms in the face of pervasive imitation and the simultaneous conception of the voices. And so it ought to be legitimate to bring to the fore and consider decisive that which is new in Zarlino's theory, the idea that complementary modes like the Dorian and Hypodorian converge to form a collective mode.

Zarlino's theory, the thought that in polyphony a mode's authentic and plagal forms are inseparably tied together, is matched by Palestrina's practice. And Bernhard Meier's[41] attempt to demonstrate that 16th-century plagal compositions were strictly differentiated from authentic ones proves to be a failure. Meier's hypothesis, that the difference between a mode's authentic and plagal variants is characterized by the ambitus of the tenor, the initial point of imitation, and the precedence of the authentic or plagal *repercussa* as a cadential degree, must mean that a strong correlation exists between these three features. That is, if it makes sense to speak of a plagal composition as opposed to an authentic one, then a plagal tenor ambitus must coincide with a plagal initial point of imitation and the prominence of the plagal *repercussa* as a "*clausula secundaria.*" The notion that the polyphonic modes, just like the monophonic ones, can be classified as authentic and plagal therefore has the character of an empirical hypothesis that can be verified or refuted—and a study of Palestrina's cycle of offertories[42] indicates that the notion is false.

1. In Palestrina's works, the norm for the number of voices is five, not four. The *quinta vox* [fifth voice] is, however, a *tenor secundus* [second tenor]. And the idea of a *"fundamentum relationis"* [basis of relationship] split between two tenors appears to be self-contradictory.

2. To refute the hypothesis of a correlation between the ambitus of the tenor, the initial point of imitation, and the precedence of the authentic or plagal *repercussa* as a cadential degree, it is sufficient to analyze a closed group of works, the eight Phrygian offertories. (The numbers in parenthesis indicate the page references in Haberl's edition.) In three compositions (27, 29, 32) the tenor's ambitus is plagal (**g–a′**), and in five compositions (35, 37, 40, 43, 46) it is authentic (**c–e′**, **e–g′**, or a-Phrygian **g–a′**). The initial points of imitation are based on answers at the fifth or fourth (tenor **b–d′–e′** answered by bass **e–g–a**, or bass **e–g–a** answered by tenor **a–c′–d′**). Answers at the fifth—the "harmonic division" of the octave—should be classified as "authentic," answers at the fourth—the partitioning of the octave by the plagal *repercussa*—as "plagal." The results, however, are perplexing: the plagal tenor ambitus is twice (27, 29) connected with a plagal imitation, once (32) with an authentic imitation. The authentic tenor ambitus is connected once (35) with an authentic imitation, four times (37, 40, 43, 46) with a plagal imitation. The result is similarly contradictory when the precedence of the authentic (the "c"-degree) or plagal (the "a"-degree) *repercussa* as a cadential degree is related to the tenor ambitus or to initial points of imitations. The prominence of the authentic *repercussa* is matched once (32) with a plagal tenor ambitus and an authentic initial imitation, twice (40, 46) with an authentic tenor ambitus and a plagal inital imitation.

In consequence, the correlation hypothesis may be considered refuted. But if it is abandoned, then the thought that polyphonic modes are differentiated into authentic and plagal forms loses its hold on the musical reality of the 16th century. A distinction may at times have been intended, but the rule is the combining of Phrygian and Hypophrygian into an indivisible e-mode.

. . .

In the 16th century, and already in the 15th century, the theoretical establishment of the modes became a difficult problem as the *octoechos*, the system of eight modes, lost the authority of dogma and the semblance of being self-evident. And it is obvious that the theorists felt troubled and challenged by the impossibility of fashioning a self-consistent, symmetrical system out of the seven octave-species, four fifth-species, and three fourth-species. None of the conceivable constructions—the conjunct and disjunct combining of tetrachords, the augmenting of fifth-species by fourths affixed above or below, or the partitioning of the octave-species into fifths and fourths—is without its flaws if one is obsessed with the phantom of symmetry. The ancient Mixolydian (**b–B**) falls outside the system of tetrachord combinations [since there is no perfect fourth below **b**]; the medieval Mixolydian (**g–g′**) shares its fourth-species (whole tone, semitone, whole tone) with the Dorian; and the procedure of partitioning all octaves not only by fifths but also by fourths leads to an asymmetrical result. That is, one either has to exclude the octave divisions **B–f–b** and **f–b–f′** or tolerate the tritone and diminished fifth as intervals for octave division along with the perfect fourth and fifth.

To be able to equate the modes with the octave-species, Gafurius denies the existence or the right to exist of the Hypomixolydian mode. "The collateral [octave] of the Mixolydian [= Hypomixolydian] did not support a mode" [Mixolydius . . . collateralem non sustinuit modum].[43] Joannes Gallicus, who died in 1473 according to the testimony of his student Nicolaus Burtius, drew the opposite conclusion from the asymmetry of the *octoechos*, from the double division of the octave **d–d′** [as both Dorian and Hypomixolydian]. He partitioned all the octave-species by fourths and fifths without taking into consideration the difference between fourth and tritone, or fifth and diminished fifth, and thus constructed fourteen modes. "Reason, that eternal mistress, thus demands that just as the fourth species of octave (**d–d′**) takes two different modes on account of their different finals and motion, so it would be well that the other six modes do the same"[44] [Aeterna idque domina ratio deposcit, ut sicut quarta diapason species (the octave **d–d′**) duos in se tonos diversos ob diversos eorum fines et motus excipit, ita quidem et aliae sex hoc agere valeant omnes]. Of course the customary eight modes are "*magis famosi, suaviores et plus exercitati*"[45] [better known, more pleasant, and more widely practiced].

Glarean's twelve modes are the result of a double division of the octave with the exclusion of the diminished fifth and the tritone; the partitionings **B–f–b** and **f–b–f′** are "*modi reiecti*," rejected modes.[46] It is in mathematics, which for him represents the essence of things, that Glarean discovers the "legal" basis for their exclusion. The harmonic and the arithmetic division of the octave—Boethius's *medietas harmonica* and *arithmetica*[47] [harmonic mean and arithmetic mean]—are to be the only legitimate principles for the construction of the modal octaves. Of course Glarean separates the *quaestio iuris* [question of law] from the *quaestio facti* [question of fact]: he denies the legitimacy of the octave partitionings **B–f–b** and **f–b–f′** but does not deny their existence as a vulgar empirical fact.[48]

The notion that the number of modes being twelve is not self-substantiated but the result of a reduction—an exclusion of what is defective *"per accidens"*—was passed down even into the 17th century. Joachim Burmeister first classes the octave **B–f–b** with the *"authentae"* as the *"Hyperaeolius"* and the octave **f–b–f′** with the *"plagii"* as the *"Hyperphrygius,"* and then rejects the *"Hyperaeolius"* and the *"Hyperphrygius"* as *"nothi"*[49] [illegitimate offspring]. And Christoph Bernhard terms the octave partitionings **B–f–b** and **f–b–f′** *"spurii"* [spurius forms] "on account of their false fourths and fifths" [wegen der falschen Quarte und Quinte].[50]

If the system of twelve modes is thus not as rigidly circumscribed as it might appear to someone accustomed to Glarean's terminology, then through Zarlino the naming and enumeration of the modes became thoroughly confused. Zarlino, whose tendency to conjure up the *"maravigliosi effetti"* [marvelous effects] of ancient music made him feel the need to cleanse the ancient tradition of medieval errors, tried to restore the ancient nomenclature to its orginal meaning. But he merely replaced the misunderstandings of the Middle Ages with his own.

Following Ptolemy and Boethius, the ancient scale system is based on a correlation between the "thetic" *mese* and the *harmoniai*, and between the "dynamic" *mese* and the *tonoi*. As *harmoniai*, the scales **e′–e, d′–d, c′–c,** and **b–B** were related to a fixed center, the "thetic" *mese* **a**. But as *tonoi*, Dorian, Phrygian, Lydian, and Mixolydian were localized in the octave **e′–e**:

	tonoi	*harmoniai*
Dorian	e′ d′ c′ b a g f e	
Phrygian	e′ d′ c♯′ b a g f♯ e	(= d′ c′ b a g f e d)
Lydian	e′ d♯′ c♯′ b a g♯ f♯ e	(= c′ b a g f e d c)
Mixolydian	e′ d′ c′ b♭ a g f e	(= b a g f e d c B)

The "dynamic" *mese* of the Phrygian tonos is **b**—the tone with the same position in the "transposed" scale as **a** in the untransposed scale. Thus the Phrygian *mese* (**b**) is a whole tone away from the Dorian *mese* (**a**), the Lydian *mese* (**c♯′**) a whole tone from the Phrygian, and the Mixolydian (**d′**) a semitone from the Lydian.

Zarlino misinterpreted the dynamic *mesen* as keynotes, the *tonoi* as *harmoniai*, and mistook the medieval method of counting tones from the bottom up for the ancient method of counting from the top down. And so Zarlino concluded from this interval schema that the ancient Dorian had become the c-mode, the Phrygian the d-mode, the Lydian the e-mode, and the Mixolydian the f-mode.[51] Alongside the ancient Dorian (**e′–e**) and the medieval Dorian (**d–d′**) there now appeared a pseudo-ancient Dorian (**c–c′**).

His discovery—which was erroneous—brought Zarlino to a dilemma: he had to either burden his philological conscience by deviating from his pseudo-ancient terminology or bewilder his reader by the difference between the customary medieval terminology and the new pseudo-ancient nomenclature. As a way out of this dilemma, in the first and second editions of the *Istitutioni harmoniche* he decided on the compromise of avoiding the names "Dorian," "Phrygian," "Lydian," and "Mixolydian" when describing the ecclesiastical modes, reverting instead to the medieval tradition of numbering the d-mode *"primo modo."*[52] Only in the *Dimostrationi harmoniche* (1571) and the third edition of the *Istitutioni* (1573) did Zarlino change the numbering to assimilate his pseudo-ancient arrangement of the modes. He declared the c-mode, the pseudo-ancient "Dorian," to be the *"primo modo."*[53] (The disagreement between Fritz Högler,[54] who viewed the primacy of the c-mode in the *Dimostrationi* as an innovation, and D. P. Walker,[55] who raised the objection against Högler that the altered arrangement of the modes had already been set forth in the *Istitutioni*, can be resolved if one takes into account the distinction between naming and enumerating.)

As its reception history indicates, the error underlying Zarlino's new numbering takes, as it were, a quantum leap in 17th-century music theory. Seth Calvisius[56] and Johann Lippius[57] adopted the numbering without understanding or paying any attention to its motivation. The c-mode is enshrined as the "first" mode and yet still as the "Ionian" mode, notwithstanding the fact that its numbering as "first" was based entirely on the presumption that it was the ancient Dorian. "If, in this series, that mode is to be placed first which arises from the first species of octave and which is composed of the first species of fifth and the first species of fourth, then that first mode will be the Ionian and its plagal. It has its basis in the first species of octave c–c′′′ [Si is modus in ordine primus collocari debet, qui oritur ex prima specie dia pason, & componitur ex prima specie dia pente, & ex prima specie dia tessaron, Jonicus cum suo remisso, primus erit. Is enim in prima specie dia pason C. c fundamentum habet . . .].[58] Adriano Banchieri[59] and Michael Praetorius take note of both the numbering of the modes from c to a, the *"Series Modorum juxta Italorum opinionem"* [Sequence of the Modes According to the Italians' Viewpoint] and the numbering from d to c′, the *"Series Modorum juxta vulgatam opinionem"* [Sequence of the Modes According to the Common Viewpoint], without deciding in favor of either one.[60]

The double misunderstanding—first, Zarlino's numbering being based on an erroneous interpretation of Boethius, and second, its then being received in a form that contradicted its original motivation—was, however, no mere confusion without any consequences or historical significance. On the contrary, the false conception of the ancient modes shaped a roundabout path toward a true conception of the modern modes. The fact that Calvisius and Lippius promoted the c-mode to the "first" mode without having considered Zarlino's pseudo-ancient motivation suggests that one should try to find a different reason for its primacy and perhaps relate the numbering of the modes to the theory of chords. According to Lippius, the c-mode is the "first" and "most natural" mode because it sets forth the "natural" triad—the "*trias harmonica naturalior*" [more natural harmonic triad]—in the "natural" register, that of the "*hexachordum naturale*" [c–a]. "The first and most natural [mode] in the music of today (against which cry many past and more recent authorities) is the Ionian along with its plagal Hypoionian, the Ionian having the appropriate harmonic triad c–e–g" [Omnium Naturalissimus & Primus in hodierna Musica (contra quam plerique Veteres & Recentiores autumant) est Jonicus cum suo Secundario Hypoionico habens Triadem Harmonicam propriam c. e. g.].[61] Out of the thoughtless reception of a misunderstanding of the ancient modes there arose an insight into the structure of the modern modes.

. . .

The quarrel over whether it is necessary or superfluous, legitimate or illegitimate to replace the *octoechos* with Glarean's system of twelve modes was brought to a conclusion and laid to rest in neither the 16th nor the 17th century. In his *Primi Albori Musicali* of 1679 Lorenzo Penna still restricts the number of modes to eight.[62] And it seems that although Glarean's theory was perceived as a possible interpretation, it was not so compelling that any unbiased musician, after having discovered it, had to recognize it as the only intelligent choice.

One might think that the classification of an a-Aeolian composition as d-Dorian or e-Phrygian was no more than an outward accommodation with the canon of the *octoechos*, that is, a naming that conceals instead of expresses the facts of the matter. But the assumption of a simple contradiction between a "Dorian" name and an "Aeolian" circumstance—thus the conjecture that although Palestrina designated a composition with an a-clausula as d-Dorian or e-Phrygian, he "composed" it as a-Aeolian—rests on an interpretative schema too crude to be uncritically accepted. The question of why one and the same composition could be conceived either as d-Dorian or a-Aeolian cannot be circumvented: the possibility of a dual interpretation must be based on the essence of modal polyphony itself.

In his *Trattato della natura e cognizione di tutti gli toni di canto figurato*

(1525) [Treatise on the Nature and Cognizance of All the Polyphonic Modes], Pietro Aaron describes the difficulties of determining the mode, and he does so with the freedom from bias of an empiricist who disdains sacrificing the ambiguity of practice to the uniformity of theory. Aaron does not recognize a c-mode or an a-mode. The "a"-degree is the Dorian *"confinalità"* and a Phrygian or Lydian *"differenza"*; the "c"-degree is the Lydian *"confinalità"* or a Mixolydian *"differenza."*[63] Thus "a-Aeolian" compositions can be interpreted as Dorian, Phrygian, or Lydian, "c-Ionian" compositions as Lydian or Mixolydian. The decision depends on the species of fourth and fifth set out at the beginning of a piece.[64]

When analyzed from the point of view of Glarean's theory, Aaron's classifications of modes transposed to *"cantus mollis"* [i.e., the ♭-system] suffer from an inconsistency that would be remedied in the system of twelve modes: in the ♭-system, the d-scale is to be considered an altered Dorian and the f-scale an altered Lydian, but the g-scale is to be considered a transposed Dorian and the a-scale a transposed Phrygian. The c-scale is either an altered Lydian or a transposed Mixolydian.[65]

Aaron's explanation of the a- and c-modes, however flawed and contradictory it may seem, was not dislodged from the musical consciousness of the time, even though Glarean subjected it to the competition of an opposing theory. The conception of mode conveyed by Palestrina's compositional practice is unmistakably that of the *octoechos*, not Glarean's system of twelve modes. In the cycle of offertories from 1593,[66] motets 5–8 are Dorian, 9–16 "Lydian" (f-Ionian), and 25–32 Mixolydian. Motets 1–4 end with an a-clausula, but must be considered d-Dorian if the cyclical arrangement of modes is not to be disturbed: the Aeolian *finalis* is intended as the Dorian *"confinalità."* Similarly unmistakable is the classification of the Magnificat compositions.[67] A work that would be "c-Ionian" or "f-Ionian" in Glarean's theory is considered a Magnificat *"sexti toni"* [plagal Lydian], one that would be "a-Aeolian" a Magnificat *"tertii,"* *"quinti,"* or *"septimi toni"* [authentic Phrygian, Lydian, or Mixolydian]. And if Palestrina thought of f-Ionian as an altered Lydian, then even d-Aeolian[68] must be understood as an altered d-Dorian.

The confusion of Ionian and Lydian is of scant importance, since no unaltered Lydian stood opposed to the Lydian modified as an Ionian: the f-mode with the tritone as the fourth degree was obsolete and avoided by Palestrina. The uncertainty in the classification of compositions that end with an a-clausula is, however, disconcerting. It seems that the tonal character of a composition would be turned on its head if the a-degree is meant to pass for the Dorian "dominant" or Phrygian "subdominant" instead of the Aeolian "tonic." According to modern concepts, the very uncertainty, the possibility of a double interpretation, endangers a work's meaning.

The same composition that one of Glarean's supporters would categorize as a-Aeolian could be understood as d-Dorian or e-Phyrgian by an opponent of the twelve-mode theory. The fact that this is possible without there being a clear line to draw between right and wrong is inexplicable as long as one clings to the idea that tone relationships must be based on a central keynote in order to establish a musical context. The keynote, the starting point and goal of tone relationships in major-minor harmony, is more a secondary factor in the modal polyphony of the 16th century. Even without a keynote—thus as a system of tones related only to each other—the diatonic degrees constitute a foundation capable of supporting a musical composition. The fifth- and fourth-relations between d, a, and e need not be grouped around a central focus to be perceived as tone relationships. The fifth establishes a relationship between two tones without the upper one having to be understood as the dominant of the lower one or the lower one as the subdominant of the upper one. In the modal polyphony of the 16th century, the relationships between the cadential degrees should be understood primarily as bilateral relationships, relationships that allow a more precise definition through the establishment of a keynote but that do not depend on one in order to be effective.

It is in the principle of bilateral relationship that one can find the basis for the possibility of dual modal determinations. Whether a composition beginning with a d-Dorian or an a-Aeolian imitation and cadencing on d, f, and a is categorized as d-Dorian or a-Aeolian seems a secondary and practically insignificant factor if a change in the classification has no effect on the meaning of the individual clausulas. The f-clausula represents neither the "subdominant parallel" in the a-mode nor the "tonic parallel" in the d-mode, nor "VI" in the one mode and "III" in the other. Rather, in each mode it is first and foremost the "f-degree."

. . .

If the possibility of a double determination of a mode forces consideration of the hypothesis that the significance of the keynote in modal polyphony was less firmly characterized than in major-minor tonality, then the thought presents itself that other categories of major-minor tonality—categories that are inseparable from the primacy of the keynote—must also be restricted in their validity if the music of the 16th century is to be adequately described. And provided that one considers the theory of functions a legitimate representation of major-minor tonality, the categorical differences between modal polyphony and tonal harmony can be formulated as antitheses between "structure" and "function," "complex" and "system."

1. In the symbol "Sp," "p" indicates a chord and "S" indicates a function that the d-minor chord shares with the F-major chord in a C-major context. The function "S" is not tied to any particular chord or even to any feature by which one group of chords is held together and contrasted with other groups. The Neapolitan chord **f–a♭–d♭′** and the chord **f♯–a–c′–d′** (which in many contexts appears as an altered subdominant) represent the same function without being connected to each other by a common tone, a "*vinculum substantiale*" [material link].

The idea of a function that can be removed from the substance through which it is represented was foreign to 16th-century musical thought and foreign to 16th-century thought in general. In modal polyphony, functions are inseparable from positions [within the diatonic system]. And one can even question whether it makes sense to speak of functions—thus whether the association between the Mixolydian *finalis* (**g**), *confinalis* (**d**), and *repercussa* (**c**) represents a system of "functions" or simply a "structure" that was recognized as Mixolydian because tradition established **g**, **c**, and **d** as the normative framework tones of the g-mode.

To be sure, "*repercussa*" was originally a designation of function. But the significance of the *repercussa* as both the reciting tone and the counterpart of the *finalis* in the higher register of the modal ambitus was undermined in polyphony. The cadential degree **c**, the modulation from the g-mode to the c-mode, shares nothing with the melodic *repercussa* **c** save its position in the scale. The function intended by the name "*repercussa*" is tied to the Mixolydian melodic archetype and cannot be transferred in the case of a modulation to the c-mode.

2. Tonal functions form a "system" in which each component, to be what it is, depends on the other components: a tonic is unimaginable without a dominant and a dominant is unimaginable without a tonic. In contrast, the defining features of a polyphonically presented mode— the *finalis* and the initial point of imitation, the ambitus and the disposition of clausulas—appear as a mere "complex" from which individual features can be detached without compromising the meaning of the others. According to Pietro Aaron,[69] in some works the dominant feature is the type of octave, the *species* of the mode, while in others it is the *finalis*. Thus if a mode is unmistakably characterized by its *species*, then the final cadence can modulate to the "*confinalità*" or the "*differenza*." Conversely, if the *finalis* is firmly established, then an opening section that diverges from the basic mode does not seem like a defect. Taken literally, Aaron's explanation can frequently lead to uncertainty in the determination of a mode because it lacks a criterion

to determine whether a work that goes from a g-Mixolydian beginning
to a d-Dorian ending should be considered Mixolydian with a clausula
on the "*confinalità*" or Dorian with an initial imitation in the mode
a fifth below. The very factor of indeterminacy, the irreducible remainder of uncertainty, is a sign that the features of a mode did not
form a "system" in which every component supported every other
component and enabled the others to exist. Instead, the features of
modal polyphony formed a mere "complex."

KEY RELATIONSHIP AND THE DISPOSITION OF CLAUSULAS

In the language of music theory, "tonal" and "cadential" harmony are
synonymous terms. The cadence T–S–T–D–T is the paradigm of a tonal
chord relationship. And according to the theory of tonal harmony, just
as chords together constitute a key, so individual keys unite to form
a collective key.

The relationship between keys is, however, in no small part defined
by features other than those between chords. In the minor mode the
prevailing disposition of keys is represented by the schema T–Tp–D–T
[i–III–V–i], not by T–S–D–T. Reasoning by analogy from chord relationships to key relationships does not do justice to musical reality.

. . .

1. At the beginning of the I–IV–V–I cadence, understanding the first
degree as the tonic is a mere assumption. The true and unabridged
meaning of the concept "tonic" devolves to the first degree only through
the very cadence from which it issues as the expected outcome. On
the other hand, the fourth and fifth degrees establish themselves as
subdominant and dominant in relation to the merely "assumed" tonic.
The initially empty notion of the tonic is the precondition for the
cadence while the fully realized notion is the result of the cadence.

The attempt to transfer the dialectic underlying the cadence to the
relationships between keys would, if done without modification, be
forced. In contrast to an initial tonic chord, an initial key can stand
on its own without appearing as a provisional and uncertain assumption.
Though an initial key may be characteristically colored by modulations
to closely related keys, it is neither established by them nor based on
them. And because a key, to be what it is, need not be related to other
keys, modulations are restricted by norms to a lesser extent than are
chord progressions. The schema T–S–D–T can be reversed to T–D–S–T
as a disposition of keys but not as a chord progression. And the schema
T–Tp–D–T in minor [i–III–V–i], which is a regular disposition of keys,
would be quite an irregular cadence.

2. The fact that chordal relationships can be subject to different rules than key relationships also comes to light through differences in the significance of individual functions. With reference to a chord, the concept of the dominant parallel in minor [♭VII] is a phantom of systematization: in A minor, the G-major chord is conceivable only as the dominant of the tonic parallel [V of the relative major]. Though the concept of the dominant parallel thus misses the meaning of the G-major chord in A minor, it nevertheless does hit on the meaning of the key of G major in an A-minor context. The dominant parallel in minor, a fiction as a chord, is a musical reality as a key.

3. Many functions whose operations are ambiguous in chord progressions are unambiguous in key relationships. It would be arbitrary or a sign of compulsive systematizing to want to determine without a shred of uncertainty whether, in the progression ii–V–I, the second degree in a major key is a dominant of the dominant due to the fifth-progression ii–V, or a subdominant parallel due to the major third shared with the subdominant. But as a key related to C major, D minor is nothing but the subdominant parallel, having in common with the subdominant key the scale with one flat.

. . .

The relationship between chordal functions and the disposition of keys is more complicated than the simple analogy from chord to key makes it seem. But this in no way alters the founding principle of tonality: that keys, just like chords, are functions of the tonic. The significance of a subsidiary key depends on its relation to the main key.

In the modal polyphony of the 16th century it would be dogmatic to presume that the relationships between the modes were based on the same or a similar principle. It is possible that the modes differ from the harmonically presented major and minor keys not only in their structure but also in the principles that establish a relationship between them. The theory and practice of the disposition of modes and clausulas has been studied by Arnold Schmitz,[1] Georg Reichert,[2] Bernhard Meier,[3] Siegfried Hermelink,[4] and Richard Jakoby.[5] Still, it remains uncertain whether a disposition of modes or clausulas differs from a scheme of keys and cadences in an essential way—in its musical significance—or merely incidentally—in its compositional structure and choice of scale degrees. Does a *clausula secundaria* on the *confinalis* fulfill a different function than a harmonically tonal cadence on the dominant, or does it fulfill the same function with different means?

Whether a mode is represented by a single clausula or by a system of clausulas—thus whether or not a clausula on a related degree signifies a change of mode—appears to have been just as hard to determine in the 16th and 17th centuries as was determining the boundary between a real "modulation" and an incidental "tonicization" in the 18th and 19th centuries. Arnold Schmitz's thesis that neither a *clausula se-cundaria*, nor a *clausula tertiaria*, nor a *clausula peregrina* implied a change of mode is, if not erroneous, then at least one-sided. "In an inflection to a *clausula peregrina* or *affinalis* no modulation or toni-cization takes place, or following the understanding and terminology of 16th- and 17th-century composers there occurs no *mutatio toni* [change of mode]—a point that is surely not unimportant for the analysis and interpretation of this period's musical artworks" [Bei dem Ein-biegen in eine Clausula peregrina oder affinalis wird nicht moduliert oder ausgewichen, es findet nach der Auffassung und Terminologie der Komponisten des 16. und 17. Jahrhunderts keine Mutatio toni statt, ein Punkt, der wahrhaftig nicht unwichtig ist für die Analyse und Interpretation der musikalischen Kunstwerke dieser Zeit].[6]

Schmitz relies on a fragmentary quotation of Calvisius purporting that a composer "already needs to take care in the use of *secundaria* and *tertiaria* but must be especially careful with the *peregrina*: 'lest it be led . . . from mode to mode instead of having the true mode be evident everywhere'" [schon beim Gebrauch der Secundaria und Tertiaria, vollends aber der Peregrina darauf zu achten: "ne . . . in alium atque alium Modum deducatur, sed ut ubique verus Modus conspicuus sit"].[7] Yet a warning about "*mutatio modi*" is not the same as the assertion that it does not exist. And in unabridged form, the quotation from Calvisius implies that unless the *clausula primaria* constantly reappears, clausulas on degrees other than the first lead to a promiscuous change of mode: "Therefore the proper clausula has its place when it is everywhere in the beginning, middle, and end of whatever *Harmonia*, lest it be led by other clausulas from mode to mode instead of having the true mode be evident everywhere" [Propria igitur clausula, cum ubique in principio, medio et fine, cuiuslibet Harmoniae locum habeat, ne per alias clausulas, in alium atque alium Modum deducatur, sed ut ubique verus Modus conspicuus sit . . .].[8] In a different chapter, Calvisius speaks about the use of the *clausula primaria*: "And the useof this clausula is at the beginning and end of a cantilena, and also when the cantilena is inflected and seems to be transposed to another mode by other chosen clausulas, then the cantilena is called back by this proper clausula and brought to order" [Atque huius Clausulae usus est, in principio et fine Cantilenarum, tum etiam, quando per assumtas alias Clausulas, Cantilena ad alium modum inclinare, et traduci videtur, per hanc enim propriam Clausulam revocatur, et in ordinem redigitur].[9] Thus it can hardly be denied that clausulas on related degrees were, or could have been, understood as "tonicizations."

Christoph Bernhard's opinion is similar to Calvisius's, though he expresses it not in a description of the disposition of cadences but in an analysis of the initial imitations in Palestrina's motets. Bernhard's study is of *"principii"* [beginnings], which according to Zarlino[10]—on whom Bernhard bases his theory of the modes—determine the mode of a composition to no less a degree than do clausulas. Thus it may be legitimate to transfer to the disposition of clausulas what Bernhard has to say about the imitations. According to Bernhard, imitations in the d-mode with the initial tones **a** and **e**, **g** and **e**, or **c** and **g** signify an *"extensio modi"* [an extension of the mode] through which one goes "beyond the proper bounds of the mode" [außer denen eigentlichen Schranken des Modi].[11] And Bernhard terms a lack of congruence between the beginning and the ending of a composition, between the first imitation and the last cadence, an *"alteratio modi"* [alteration of the mode][12] or, in another place, a *"mutatio toni"* [change of key].[13]

The problem of when a transition to different initial points of imitation or to different clausula degrees should be understood as an *extensio modi* and when it should be understood as a *mutatio toni* is reminiscent, as mentioned, of the difficulties in tonal harmony of marking off the boundary between "modulation," which implies a change of key, and mere "tonicization." The problem, however, can be solved following other criteria.

In major-minor tonality, the distinction between incidental tonicization and real modulation depends not only on harmonic, but to a nearly equal degree on formal, considerations. A succession of keys that would be a mere tonicization in the second theme of a sonata form could appear as a modulation in an ABA song form. At least two explanations are possible. First, the caesuras of the song form throw into bold relief the factor of modulation, while the tonal integrity of the second theme emphasizes the factor of tonal dependence. And second, in a smaller form like ABA—in connection with listening to shorter stretches of music—the tendency to understand closely related keys as cofactors of the main key is weaker than in the larger form of the sonata.

If the decision between a modulation and a tonicization depends on a composition's formal type, so the decision between a *mutatio modi* and an *extensio modi* depends on the relation of clausulas to the structure of the text. For Calvisius, the terms *"propria"* and *"impropria"* characterize not the mere position of a clausula in the modal scale but its relation to the text. A *clausula tertiaria* or *peregrina* is considered *"propria"* provided it fulfills its function of musically representing a comma; *"impropria,"* on the other hand, if it comes at the end of a poetic period. *"Clausulae impropriae,"* however, change the mode.

"Other clausulas for expressing a comma and for moving the affections should, however, be taken up with great care lest, with the mode changed by improper clausulas, the *Harmonia* be thoroughly destroyed" [Aliae clausulae ad commata exprimenda, et ad affectus movendos assumuntur, magno tamen iudicio, ne Modo per improprias clausulas immutato, Harmonia prorsus destruatur].[14] Thus, according to Calvisius's criteria, the disposition of clausulas 1:C, 2:d, 3:a, 4:C [numbers indicate verses, letters indicate keys] implies a *mutatio modi* if verse 2 is marked off by a period, but a mere *extensio modi* if by a comma.

· · ·

In tonal harmony, doubt over which degree a cadence falls on is impossible or at least rare. The rules that the lowest tone of the "stack of thirds" forms the root and that a chord reached through a deceptive cadence is to be understood as the "parallel" of the "proper" cadential chord allow for a determination of cadential chordal degrees to which clings hardly a trace of uncertainty.

The clausulas in modally oriented intervallic composition, however, are frequently ambiguous. The method of perhaps placing the bass progressions **g–d** or **g–f** under an a-Phrygian discant-tenor clausula

( )—a procedure that was handed down even into the 17th

century[15]—makes it difficult if not impossible to stipulate, without being arbitrary, whether the clausula should be viewed as an a-cadence or as either a d-cadence or an f-cadence.

One might suppose that from an analysis of compositional structure it ought to be possible to decide whether the tenor or the bass is the *"fundamentum relationis"* [the basis of relationship], and from that to decide which tone of the clausula represents the cadential degree. But except in cantus-firmus composition, which became obsolete in the 16th century, the features are lacking on which one could base such a judgment. Ernst Apfel's hypothesis[16]—that whenever the bass is necessary to justify fourths or diminished fifths between tenor and discant, it must be considered the *"fundamentum relationis"*—is subject to doubts inasmuch as it frequently runs counter to the only sure criterion of a hierarchy of the voices, the cantus-firmus principle. The fact that the tenor is the cantus-firmus voice, thus that the clausulas in the tenor represent the cadential degrees, does not rule out the occurrence of fourths or diminished fifths between tenor and discant that must be supported and legitimized by the bass.

On the other hand, even in works unequivocally marked by a

discant-bass structure, the possibility needs to be considered that the composer shares the theorist's inclination to cling to the tenor principle in determining the mode even when this principle is compositionally thwarted by the primacy of the bass: the direct impression made by a clausula need not correspond with its modal meaning. If Johann Lippius defines the tenor voice as *"melodia regularis"* [ruling voice] and the bass voice as *"melodia fundamentalis"* [fundamental voice],[17] then it seems that his terminology expresses the distinction between a voice as the determinant of the mode and a voice as the foundation of compositional technique.

It would, of course, be wrong to view the tenor formula **d'–c'** as the sole expression of a clausula's modal meaning and to see the discant formula **b'–c″** as a mere contrapuntal addition. Rather, the clausula first establishes itself through the collaboration of the voices in the 6–8 interval progression. And the 6–8 progression—as a succession of consonances—is not merely an external constraint on the compatibility of different melodic formulas, but an essential feature of the clausula. In fact, in Gioseffo Zarlino's descriptions of clausulas the subject is exclusively interval progressions such as 3–1, 6–8, and 10–12, not melodic formulas.[18] According to Zarlino, the mark of a *"cadenza"* is the progression from an imperfect to a perfect consonance with a half-step progression in one of the voices. The interval progressions

, , , and are considered simple

clausulas, while the progressions and are considered

combined clausulas. (The German theorists of the 16th century— following the example of Nicolaus Wollick or Melchior Schamppecher in the *Opus aureum* of 1501—place the accent on melodic formulas instead of interval progressions.)

The transition from the melodic to the harmonic conception of the cadence would scarcely be understandable without the intercession of the concept of interval progression. Yet however clearly the main features of the development from modal intervallic composition to harmonically tonal chordal composition stand out, it remains equally difficult to determine in individual cases, without being arbitrary, how a clausula or cadence should be understood. A judgment over whether the Ionian and Aeolian clausulas of the 16th century can or cannot be considered major and minor cadences depends less on objective facts evident in the musical notation than on the basic principles used in the interpretation. In the first place, it is uncertain to what extent the theorists ought to be taken as authorities. Second, it is problematic whether a cadence can be thought of as being harmonically tonal if its larger musical context is not—thus whether it is legitimate to see within the conception of what is harmonically tonal a principle that asserted itself first in the cadence in order then to branch out gradually over entire compositions. And third, one is forced to choose between the self-contradictory principles of ascribing to a situation its later, historically secondary meaning either as soon as it appears possible or not until it is absolutely necessary. A harmonically tonal interpretation of the Ionian and Aeolian clausulas is possible from as early as when their external forms are no longer distinguishable from those of the major and minor cadences, thus since 1500.[19] But such an interpretation is absolutely necessary only from the second half of the 17th century when the conception of what is harmonically tonal asserted itself in the parlance of the theorists.

The transition to a terminology influenced by harmonic criteria—the shift from the last vestige of the old to a vague recognition of the new—can be detected in the terms used by Wolfgang Caspar Printz in his *Satyrischen Componisten* to characterize the "*clausulae finales primariae*" [primary final clausulas]:[20]

Example 66

The term "*clausula dissecta imperfecta*" [interrupted imperfect clausula] [ex. 66f] allows for two different interpretations. It is conceivable that Printz intended the expressions "*perfecta*" and "*imperfecta*" merely to accentuate the contrast between the perfect cadence and the half cadence—the "*clausula totalis*" [complete clausula] (66a) and the "*clausula dissecta*" [interrupted clausula] (66f). But then again, it is not out of the question that the "*dissecta imperfecta*" (66f) was meant to be contrasted with the "*dissecta acquiescens*" [resolved interrupted clausula] (66b) and the "*dissecta desiderans*" [unresolved interrupted clausula] (66e), and that Printz perceived it as "imperfect" [in the sense of "incomplete"] because the IV–V progression is more compelling in requiring a further continuation, thus tolerating an interruption less well than the IV–I and I–V progressions of the "*dissecta acquiescens*" and "*dissecta desiderans.*" In the second interpretation, the term "*imperfecta*" is a sign of a harmonically tonal mode of listening. And this suggests itself more strongly since even the term "*dissecta acquiescens*"—in fact due to a hidden internal contradiction—expresses the transition from a melodic-contrapuntal to a harmonic understanding of clausulas. The clausula is "*dissecta*" [interrupted] because the interval progression and the melodic formulas break off on the penultima. But on the other hand, it is "*acquiescens*" [resolved] because it has harmonic closure. If the melodic-contrapuntal aspect, the interruption of the interval progression and melodic formulas, was the deciding factor, then this clausula, analogous to the "*dissecta desiderans,*" had to be viewed in relation to its missing final degree, and thus classified as a d-cadence. But the fact that Printz sees it as an a-cadence implies that he is calling attention to the clausula's harmonically tonal aspect.

Similarly ambiguous is the contrast between the "imperfect" clausula of ex. 66g and the "perfect" clausula of 66c. In 66c, the bass takes over the discant formula **g♯–a**, and it is conceivable that 66g is "imperfect" because the second-progression **e–f♯**, in contrast to **g♯–a**, is not a regular melodic formula. But it is more likely that Printz was thinking of the six-three chord when he labeled 66g as "imperfect." After all, 66h is also classified as "imperfect," and since the descent of a third in the bass of 66h is the regular alto formula—a "*clausula altizans*" [alto clausula]—the "imperfection" must be based not on melodic aspects but on the sonority itself.

· · ·

In the modal polyphony of the 16th century, the disposition of clausulas is neither completely irregular nor subject to a fixed principle that would be exactly same in the Phrygian as in the Ionian mode. Zarlino's I–V–III schema, the rule that in every mode the *clausula primaria* should be on degree I, the *clausula secundaria* on degree V, and the *clausula tertiaria* on degree III, is speculative and not based on empirical evidence.[21] Yet the opposite extreme—the impression of caprice—is based on the disappointment of a false expectation, the idea that a modal clausula—just like a tonal cadence—must form the "goal" of a "development." In misunderstanding the clausula's purely syntactical significance,[22] a function is attributed to it that it was not meant to fulfill.

The general I–V–III schema, which according to Zarlino is recurrent in every mode, is too rigid to do justice to musical reality. The individual modes are characterized by different arrangements of cadential degrees, typical dispositions of clausulas by which one mode is distinguished from the next. The studies of R. O. Morris on "modulations" in vocal polyphony,[23] of Georg Reichert on the caesural cadences in Lasso's chansons,[24] and of Siegfried Hermelink on the clausula degrees in Palestrina's masses and motets[25] differ so trivially in their findings that one can without exaggeration speak of established norms.

The "old" modes—Dorian, Phrygian, Lydian, and Mixolydian—are unmistakable in their dispositions of clausulas:

d-Dorian:	d	a	f		=	I	V	III	
e-Phrygian:	e	a	c	g	=	I	IV	VI	III
f-Lydian:	f	c	a		=	I	V	III	
g-Mixolydian:	g	c	d		=	I	IV	V	

The norm for Aeolian matches the Dorian, and the norm for Ionian matches the Lydian:

a-Aeolian:	a	e	c	=	I	V	III
c-Ionian:	c	g	e	=	I	V	III

Melodic structure and the succession of clausulas are closely inter-connected, though without the relation between them being so immediately evident as that between chord relationships and the disposition of keys in tonal harmony. In Johannes Cochläus's "*exercitium cantus choralis*" [the practice of chant], the degrees representing the regular clausulas—the *clausulae primariae, secundariae,* and *tertiariae*—recur as the structural tones of modally characterized melodies. "In the first mode [authentic Dorian] the most frequent is the fifth from **d** to **a**, while in the second mode [plagal Dorian] it is the minor third from **A** to **c** or from **d** to **f** . . . The minor sixth from **e** to **c′** ought not to be overlooked because it is most frequent in the third mode [authentic

Phrygian] and exceedingly mild. In the fourth mode [plagal Phrygian] the fourth is common from **e** to **a** and vice versa . . . In the fifth mode [authentic Lydian] the following thirds are common, **f** to **a** and **a** to **c'** . . . The fifth from **g** to **d'** and then down to **b** and rebounding again to **d** is a frequently celebrated usage with melodies in the seventh mode [authentic Mixolydian] . . . The eighth mode [plagal Mixolydian] frequently turns to the fifth above the final and especially the fourth from **g** to **c'"** [In primo tono frequentissima est diapente a D ad a, in secundo vero semiditonus ab A ad C vel a D ad F . . . Mollis sexta ab E ad c non est negligenda, quod in tertio frequentissima sit et plurimum suavis. In quarto tono frequens est diatessaron de E ad a vel e contra . . . In quinto crebre sunt istiusmodi tertiae ex F in a et ex a in c . . . Quinta ex G in d et rursus tertia ex d in b iterum resiliens in d frequenti celebrantur usu in cantu septimi toni . . . Octavus tonus frequenter versatur in diapente supra finalem et maxime in diatessaron ex G in c . . .].[26]

The fact that the same hierarchy of degrees underlies both the melodic structure and the disposition of the clausulas can be understood from the character of the modes as archetypes. The relationship between melodic structural tones and dispositions of clausulas— "modulations" to use Morris's term—can hardly have the rational basis (or the rational basis to anything like the same degree) of the relation between the disposition of keys and the cadence in tonal harmony. One can deduce the relationship between the keys of C major and G major from the V–I cadence, but not, or not in the same sense, the affinity between the Phrygian and Ionian modes from the relationship between the Phrygian *finalis* (**e**) and *repercussa* (**c**). From the point of view of tonal "logic," there seems to be a missing link that if present would make it possible to see how a relation between keys or modes can result from melodic functions. But such a link turns out to be superfluous if one realizes that the correspondence between a melodic framework and a disposition of clausulas represents a different principle than that of tonal "logic," not the same principle expressed in an imperfect fashion. The distinction between primary and secondary degrees is a means of characterizing a mode that can be applied not only to the melodic structure but also to the disposition of clausulas and modes. And neither phenomenon is the basis or the result of the other. The relationship should be understood as one based on analogy and not as one between a basic principle and its derivative result.

Even final cadences, enumerated by Pietro Aaron in his *Trattato della natura e cognizione di tutti gli toni di canto figurato*,[27] are subject to the same norm as are melodic structural tones and the disposition of cadences. According to Aaron, the legitimate endings are:

in	d-Dorian	the degrees	d and a
	e-Phrygian		e, a, and g
	f-Lydian		f, c, and a
	g-Mixolydian		g and c.

Aaron claims that the determination of whether a final cadence on **a** is Dorian *"confinalità"* or Phrygian or Lydian *"differenza,"* and whether a final cadence on **c** is Lydian *"confinalità"* or Mixolydian *"differenza,"* must be made on the basis of the *"species,"* the types of fourth and fifth underlying the melodic structure of the tenor.

Aaron's schema of the disposition of clausulas is, in contrast to his enumeration of final cadences, too inclusive to be discriminating:[28]

d-Dorian	**d**	**f**	**g**	**a**		
d-Hypodorian	**A**	**c**	**d**	**f**	**g**	**a**
e-Phrygian	**e**	**f**	**g**	**a**	**b**	
e-Hypophrygian	**c**	**d**	**e**	**f**	**g**	**a**
f-Lydian	**f**	**a**	**c'**			
f-Hypolydian	**c**	**d**	**f**	**a**	**c'**	
g-Mixolydian	**g**	**a**	**b**	**c'**	**d'**	
g-Hypoixolydian	**d**	**f**	**g**	**c'**		

The only norm that one might abstract from this table is the negative rule that in a plagal mode one should avoid the cadential degree that divides the ambitus by a fifth (d-Hypodorian **A–e–a**) instead of by a fourth (d-Hypodorian **A–d–a**). Thus in d-Hypodorian, **e** is missing, in f-Hypolydian, **g**, and in g-Hypomixolydian, **a**.

The norms for the modal cadences, the schemata

d-Dorian:	d	a	f
e-Phrygian:	e	a	c
f-Lydian:	f	c	a
g-Mixolydian:	g	c	d
a-Aeolian:	a	e	c
c-Ionian:	c	g	e

are clearly characterized in both the melodic structure and the disposition of clausulas. Yet this clarity is equaled by the difficulty of recognizing a "system" in these schemata. Three interpretations are possible.

1. The *clausulae secundariae* and *tertiariae* of the four "old" modes—Dorian, Phrygian, Lydian, and Mixolydian—are none other than the *repercussae* of a mode's authentic and plagal forms. (And a-Aeolian is the analogue of d-Dorian, c-Ionian of f-Lydian.) The fact that the authentic and the plagal *repercussae* exist side by side in the disposition of the clausulas—the authentic as the *secundaria*, the plagal as the *tertiaria*—is a feature by which the polyphonic presentation of the modes differs from the monophonic. The authentic ambitus of the tenor and the plagal ambitus of the bass, or the plagal ambitus of the tenor and the authentic ambitus of the bass, go together to form a *"modus mixtus."*[29] And the fact that both *repercussae* appear as clausula degrees in the same composition justifies speaking—in contradiction to the theorists' dogma that the authentic or plagal ambitus of the tenor marks a composition as authentic or plagal—of a collective Dorian or Phrygian mode that combines the respective authentic and plagal variants.

2. The thought of attributing the connections between the clausula degrees to relationships of fifths and fourths may impress one as anachronistic. The appearance that such an idea is due to a bias toward the categories of major-minor tonality is, however, deceiving. Even if the relationships between the *clausulae primariae* and *secundariae*—the degree relations **d–a**, **e–a**, **f–c**, **g–c**, **a–e**, and **c–g**—are explained as fifth-relations, the concept of "fifth-relation" must at the same time be understood differently than in major-minor tonality. In the harmonically tonal fifth-relation, two features are intertwined: first, the fifth-relation as a two-sided, "bilateral" relation without a sense of a particular alignment, and second, the "tendency" of the one degree toward the other. In contrast, only the first factor is operative in the modal fifth-relation. There is a relationship between **a** and **e**, but it does not include a dependence of one degree upon the other. The fifth-relation is nothing but a bilateral relation, and it was perceived as such without **e** being related to **a** as a dominant, or **a** to **e** as a subdominant. A listener who has grown up in the tradition of major-minor tonality may find it difficult to discontinue hearing a sense of alignment in degree relationships, but to do so is not impossible.

If the fifth-relation and analogously the third-relation are understood as bilateral relations, then the sense emerges of a phenomenon that could be negatively—and inadequately—termed modal indeterminacy. The concept of the bilateral relation means that the fifth-relation establishes a connection between **e** and **a** that is independent of the dilemma of choosing whether **e** should be considered the *finalis* and **a** the *repercussa* or, conversely, **a** the *finalis* and **e** the *repercussa*. If, however, the meaning of the relation between **e** and **a** is unaffected by the uncertainty about the *finalis*, then the decision between **e** and a can be left open without jeopardizing the relationship's intelligibility. The bilateral relation is the primary factor, the establishment of a *finalis* the secondary factor.

The first four compositions from Palestrina's cycle of offertories[30] provide an example of modal indeterminacy. Offertories 5–8 are unmistakably in d-Dorian, 9–16 in e-Phrygian, 17–24 in f-Ionian ("Lydian"), and 25–32 in g-Mixolydian. From the arrangement of the cycle, based on the numerical scheme 8 + 8 + 8 + 8, it can be inferred that the mode of offertories 1–4 is meant to be d-Dorian. The actual mode, however, is a Dorian-Aeolian *"modus commixtus"*:[31] the final cadences have the chords d–A, E–A, d–A, and E–A; the *"species"* of the initial imitations are **a'–d"** | **d'–a'**, **a'–e"** | **d'–a'**, **a–e'** | **d–a**, and **a'–e"** | **d'–a'**. And if Glarean's theory of the modes had been elevated to the level of official doctrine, Palestrina could even have established **a** instead of **d** as the *finalis* without changing the meaning of these compositions in the least.

The essence of a Dorian-Aeolian *"modus commixtus"* is not the fluctuation, the "modulation," between Dorian and Aeolian but the "bipolar" relationship as a permanent state of affairs. The precondition for the feasibility of a double mode is, however, the understanding of the fifth-relation as a bilateral relation without the sense of a particular alignment.

This second interpretation of modal norms should be understood not as a contradiction of the first but as its complement and continuation. It only says that the factor of the fifth-relation is accentuated and raised to an independent status by the relationship between *finalis* and *repercussa*, and that this independence makes possible the phenomenon of the *"modus commixtus,"* a double mode in which a judgment for one or the other modal classification is of secondary importance. The derivation from the relation between *finalis* and *repercussa* is "set aside" in the modally ambiguous fifth-relation. But if this second interpretation is a description of a later stage of development, then there can be yet a third interpretation alongside the first two, an interpretation that tries to express through a formula the transition from the system of the modes to major-minor tonality.

3. The *repercussae* or *clausulae secundariae* of the four "old" modes— **a** in Dorian and Phrygian, **c** in Lydian and Mixolydian—are identical to the *finales* and *clausulae primariae* of both the "new" modes. Accordingly, **c** and **a**, the tonics of the later major and minor, are already found in the system of the modes as "primary points of attraction." And just as it would be wrong to draw the conclusion that Mixolydian and Phrygian are nothing but major and minor with irregular endings on their dominants, so it would be dogmatic to deny

the possibility that the "points of attraction" **c** and **a** gradually asserted themselves as "centers" through the mutual effects of the modes. Modes having a mutual effect on each other is one of the features that differentiates a polyphonic presentation of the modes from a monophonic one.[32] And the hypothesis that its result was, or could have been, the increased prominence of **c** and **a** — the very degrees on which the schemata of the different modes coincide — makes it possible to understand the transition to major-minor tonality as an internal development of polyphony. Of course the mutual effect of the modes was not the sole factor tending toward major-minor tonality, and the magnitude of its significance can only come to light in the analysis of individual works.[33]

   · · ·

The transition from description to prescription, from describing the modal dispositions of clausulas to deducing them from a given principle, was accomplished by Gioseffo Zarlino in 1558. Of course there are two faces to Zarlino's theory. On the one hand, the theory distorts many of the modal norms. On the other hand, though it shares with major-minor tonality the formal feature of being a system, it does not, as Riemann thought, share its content. Only its systematic character *per se* was important for the recognition of harmonically tonal cadence and key relationships. The actual content of Zarlino's theory was a hindrance preventing most 17th-century theorists from gaining insight into what was going on in musical practice.

According to Zarlino, the meaning of a work is determined not only by the form in which it is realized but also by the goal toward which it strives. When making a judgment of the mode, one must consider not only the *finalis*, the "goal" of a composition, but also its "form." And provided the "form" is unmistakable, no defect is implied if the composition ends on the fifth, the "*chorda mezana*," instead of the keynote, the "*chorda finale*." "If I had to make such a judgment, I would, as is reasonable, judge not simply from the final, as some have wanted to do, but from the entire form contained in the composition. Hence I say that if I should have to judge a composition by its form, that is, by the way it proceeds, as one ought, it would not be out of place if the principle mode should end on the mean tone of the harmonic division of its octave [= the fifth] and the same for the plagal mode ending on the extremes of the arithmetic division of its octave [= the same fifth], putting aside its final" [Giudicarei, che fusse ragionevole, che non dalla chorda finale semplicemente; come hanno voluto alcuni: ma dalla forma tutta contenuta nella cantilena, se havesse da fare tal giuditio. Onde dico, che se io havessi da giudicare alcuna cantilena da tal forma, cioè dal procedere, come è il dovere; non haverei per inconveniente, che il Modo principale potesse finire nella chorda mezana della sua Diapason harmonicamente tramezata; & cosi il Modo collaterale nelle estreme della sua Diapason arithmeticamente divisa; lassando da un canto la chorda finale].[34] (Siegfried Hermelink[35] reads "lassando ad un canto" [leaving to an upper voice] instead of "lassando da un canto" [putting aside]. And in his exegesis of the passage he states not that the *"chorda finale"* can be lacking but that it appears in the cantus instead of the tenor. Zarlino's term for the upper voice is, however, *"soprano,"* not *"canto."*)

Besides the ambitus of the voices,[36] the features of modal "form" are the initial tones—Hermelink's translation of *"principii"* as "main tones" is in error[37]—and the disposition of clausulas. In addition to the tonic and the fifth, Zarlino allows the third of the mode as one of the regular first tones. "And although the true and natural initial tones not only of this mode (the first mode) but also of every other mode are the outer tones of their fifth and fourth [=final and fifth] and the mean tone that divides the fifth into a major and a minor third [=the third], one still finds many compositions that have their initial tones on other degrees" [Et benche li veri, & naturali Principii, non solo di questo (the first mode), ma anche d'ogn' altro Modo, siano nelle chorde estreme della loro Diapente, & della Diatessaron; & nella chorda mezana, che divide la Diapente in un Ditono, & in un Semiditono; tuttavia se trovano molte cantilene, che hanno il loro principio sopra le altre chorde].[38] (For Pier Francesco Valentini, a theorist from the first half of the 17th century, allowing the third as an initial tone was "an artistic license for writing imitations and taking counterpoints" [licenza di fare le imitationi e pigliare in contrapunti].)[39]

Zarlino subjected the disposition of clausulas to a fixed schema, one based less on empirical evidence than on speculative theory. The hierarchy of degrees is the same in every mode: the proper position for a *clausula primaria* is on degree I, for a *clausula secundaria* degree V, and for a *clausula tertiaria* degree III. "Hence it will be sufficient to say here once and for all that the cadences are of two types, that is, regular and irregular. The regular ones are those that occur at the outer sounds or tones of the modes where each mode's octave is divided harmonically or arithmetically . . . similarly where the fifth is divided by a mean tone into a major and a minor third . . . These then are the regular cadences of the first mode, which occur on these tones: **d**, **f**, **a**, and **d'**" [La onde bastarà in questo luogo solamente dire hora per sempre; che le Cadenze se trovano di due sorti, cioè Regolari, & Irregolari. Le Regolari sono quelle, che sempre se fanno ne gli estremi suoni, o chorde delli Modi; & dove la Diapason in ciascun Modo harmonicamente, overo arithmeticamente è mediata, o divisa della chorda mezana . . . simigliantemente dove la Diapente è divisa da una chorda mezana in un Ditono, & in uno Semiditono . . . Sono adunque le Cadenze regolari del Primo modo quelle, che se fanno in queste chorde D, F, a, & d].[40]

It is obvious that the I–V–III schema distorts musical reality by suppressing the importance of degree IV in the Phrygian and Mixolydian modes. Just as obvious is the speculative relationship that in Zarlino's system combines the theory of initial tones and clausula degrees with the explanation of triad—with the method of constructing the chords c–e–g and d–f–a by the harmonic and arithmetic division of the fifth (15:12:10 and 6:5:4 [in string lengths]).[41] For Zarlino, the thought that the arrangement of cadences and the choice of initial tones were subject to the same principle as the structure of the triad seemed like an insight into the "natural system" of music—whatever falls outside this system is considered vulgar sensation devoid of intellectual relevance. The connection between the cadential degree schema and the deduction of triads does not mean that in Zarlino's system the explanation of chordal relationships was based on an analysis of chordal structures. Rather, it means that the relation between those degrees meant to occur at the end of periods comes under the same mathematical rule as the relation between the tones that form a triad. The principle of analogy operative in the practice of modal norms[42] is brought by Zarlino under a mathematical formula. Phenomena that evade interpretation by the formula are explained as incidental anomalies.

Of course Zarlino noticed and even emphasized the fact that the I–V–III clausula schema does not conform to the reality of the Phrygian and Mixolydian modes. But he understood this not as a refutation of his theory but as a deficiency and "impurity" in musical practice. The affinity of the Phrygian and Mixolydian modes for degree IV appeared to him as the sign of a "*mixtio modorum,*" of a supplanting of the authentic Phrygian octave (e–b–e′) by the plagal Aeolian octave (e–a–e′) or of the authentic Mixolydian (g–d′–g′) by the plagal Ionian (g–c′–g′). "First take note that even though one finds an almost infinite number of compositions in each of the demonstrated modes, nonetheless there are many of them that are composed not in their simple mode but in a mixed mode. For that reason we will find the third mode [authentic Phrygian] blended with the tenth [plagal Aeolian], and the eighth [plagal Mixolydian] with the eleventh [authentic Ionian]" [Primieramente se de avertire, che quantunque se ritrovino quasi infiniti le cantilene di ciascuno delli mostrati Modi; nondimeno molte di loro se trovano, le quali non sono composte ne i loro Modi semplici, ma nelli Misti: Imperoche retrovaremo il Terzo modo mescolato col Decimo, l'Ottavo con l'Undecimo].[43] (Zarlino contrasts **d–g–d′** with **c–g–c′** instead of **g–d′–g′** with **g–c′–g′**.) He thus distinguishes between that which is and that which, according to the mathematical nature of things, should have been—a difference that Hermelink failed to recognize.[44] Zarlino held a dogmatic opinion without being blind to musical reality.

Zarlino founded a tradition of clausula theory that extends down to Johann Gottfried Walther, who in his *Praecepta der Musicalischen Composition* of 1708 still repeats the thesis that the proper positions for the "*clausulae essentiales*" are on degrees I–III–V, in major as well as in minor.[45]

Giovanni Maria Artusi's explanation of the "*cadenze regolari*"[46] is quoted from Zarlino.[47]

Adriano Banchieri does mention the norms that underlay the disposition of clausulas in compositional practice—Dorian **d–a–f**, Phrygian **e–c–a**, Lydian **f–c–a**, Mixolydian **g–d–c**—but refers to them only as a rule for "*intuonationi*" [intonations: organ preludia].[48] His enumeration of cadential degrees is based on Zarlino's I–III–V schema: "Every mode has three cadences: the final, the indifferent, and the mean. Modes 1 and 2 have cadences on the notes D, F, and A. Modes 3 and 4 have cadences on the notes E, G, and B . . . " [Ogni tuono hà tre cadenze, finale, indifferente, & mezana. 1. & 2. tuoni hanno le cadenze negli tasti, D. F. & A. 3. & 4. tuoni hanno le cadenze negli tasti, E. G. B . . .].[49] Banchieri's terminology can be related to Zarlino's characterization of the tones of the triad. Zarlino names "*chorda mezana*" [mean tone] not only the fifth resulting from the division of the octave but also the third resulting from the division of the fifth. But in his terminology, "indifferent" refers to the fifth. The "indifferent," unchanging fifths contrast with the "different" thirds, which have a different arrangement in major than in minor. "The outer tones of the fifth are invariable . . . but the outer tones of the thirds are placed differently between this fifth" [Gli estremi della Quinta sono invariabili . . . però gli estremi delle Terze si pongono differenti tra essa Quinta].[50]

In his *Duplitonio*,[51] Pier Francesco Valentini adopted Zarlino's I–V–III schema but modified it by a detour through his construction of twenty-four instead of twelve modes. Valentini's theory of the modes is based on the idea that the concept of the plagal mode must be separated from that of the arithmetically divided octave. "Plagal" is the registral exchange of fifth and fourth, the inversion of **d–a / a–d′** to **A–d / d–a**. But an arithmetic division intended to pass for Dorian must be based on the Dorian octave **d–d′**, not on the Hypodorian octave

A–a. Thus four, instead of two, modes should be based on the keynote d: (1) a "harmonic-authentic" mode with the harmonically divided Dorian octave in an authentic register (d–a–d′); (2) a "harmonic-plagal" mode with the harmonically divided Dorian octave in a plagal register (A–d–a); (3) an "arithmetic-authentic" mode with the arithmetically divided Dorian octave in an authentic register (d–g–d′); and (4) an "arithmetic-plagal" mode with the arithmetically divided Dorian octave in a plagal register (G–d–g). Valentini's construction of the "arithmetic" modes[52] is not as absurd as it seems to be. On the one hand, it can be based on the observation that in initial imitations the main mode is often linked with the mode a fifth below. And on the other hand, Valentini's splitting of the modes—an admittedly complicated but still not aimless detour—does justice to the fact that in compositional practice the *clausula secundaria* of the Phrygian and Mixolydian modes is degree IV, not degree V. Valentini reckons degrees I, IV, and III as the "*cadenze regolari*" [regular cadences] of an "arithmetic" mode and supplements them with degree VI as a "*cadenza aggiunta*" [adjunct cadence].[53] The result of Zarlino's schema of cadential degrees and Valentini's *idée fixe* of splitting the modes is thus the actual Phrygian disposition of cadences—e–a–c–g.

The first German theorist to adopt Zarlino's I–V–III schema was Seth Calvisius. It is with him that the terms "*clausula primaria*," "*secundaria*," and "*tertiaria*" appear to originate. "They form the clausulas of the mode of this same name . . . the primary clausula on the mode's final, which is the lowest note in the fifth of this mode . . . the secondary clausula, on the other hand, on its harmonic mean [= the fifth], which is the highest note in the fifth; and the tertiary clausula is formed on the mean of the lesser principal tone [= the third], namely the mean of the fifth, which can be divided both harmonically and arithmetically" [Clausulas autem formant eiusdem nominis Modi . . . Primariam in ipsa Clave finali, quae est infima in diapente eius Modi . . . Secundariam vero, in ipsa medietate Harmonica, quae est suprema Clavis in diapente; et tertiam in medietate minus principali, intervalli scilicet diapente, quod et Harmonice et Arithmetice dividi potest].[54] Johann Lippius has a more laconic formulation: "The primary fugue and clausula is on the prime tone of the proper triad, the secondary on the highest tone [= fifth], and the tertiary on the middle tone [= third]" [Primaria Fuga et Clausula est a Prima Triadis Propriae: Secundaria a Suprema: Tertiaria a Media].[55]

Joachim Burmeister confuses the terms. He labels the fifth degree, the old "*affinalis*" or "*confinalis*," the "*minus principalis*" [lesser principal tone] and the third degree, Calvisius's "*medietas minus principalis*" [mean of the lesser principal tone], the "*affinalis*." (The *"medietas principalis"* is the division of the octave by the fifth, the *"medietas minus principalis"* the division of the fifth by the third.) "1. The main tone occurs when a rest from motion is made by the introduction of a clausula whose third part, properly called the final, is given by the lowest tone of the tenor octave in the principal mode. 2. The lesser principal tone is taken on the emmesepistrophic tone [= the fifth]. 3. The *affinalis* is made on the tone called emmeles [= the third]" [1. Principalis est, quando quies a modulando fit introductione Clausulae, cuius tertia pars, proprie Finis dicta, in Modi Principio, Tenoris Diapason infimo sono, datur. 2. Minus principalis est, qui a sono Emmesepistropho excipitur. 3. Affinalis, qui fit in sono, qui Emmeles dicitur].[56] (By the terms *"sonus emmesepistropho"* and *"emmeles"* he means, respectively, the quality of the fifth as the middle of the octave and that of the third as a mode's characteristic melodic degree.) Christoph Bernhard corrected Burmeister's reversal of word meanings: degree V is defined as the *"confinalis principalis"* [principal confinal], degree III as the *"confinalis minus principalis"* [lesser principal confinal].[57]

Those late 16th- and 17th-century treatises that give a disposition of clausulas differing from Zarlino's I–V–III schema must be considered from diverse and even antithetical points of view. Their divergence can be based on modal or tonal considerations, that is, on an appeal to the norms of 16th-century practice or on observations that asserted themselves in connection with the transition to major-minor tonality. And it is sometimes difficult to draw clear lines between them.

The dispositions of cadences in the Dorian and Aeolian modes are historically neutral. One cannot detect in them the change of systems, the transition from modality to major-minor tonality. As far as the d- and a-modes are concerned, Zarlino's I–V–III schema coincides not only with the norms of 16th-century practice—with the principle that the authentic *repercussa* becomes the *clausula secundaria* and the plagal *repercussa* becomes the *clausula tertiaria*—but also with the key relationships in the minor mode of tonal harmony. In those 17th- and 18th-century works whose harmonically tonal character cannot be doubted, the primary disposition of keys in minor is T–Tp–D–T, not T–S–D–T. In minor, unlike major, the arrangement of keys is not an image of the cadence.[58]

Similarly neutral is the Mixolydian mode. In 1597, Thomas Morley mentions that the g-mode is connected to the c- and d-modes by a natural affinity: "And though the ayre of everie key be different one from the other, yet some love (by a wonder of nature) to be joined to others so that if you begin your song in Gam ut, you may conclude it either in C fa ut or D sol re, and from thence come againe to Gam ut."[59] It would be a mistake to conclude from this comment that Morley had a functional conception of key relations. The disposition I–IV–V–I is not only characteristic of the key of G major but was already characteristic of the g-mode in the 16th century. Presumably Morley's divergence from the I–V–III schema should be understood as a revision of Zarlino's speculatively based dogma by an empirical observer of modal practice and not as an expression of a harmonically tonal sensibility. Only the generalization of the I–IV–V schema from a feature of the g-mode to a norm of the f-and c-modes as well, a subject which Morley does not discuss, would qualify as an unambiguous sign of the transition to major-minor tonality.

Angelo Berardi, alongside Bononcini the most important Italian theorist of the late 17th century, gives thirty-six examples in his *Il Perchè musicale ovvero staffetta armonica* of the "harmonic clausulas of the twelve keys that give the *repercussae* and measures of the modes at the beginning, middle, and end according to their nature" [Clausule Armoniche delli 12. Tuoni, che danno le ripercussioni, e misure de' modi nel Principio, Mezzo e Fine secondo la loro natura].[60] Berardi classifies the cadences according to their position in the overall form: the *clausula secundaria* occurs at the beginning, the *tertiaria* in the middle, and the *primaria* at the end. Transferring the *clausula primaria* to the initial position results in the table below.

d-Dorian:	authentic & plagal	d	a	f	=	I	V	III
e-Phrygian:	authentic	a	g	a	=	IV	III	IV
	plagal	e	g	b	=	I	III	V
f-Lydian:	authentic & plagal	f	c	a	=	I	V	III
g-Mixolydian:	authentic	g	d	e	=	I	V	VI
	plagal	g	d	c	=	I	V	IV
a-Aeolian:	authentic & plagal	a	e	c	=	I	V	III
c-Ionian:	authentic	c	g	a	=	I	V	VI
	plagal	c	g	e	=	I	V	III

Zarlino's norm is valid for the "indifferent" minor modes, Dorian and Aeolian. Among the major modes, it is valid for Lydian, which had become an archaism, but also for the plagal Ionian, which had not. The fact that in the authentic Phrygian and plagal Mixolydian modes Berardi locates the *clausula tertiaria* on degree IV conforms to 16th-century modal practice. But it is noteworthy that in the authentic Phrygian mode the *clausula primaria*, as well as the *tertiaria*, occurs on the a-degree instead of the e-degree. Provided the deviation from the accustomed degree is not to be understood as a *"differenza"* in Aaron's sense[61] but as a reinterpretation of the Phrygian mode as a secondary key within the Aeolian mode, it then supports the hypothesis that the consolidation of the modal "points of attraction" **a** and **c** into tonal centers was one of the factors that facilitated the transition from the system of modes to major-minor tonality.

In establishing degree VI as the *clausula tertiaria* of the authentic Mixolydian and Ionian modes, Berardi diverges not only from Zarlino's speculative norm but also from the norms of 16th-century practice. One might conjecture that he had observed the relative minor in harmonically tonal compositions to be a more closely related key than the mediant. But one can find little or no trace of a harmonically tonal foundation in the examples that set forth degree VI through the plagal cadences a–E in g-Mixolydian and d–a in c-Ionian.

While the clausula theory that Lorenzo Penna develops in the third book of his *Primi Albori Musicali*[62] is two decades older than Berardi's table, it nonetheless represents, even if in a confused form, a later stage in the development of a tonal consciousness. Penna counts only eight instead of twelve modes. He deduces the authentic modes from the harmonic division of the octave (Dorian **d–a–d′**) and the plagal modes from the arithmetic division (Hypodorian **A–d–a** = **d–g–d′** in the ♭-system). Since he bases the arithmetic division on the same octave as the harmonic division, the plagal modes appear transposed a fourth above, thus in the ♭-system. To be sure, d-Dorian and g-Hypodorian are the only modes that Penna constructs in a regular fashion without mistakes or modifications. In connection with the arithmetic division of the octave **e–e′**, the transposition sign ♭ is left out: thus the mode meant to be plagal a-Phrygian is plagal a-Aeolian. Penna bases the fifth and sixth modes on the octave **c–c′** instead of **f–f′**. This octave is harmonically divided into what is really an authentic c-Ionian (**c–g–c′**) and arithmetically divided into what is really a plagal f–Ionian (**c–f–c′** in the ♭-system). Thus the "new" modes, which Penna seemingly denies by hanging on to the eight-mode system, work their way into his modal theory through a circuitous route, that of transforming the plagal Phrygian into the plagal Aeolian and the Lydian into the Ionian. And Penna's recasting of the old modes comes closer to major-minor tonality than does Glarean's adding to them.

Penna's construction of the Mixolydian mode can scarcely be untangled. First, he bases the seventh and eighth modes on the octave **d–d′** instead of **g–g′**. Second, instead of dividing it harmonically and arithmetically, he divides it twice arithmetically (**d–g–d′**), first in the ♭-system and then in the ♮-system. And third, as the *finalis* of the octave **d–g–d′** in the ♭-system, he stipulates **d**, not **g**. His seventh mode is thus

Valentini's "arithmetic-authentic" Aeolian mode, his eighth the regular
g-Hypomixolydian.

mode 7

Qui la Cadenza di C sol fa ut è per Accidente

mode 8

Qui la Cadenza di C sol fa ut è per Accidente

Example 67

The basis for these contradictions seems to be a contrast between modal
dogma and harmonically tonal practical experience. And while Penna
perceived the contrast, he failed to fully grasp it, so that he sought
an accommodation where clear distinctions were needed. The result
is confusion.

The transition to major-minor tonality is accomplished in Penna's
disposition of the cadences:

d-Dorian:	d	a	f	=	I V III
g-Dorian	g	d	b♭	=	I V III
e-Phrygian	e	b	a	=	I V IV
a-Aeolian	a	e	c	=	I V III
c-Ionian	c	g	f	=	I V IV
f-Ionian	f	c	b♭	=	I V IV
d-"Aeolian"	d	g	c	=	I IV VII
g-Mixolydian	g	d	c	=	I V IV

The minor modes d-Dorian, g-Dorian, and a-Aeolian follow the I–V–III
schema, the major modes c-Ionian, f-Ionian, and g-Mixolydian the
I–V–IV schema. The reinterpretation of the modal *finales* and *repercussae* as the tonal functions T–D–Tp in minor and T–D–S in major
is obvious and unmistakable.

BETWEEN MODALITY AND MAJOR-MINOR TONALITY

The diatonic system is the embodiment of all the modes. And, as a result of the modes' mutual effects in polyphonic contexts, it can emerge as the dominant factor, the factor with the primary role in determining the overall musical impression. The modal characters of the Dorian, Phrygian, and Ionian species of fifths and fourths do not become completely effaced by their joint encounters within the narrow ambitus of a polyphonic composition. Nevertheless, the constant intertwining and crossing of different melodic modes results in a network of interrelationships that assists the diatonic, the comprehensive system, in achieving precedence over the individual modes. Thus the position in the scale, not the position in the mode, becomes the primary factor in defining a tonal degree.

In order to cling to the characterization or classification of mode as the sole principle of interpretation, both Tinctoris and Glarean insist on a separation of the voices. The separation, however, is a fiction. In musical reality, counterpoint is the interrelationship of the voices, not their complete independence. And the mutual effect of the voices does not leave untouched the modal characters of the species of fifths and fourths. The interrelationship can be experienced either as a contrast to, or as a neutralization of, the melodically characterized modes. A contrast, if it is not to shrivel to pure unconnectedness, presumes a consciousness of a factor common to the contrasting modes: the diatonic system. And a neutralization leaves this same diatonic system as the sole feature remaining to define a tonal degree.

Jacques Handschin's thesis that the diatonic system, the circle of fifths from **f** to **b**, is fundamental[1] and logically prior to any particular mode, accordingly gains relevance in connection with modal polyphony. The interrelationship of the modes removes, as it were, the definition of the diatonic system as "substructure" from the thin air of abstraction and transfers it to musical reality. But of course the "emancipation" of the diatonic system to an existence and effect not bound to a modal Gestalt is a "second-stage sense of direct relationship" [*zweite Unmittelbarkeit*], not the first stage as Handschin made it appear.

.   .   .

It seems, of course, that at the very moment the diatonic system achieved precedence over the modes it was once again suppressed. In polyphony, the positions of the tones in the scale are modified or even neutralized by the various sonorities, just as the modal characters of the species of fifths and fourths are modified or neutralized by the mutual effects of the voices. The fifth in **g–b–d′** is a "different" **d′** than the bass tone of **d′–f′–a′**.

The position of an individual tone in the scale is "suppressed"— preserved and at the same time altered—by its position within a particular sonority. It would be a mistake, however, to transfer the chord theory of the 17th and 18th centuries to modal polyphony and to presume that six-three chords are inversions of five-three chords.

Rameau's concept of chordal inversion includes three factors that must be kept separate if the differences between tonal harmony and the chordal technique of the 16th century are to become clear: (1) octave equivalence; (2) the establishment of the lower tone of the third and fifth—thus the upper tone of the sixth and fourth—as a "*centre harmonique*"; and (3) the identification of the character of the six-three chord (**f–a–d′**) with that of the root-position chord (**d–f–a**).

1. Octave equivalence, the idea that the sonority **e–g–c′** consists of the "same" tones as **c–e–g**, was never in doubt. But it does not imply a precedence of the five-three over the six-three chord. In the 16th century, just as in the period of tonal harmony, the clausulas

and were taken to be equivalent. But

d′–f′–b′ was not conceived as an "inversion" of **b–d′–f′**. Rather, **b–d′–f′** was conceived as a variant of the basic form **d′–f′–b′**, as a variant resulting from the displacement of the soprano formula **c″–b′–c″** to the lower voice.

2. The principle of octave equivalence is negated by Zarlino's characterization of sonorities, that is, marking the major triad as "*allegro*" [gay] and the minor triad as "*mesto*"[2] [sad]. This characterization is not an unsupported assertion but rests on a psychological interpretation of the "*regola delle terze e seste*" [the rule of thirds and sixths], the norm that a major third or sixth resolves to a fifth or an octave by "expansion" (or) and a minor third or sixth resolves to a unison or fifth by "contraction" (or). "Hence the larger imperfect consonances want to become still larger, while the smaller ones have the opposite nature. That is, the major third and major sixth want to make themselves larger, the one going to the fifth and the other to the octave; and the minor third and minor sixth love to make themselves smaller, the one going toward the unison and the other toward the fifth" [Onde le imperfette maggiori desiderano di farse maggiori; & le minori hanno natura contraria:

conciosia che il Ditono, et lo Essachordo maggiore desiderano di farsi maggiori, venendo l'uno alla Quinta, & l'altro alla Ottava; & il Semiditono, & lo Essachordo minore amano di farsi minori, venendo l'uno verso l'Unisono, & l'altro verso la Quinta].[3] According to the physiological theory of "animal spirits" [*Lebensgeister*], the distinction between the "lively" and the "lifeless" impression produced by the intervals is based on the contrast between "expansion" and "contraction." "The property or nature of imperfect consonances is that some of them are lively and gay, accompanied by great sonority, while others, however sweet and mild they may be, tend a little toward the sad or languid. The former are the major thirds and sixths and their octave duplications; the latter are the minor thirds and sixths" [Il proprio, o Natura delle Consonanze imperfette è, che alcune di loro sono vive & allegre, accompagnate da molta sonorità; & alcune, quantunque siano dolci, & soavi, declinano alquanto al mesto, overo languido. Le prime sono le Terze, & le Seste maggiori, & le replicate; & le altre sono le minori].[4]

If taken literally, Zarlino's characterization of sonorities excludes the idea of chordal inversion. In addition to the major triad **c–e–g**, it is the "minor six-three chord" **c–e–a** composed of a major third and a major sixth, not the "major six-three chord" **e–g–c'**, that is considered "*allegro*." The displacement of the bass tone to the upper voice thus brings about a reversal in a triad's character: **e–g–c'** is "*mollar*" and "*mesto*" just like **e–g–b**, not "*dural*" and "*allegro*" like **c–e–g**.

3. There seems to be an irreducible contradiction between Zarlino's characterization of sonorities and the principle of octave equivalence. Yet the attempt at a reconciliation is neither superfluous nor futile.

As sonorities, the intervals differ in their degree of "stability" or "instability," a factor independent of the stylistic difference between modal counterpoint and tonal harmony. A minor third has a more "unstable" effect than a major third, and the lower tone is a weaker root in the minor third than in the major third. The precedence of the bass tone, undisputed in the major triad, in the minor triad is exposed to the competition of the middle tone, the "root" of the major third. But the fact that the third of the minor triad appears as a "second root" is not without some bearing on the meaning of the six-three chord: the minor six-three chord is an inversion of the root-position chord to a lesser degree than is the major six-three chord.

While the differentiation is unmistakable as a phenomenon in tonal harmony, it is irrelevant for the "harmonic logic." One can ignore the fact that the six-three chord **f–a–d'** is not a completely equivalent variant of the root-position chord **d–f–a** because the difference has no effect on the six-three chord fulfilling the same function as the root-position chord. But if instead of the "function" one is to establish the simple "position" of the sonority in the scale, then an essential significance devolves on the distinction between independent and dependent six-three chords. As the "primary" tone that determines the position of a six-three chord in the scale, it is more the highest tone in the six-three chord with minor third and sixth, and more the lowest tone in the six-three chord with major third and sixth. For **e–g–c′**, the similarity with **c–e–g** (not **e–g–b**) is the more pronounced, for **f–a–d′**, the similarity with **f–a–c′** (not **d–f–a**).

If one groups sonorities as "stable" and "unstable," then the possibility presents itself of a reconciliation between Zarlino's characterization and the principle of octave equivalence: the equivalence of **e–g–c′** and **c–e–g** accords with the principle of octave equivalence, the analogy between **f–a–d′** and **f–a–c′** with Zarlino's schema.

4. The hypothesis that the tone perceived as "primary" was the lowest tone in the six-three chord **f–a–d′** but the highest tone in **e–g–c′** corresponds to 16th-century practice concerning chromatic alterations. Flatting a tone was considered an "essential" alteration, an operation changing the scale, while sharping a tone was considered an "accidental" alteration, an incidental, transient modification. But over a flatted degree in the bass the sixth is major (**B♭–g**), over a sharped degree minor (**f♯–d′**). And the "stability" of the **B♭** matches the independence of the major sixth, the "instability" of the **f♯** the dependence of the minor sixth. The fifth can be substituted for the sixth over **B♭** but not for the sixth over **f♯**. And from the fact that **f♯** was employed as the third of a five-three chord (**d–f♯–a**) and the bass of a six-three chord (**f♯–a–d′**) but not as the bass or fifth of a five-three chord (**f♯–a–c♯′** or **B–d–f♯**), one can conclude that **f♯–a–d′** was conceived not as a variant of **f♯–a–c♯′** but as an equivalent of **d–f♯–a**. **B♭–d–g** is primarily an analogue of **B♭–d–f** (and not of **G–B♭–d**); **f♯–a–d′**, on the other hand, is primarily an analogue of **d–f♯–a** (and not of **f♯–a–c♯′**).

5. If one attempts to sketch out a symbol system that does justice to 16th-century chordal technique, then the practice of designating major triads with upper-case letters and minor triads with lower-case letters must be supplemented with additional symbols. From the stock symbols of figured-bass practice one can adopt the method of expressing the incidental character of chromatic alterations by sharps or flats preceding numbers—thus symbolizing an a-clausula with raised third as a$^{\sharp 3}$ and not as A. But the use of numbers for six-three chords is ambiguous. From a thoroughbass perspective the symbol e^6 means the chord **e–g–c′**, but from the point of view of functional harmony it means **g–b–e′**. To avoid confusion, one could designate sixths with letters and indicate which tone is "primary" by their order. F^d would then be the symbol for the sixth-three chord **f–a–d′** with **f** as the primary tone, C$_e$

the symbol for **e–g–c′** with **c′** as the primary tone. The change between superscript and subscript letters could express the "inversion" of sonorities: **d–f–b** would be symbolized as d^b, **b–d′–f′** (with **d′** as the primary tone) as d_b.

. . .

Any attempt to formulate the concept of the chordal scale degree in such a way as to avoid a contradiction with the hypotheses of "intervallic composition" would remain fragmentary without a description of the context into which the degrees fit. Corresponding with a modified concept of degrees there must be a conception of a system of degrees that diverges from major-minor tonality.

1. To appear as part of a context, a degree can be defined either by its relation to a center or by its position in a closed system. The two possibilities should not be understood as mutually exclusive alternatives. The fact that the chords in a major or minor key are defined by their relationships to the tonic does not exclude a key's set of chords from being limited to the system of diatonic scale degrees—the theory of functions emphasizes the relation to a center, the theory of fundamental progressions the limitation by the diatonic system.

Of course these features coexist with unequal claims to validity. In major-minor tonality the relationship with the tonic chord is unquestionably the primary factor. Even so simple a situation as the "tonicization" of secondary degrees by secondary dominants preceding the tonic and subdominant parallels is already scarcely intelligible under the assumptions of degree theory. The symbols III$^{\sharp 3}$–vi and VI$^{\sharp 3}$–ii are inadequate because they generally ascribe to the secondary dominants a chromatic-accidental character that they have only in rare instances. And the formulas (V) vi and (V) ii [V/vi and V/ii] imply a concession to functions theory. The "V" is not meant as the degree of a transposed scale but as a symbol of dominant function.

If the relation to a center is accordingly the primary criterion of defining a chord in major-minor tonality and the position in the system is secondary, then the reverse is true for broad stretches of 16th-century chordal technique. To borrow Handschin's phrase, the diatonic degrees form a "closed society" in which each sonority is unambiguously defined by its position. The fa-degree stands in sharp contrast to the mi-degree. And the various sonorities are unmistakably set off from each other by the dissimilarity in their relationships to the system's extremes—the fa-degree and the mi-degree.

The unambiguous nature of the positions is not endangered by chromatic alterations. As soon as the mi- and fa-degrees are established, an alteration can be recognized as merely an incidental occurrence. In the progression F^d–$e^{\sharp 3}$–$a^{\sharp 3}$–$d^{\sharp 3}$–G, the Phrygian cadence is sufficient to make possible, in spite of the accumulation of accidentals, a clear differentiation between diatonic and chromatic tones.

2. In major-minor tonality, it is not only difficult but inadequate to separate the idea of a system of degrees from the idea of a key. A series of chords in the scale with b♭ becomes, as it were, diminished in its musical reality if it is uncertain whether F major or D minor is intended as the key. Yet for our consciousness of the music, even the least tendency toward a determination of the key is sufficient to lift the state of indeterminacy.

Objections seem to suggest themselves. To maintain that while indeterminacy is an exception, its existence and musical right to exist are nonetheless indisputable, one could refer to the method of modulating through common or "neutral"[5] chords. Yet the concept of "neutral" chords is itself questionable. Chords that intervene between two keys to the extent that they can be classed with both the preceding one and the following one are more doubly determined than undetermined.

If a system of degrees in major-minor tonality is thus principally a system of degrees within a key, then the compositional technique of the 16th century, as will be demonstrated in greater detail in analyses of individual works, leads to a separation of these categories. A progression like G–F–$a^{\sharp 3}$ can be defined neither in terms of harmonic tonality nor in terms of a mode. In a harmonically tonal context, since it characterizes no key, it would scarcely be intelligible—a blind spot. In a 16th-century work, on the other hand, it makes sense even without a modal characterization because the positions in the scale are sufficient to make a determination of the sonorities and to give them musical significance. Of course the determination is incomplete: the progression can be understood as G–F–$a^{\sharp 3}$ in the ♮-system, but also as $g^{\sharp 3}$–F–$a^{\sharp 3}$ in the ♭-system. The fact that the ♮-system is intended only becomes established when, in addition to the fa-degree, the mi-degree presents itself.

3. Since a modal characterization is often lacking, the determination by the diatonic system appears as the fundamental factor of 16th-century chordal technique. The fact that defining the mode can be omitted without invalidating the sense of the music does not mean that mode is a matter of indifference. Sonorities are often doubly determined. And the degree to which the location of a sonority as a modal degree permeates its position as a degree within the diatonic system can be determined only on a case-by-case basis.

4. Tonal harmony is "dynamic." A tension exists between chords with

subdominant and dominant function, a tension that presses toward resolution in the tonic. This tension can be more clearly expressed with dissonances—the sixth above the subdominant triad and the seventh above the dominant triad—but it is not based on them.

Apart from sporadic cases, 16th-century music lacks the functional tensions that constitute the essence of tonal harmony. A progression like G–F , whose structural framework is the interval progression 10–12 ( ), can stand on its own without requiring a continuation or having the effect of a musical non sequitur. This does not mean that 16th-century chordal technique was "devoid of tension." As an imperfect consonance, the major sixth (**f–d′**) strove for "perfection" through resolution in the octave (**e–e′**). But the factor of unrest was perceived exclusively in individual imperfect sonorities, not in the relation between chords. The Phrygian clausula F^d–e$\sharp^3$ formed a self-contained progression, not a fragment of an A-minor cadence.

5. The fact that tonal harmony is "dynamic" signifies both that there are functional tensions between chords and that the meaning of a chordal degree depends on a context. This implies that the meaning of a degree is not fixed but can change even without "modulating." Not only degrees iii and vi, which function in major either as parallels of the dominant and tonic or as *"Leittonwechselklänge"* of the tonic and subdominant, but also degrees ii and I are equivocal. In the chord progression I–ii–V–I, degree ii changes from the function of the subdominant parallel to that of the dominant-of-the-dominant. And at the beginning of the I–IV–V–I cadence, degree I changes from the function of the tonic to that of the dominant-of-the-subdominant. Functions are not tied to degrees and degrees are not tied to functions, a circumstance concealed by the custom of using functional symbols to indicate degrees.

The notion of an ambivalence of meanings and of a dialectical relationship between degree and function seems to have been foreign to the 16th century. In intervallic composition, the sonorities are defined as positions whose meaning is independent from the sequence in which they appear. In C major, the e-minor chord in the progression C–e–G is more the *"Leittonwechselklang"* of the tonic and in the reverse progression G–e–C more the "parallel" of the dominant. But in c-Ionian, it is a mi- or la-degree—yet incompletely determined. And an occurrence of the fa-degree is sufficient for its complete determination as a mi-degree. The larger context in which the e-minor sonority appears is irrelevant.

6. In the 16th century, it is uncertain whether an incomplete determination was perceived as tension. The procedure of putting off the

mi- or fa-degree to hold the exact meaning of sonorities in suspension would bring a "dynamic" factor to 16th-century chordal technique that could make up for its lack of functional tensions. But it is difficult to determine, without being arbitrary, whether the interpretation of incomplete determination as a "dynamic" factor is reading too much into it, or whether the opposite interpretation as passivity devoid of tension is too superficial.

7. In the 16th century, as mentioned, the fifth-relation was understood as a bilateral relationship that implied no subordination of the one degree by the other. The fifth establishes a close relationship between **d** and **a** without **a** being understood as the dominant of **d** or **d** as the subdominant of **a.**

Similarly bilateral is the effect of the "third-relation," the relation between the C-major and e-minor sonorities. But one should not fail to recognize that the "third-relation," the linking of sonorities by two common tones, differs in essential respects from the fifth-relation based on the principle of consonance. The fifth-relation is "logically" based, the "third-relation" more "materially" based. And if one designates the fifth-relation as a "relationship," then the relation between sonorities a third apart should be defined as a "partial congruence" since the deciding factor is not the interval of a third but the common tones.

In major-minor tonality, "partial congruence" is a secondary feature. The functional analogy between the C-major and a-minor chords, or F-major and d-minor chords, while it is certainly connected with the fact that parallel chords have two tones in common, is not primarily based on it. The attempt to deduce the functions from "material" factors would be misplaced and would become entangled in contradictions. (In major, degrees ii and vii form a functional contrast, even though they have two tones in common.)

On the other hand, in 16th-century compositional technique the number of common tones does appear as a primary factor in defining the relationship between sonorities. There is a contrast between the C-major and d-minor sonorities, but a close relationship of "partial congruence" between the C-major and e-minor sonorities.

The relations between 16th-century sonorities are effective only (or almost only) directly, not indirectly. In tonal harmony the contrast between chords without a common tone is "dynamic"—it induces further consequences. In the I–ii–V–I cadence there is a tension between I and ii that is resolved by V. By comparison, in 16th-century chordal technique the contrast between sonorities without a common tone appears as a self-contained event. The progression G–F does not need to be followed by anything, and F^d–$e^{\sharp 3}$ is a cadence.

8. A contradiction undeniably exists between the thesis that the

chordal degrees formed a closed system in the 16th century and the admission that the system, the diatonic system, allowed for an expansion through the b♭-degree. The contradiction is, however, not irresolvable.

The closure of the system is the correlate of the immutability of the degrees. The system's closure is the precondition for the degrees' immutability and vice versa. Provided that **e** and **f** establish themselves as the mi- and fa-degrees of the ♮-system, then the d-sonority, even with raised third, is unequivocally determined as the re-degree. But if the degrees are set out unmistakably, then it is possible to insert a b♭-degree that expands the system without endangering the degrees' unequivocal status. The practice of placing a Phrygian-like cadence on the a-degree, without the lowering of **b** to **b♭** affecting the overall context, only admits of one explanation: that the a-sonority, in spite of the b♭, represents the la-degree and does not change into the mi-degree of the ♭-system.

The appearance of a contradiction between the closure of the system of degrees and the possibility of an expansion thus vanishes if one takes into consideration the course of time—what came earlier and what comes later. The closure on which is based the immutability of the degrees is a starting principle.

9. In the 16th century, composition with chordal degrees was subject to a peculiar dialectic. The idea of understanding the degrees as a "closed society" in which sonorities are defined by their positions sufficed to establish a "harmony" that was insignificant in comparison with counterpoint. The system of six interrelated degrees fulfilled its function as long as it formed the background for polyphonic techniques and thus remained a simple foil of which one did not need to be conscious to experience its effect in the impression of "closure." But if chordal technique is elevated to the ruling principle of composition, then the system of degrees proves to be narrow and rather meagre, almost as though there is an externalization of an implication that the system itself cannot support. Willaert's procedure of combining all the degrees in close proximity without repeating any of them appears as an explicit representation of the closed system. The same period, however, saw the rise of the chromatic harmony that Edward E. Lowinsky has described as "triadic atonality."[6]

· · ·

The thesis that scale degrees in 16th-century chordal technique were understood primarily as degrees in a diatonic system and only secondarily as degrees in a mode must, to avoid any misunderstanding, be defined more precisely.

1. The precedence of the system over the mode is evident in the fact that works without a mode—Pietro Aaron named them "*canti euphoniaci*" [consonant songs][7]—could still make sense. The determination of the mode could be uncertain or even entirely omitted without endangering the significance of the simultaneities, a significance based on the positions within the system.

2. The mere fact that the mode of a polyphonic composition is not presented by the disposition of sonorities does not prove that a mode is lacking. In modal polyphony, the modes are primarily characterized by the schemata for imitative entries and the species of fourths and fifths that form the general melodic framework—the independence of the sonorities from the mode is matched by an independence of the mode from the sonorities. And however strange the idea may seem that a nonmodal chordal technique can coincide with a nonchordal presentation of a mode, it is nevertheless unavoidable.

3. One could object that the clausula degree—thus a factor of chordal technique—also belongs among a mode's defining features in company with the ambitus and the schema for imitations. But the modal clausula, in contrast to the tonal cadence, is not the result of a harmonic progression. To be sure, the mode can be detected from the clausula, but the clausula forms neither the center around which the sonorities group themselves nor the goal toward which they strive. The clausula is used much like a "sign" of the mode, without the mode being the principle that governs the disposition of the other sonorities. In modal polyphony, unlike tonal harmony, it is seldom possible to predict on which clausula degree a series of sonorities will end.

4. The fact that the type of harmonic progressions which would result in a particular clausula fail to appear, or appear only in rudimentary form, does not of course rule out a mode's primary degrees—the "*clausula primaria*" and "*secundaria*"—from being clearly prominent, even if only through the sheer preponderance of their occurring more than other sonorities. Yet it is precisely in the "homophonic" compositions of the 16th century that one can observe a tendency toward a uniform and thus modally neutral utilization of degrees[8]—a precedence of the principle of *varietas* over the presentation of the mode.

. . .

In the 16th century, the effect of the idea that six or seven degrees form a "closed society" and need not be related to a single center to establish a musical context was not limited to the narrow sphere of the disposition of individual sonorities. In a large number of works this same idea underlies more remote and indirect relationships as well, the relations between the clausula degrees. The clausula dispositions I–IV–III in Phrygian or I–IV–V in Mixolydian are "*indifferente*" [indifferent] to the "characteristic" dispositions such as I–V–III in Dorian, and allow for neither a modal nor a harmonically tonal interpretation. But the indeterminacy is not a defect. Instead, it means that clausula degrees, just like chordal degrees, form a system primarily of simple interrelationships that instead of being based on a tonic chord are, as it were, self-supporting.

1. Just because a disposition of clausulas is not modal does not mean that it has to be harmonically tonal. The notion that modality and major-minor tonality form a dichotomy that excludes all other possibilities is erroneous. A false conclusion is reached when Franklin B. Zimmerman supposes that "an advanced tonal design" can be detected in William Byrd's "cadential arrangements" because they are irregular according to the criteria of modal theory.[9]

The coordinate, as opposed to subordinate, relationship of degrees is one of the features by which "*indifferente*" dispositions of clausulas differ not only from modal but also from harmonically tonal dispositions. If one compares the c-Ionian and g-Mixolydian compositions in Byrd's *Psalms, Sonnets and Songs* of 1588,[10] it is evident that without exception they employ the same clausula degrees: **c**, **g**, **d**, and **a**.

A modal interpretation is out of the question. An attempt to distinguish the "proper" from the "improper" clausulas according to the letter of modal theory, thus to define the d-clausula in the g-mode as a "*clausula propria*" and the same clausula in the c-mode as a "*clausula impropria*," can find no justification. In Byrd's c-mode, the d-clausula does not appear where the text speaks of mistakes and troubles, nor does the disposition of the clausulas allow one to conclude that Byrd perceived those clausulas which modal theory would classify as "*impropriae*" as deviations toward what is exceptional and remote. In his c-mode, the d-clausula stands with equal rank alongside the c- and g-clausulas.

No less misplaced would be a harmonically tonal interpretation. It would have the absurd consequence of suggesting that Byrd submitted to the rule of modulating, when in "C major," to the "tonic parallel" but not to the "subdominant" and conversely, when in "G major," to the "subdominant" but not to the "tonic parallel."

Byrd's procedure admits of no other explanation but that the clausula degrees **c**, **g**, **d**, and **a** form a self-supporting system of interrelationships that is only secondarily and "formally," not functionally, based on an underlying mode. If the opening lines cadence on the degrees **g** and **d**, then the mode established by the final cadence can be not only g-Mixolydian[11] but also c-Ionian.[12] The principle underlying the disposition of clausulas is that of coordinate, not subordinate, structure.

2. In a system of degrees primarily related one to another and only secondarily related to a center, the sequence in which the clausula degrees appear—thus the distinction between whether the movement from the c- to the d-clausula is mediated by a g-clausula or whether the d-clausula follows the c-clausula as a contrast—is of no less but of a different importance than in a major key.

To be significant, the contrast between the d-clausula and the c-clausula does not need to be more precisely determined nor does it need to be resolved. The contrast is musically effective without there being any necessity to interpret the c- and d-degrees functionally as the tonic and the subdominant parallel in C major or as the subdominant and the dominant in G major. Instead of having "harmonic logic" tie the resolution of the contrast to the reconciling g-degree, 16th-century chordal technique leaves the choice of a continuation to the composer, a choice limited only by the boundaries of the system.

If the contrast between the c- and the d-clausulas is consequently a self-contained event from which no consequences need be drawn, then the movement from **c** through **g** to **d** differs from a harmonically tonal modulation in its lack of functional tensions. In C major, the dominant-tonic relation **g–c** is a qualitatively different fifth–relation than the Sp–D relation **d–g**, which tends toward resolution in the tonic and thus resembles in its effect the constrast of a second. By comparison, the fifth-relations between clausula degrees are nothing but fifth-relations, that is, close relationships that are self-contained instead of pointing to something beyond themselves. They do not urge the harmonic progression in a fixed direction but are, as it were, "lacking in tendency."

It is thus erroneous when, from the observation that William Byrd often places clausula degrees a fifth apart, Franklin B. Zimmerman[13] draws the conclusion that the a-degree in the c-mode was understood as an extension in the "dominant direction." Zimmerman's hypothesis is evidently negatively motivated. That is, since the a-degree, when situated between a d- and a g-clausula, cannot be understood as a "tonic parallel," it ought to be considered a "dominant of the dominant of the dominant." But the idea expressed or implied by the term "dominant of the dominant of the dominant" is either tautological or false: tautological if "dominant" is intended as a synonym for "interval of a fifth" and false if intended as a harmonic function.

3. The system of clausula or cadence degrees—degrees related primarily to each other and not to a fixed center—is based on neither

modality nor harmonic tonality. Thus its existence and right to exist
is independent of the modal or harmonically tonal characterization of
the chord progressions between cadences, of the so-called "component
modes" or "component keys." And for the very reason that the system
stands apart from these two alternatives, it takes on the historical
function of making possible the transition between them. But if the
"nongravitational" system of degrees has significance as a mediator,
then it is still consistent with its meaning if the form of the individual
"component modes" or "component keys" remains indecisively and
ambiguously in the middle between a clear expression of modality and
harmonic tonality. In the music of William Byrd it is no accident that
the intermediate forms between Mixolydian and major, or Dorian and
minor, predominate.

In the early 17th century, the differences between the "*modi naturaliores*" [more natural modes]—Ionian, Lydian, and Mixolydian—
shrivel to insignificant vestiges of the past. Through the accidentals b♭
and f♯, which spread "backward" from the cadence, the f- and g-modes
were assimilated into the c-mode, the "*modus naturalissimus*" [the most
natural mode] to use the words of Johann Lippius. The g-mode falls
into a twilight in which it becomes difficult to determine, without being
arbitrary, whether the *subsemitonium modi* [the semitone below the
keynote] should be considered a mere accidental, or conversely,
whether the "Mixolydian seventh" should be considered only a picturesque departure from the major scale.

The mutual assimilation of the "*modi molliores*" ["softer" modes]
was accomplished more slowly. In the late 17th century, Phrygian still
formed a third type alongside major and minor. And whether Aeolian
or Dorian was the paradigm of a "*modus mollior*" remained largely
undetermined. The realization that Aeolian minor stands between
Dorian and Phrygian just as Ionian major stands between Lydian and
Mixolydian was negated by the custom of counting Dorian as the first
"*modus mollior*" and, for that reason, perceiving it as primary. Well
into the early 18th century, theorists clung to the method of representing
the minor triad as re-fa-la in the natural hexachord, thus as the tonic
chord in the Dorian mode.

. . .

The transition from modality to major-minor tonality was facilitated
by a intermediate stage of indifference and uncertainty that can be seen
not only in the relations between individual tones but also in the
relations between chords and the clausula degrees.

1. The crossing and interrelating of melodic modes and modal fragments in polyphonic composition had the result that what often stood out was not the specific modes but their common factor, the autonomous diatonic system.

2. A mode was characterized by melodic formulas, schemata for initial imitations, and dispositions of clausulas. But the chordal technique could be separated from the presentation of the mode. Six chordal degrees form a closed system. And the significance of one degree depends less on its relation to a center than on its position in the system, that is, on how near or far it is to the extremes, the mi- and fa-degrees. It seems as though the six-three chord **f–a–d'** is more representative of the f-degree than the d-degree, while the six-three chord **e–g–c'** is more representative of the c-degree than the e-degree.

3. Analogous to individual chordal degrees, clausula degrees and the sections whose endings they formed could also be understood as elements in a system of simple interrelationships that was not, or only secondarily, related to a central point and to a single mode. The mode withered to a merely "formal" designation expressed by a few features or "signs." And it was in the chordal technique, since it was separable from the presentation of the mode, that tonal harmony could develop.

CHAPTER IV

ANALYSES

Josquin des Prez: Motets

The attempt to demonstrate in Josquin's motets the significance, or lack of significance, of the C- and a-modes—the "proto-forms" of major and minor—is tied to two preconditions.

First, it is necessary to describe the function of ♭, which sometimes seems to work against an unambiguous determination of the mode. The practice of notating the voices with divergent key signatures is certainly the exception in Josquin's motets.[1] Yet it is often uncertain whether the tonal system is meant to be heptatonic or octatonic.

And second, one should describe the importance that Josquin assigned to an unambiguous presentation of the mode.

.   .   .

The dual degree of b♭/b♮, or e♭/e♮ when the signature has one flat, evades an attempt at a fixed definition. It seems to have become the common opinion that a b♭, unless prescribed by the key signature, should be understood as an "accidental," as a mere auxiliary tone. That is, it should be viewed as a supplement to the set of tones that, while indispensable for the avoidance of the tritone and the diminished fifth, represents a "chance occurrence" in relation to the tonal system and thus has no significance even for the mode. Compared with the "essential" b, the "accidental" b♭ appears as a tone of lower rank that instead of forming its own scale degree participates in that of b♮.

The concept of "accidence" is too weak and narrow to express the unabridged meaning of the incidental b♭. But on the other hand, if one concedes that b♭ is not merely an incidental "coloration" of b♮ but an independent degree in its own right, then some other difficulties arise.

If one allows b♭ as a proper degree alongside b♮, then b♭ signifies either an expansion of the heptatonic scale to an octatonic scale or a change of system, a transposition of the scale. And the difference between the untransposed and the transposed scale again presents itself in two forms: as a simultaneous contrast or as a successive contrast—as "bitonality" or "modulation."

As an "accidental," b♭ is a "colored" b♮. On the other hand, as an "eighth" degree it forms the opposite extreme of b♮ in the circle of fifths b♭–f–c–g–d–a–e–b♮. And in connection with a "contrast of diatonic system," the b♭-degree in the transposed scale becomes the analogue of the f-degree in the untransposed scale. The differences between these interpretations suggest mutually exclusive alternatives. But Josquin's works, through their ambiguity, avoid the clarity of these opposing concepts and shun the compulsion for either-or categories.

While each of the three interpretations of the incidental b♭ can be supported by analyses of individual Josquin motets, it is nonetheless impossible to draw fixed boundaries between them. The categories of "accidence," "octatonicism," and "contrast of diatonic system" are mutually exclusive. But the phenomena that suggest one or the other concept are not sharply divided—they subtly blend into each other.

Were the differences intended as they appear in the three categories, then they should be "composed out" in the music. Yet they are not. So the unavoidable alternative is to make a single concept from the meaning of the b♭-degree, a concept that enables the apparent antitheses—accidence, octatonicism, and change of system—to be understood as mere variants, different specifications, as it were, of a single type. Of course it is probably futile to search for a single term that would express in a precise and unabridged fashion the circumstance that b♭ remains in an ambiguous middle ground between the meanings of heptatonicism/octatonicism, accidence, and transposition. And so it must suffice if the analyses bring out an idea that is clear, though a word is lacking to name it.

The *prima pars* [first part] of the motet *Qui velatus facie fuisti*[2] is divided into nine lines of text, all based on two melodic formulas. These formulas are repeated and modified according to the following schema:

$$a^1 \quad a^1 \quad b^1 \quad a^2 \quad a^2 \quad b^2 \quad b^3 \quad b^4 \quad b^5$$

measures 1–15 16–30 31–34 35–40 41–46 47–52 53–58 59–64 65–70

Formula "b" consists of a descending fourth-progression in the soprano over a series of sonorities whose lowest voice seems to anticipate the Romanesca bass (**b♭–f–g–d | b♭–f–g–d–G**). Example 68 shows sections b² and b³ in mm. 47–58.

Te pe - ti - mus at - ten - ti - us,

e - sto no - bis pro - pi - ti - us

Example 68

A functional interpretation of the sequence as T–D–Tp–Dp | Tp–
Dp–S–T seems obvious, but it would nevertheless be mistaken because
the composition's underlying mode is e-Phrygian, not f-Ionian. The
a-degree, not the f-degree, forms the "center" of the just-cited measures. In section b⁵, the F–C–d–a series of sonorities heard in b² closes
with a 3–5 clausula on the a-degree (mm. 69–70:   ). And the
a-degree is none other than the *repercussa* of the e-Phrygian mode:
in b⁵, the a-clausula is followed by a turn toward the finalis **e** as a coda
to the *prima pars*.

It would be absurd to interpret the **B♭** appearing as a "root" in mm.
56 and 69 as a mere accidental. But neither can one speak of a change
of diatonic system, a "modulation," from a-Phrygian to e-Phrygian. In
section b⁵, the progression   is immediately followed, without
an intervening degree, by the turn toward the concluding e-sonority.
The caesura is missing that would be assumed by the concept of a
"change of system," if it is not to be an empty phrase. And so one
is unavoidably led to understand the b♭ as the eighth degree of an
octatonic system.

The octatonicism of the motet *Qui velatus facie fuisti* is not a special
case. In *O Domine Jesu Christe*[3] and *Stabat mater dolorosa*[4] the B♭-
and e-chords, or the E♭- and a-chords when the signature has one flat,
are likewise juxtaposed in contexts that do not permit straightforward
parsings, thus excluding the notion of a change of system.

The simultaneous contrast of systems, which Willi Apel and Richard H. Hoppin[5] would call "bitonal," forms the opposite extreme of octatonicism. The motet *Dominus regnavit*[6] has been handed down with divergent signatures: soprano and tenor (ambitus **c′–c″** and **c–d′**) are notated in the ♭-system, bass and alto (ambitus **F–g** and **f–g′**) in the ♭♭-system.[7] The divergence is motivated by compositional technique: the alto imitates the soprano at the lower fifth, as does the bass the tenor. In fact, apart from the clausulas, for long stretches the imitation is canonic.

An interpretation of this motet as "bitonal" may seem natural, but it would be neither unobjectionable nor the only possible explanation.

1. The difference between a canon at the lower fifth that can be notated with divergent signatures and a sporadic imitation at the lower fifth that can be notated with incidental flats is not so fundamental as to justify speaking of "bitonality" in the one case and not in the other. If this were nonetheless the case, then in view of the prevalence of imitation at the lower fifth, one would be forced to regard "bitonality" as one of the basic categories of Josquin's imitative technique. There is no support, however, for such a conclusion. In Josquin's motets, no firm lines can be drawn between "bitonal" and "monotonal" imitations at the lower fifth because the placement of the accidentals is often problematic. In fact, the uncertainty about accidentals does not rest on our ignorance of the "*Selbstverständlichkeiten*" [things once self-evident (Riemann)] in 15th- and 16th-century practice but is instead an intrinsic feature of the subject itself. Whether an imitation at the lower fifth is carried out "bitonally" or "monotonally" is a secondary factor. But a "bitonality" whose relation to its opposite is indifferent rather than contradictory hardly deserves the name.

2. In the *prima pars* of the motet *Dominus regnavit* (mm. 1–84), **e** appears in the soprano and tenor only as the *subsemitonium* [leading tone] in f-clausulas. Thus it can be understood as an incidental alteration of the ♭♭-system. The *secunda pars* is more complicated. The beginning (mm. 85–103) and the end (mm. 148–76) are in the ♭♭-system with a quasi-incidental **e**, the middle (mm. 115–26) is in the ♭-system—e♭′ is avoided in the alto and bass. The transitional or connecting sections are shaped by passages in which the ♭- and ♭♭-systems cross over each other (mm. 103–14 and 126–47):

Example 69

It thus appears that the *secunda pars* is based on a schema that could be interpreted as a "plan of modulation":

$$\flat\flat \qquad \flat\flat/\flat \qquad \flat \qquad \flat/\flat\flat \qquad \flat\flat$$

measures   85–103   103–14   115–26   126–47   148–76

Instead of being a basic conception, "bitonality" would consequently be a mere cofactor.

Like *Dominus regnavit*, the motet *Tribulatio et angustia invenerunt me*[8] is based on imitations at the lower fifth between soprano and alto, tenor and bass. But all the voices have only one ♭ in their signatures, and in several passages it is doubtful whether a second flat could be added to the alto and bass. At the beginning (mm. 1–15) and at the end (mm. 50–57) the second ♭, the result of strict imitation at the lower fifth, is written as an accidental. But in the second section (mm. 16–21) the imitation schema leads to a contradiction with the chordal structure.

Example 70

Soprano and tenor form an a-Phrygian voice pair, alto and bass a d-Phrygian voice pair, so that it seems as though the composition was conceived "bitonally." But it is questionable whether the e′ in the alto can be replaced by e♭′ because the alteration would result in a "*relatio non harmonica*" [a relation contrary to harmony], the diminished fifth a–e♭′. The conflict cannot be resolved by appealing to "*verloren gegangene Selbstverständlichkeiten"* [things once self-evident but now lost to the past (Riemann)] in the performance practice. And the fact that the alternative between the distortion of an imitation and the deformation of a sonority was at all possible reveals that the basis for this dilemma, the difference between **e'** and **e♭'**, represented a secondary factor that could be left ambiguous. Josquin composed as though every conflict could be avoided through the possibility of interchanging **e'** with **e♭'**. The fact that this assumption did not always prove correct was unimportant to him.

In section three (mm. 21–30) the **e♭'** in alto and bass is obviously the *"nota supra la"* of the **f–d'** hexachord [the "note above la" was sung as fa in the next higher hexachord]. But in section four (mm. 31–41) the imitation schema collides with the mode represented by the clausula.

Tri - bu - la - ti - o - nem et   do - lo - rem   in - ve   -   ni

Example 71

Changing **e'** to **e♭'** is suggested by the imitation at the lower fifth but hindered by the clausula. This is because an a-clausula in the ♭♭-system, corresponding to a b-clausula in the untransposed system, would be a singular event. Section five (mm. 40–49) is in the ♭-system: soprano and tenor are limited to the natural hexachord, alto and bass to the "soft" hexachord.

That the distinction between b♭ and b♮ or e♭ and e♮ represented a secondary factor is also shown by a conflict in the motet *Misericordias Domini in aeternum cantabo,*[9] a conflict that cannot be resolved as long as one understands the ♭ as a sign of transposition. A Phrygian theme that includes the tones **c'–b–a** is, in mm. 50–63, transposed from the cadence degree **a** to **d**, **g**, and **c**, thus led through a "modulation by descending fifths." That the **b♮** must be changed to **b♭** in the third-progression above **g**, the analogue of **c'–b–a** and **f–e–d**, is prescribed in the alto (m. 57) and is thus self-evident in the bass (m. 55) and soprano (m. 59) as well. But whether one should read **e♭'–d'–c'** for the notated **e'–d'–c'** in the tenor (mm. 61–63) could be questioned and is more than likely improbable.

ple - na   est ter   -   ra

Example 72

First, in the ♮-system the e♭′ was considered beyond the pale. And second, going from a c-clausula in the ♭♭-system to an a-clausula in the ♮-system—the result of the chromatic alteration (mm. 63 and 68)—would be even more abrupt and strange than the transition given in the text from a g-clausula in the ♭-system to a c-clausula in the ♮-system (mm. 61–63). Thus, if one wishes to preserve the boundaries of the tonal system, then one must forfeit the identity of the theme.

On the other hand, the problematical nature of the placement of accidentals in *Misericordias Domini* points out that the tranposition to the lower fifth, from **d** to **g** (mm. 53–57), need not be intended as a change of system, even though b♭ is substituted for b♮. The supposition that the theme appears in the ♮-system on **a** and on **d**, in the ♭-system on **g**, and again in the ♮-system on **c** would attribute to Josquin a lack of compositional logic, a contradiction between the unfolding of the imitations and the modulations that would be strange indeed. To recognize the logic in the imitative passages one must conceive of them as thematic modulations to four degrees of an octatonic system, a system that permits the alteration of b♮ to b♭ but not of e♮ to e♭.

As the examples of conflicting cases show, both the simultaneous contrasting of systems—"bitonality"—and the successive—"modulation"—tend toward octatonicism. And in *Rubum quem viderat Moyses*[10] one can see still more clearly than in the previously cited motets that octatonicism represents the comprehensive category: an octatonicism in which the two forms of the dual degree constitute the opposite extremes of the system and yet are interchangeable. On the one hand, the difference in the two forms can be so abrupt that the change between e♭′ and e′ or b♭ and b has the effect of a "modulation," and on the other hand it can shrink to an irrelevance that makes it possible to understand e♭′ or b♭ as mere "colorations," as incidental substitutions for e′ or **b**.

Rubum quem viderat Moyses is based on an e-Phrygian chant[11] that is transposed in the motet to a-Phrygian. The initial series of imitations is octatonic: the first phrase, **d–e–f–g** in the chant, is set forth in the motet in three different species of fourths, Dorian in the tenor and soprano (**g–a–b♭–c′** and **g′–a′–b♭′–c″**, respectively), Phrygian in the bass (**d–e♭–f–g**), and Ionian in the alto (**c′–d′–e′–f′**). It is not out of the question that the disagreement of the fourth-species is intended as a characterization of the thorn bush referred to in the text. The middle sections (mm. 15–32, 32–49, 48–57) are based on "bitonal" imitations at the fifth between soprano and alto, tenor and bass. Soprano and tenor are notated in the ♭-system, alto and bass in the ♭♭-system. The concluding passage (mm. 57–64) could be understood as a "modulation"—the plagal cadence ♪ is imitated at the lower

fifth ♪ . But the motet's octatonic beginning demonstrates in
an all but programmatic fashion how one should understand "bitonality" and "modulation": not as fundamental principles but as an
unfolding of cofactors that are resolved within octatonicism.

. . .

It seems to be a foregone conclusion, one requiring no special proof,
that the tonal or modal character of a work can be detected in its
disposition of cadences. The classification of clausulas into "*primariae*,"
"*secundariae*," "*tertiariae*," and "*peregrinae*" developed by the theorists
of the 16th and 17th centuries unequivocally stipulated which cadential
degrees were proper to a mode and which were foreign. But in works
based on a canonic framework the presentation of the mode is frequently compromised by the compositional conception. And one could
imagine Josquin sacrificing the clarity of the mode for the sake of that
"*ostentatio ingenii*" [display of talent] attributed to him by Glarean.
So to be able to determine the degree to which Josquin felt the
presentation of a mode was an essential or an incidental factor of
composition it is probably not the worst procedure to investigate
compositions in the highly constrained "*stylus ligatus*" ["bound style,"
meaning bound by or tied to canons, mensuration schemes, or other
constraining artifices].

The motet *Ut Phoebi radiis*,[12] which ought to be classified as f-Lydian
or f-Ionian according to its *finalis*, is based on a "*soggetto cavato dalle
vocali*" [a subject carved out of the hexachord syllables]. The degrees
of the hexachord are presented—ascending in the *pars prima* (mm.
1–73), descending in the *pars secunda* (mm. 74–151)—in a progressive
process of addition. The two lower voices, in canon at the fourth, first
intone one degree of the hexachord (ut in the *pars prima*, la in the
pars secunda), then two degrees (ut–re and la–sol respectively), and
so forth. Specifically, the bass presents the natural hexachord (**c–a**),
the tenor the soft hexachord (**f–d′**). In the second part, the cadences—
on **g** (m. 85), **f** (m. 96), **e** (m. 108), **d** (m. 121), and **c** (m. 135)—are
determined by the *soggetto*. The endings of the canonic passages, for

example, la–sol = ♪ or la–sol–fa = ♪ , suggest

interpretations as the penultimate and final of 6–8 cadences that could be supplemented by **f♯'–g'** or **e'–f'**, respectively. By contrast, in the first part it is not the ending but the beginning of the canonic passages (ut–re = 𝄢) that is destined to be the penultimate and final of a cadence, namely an f-clausula with "supposed" third (**d**). Yet the hidden f-clausulas (mm. 20–21, 31–32, 43–44) hardly suffice to characterize the motet as being unambiguously f-Lydian or f-Ionian. In relation to the compositional design, the presentation of the mode takes place in the background.

While the disposition of cadences in *Ut Phoebi radiis* accordingly depends on the *soggetto*, other motets with a canonic framework show that Josquin took pains to achieve an unequivocal presentation of the mode in spite of obstacles springing from the compositional design. The motet *Pater noster*[13] is in g-Dorian. The first part (mm. 1–120)—the second part is an *Ave Maria*—is based on the framework of a canon at the fifth. The alto follows the tenor at a distance of three breves. The cadential degrees in the chant melody [given by the tenor] match the *parallelismus membrorum* of the text [the paired phrases of structured Biblical texts, e.g., "Our Father who art in Heaven; Hallowed be Thy name"]. "Commas" cadence in the tenor on the subtonic **f** (in the alto on **c'**), "periods" on the final **g** (in the alto on **d'**). Only the phrase "Adveniant regnum tuum" [Thy kindom come] (III), which stands on its own, interrupts the *parallelismus membrorum*. And the motet divides the period "Et dimitte debita nostra, sicut nos dimittimus debitoribus nostris" [And forgive us our trespasses as we forgive those who trespass against us] into three parts (VIII–X) instead of two.

Closing Tones in the Chant	f	c'	g	d'	f	c'	f	c'	g	d'
Tones in the Bass	d	a	g	g	d	a	d	a	g	g
Measures	14	17	26	29	36	39	46	49	56	59
Sections	I		II		III		IV		V	

f	c'	g	d'	f	c'	g	d'	g	d'	f	c'	g	d'
d	a	g	d	d	c	g	g	g	g	d	c	g	g
66	69	72	75	80	83	88	91	95	98	105	108	115	118
VI		VII		VIII		IX		X		XI		XII	

Josquin interprets the subtonic **f** in the tenor as the third above **d**, the corresponding **c'** in the alto as the third above **a'**, or less often as the octave above **c'**. But at the ends of periods he breaks the correspondence between tenor and alto so as to avoid a predominance of the d-degree that would endanger the clarity of the mode. Only once (section VII) does **d'** appear as the octave above **d**. But in the remaining five cases **d'** is the fifth above **g** so that the preeminence of **g** as the *finalis* is preserved.

The same procedure underlies the presentation of the mode in the motet *O virgo prudentissima*.[14] Tenor and alto form a canon at the fifth on the antiphon *Beata mater . . . intercede pro nobis*. The chant is transposed from d-Dorian to g-Dorian and changed in a few places for the sake of the canonic structure. The concluding tones of the individual "*membra*" [phrases] of text alternate between the subtonic (once the supertonic) and the *finalis*. And as in the motet *Pater noster*, a predominance of the d-degree is avoided by setting the cadence tone **d'** in the alto not as an octave but as a fifth above the bass. The fact that a **c** is supposed under **g**—the *finalis* in the tenor in mm. 58, 63, and 101—is based on the canonic structure: tenor and alto form the sixth **g–e'**, which allows only **c** or **e** for its bass.

Chant	f	c'	f	c'	g	d'	g	d'	a	e'	g	d'	g	d'
Bass	d	a	d	a	c	g	c	g	d	c	c	g	g	g
Measures	37	39	44	46	58	60	63	65	91	93	101	103	105	107

If the obstacles impeding an unambiguous presentation of the mode are already substantial in *O virgo prudentissima* and *Pater noster*, then in the sequence *Veni, sancte Spiritus*[15] they seem to grow to mammoth proportions. For its compositional framework, this six-voice motet has a double canon at the fifth. *Quinta vox* and *superius* form a first canon; bass and tenor form a second. The *comites* [canonic answers] follow the *duces* [canonic subjects] at the distance of six semibreves, which make up two *tempora* in the *tempus perfectum* [3/1 time] of the *pars prima* (mm. 1–65) and three *tempora* in the *tempus imperfectum diminutum* [2/1 time] of the *pars secunda* (mm. 66–177). The *duces*— *quinta vox* and bass—combine to form a first pair of voices, and the *comites*—*superius* and tenor—combine to form a second. One can thus describe the double canon as an interlocking of two duos at the interval of a fifth:

Superius			....			....			
Quinta vox	....				....				
Tenor			——————			—			
Bass	——————				——————				
Measure	1	2	3	4	5	6	7	8	9

Superius and *quinta vox* carry the chant melody, which is transposed from d- to g-Dorian and altered in a few places. Since all the parts have a ♭ in their signatures, the *quinta vox* with **g** as its *finalis* represents the underlying mode. (Thus if one took this voice's function into consideration it ought to be designated the "tenor.") The form of the sequence, its "progressive repetition," is strictly preserved and polyphonically "composed out": the motet is divided into five double versicles, each of which contains three lines of text.

A	A	B	B	C	C	D	D	E	E
abc	abc	def	def	ghi	ghi	klm	klm	nop	nop
1–17	18–34	35–48	49–62	66–83	84–101	102–20	121–39	141–57	155–171

In the motet's last double versicle the exposition overlaps the repetition: the first line of the repetition in the *quinta vox* forms the counterpoint to the third line of the exposition in the *superius* (mm. 155–57).

In the motets *O virgo prudentissima* and *Pater noster*, Josquin was able to avoid having the canon of chant melodies at the fifth, where g-clausulas are answered by d-clausulas, lead to a predominance of the fifth degree in relation to the *finalis*. But in a double canon, the correspondence of clausulas at the interval of a fifth seems to be inevitable. And the obstacles that confront an accentuation of the *finalis* are sooner heightened than moderated by the chant's own disposition of cadences, since along with the *finalis* **g**, the fifth degree—not the subtonic as in *O virgo prudentissima* and *Pater noster*—also has a prominent position:

$$g \quad d \quad g \; \|{:} \; g \quad f \quad g \; \|{:} \; d \; b^\flat g \; \|{:} \; c \quad g \quad d \; \|{:} \; d \; b^\flat g \; \|$$

The answering of d-clausulas (*quinta vox* and bass) by a-clausulas (*superius* and tenor) results in a changeover toward a-Phrygian, "*a Dorio ad Phrygium*" [from Dorian to Phrygian], which in Glarean's words leads a piece into remote and strange areas, "*a proposito aliquo in longe diversum*" [from a given subject to something far different].[16] While the obscuring of the mode by the predominance of the "sharp side" may seem unavoidable, an analysis nevertheless clearly shows that Josquin still tried to preserve the unambiguous sense of the g-Dorian mode. First, he reinterprets g-clausulas as c-clausulas, and the corresponding d-clausulas as g-clausulas. The cadence in the chant is treated as an alto formula instead of as a discant formula [the discant formula would have had **c♯** as its penultima] (mm. 3–4 and 5–6, 15 and 17, 111–12 and 114–15):

(Chant cadence)

(Ve) - ni san - cte spi - ri - tus

Example 73

And second, he avoids the Phrygian a-clausula in the first double versicle (the answer at the fifth of the d-clausula) by not cadencing the voices of the second canon (bass and tenor) together with those of the first (*quinta vox* and *superius*). Instead, he allows bass and tenor to disregard the caesuras in the chant sung by *quinta vox* and *superius* (mm. 10 and 12). And in the third double versicle, just as in the first, the a-clausula is once again circumvented. Instead of forming voice pairs (bass/*quinta vox*, tenor/*superius*) that cadence as mutually independent duos, the two canons combine into a four-voice imitative passage without a clausula (mm. 66–74).

Thus, in spite of Glarean's skepticism,[17] Josquin concerned himself with a clear and unambiguous presentation of the mode even when technical constraints made it far more difficult. All the more significance then rests on the solution he furnished to the problem of the a- and c-modes, the prototypes of minor and major.

. . .

The fact that the Ionian and Aeolian modes are missing from the *octoechos* [eight modes] and yet represent the prototypes of major and minor tempts people to create antitheses whose simplicity may be attractive but into which historical reality fits only reluctantly. Hugo Riemann constructed an antithesis between "natural" major-minor tonality and "artificial" modality, a modality that confirmed its artificiality by suppressing what was "natural" and disparaging it as "common." Riemann's thesis includes the notion that an Ionian or Aeolian composition represents not a mode but the opposite of modality: major-minor tonality. And Edward E. Lowinsky, who tries to demonstrate that the c-Ionian compositions of Dunstable, Dufay, and Josquin have an "art of tonal organization" opposed to that of the "ecclesiastical modes," seems to share Riemann's assumptions.[18]

Glarean, who augmented the *octoechos* with the Ionian and Aeolian modes in 1547, understood what he wrote differently from how Riemann interpreted it. Glarean discovered the modes he named "Ionian" and "Aeolian" in Gregorian chant and in 15th- and 16th-century polyphony. And he conceived them not as something new and antithetical to the modal system but as something in existence for a long time that had nevertheless gone unrecognized. Even Pietro Aaron[19] mentions compositions that end on **a**. But he interprets **a** not as the *finalis* but as the d-Dorian "*confinalis*" or the e-Phrygian "*repercussa*."

An attempt to define the extent to which Josquin's "Aeolian" mode tends toward the "harmonically tonal minor" is thus unsupported as long as it is uncertain whether it was Aaron's interpretation or Glarean's theory that conformed to the composer's practice. An "Aeolian" mode that proves to be Phrygian on closer analysis cannot be declared the prototype of the "harmonically tonal minor."

Among the seventy motets published in Josquin's complete works, eight end either on **a** in the ♮-system[20] or on **d** in the ♭-system.[21] Motets number 52, *Qui habitat in adjutorio altissimi* (Psalm 91),[22] and 70, *Levavi oculos meos in montes* (Psalm 121),[23] have some traits in common that connect them all the more closely since the features in question are unusual in the early 16th-century motet. First, the opening imitations are repeated at the end (no. 52, mm. 1–10 = 271–80: "Qui habitat in adjutorio altissimi"; no. 70, mm. 1–11 = 170–80: "Levavi oculos meos in montes"). Second, the initial imitations, whose themes are clearly g-Dorian, are supplemented with short appendices when repeated so that they end with "perfect" cadences on **d** (mm. 280–82 in no. 52 and mm. 180–83 in no. 70). Thus it seems as though at the end of the motets the Aeolian mode is substituted for the Dorian. And

third, the *primae partes* end with half cadences on **a** ( ) that

seem to confirm the two works' Aeolian character. Of course these a-cadences result from the transposition a fourth lower of g-Dorian passages ending on **d** (no. 52, mm. 148_2 to 150/151–55; no. 70, mm. 99–102/103–6).

Yet for all that, the mode of both motets is still g-Dorian. Not counting the return of the beginning at the end, *Qui habitat in adjutorio altissimi* comprises sixteen verses. Thirteen end with g-clausulas (mm. 24, 47, 56, 79, 109, 127, 140, 188, 202, 220, 233, 246, and 270). And the first halves of the verses, the "commas," are several times contrasted with the verse endings by having clausulas on secondary degrees—on **d** (mm. 32, 135, 225), **b**♭ (mm. 92, 145, 260), or **a** (m. 73). Verses four and ten do not cadence. The theme of the imitations in verse four is Dorian (mm. 63–68: **c–G–c–B♭–G** = **g–d–g–f–d**). In verse ten, which merges with the first half of verse eleven, the theme is modally ambiguous (mm. 156–82: **g–b♭–g–f–b♭–a = d–f–d–c–f–e = a–c′–a–g–c′–b♭**).

The mode in *Levavi oculos meos in montes* is similarly unmistakable. Of the eight verses, six end with g-clausulas (mm. 60, 80, 128, 137, 155, and 172). The first halves of the verses cadence on **d** (mm. 51, 116, and 132) or on **b♭** (mm. 88 and 151). To be sure, the end not only of the *prima pars* (m. 105) but also of the first verse (m. 40) stands out from the g-Dorian context by virtue of an a-clausula. But g-clausulas precede the a-clausulas (mm. 28 and 98), and in fact the passages cadencing in g-Dorian set the same verse halves as those cadencing in a-Phrygian ("unde veniet auxilium"; "qui custodit Israel").

The cadences on **d** and **a** in motets 52 and 70, even though placed at the ends of the *prima* or *secunda pars*, are therefore incidental deviations that certainly cloud the Dorian character of the compositions but do not make it unrecognizable.

· · ·

It should also be mentioned that the transmission of the motets is not without problems. First, in the manuscript Cambrai 125–128, a g-chord is appended to the d-cadence in *Qui habitat in adjutorio altissimi*.[24] And whether the version in the other sources merits the precedence granted it by the Complete Edition can only be determined after studies of the filiation of the sources, studies that permit an estimation of their importance. Second, the Aeolian appendices to the two motets are in almost note-for-note agreement.

Al - tis - si - mi.

mon - tes

Example 74

And while the motivic material of the cadential formula is prepared earlier in *Qui habitat in adjutorio altissimi* (mm. 276–78), it is not in *Levavi oculos meos*. So it is not out of the question that in *Levavi oculos meos*—the motet is preserved in only a single and quite late source—the Aeolian appendix is an extraneous addition: a "revision" after the pattern of *Qui habitat in adjutorio altissimi*.

· · ·

A similar conception underlies the motet *Memor esto verbi tui* (Psalm 119, verses 49–64).[25] Although the motet ends with an a-clausula, its mode is d-Dorian.[26] Of the seventeen verses—the psalm text is augmented by the *Gloria Patri* [the doxology]—thirteen end on **d** (mm. 21, 39, 66, 82, 96, 144, 174, 192, 211, 228, 279, 296, 310) and two on **e** (mm. 123, 164). The "commas," the first halves of the verses, cadence on **a** (mm. 86, 112, 197), **f** (mm. 30, 54, 218, 291), or **e** (mm. 136, 184, 268). Verses sixty-one and sixty-two are executed in strict canonic imitation without clausulas.

The features that make for a close connection between *Levavi oculos meos ad montes* and *Qui habitat in adjutorio altissimi* reappear in *Memor esto verbi tui*. First, the beginning, verse forty-nine, is repeated at the end (mm. 311–28)—in fact in a similar and even partly identical musical setting (mm. 319–21 = 9–11). Second, the ending turns toward **a**, the fifth degree. And third, a plagal half cadence on **e** (a–e) at the end of the *prima pars* (mm. 163–64) corresponds to the a-clausula of the *secunda pars*.

That three unusual features—the repetition of the beginning at the end, the appended cadence on the *confinalis*, and the half cadence at the end of the *prima pars* that corresponds to it—should coincide in different motets, as if one were the precondition of the other, cannot be dismissed as chance. But the relationship that seems to exist between the "reprise technique" and the "divergent cadences" is far from clear. The thought that Josquin had in mind a balance between the "closed" nature of the form and the "open" nature of the disposition of cadences would hardly be more than a vague conjecture.

The motet *Miserere mei, Deus* (Psalm 51, verses 3–21)[27] ends on **a**. But **a** is meant not as an "Aeolian *finalis*" but as a "neutral" degree that can be interpreted as a Dorian *confinalis* or as a Phrygian *repercussa*. As Bernhard Meier has shown,[28] the motet is based on the principle of "*commixtio modorum*" [a mixing of different modes], the movement "*a Dorio ad Phrygium*" [from Dorian to Phrygian] (Glarean) or vice versa. The change between modes is facilitated by clausulas on **a** (mm. 21, 51, 96, 157, 229, 252, 347). Less often, the modes are abruptly contrasted (mm. 35–40, 131–35, 278–83). It is uncertain whether, as Meier believes, Phrygian is to be understood as the basic mode and Dorian as a modulation. At the ends of verses, nine Phrygian cadences (mm. 58, 74, 111, 160, 183, 213, 245, 283, 413) confront seven Dorian cadences (mm. 40, 91, 135, 198, 226, 262, 333). And the fact that an a-clausula is placed at the end of the motet seems to indicate that an ambiguity forms the basic character of the work, an ambiguity that cannot be resolved into a primary and a secondary factor.

The motets *Huc me sydereo descendere jussit Olympo*[29] and *Ave nobilissima creatura*[30] are based on the same cantus firmus. The antiphon *Plangent eum* given in the tenor of *Huc me sydereo* is melodically identical to the antiphon *Benedicta tu in mulieribus*, which forms the cantus firmus of *Ave nobilissima creatura*. And even the technique for the mensural realization of the antiphons—it has been described by Rolf Dammann as a "late form of the isorhythmic motet"[31]—is the same in both motets.

. . .

The antiphon *Plangent eum* (*Huc me sydereo*) is performed in three mensurations: in longs and breves (m. 49), breves and semibreves (m. 140), and semibreves and minims (m. 176). Or expressed in another way, the same notation, written in breves and semibreves, appears under three different signs of proportion, O, ¢, and ₵.[32] The relation between the three mensurations cannot be formulated as an exact proportion, because while the semibreves of *tempus perfectum* and those of *tempus imperfectum diminutum* are in the ratio of 2:1, the breves vary. They are either in the ratio of 3:1 or—if they are imperfected [i.e., reduced to two-thirds their normal length] in *tempus perfectum*—in the ratio of 2:1. Dammann, who interprets the technique as "isorhythm" and defines the proportions of the three mensurations as 6:2:1, is first forced to disregard the imperfecting of the breves and then constrained to relate them only to each other. Yet the sign O means not only that the breve is perfect (and not imperfect as in C) but also that semibreve is imperfect (and not perfect as in ⊙). To speak of "isorhythm" may thus be in error. What reappears is not a rhythm but a particular notation subjected to differing rhythmic interpretations.

The realizations of the antiphon *Benedicta tu in mulieribus* (*Ave nobilissima creatura*) are based on the mensurations O, C, and ¢ (mm. 49, 161, and 237).[33] But to speak of a proportion—Dammann defines it as 3:2:1—is inadequate because, just as in *Huc me sydereo*, deciding between 2:2:1 and 3:2:1 is impossible without being arbitrary.

. . .

The modal character of the cantus firmus is contradictory. Without transposing the melody, Josquin places a ♭ in the signature, thus in the third line changing **b♮** to **b♭**. (The added **b♭** in the fourth line is not foreign to the melodic archetype of the antiphons. It can be found—notated as **b♭**—in the antiphon *Expectetur sicut pluvia*.)

Si - cut ros   De - us   no - ster

Example 75

Josquin's interference with the chant tradition is not as arbitrary as it seems. In the original chant version the melody ends on **a** and spans the ambitus from **f** to **e'**. In Glarean's twelve-mode system it should thus be classified as Hypoaeolian. But in the Middle Ages the Aeolian mode was considered illegitimate. So to be able to fit the melody into the *octoechos*, one had to categorize it either as Hypophrygian or as Hypodorian. In the one case an **f♯** resulted in the third line (e-Hypophrygian with the ambitus **c–b**), in the other a **B♭** in the fourth line (d-Hypodorian with the ambitus **B♭–a**). The classification as Hypophrygian carried the day, but the melody was left where it was in the ambitus **f–e'** (instead of **c–b**). That is, to conceal the chromatic **f♯** one notated the melody with the *finalis* **a** instead of **e**. (Only in the antiphonary of Lucca is the melody handed down with the *finalis* **e**, and there the **f♯** is omitted.[34]) Under the assumption that the melody is Hypophrygian, the avoidance of the chromatic degree is, however, a mere fiction. The **a** needs to be understood as the *finalis*—were it thought of as the Phrygian *repercussa* then the melody should have been attributed to the third, not to the fourth, mode. But if **a** is the Hypophrygian final, then **b♮** is a transposed **f♯**. (And in the antiphon *Expectetur sicut pluvia*, it is not the **b♭** that is a lowered degree, but the **b♮** that is raised.)

In view of the dilemma that either categorizing the melody as Hypophrygian or avoiding the chromatic degree results in a mere fiction, Josquin's notation loses the appearance of arbitrariness that one might attach to it from a cursory observation. To resolve the contradiction plaguing the chant tradition, Josquin altered the melody: his version is unequivocally Hypophrygian.

On the other hand, it seems as though the effort to make the melody modally more precise is once again canceled by the polyphonic context, and that the a-Phrygian cantus firmus is reinterpreted as d-Aeolian. In *Huc me sydereo*, a d-cadence in the other voices (m. 192) is appended to the Phrygian a-cadence that ends the cantus firmus (m. 189). And in *Ave nobilissima creatura,* the bass places the lower fifth **d** (m. 265)

beneath the discant-tenor clausula on **a** (). For cantus-firmus

motets, however, Tinctoris's rule that the tenor, as the *"fundamentum totius relationis"* [basis of the whole relationship], is the voice that determines the mode, should probably be valid without qualification. As a consequence, the **d** in the bass would be modally irrelevant.

It seems as if the "Aeolian" mode can be reduced either to the Dorian mode or to the Phrygian. And regarding the question of whether Glarean's category "Aeolian" can be transferred to Josquin's motets, even *Misericordias Domini in aeternum cantabo*[35] is affected, though the *prima pars* ends with a half cadence on **e** (a–e) to which an a-clausula is appended and the *secunda pars* and *tertia pars* end with "perfect cadences" on **a**.

The text is a compilation. At the beginning there is the second verse of Psalm 89 ("Misericordias Domini in aeternum cantabo"), at the end the first verse of Psalm 71 (=verse two of Psalm 31: "In te, Domine, speravi; non confundar in aeternum"). In terms of compositional technique, the motet is based on the principle of variation: five "motives" are manipulated in various forms. "Motive" α is characterized by an ascending leap of a fifth (mm. 1–9, 134–48), β by a rising third and a falling fourth (mm. 15–34, 106–19, 160–75), γ by a Phrygian second (mm. 33–50, 51–68, 125–33, 201–14), δ by an ascending leap of a fourth (mm. 69–82, 176–82, 228–45), and ε by a sequencing of falling thirds in close four-voice imitation (mm. 82–92, 149–59, 221–27).

The motet is modally characterized—analogously to *Miserere mei, Deus* and *Memor est verbi tui*—by "commixtiones" [mixtures] of Phrygian and Dorian. The opening motive in the tenor is set forth on **d** and **e** (mm. 1–9),

Example 76

the final phrase in the *superius* on **e′** and **d′** (mm. 259–69).

In te, Do - mi - ne, spe - ra - vi,

in te, Do - mi - ne, spe - ra - vi,

Example 77

The fifth **A–e** (**a–e'**) of the initial imitation in the bass and alto and the a-clausula in the closing passage are indeed ambiguous or seem to be. One can view the **a** as a reconciliation of the contrast between Dorian and Phrygian—in d-Dorian as well as in e-Phrygian it forms the second primary degree after the *finalis*—or interpret it as an Aeolian *finalis*, as a "tonic" surrounded by its "subdominant" and "dominant."

First, one can judge the fact that a notion of "*commixtio modorum*" underlies the fluctuation between Phrgyian and Dorian from the piling up of "modulating" passages in which themes are transposed to four different degrees—**b**, **e**, **a**, and **d** (mm. 15–34, 33–50, 51–68). Each theme ends a second lower than its initial tone, for example (mm. 51–53):

mi - se - ri - cor - di - a

Example 78

Therefore the beginning tones **b–e–a–d** (mm. 15–34: **a–d–e–b**) are matched by the ending tones **a–d–g–c** (mm. 15–34: **g–c–d–a**). But the accent falls on the beginning tones, not the ending tones. The circle of fifths **a–d–g–c**, if one emphasized it, would signify an unmotivated "tonicization" of the g- and c-modes. On the other hand, the circle of fifths **b–e–a–d**, which sets the Phrygian fifth against the Dorian fifth, is characteristic of the modal conception of the motet—the fluctuation between Phrygian and Dorian.

Second, the Phrygian and Dorian modes in *Misericordias Domini* are not only mixed, but they are also set out separately. Imitations with the structural tones **d** and **a** are unequivocally Dorian (mm. 69 and 175), those with **e** and **a** Phrygian (mm. 106 and 160). The **a** does not appear as a central focus—as a tonic that gathers around itself a subdominant and dominant—but as a mediating "neutral element" between Phrygian and Dorian.

Even the last of Josquin's apparently Aeolian motets, *Qui regis Israel intende*,[36] can be reduced to another mode—Phrygian. The text is a paraphrase of fragments from Psalm 80.

Psalm	Motet
2: Qui regis Israel intende qui deducis velut ovem Joseph. Qui sedes super cherubim manifestare	Qui regis Israel intende Qui sedes super solem et lunam, custodi nos. Qui regis reges, miserere nobis et vide afflictionem nostram.
3: Excita potentiam tuam, et veni ut salvos facias nos.	Excita potentiam tuam, et veni ut salvos nos facias.
6: (Quousque) cibabis nos pane lacrimarum, et potum dabis nobis in lacrimis in mensura?	Ne cibes nos amplius pane lacrymarum ne amplius poculum meum cum fletu misceas.
8: Et ostende faciem tuam, et salvi erimus.	Ostende faciem tuam
15: Rispice de coelo et vide, et visita vineam istam.	et respice de caelo et vide, et visita populum tuum in pace.

To begin with, the motet seems to be Aeolian. Five of its six sections of text end on **a** (mm. 13, 35, 50, 87, and 109) and one ends on **d** (m. 72). The "commas" cadence on **a** (m. 43), **f** (m. 78), and **e** (m. 99). Yet the melodic structure of the tenor, which determines a composition's modal character, is unmistakably Phrygian. It clearly centers around the structural tones **e–g–a–c′**. And according to Zarlino's theory of *"fuggir le cadenze"* [evading cadences], the "plagal half cadences" on **a** in mm. 13, 22, and 59 can be interpreted as "impeded" e-clausulas.

Example 79

Thus, however disappointing it might seem, the conclusion is clear: the Aeolian mode, the prototype of the harmonically tonal minor mode, was foreign to Josquin.

. . .

The Ionian mode, writes Glarean, is *"omnium Modorum usitatissimus"* [the most used of all the modes].[37] First, however, the superlative is an overstatement. In Josquin's motets the predominant modes are Dorian (28 compositions)[38] and Phrygian (21 compositions).[39] And second, it is uncertain how the mode that Glarean named "Ionian" was understood in the early 16th century. It was generally notated as an f-mode with **b**♭, less often as a c-mode. "But in our day [this mode] is banished a fourth away from its proper place to the Lydian *finalis*, that is, **f**, not, however, without fa on **b**♭" [Sed nostra ætate sede propria exulans per diatessaron in Lydii finali claui, hoc est, F. non tamen absque fa in b claui cantus finit].[40] But the f-mode with **b**♭ could also be understood as a modified Lydian mode instead of as a transposed Ionian so that the modal canon restricting the number of scale types to the original *octoechos* remained intact. In the period around 1500, the unaltered Lydian—counteracted by the prohibition of the tritone—was a rarity.

In the motet *Ave verum*[41] the f-mode is notated without a ♭ in the signature, and an incidental ♭ is only sporadically indicated in the tenor, the cantus-firmus voice (mm. 8, 32, 104). Doubtless, however, Josquin assumed that the chromatic alteration was a matter of course that did not need to be made explicit. In the chant model, the prosa *Ave verum corpus natum*, the **b**♮ is already regularly displaced by **b**♭. On the other hand, it is hardly a superficial matter that the notation of the Petrucci print of 1503, which may be taken as authentic, maintains the appearance of the mode being Hypolydian. The very indeterminacy itself is what is characteristic. Since the tonal system held itself in a vague middle ground between heptatonicism and octatonicism, the question of whether the **bb** was essential or incidental could be left open. One is forced to define the mode as an Ionian that was considered a Lydian. The fact that it is Ionian remained concealed by Josquin's notation. Only Glarean, who wanted to demonstrate the existence of the Ionian mode, placed a ♭ in the signatures of all the voices when he printed Josquin's *Ave verum* in his *Dodekachordon*.

The motet *O admirabile commercium*[42] is based on an antiphon in the sixth mode—Hypolydian. It is realized as a tenor cantus firmus transposed from **f** to **bb**. Josquin gives a signature of one ♭, not two, thus adhering to the idea that the mode is Hypolydian. But in the chant model the fourth degree is already regularly lowered. And in the motet, the "incompleteness" of the signature is not meant to preserve the "Lydian fourth" but is instead based on hexachords. In the tenor the second flat was superfluous since the e♭′ always appears as the "*nota supra la*" (mm. 51, 57, 67, 68, 90, 97). And in the bass, e♭ is separately indicated twenty times because its placement in the signature would not have been without problems. It would have provoked a chromatic alteration of **a** to **a♭**, the "*nota supra la*" of the hexachord **B♭–g** (mm. 40, 74).

Even more clearly than *Ave verum* and *O admirabile commercium*, the third (and last) of the "Lydian" notated motets, *Ut Phoebi radiis*,[43] demonstrates that the tonal system tends toward octatonicism, so that the problem of whether the f-mode should be classified as "Lydian" or "Ionian" loses much of its relevance. The motet's *soggetto* [subject], the hexachord theme ut–re–mi–fa–sol–la, is sung by the tenor in the "soft" hexachord, by the bass in the "hard" hexachord, and in mm. 55–62 the alto joins in to make a three-hexachord combination [where bass sings the natural, tenor the soft, and alto the hard hexachords]:

Example 80

If the f-mode with b♭ is considered a modified Lydian, then the c-mode must be understood not as a model for, but as a copy of, the f-mode. That is, the c-mode is sooner a transposition of the f-mode with b♭ than the f-mode with b♭ a transposition of the c-mode. The conclusion may be perplexing but it is unavoidable.

The fact that Josquin, who based four compositions on the c-mode,[44] understood it as a transposed f-mode can be determined from the cantus-firmus technique in the motets *Homo quidam fecit coenam magnam*[45] and *Alma redemptoris mater*.[46] The responsory in the sixth mode,[47] not the antiphon in the third, forms the cantus firmus of *Homo quidam*. In the chant model, the Hypolydian mode is notated as an f-mode with incidental b♭s. But Josquin transposed the melody from **f** to **c** and set the cantus firmus as a canon at the lower fourth in the *prima pars* of the motet (*contratenor primus*: **c'**; tenor: **g**), and as a canon at the unison in the *secunda pars* (*contratenor primus* and tenor: **c'**). In the canon at the lower fourth, the melody transposed to **g** appears as the *comes* [canonic answer], which then forms the reference voice in the cadences. Yet Josquin avoids a preponderance of "*clausulae secundariae*" on **g** compared to the "*clausulae primariae*" on **c**. Instead of supplementing the **a–g** cadential progression of the *comes* with the discant clausula **f♯'–g'**, he interprets the **g** ending the chant passages as the penultima of a c-cadence in the other voices (mm. 34, 53, 83).

Motet no. 21 is a double motet on the Marian antiphons *Alma redemptoris mater* and *Ave regina coelorum*. *Alma redemptoris mater* is realized in the superius and bass, *Ave regina coelorum* in the alto and tenor. The c-mode should be understood as a transposed f-mode since the chant model of *Alma redemptoris mater* is notated in the f-mode with b♭ and only transposed from **f** to **c** in the motet. The second cantus firmus, *Ave regina coelorum*, is, however, modally ambiguous. The chant, which spans the ambitus **g–g'** and ends on **c**, is ascribed to the sixth mode and thus categorized as f-Hypolydian transposed up a fifth. But the melody's alternation between the use of b♭ (first and second distinctions [=chant phrases or segments]) and b♮ (fourth and sixth distinctions) suggests understanding the c-mode as a transposition of g-Hypomixolydian up a fourth. The juxtaposition of **f** and **f♯** in g-Hypomixolydian—suspect as chromaticism—would be legitimized in that it would be notated as the alternation between b♭ and b♮. Thus the categorization of the melody as Hypolydian is questionable and apparently based on reasoning by analogy. A feature of the untransposed f-mode, the interchangeability of b♮ and b♭, was transferred to the transposed version. And so it was possible to classify the transposed Hypomixolydian as transposed Hypolydian.

In the actual motet the modal characters of both chant models are, as it were, interchanged. The flatting of the seventh degree is avoided in *Ave regina* even though the chant prescribes it (mm. 1, 9, 17, 22), and it is prescribed in *Alma redemptoris mater* even though the chant does not include it (mm. 15, 30, 101, 153). Josquin thus confirms the touch of Mixolydian, even if through a kind of modal inversion.

It must remain an open question whether the c-mode in the motets *Mittit ad virginem*[48] and *Ave Maria*[49] is intended as a transposed f-mode. Reasoning by analogy from the underlying chants would be, if not illegitimate, then at least dubious. The melody of the sequence on which the motet *Mittit ad virginem* is based[50] is already notated in the c-mode in the chant model. And it is uncertain whether the *Ave Maria* is based on a *cantus prius factus* [a pre-existing chant]—Ludwig Senfl's *Ave Maria*[51] is a parody motet of the Josquin work and thus allows no conclusions to be drawn concerning a chant model. The text consists of two introductory ten-syllable lines (the annunciation, with altered ending), five strophs each with four eight-syllable lines in a paired rhyme schema (*a a b b*), and two concluding five-syllable lines. Melodically, the strophes are each independent, giving little support to the conjecture that Josquin used preexistent material. On the other hand, in strophes 2–5 the pairing of the rhyme (*a a*, but not *b b*) is underscored by melodic repetitions that would be unusual were the composition not based on a *cantus prius factus*. One could, of course, object that the repetitions in strophes 2 and 3 are based on the particular compositional technique, on the method of paired imitation (mm. 55–65 and 78–84). But this explanation breaks down in strophes 4 and 5 (mm. 94–101 and 111–27).

An Ionian mode that leaves open the possibility of being understood as modified Lydian distinguishes itself from the harmonically tonal major mode by the scant significance of degree IV: in the f-mode, a b♭ that can be interchanged with b♮ is no subdominant. And according to Zarlino, it is degree III, not IV, that forms the third clausula of the f-mode (along with the cadences on **f** and **c**). Zarlino's modal theory may suffer from some errors induced by a compulsion for systematization. But the assertion that I–V–III represents the hierarchy of degrees in the f-mode—that degree I functions as the "*clausula primaria*," degree V as the "*secundaria*," and degree III as the "*tertiaria*"—is unquestionably sound.

In the motet *Alma redemptoris mater*,[52] the Marian antiphon is realized as a canon at the unison in the middle voices. The *comes* (tenor) follows the *dux* (alto) at the interval of three breves. In the disposition of clausulas Josquin was thus both tied to the chant melody and subject to the constraints of canonic construction. But the deviations from the chant model are not contrapuntally motivated. Instead, they sharpen the presentation of the f-mode. The motet's disposition of cadences is "more regular" than the chant's: the four main sections of the text end on **f**, **a**, **c**, and **f** (mm. 37, 53, 80, and 116) instead of on **a**, **a**, **f**, and **f**. First, Josquin emphasizes the precedence of the "*clausula primaria*" (**f**). Second, he permits a main section of the text to end on a "*clausula secundaria*" (**c**) in addition to the "*clausula tertiaria*" (**a**) already present in the chant model. And third, for the sake of "*varietas*" [variety], he avoids the immediate repetition of a cadence. In place of the clausula sequence **a–a** (end of the first "period" and the first "comma" of the second) he substitutes **f–a** (mm. 37 and 44), and in place of **f–f–f** (the comma and end of the third period followed by the first phrase of the fourth period) **f–c–f** (mm. 73, 80, and 89). One might suppose that the changes to the ends of the first and third periods were based on the motet's canonic construction and thus not to be understood as expressing Josquin's conception of the f-mode. Yet in the first period it would not only have been possible but even obvious to set the rhythm of the chant phrase **c′–f–g–a–b♭–a** ("*manes*") so that the second-progression **b♭–a** in the *dux* would have formed an a-clausula with **g–a** in the *comes*. Nor is the c-clausula at the end of the third period contrapuntally motivated. The c-clausula is actually forced on the chant melody. Josquin interprets **f–g–f** not as the antepenult, penult, and final of a tenor clausula on **f**, but as the penult, final, and continuation of an alto clausula on **c** (mm. 79–80).

Example 81

To accomplish the regular disposition of cadences **f–a–c–f**, Josquin does not shrink from a forced treatment of certain details.

The third degree of the Ionian ("Lydian") mode becomes a problem in connection with strict imitation at the upper fifth. In the motet *Inviolata, integra et casta es, Maria*,[53] the melody of the Marian sequence is realized in a canon at the upper fifth with a progressive narrowing of the time interval between the voices. The *comes* (*tenor primus*), the upper voice of the canon, follows the *dux* (*tenor secundus*) after three breves in the *pars prima*, after two breves in the *pars secunda*, and after one breve in the *pars tertia*. The versicles of the sequence end in the *dux* on **a** (I, 1 and 2, II, 1 and 2, IV, 1 and 2) and on **f** (III, 1 and 2, V, 1–3, VI), in the *comes* thus on **e** and **c**.

But the e-clausula, which would compromise the f-mode, is evaded or concealed. The discant formula **d′–e′** appears in a Phrygian clausula (𝄢) with a descending leap of a fourth placed under it in the bass (**d–A**, mm. 49–50 and 62–63), in an "impeded" cadence (𝄢) instead of 𝄢 : mm. 23–24), or as the alto formula of an a-cadence (𝄞 : m. 36). The tenor formula **f′–e′** appears in an "impeded" cadence (𝄢 instead of 𝄢 : mm. 92–93) or in a "plagal half cadence" (𝄢 : mm. 105–6). And so the clarity of the f-mode is strictly preserved.

For the lamentation of David, *Planxit autem David*,[54] Josquin selected the f-mode with a ♭ in all the signatures. The text comprises verses seventeen to twenty-seven from the first chapter of Second Samuel (verse 18, 1 is lacking; verse 26 consists of two periods). Ten of the twelve periods cadence on **f** (mm. 23, 46, 106, 194, 220, 245, 269, 294, 313, 335), and the other two end with a-clausulas (𝄞) under each of which is placed the descending leap of a fourth **g–d** (mm. 64–65 and 154–55). These two "plagal half cadences" appear to be motivated by the text, that is, by interrogative or negative formulations ("quomodo ceciderunt fortes in proelio?" [How are the mighty fallen in the midst battle?] and "quasi non esset unctus oleo" [not annointed with oil]). Among the clausulas corresponding to commas, the "*primaria*" **f** predominates (mm. 55, 73, 140, 172, 183, 204, 213, 236, 319) followed by the "*tertiaria*" **a** (mm. 122, 129, 227, 256, 280, 305), so that the f-mode appears "tinged" with a-Phrygian. The "*secundaria*" **c** (mm. 13 and 83), like the "*peregrina*" **g** [lit. "wanderer"; often means "extra"] (mm. 36 and 92) occurs but rarely. A gradation of clausulas that matches the syntax of the text can, however, be determined not only from their positions but also from their forms. At the ends of periods a perfect cadence with discant, tenor, and bass formulas is the rule (mm. 23, 106, 194, 220, 245, 269, 294, 313, 335) and the 6–8 cadence the exception (m. 46). By contrast, at the ends of commas 6–8 clausulas (mm. 13, 55, 83, 122, 129, 183, 204, 227, 256, 280, 305, 219) or cadences with interrupted bass formulas (𝄢 : mm. 73 and 92) predominate over perfect cadences (mm. 36, 140, 172, 213, 236).

Josquin's choice of the f-mode with b♭ for the lamentation of David seems nonsensical and only becomes comprehensible if one understands the f-mode not as Ionian but, in spite of the b♭, as Lydian—in fact as plagal Lydian. According to Glarean, Hypolydian is a "serious" mode, and Zarlino characterizes it as plaintive. "Therefore one finds in their works many songs composed in this mode, about which they say that it is neither very gay nor elegant and thus they use it in sad and devotional compositions pertaining to commiseration, and they employ it in accompanying those texts that call for tears" [Imperoche se trova ne i loro libri molte cantilene, composte sotto questo modo, ilquale dicono, non esser molto allegro, ne molto elegante; & però lo usarono nelle cantilene gravi, & devote, che contengono commiseratione; & lo accompagnarano a quelle materie, che contengono lagrime].[55] To be sure, the ambitus of the tenor (B♭–f′) in *Planxit autem David* is ambiguous. It spans the authentic as well as the plagal octaves. But the discant is limited to the Hypolydian octave c′–c″ (once, in mm. 152–55, it goes below it to b♭, a, and g), and four times it cites the psalm formula of the first tone [= Dorian] (f–g–a . . . b♭–a–g–a: mm. 55–65, 175–78, 257–65, 314–20), which can be taken as a variant of the psalm formula for the sixth tone [= Hypolydian] (f–g–a . . . g–a–f) with which it shares the *initium* [opening motive] f–g–a and the *repercussa* a.

In *Planxit autem David*, the third degree a is characterized in two distinct ways. On the one hand, to be able to comprehend the choice of the f-mode one must ignore the alteration of b♮ to b♭ and understand the mode as Hypolydian, thus conceiving the a as the Hypolydian *repercussa*. But on the other hand, the ♭, when it appears in all the signatures, is not an "accidental" in the sense that it could be absent. It allows the a-clausula to become a Phrygian cadence, and Phrygian— more precisely, Hypophrygian—is classed, like Hypolydian, among the keys that have the power to express a lament. The ♭ is thus both "accidental" and "essential"—the contradiction was possible because it was undecided and would remain an open question whether the tonal system was heptatonic or octatonic.

It seems as though a plagal type of f-mode emphasizing the *repercussa* a contrasts with an authentic type in which, along with degree I, there is a predominance of degree V. Of course the differentiation between them is often vague and indeterminate. In the motet *Ave Maria*,[56] even though the ambitus of the tenor is plagal c-Ionian ("Lydian"), g-clausulas (mm. 84, 119, 127) predominate over the sole e-clausula (m. 39). Conversely, degree V is only faintly expressed in the motet on Psalm 113, *Laudate, pueri, Dominum*,[57] which is characterized as authentic f-Lydian by the utilization of the fifth psalm tone. The reference to the melodic model is more clearly manifested at the beginning and end, verses one, ten, and eleven (mm. 1, 161, 181), and less so in the middle, verses two, five, and six (mm. 13, 64, 89). Ten of the twelve periods end on **f** (mm. 22, 39, 63, 79, 88, 103, 122, 161, 180, 203), and the other two end on **d** (mm. 11–12 and 196–98). These two divergent cadences, the *"clausulae peregrinae,"* are motivated by the psalmization formula: Josquin places the fifth **a–d** below the falling third **c′–a** in the cantus firmus.

Only the authentic type of f-mode, not the plagal, can be conceived as a prototype of the harmonic major mode. And it was with an example of an authentic Ionian ("Lydian") motet, *Benedicite omnia opera Domini Domino,*[58] that Edward E. Lowinsky attempted to define "Josquin's role in the evolution of tonality."[59]

The Song of the Youths from the Book of Daniel (chap. 3, verses 57–74 [omitted from some Bibles]) forms the motet's text. In verses 58–73 the motet lacks the continually recurring half verse "laudate et superexaltate eum in saecula." The *parallelismus membrorum* is thus broken up, though it is reestablished by the motet's disposition of cadences. The even-numbered verses 58, 60, 62, and 64 end on the *repercussa* **c** (mm. 34, 57, 78, and 96) while the odd-numbered verses 59, 61, 63, and 65 end on the *finalis* **f** (mm. 45, 66, 87, and 106). Verse 66 is characterized as a "comma" by the lack of a *"clausula formalis"* (m. 119) and is thus connected to the period ending of verse 67 (m. 129). Verse 72 ends with the half cadence F–C (m. 169), verse 73 with the full cadence G–C (m. 181).

. . .

The melodic motives underlying the individual sections each evolve separately through "developing variation" [*progressive Variation* (Schoenberg)]. The first half verse sets out motive a[1] (m. 1: "Benedici-te"), the second half verse a contrasting motive, b[1] (m. 16: "Laudate").

Example 82

Motive a[1] is not only repeated—whether in the original form (m. 72), in diminution (m. 46), or in a simplified form (mm. 88 and 152)—

sol et lu - na Be - ne - di - ci- te Be - ne - di - ci - te

Example 83

but also modified. The beginning of the second verse, a^2 (m. 25), is derived from a variant of a^1, and the beginning of the third verse, a^3 (m. 33), is in turn derived from a^2.

Be - ne - di - ci - te Be - ne - di - ci - te

Example 84

But at the same time a^2 suggests b^1, and the motives developed from a^2—motive $a^{2/x}$ (mm. 57 and 110), $a^{2/y}$ (m. 78), and $a^{2/z}$ (m. 129)—express the relation to motive b ever more clearly through their progressive distancing from motive a.

Be - ne - di - ci- te Be - ne - di - ci- te Be - ne - di- ci- te

Example 85

The counterpart to this richly developed art of variation is a simplified chordal technique, one in which Lowinsky believed he recognized a tendency toward harmonically tonal chordal composition. "Repetition of chords and of chord progressions solidifies tonal feeling."[60] Yet the harmonic sequences cited by Lowinsky, rather than being the point of departure for the technique of imitation, are the product of that technique. In the realizations of motive a^1, the primary factor is the canonic schema, the imitation at the distance of one semibreve. The I–IV–V–I chord progression is secondary.

According to Lowinsky, a progressive dissonance treatment corresponds with the transition from modal counterpoint to harmonically tonal, chordal composition. "In his pursuit of harmonic logic he came as close to using the dominant seventh chord as sixteenth-century practice allowed—and it should be added that, fifty years after Josquin, Palestrina felt he could not go so far."[61] To support his thesis, Lowinsky cites mm. 104–6 and 116–17.

Example 86

But the tones that Lowinsky interprets as "dominant sevenths" are nothing more than accented passing tones, and the attempt to explain them as chordal dissonances is questionable.

1. In *Benedicite omnia opera Domini Domino* the accented passing tone appears not only as a "dominant seventh," but also in contexts that exclude an interpretation as chordal dissonance (mm. 8, 41, 44, 76, 77, 84, 95, 121, 127, 179, 184).

Example 87

Were one to grant Lowinsky's hypothesis, then one would be forced to take phenomena that fall under a single concept in the theory of counterpoint—that of the accented passing tone—and apportion them between two categories, speaking in some cases of "chordal dissonances" and in others of "nonharmonic tones." As a chordal dissonance, the seventh induces the root progression V–I, and the very fact that it does induce this root progression is the criterion of its validity as a chordal dissonance. Measures 8 and 121–22 of the motet, however, unmistakably demonstrate that in the early 16th century it was not felt necessary to draw harmonic consequences from the accented passing seventh.

Example 88

2. Measured by the norms of the Palestrina style, the accented passing tone was considered an archaism or a stylistic vulgarity in the late 16th century. Of course in the 17th century it was once again legitimized and explained as a "figure," as a permissible exception to the rule. Yet one cannot transfer the significance that it received in the emancipation from the strict style to a time before the cultivation and codification of "pure composition" [*reiner Satz*]. In the early 16th century the accented passing tone was a phenomenon that was destined for obsolescence and oblivion in the lower reaches of unrefined counterpoint and must therefore be conceived not as a progressive factor but as something behind the times.

3. It is doubtful whether the motet *Benedicite omnia opera Domini Domino* should be considered one of Josquin's works. It survives only in three mutually dependent German prints from the years 1537, 1553, and 1559,[62] and thus must have been, if authentic, a late work. The use of the under-third clausula (mm. 21–22 and 65–66) and some contrapuntal "crudities"—not to be confused, of course, with the misprints in the complete edition[63]—make it possible to conjecture that the attribution to Josquin is in error. The rough treatment of dissonance in m. 115 must be blamed on the composer, not the work's transmission, because each of the mutually incompatible tones has a discernible motivation: alto and tenor form a clausula, and **a′** in the discant is thematic.

Example 89

Other errors that cannot be corrected are the parallel fourths in the outer voices at m. 124

Example 90

and the parallel fifths in mm. 136–37.

Example 91

While the discant relates to the tenor, and the alto to the bass, the relationship between the outer voices is ignored.

"Josquin's role in the evolution of tonality" [Lowinsky] is thus doubtful.

Marco Cara and Bartolomeo Tromboncino: Frottolas

The "Libro primo" of frottolas published in 1504[1] includes as its second number a frottola by Marco Cara, *Oimè el cor*,[2] seemingly so simple or even primitive that it admits of opposite interpretations of its compositional technique. Edward Lowinsky cites the bass of *Oimè el cor* in his *Tonality and Atonality in Sixteenth-Century Music* and characterizes it as a variant of the passamezzo antico.[3] According to Lowinsky, ostinato "bass patterns" form "an organic part of the emergence of harmony and of tonality."[4] And it is on compositions such as *Oimè el cor* that Lowinsky bases his judgment "that the creative impetus for the new harmonic language and for modern tonality came from Italy."[5]

According to Lowinsky, the bass in *Oimè el cor* presents the roots of a harmonically tonal chordal composition. But in sharp contrast to Lowinsky's interpretation, the same bass can be understood as a secondary voice, as a mere addition to a cantus-tenor framework. The upper voices, cantus and tenor, form a two-voice composition that can stand on its own[6] and does not need to be supported by the bass (mm. 1–12).

Example 92

In the first interpretation, the passamezzo antico bass formula **d–c–d–A** (mm. 3–5) appears as the foundation of a chord progression. But according to the second interpretation it results from the method of supplementing a pre-existent cantus-tenor composition with a *contratenor bassus* whose voice leading is regulated not by considerations of harmonic tonality but by the prohibition of dissonances and parallel perfect consonances.

Leaps of fourths and fifths in the bass are not as reliable a criterion of a conception of harmonic tonality as Lowinsky thinks they are. After all, if one is to avoid parallel fifths, parallel octaves, and the unstable six-three chord, then a pre-existent chain of thirds in the upper voices,

, also forces the **f–c–d–A** voice leading in the bass.

The method of supplementing a cantus-tenor composition with a contratenor originated in the 15th century. And provided that the significance of a composition depends on the tradition out of which it arose—provided therefore that a procedure's origin determines its meaning—then a frottola like *Oimè el cor* must be characterized as a two-voice composition with a supplemental bass. And in other frottolas by Marco Cara, *Hor venduto*[7] for instance, the origin of his compositional technique in cantus-tenor compositions of the 15th century is even more conspicuous than in *Oimè el cor* (*Hor venduto*, mm. 19–27):

Example 93

Not only the octave-leap clausula at the end of the verse but also the harmonically unmotivated bass pattern in mm. 19–21—a pattern forced solely by the prohibition of parallel fifths and octaves—reveals that the bass is merely a supplement, not the foundation.

On the other hand, frottolas do exhibit an unmistakable tendency toward a style of composition where the bass is the foundation. The upper voices in mm. 7–12 of *Oimè el cor* can, of course, stand alone. But their voice crossing would hardly be comprehensible had the cantus and tenor not been jointly planned with a view to the bass tones **d–A–e–A**. Hence the tradition is not only preserved but also reinterpreted. The originally supplemental voice leadings of the bass consolidate into "patterns" that take on the function of a compositional foundation. And the connection that Lowinsky discovered with the passamezzo antico is undeniable. Of course the supposition that the bass of *Oimè el cor* was a variant of the passamezzo antico is poorly substantiated. The reverse is more plausible: many phrases that frequently recur in the added basses—phrases determined by the typical parallel thirds and sixths of the upper voices—marked themselves as stock formulas and became "emancipated" to an independent existence and meaning. Thus the bass in *Oimè el cor* represents more the prototype of the passamezzo antico than a transformation of it.

The fact that the structure of some—not all—of Cara's frottolas is grounded in the tradition of cantus-tenor compositions does not mean that Lowinsky's interpretation is wrong. But it does mean that it is not the only interpretation possible. Lowinsky's interpretation presumes that the tradition of compositional technique was reinterpreted in the frottola so that the bass, which originated as a added voice, became conceived as a fundamental, not a supplemental, voice. And there is no lack of arguments with which one could support the conjecture that the bass changed its function.

In the frottolas by Marco Cara and Bartolomeo Tromboncino, cantus-tenor composition was but one type among many. And it is not out of the question that under the influence of cantus-bass composition, which existed alongside cantus-tenor composition, the significance of the bass changed in cantus-tenor composition.

Among the frottolas by Cara, the cantus-tenor type of composition is represented by—in addition to *Oimè el cor* and *Hor venduto*—*Udite, voi finestre*[8] and *O Pietà, cara signora*.[9] The beginning of *Udite, voi finestre* (mm. 1–4) is characteristic:

Example 94

The end of the first verse (m. 2) would be absurd in a cantus-bass composition. To be understood as a consonance, the **g'** in the cantus must be related to the tenor, not to the bass. (The half rest in the cantus stands in place of a suspension prepared by the octave **g–g'** and resolved by the sixth **a–f'**.)

Among the frottolas by Bartolomeo Tromboncino, *Vale, diva mia*,[10] *Deh! per dio!*,[11] *Ah, martiale e cruda morte*,[12] and *Più che mai*[13] are based on a cantus-tenor framework. In *Vale, diva mia* the half rest in the bass of m. 2, inexplicable in a cantus-bass composition, is the expression of an embarrassment:

Example 95

The pre-existent cantus-tenor framework allowed for no tone in the bass that would not have violated a rule of counterpoint. In *Deh! per dio!* the isolated **B♭** in the bass (m. 11), a tone foreign to the diatonic system of the g-Mixolydian mode, is contrapuntally induced (mm. 10–12):

Example 96

Were parallel fifths and octaves to be avoided in mm. 10–12, then no voice leading in the bass would be possible without the irregular **B♭**—neither **d–c–g** nor **d–a–g**.

Cantus-bass composition, in which the outer voices form a framework filled in by the inner voices, is rare in unmodified form. A paradigm of the type is Cara's *Chi me dara*.[14] In their measured motion and the clarity of their articulation of the text, the outer voices set themselves apart from the inner voices, which are rhythmically more active and disregard the caesuras between the verse lines.

In terms of compositional technique, the simplest form of cantus-bass composition is represented by Cara's *La fortuna*:[15] the outer voices move almost entirely in parallel tenths. But voice leading in parallel tenths is incompatible with a conception of harmonic tonality. Hence the fact that the cantus is related primarily to the bass instead of the tenor does not imply that the bass forms the foundation of chord progressions that should be understood as being harmonically tonal.

Cantus-tenor composition and cantus-bass composition derive from different traditions. Most frottolas by Cara and Tromboncino, however, evade an unequivocal categorization. Features of one compositional type stand alongside those of the other. And the fact that cantus-tenor and cantus-bass composition permeate each other—instead of being unmistakably contrasted—seems to support the conjecture that the bass of cantus-tenor compositions was reinterpreted from a supplemental to a fundamental voice. And so Lowinsky's attempt at a harmonically tonal interpretation of compositions like Cara's *Oimè el cor* need not contradict the fundamental principles of the frottola's compositional technique.

In Tromboncino's *Se mi e grave*[16] and *Crudel, come mai potesti*,[17] the octave-leap cadence, one of the distinguishing features of cantus-tenor composition, stands alongside the parallel tenths in the outer voices, a feature of cantus-bass composition.

Example 97

And the displacement of the 6–8 clausula in Cara's *Se non hai perseveranza*[18] and Tromboncino's *A la guerra*[19] is due to a similar alternation between reference to the tenor and reference to the bass.

Example 98

The compositional process underlying these citations is, or seems to be, self-contradictory. On the one hand, it would seem forced to call the bass of *Se non hai perseveranza* the fundamental voice in the clausula and then in the next measure to demote it to the status of an added voice, as a mere supplement to the cantus-tenor clausula . On the other hand, the 6–8 progression is the common, and thus the essential, feature of both cadences.

On closer inspection, however, the contradiction loses its relevance because the question of whether a composition's lowest voice did or did not function as a point of reference mistakes the intention underlying the compositional technique of Cara and Tromboncino. The distinction between voices that determine primary relationships and those that are determined by them—the difference between a compositional framework and the supplementary voices that fill it out—has structural significance not only for the cantus-tenor and cantus-bass compositions of the 15th century but also for the harmonically tonal chordal compositions of the 17th century. But the goal that Cara and Tromboncino had in mind, a goal they did not entirely realize, was the abolition or attenuation of the difference between the primary voices and the secondary voices dependent on them—a postulate formulated by Aaron in 1525. The method of crossing cantus-tenor and cantus-bass formulas tends less toward composition with a fundamental bass than toward a polyphony in which all the voices collaborate with the same or nearly the same rights.

The attempts at imitation in Tromboncino's frottolas[20] are no doubt meagre and melodically limited to stereotyped formulas or ornaments. But the fact that the alto, which in frottolas can still generally be recognized as the last voice to be composed,[21] is involved in imitation along with the traditional main voices is indicative of Tromboncino's tendency to ennoble the genre. And it was in this genre that there appeared the transition from the framework technique—the method of drafting a two-voice counterpoint and then supplementing it with added voices—to a simultaneous conception of all the voices.

Of course many details reveal that the compositions were "pieced together." In Tromboncino's *Poi che l'alma*,[22] besides the bass, the cantus and alto also temporarily function as the lowest voice (cantus, mm. 14 and 26; alto, mm. 27–30). This is probably the result of the process of developing a four-voice composition out of two-voice cells whose localization—in contrast to the traditional framework technique—fluctuates among the voices.

A parallel fifth between cantus and alto in Cara's *Come chel biancho cigno*[23] (mm. 5–6) is the result of a crossing of two voice-pairs:

Example 99

The cantus is related primarily to the tenor, the alto to the bass. And in m. 11 of Cara's *Io non compro*,[24] the fact that the alto and tenor voices cross without any apparent motivation is based on the custom of leaving it to the tenor to join the cantus in forming the 6–8 progression of the cadence [ex. 100].

Example 100

A simultaneous conception of the voices is the assumption not only of 16th-century polyphony but also of 16th-century chordal composition. And both lines of development are marked in the frottolas even if the tendency toward polyphony lacks emphasis. Many details cannot be explained without recourse to the concept of a chord—to the perception of a three- or four-tone sonority as a directly given unity.

The passing-tone **b′** in the cantus of Cara's *Defecerunt*[25] (m. 2) relates to the chord as a whole, not to one voice. But the tendency toward chordal composition does not imply that the harmony is tonal.

Example 101

Cara's *Deh si, deh no*[26] is conceived as a chordal composition, even though the underlying basis of cantus-tenor composition may still be detectable. And the key is c-Ionian. But between the verses that cadence on degrees I and V (mm. 1–4: C–F–C–G–$^{f\sharp}_a$–G; and mm. 9–12: C–F–d–G–C) there is the sharp contrast of a chord progression that is reminiscent of the folia model and in a harmonic interpretation should relate to G minor: B♭–F–g–d–G (mm. 5–8). The abrupt juxtaposition forces one to assume that chord progressions, even apparently harmonic cadences, were understood as mere formulas that could be pieced together without being functionally interrelated. And it is precisely in the method of joining together things that are "unconnected" that the line of development of 16th-century chordal composition clearly distinguishes itself: "emancipated" chordal composition—no longer tied to a two-voice framework—tends toward harmonic "*varietas*" [variety], toward an expansion of the wealth of sonorities, an expansion that is at the same time independent of a need for tonal centering.

CLAUDIO MONTEVERDI: MADRIGALS

Giovanni Maria Artusi's polemic against Monteverdi[1] is often mentioned but has scarcely been analyzed. It seems well established that the aggravated theorist was wrong about the composer. But the attacks that Artusi mounted against the treatment of dissonance and the use of keys in Monteverdi's fifth book of madrigals are not incomprehensible, however crude and pedantic their formulation. Nor is it sufficient to dismiss Artusi's arguments as pure misunderstandings by pointing out that he overlooked the expressive character of the passages he cited. After all, expressive features are not exempt from the requirement that they be comprehensible in terms of compositional technique. And no less inadequate would be the explanation that Monteverdi's method can be attributed to a new, and therefore to Artusi a strange, principle, that of tonal harmony. No matter how far the harmony of the fifth book of madrigals departs from the norms of the 16th century, it is still not tonal in the sense of major-minor tonality. It represents a stage of development that evades simple classification under the alternatives of modality or harmonic tonality.

The beginning of the madrigal *O Mirtillo, Mirtillo anima mea*,[2] which leaves the key in doubt, provoked Artusi's indignation. For Artusi, the fact that a composition ending with a D-cadence begins with an F-cadence, in fact with its fourth degree Bb major, appeared as an "*impertinentia d'un principio*" [inappropriate beginning].[3] And it is, without question, difficult to make an unequivocal determination of the madrigal's key. Apparently it is meant to be g-Mixolydian, since not only is the F-cadence (mm. 1–2) at the beginning transposed to G, but also the final passage, in D (mm. 63–69), is an exact transposition of a section in G (mm. 57–62). But a proof and justification of this determination of key is not possible without numerous detours.

The customary features of a mode—melodic formulas and schemata for imitations, a clear marking of the octave species, and a characteristic disposition of cadences—are all missing in *O Mirtillo*. Edward E.

Lowinsky would likely have been tempted to speak of "triadic atonality." With five cadences or verse endings (mm. 5, 29, 43, 56, 62), the G-major chord, the root chord of the primary key, is scarcely more prominent than the d-minor chord (mm. 41, 51, 53, 69), the a-minor chord (mm. 12, 31, 35, 46), the F-major chord (mm. 2, 10, 59), or the C-major chord (mm. 14, 65). Instead of being grouped around a center, the cadences are uniformly distributed over the degrees of the natural hexachord—only the E-major chord occurs but once (m. 8).

It is evident from the madrigal's beginning that the triads in *O Mirtillo* must be understood as chords, as directly perceived unities, and not as the results of a combining of intervals. If the key relationships that make g-Mixolydian prominent as the main key are not to become unrecognizable, then mm. 3–5 must be perceived as a transposition of mm. 1–2. But outside of the bass, none of the voices or interval progressions in mm. 3–5 reappear unaltered. The identity of the passage is preserved only by the sequence of chords and the bass that represents that sequence. As a result, the chords must be considered primary unities.

Chordal composition does not, however, imply tonal harmony. If by "tonal harmony" one understands an association of chords based on dominant, subdominant, and parallel connections to a tonal center, then verses two and three of *O Mirtillo* cannot be defined as being "tonal."

Example 102

Neither the relations between the d-minor and E-major or the G-major and F-major chords ["d-minor" assumes the implied resolution of the tied **e″** to **d″** on the word "qui"], nor the connection between the verse endings on E-major and F-major chords can be attributed to dominant, subdominant, or parallel relationships. The reconciling a-minor and C-major chords, indispensable in a tonal context, are lacking. And it hardly need be pointed out that an interpretation of the chordal relationships in *O Mirtillo* as "harmonic ellipses" would be anachronistic: the omission of the obvious, which was possible in the 19th century during the final stage in the development of tonal harmony, was inconceivable around 1600, when what was later trivial was still unfamiliar. The chord sequences d–E, E–D, and G–F are not "harmonic ellipses," not abbreviations for d–E–a and G–F–C, but self-substantiated progressions that owe their convincing effect to the tradition of intervallic composition. There, a progression in contrary motion with a half-step connection in one of the voices (,) had a meaning similar to that of a dominant or subdominant relation in tonal harmony. Of course the effect of these progressions fades during the transition from intervallic to chordal composition.

Though the technique of chordal composition used by Monteverdi in *O Mirtillo* is therefore not harmonically tonal, it would also be meaningless to classify it as "modal." "Mode," as a category of polyphony, is a concept that embraces melodic formulas, schemata for imitations, the ambitus of each voice, and dispositions of cadences. But it includes no norms or models for the sequence of chords. In the progression that ends *O Mirtillo*, D–G–E–a–G–C–F–G–D–a–G⁶–D⁶–A–D, one can find no trace of its being determined by the mode, no tendency toward the D-major chord as the goal and conclusion. And therefore it seems that the definition of *O Mirtillo* as Mixolydian shrivels to an empty categorization.

The impression of indefiniteness disappears, however, if the G-key is understood as part of a system or, as Jacques Handschin would say, part of a "society." The succession of chordal roots in mm. 3–5, C–G⁶–D–G = G: IV–I–V–I, leaves open the question of whether the G-key represents the Mixolydian or the Ionian mode, thus whether f♯ is intended as a diatonic and essential, or a chromatic and incidental, *subsemitonium modi* ["leading tone"; chromatic in g-Mixolydian, diatonic in g-Ionian]. Only the context makes the G-cadence recognizable as Mixolydian. The Phrygian cadence d⁶–E (mm. 7–8) and the Lydian cadence G–F (mm. 9–10) establish the ♮-system as the diatonic system to which the G-cadence should be referred.

The G-cadence, ambiguous when taken by itself, is defined as a sol-cadence, as Mixolydian, by its relationship to the E-major and F-major verse endings, the mi and fa degrees of the ♮-system. This modal characterization is not contained in the G-cadence itself but results from its relationship with the Phrygian E-cadence and the Lydian F-cadence. Consequently g-Mixolydian in *O Mirtillo* is not a self-sufficient mode but a "component key" [*Teiltonart*] whose position and meaning are derived from the system to which it belongs.

A description of the stage of development that Monteverdi's madrigals represent in the history of harmony thus must consist primarily
of an attempt to provide a more precise definition of the concept of
a "component key."

1. A diatonic system's six component keys, represented by the
cadential degrees ut, re, mi, fa, sol, and la (Ionian, Dorian, Phrygian,
Lydian, Mixolydian, and Aeolian), stand apart as independent entities
that cannot be reduced one to the other. It would be precarious to
categorize the E- and F-major cadences of the second and third lines
of *O Mirtillo* as degrees VI and VII of the g-Mixolydian mode. The
symbols VI and VII would represent nothing but empty ordinal numbers
without musical relevance. (It was already pointed out that an attempt
to give them meaning through a harmonically tonal interpretation of
the E-major and F-major chords as dominant of the subdominant
parallel [V/ii] and as double subdominant [IV/IV] would be misplaced.)
The musical significance of the E-major and F-major chords consists
in nothing more than representing the Phrygian mi-degree and the
Lydian fa-degree. And the chordal characters of the degrees are
independent of the main key. The F-major cadential degree is the
fa-degree in relation not only to the d-mode but also to the G-mode.
The symbols "d: III" and "G: VII" would either be meaningless or—if
they imply that the F-major cadential degree viewed as "d: III" would
have a different meaning than when in the position of "G: VII"—
erroneous.

2. The main key of a composition is not a center to which the
remaining component keys are related as secondary keys, but merely
a *primus inter pares* [first among equals]. To be sure, it is a "main"
key insofar as it is set off from the society of component keys by its
frequent recurrence and by its position at the beginning and end—or,
as in *O Mirtillo*, by its location in the third-to-last and second-to-last
positions. But it does not form a "basic" key from which the dependent
keys are derived. In *O Mirtillo,* the *raison d'être* of the component keys
e-Phrygian and f-Lydian cannot consist of a nonexistent relationship
with g-Mixolydian. On the contrary, the system of component keys,
which includes e-Phrygian and f-Lydian along with g-Mixolydian, is
"logically prior" to the establishment of g-Mixolydian as the main key.
In *O Mirtillo*, "main key" is more of an extrinsic, formal category than
one that establishes the basis of musical coherence.

3. The fact that the component keys in Monteverdi's madrigals are
independent of one another does not mean that dominant, subdominant, and parallel relationships were excluded or as such were not
effective. While they can be a means for tying together the component
keys, they are not fundamental to the system. It is possible, if not

unavoidable, to conceive of the cadential degrees in the chordal sequences D–G–D–G | a–E–a | C–G–C | d–A–D | D–g–D (mm. 42–52) as a complex of subdominant and parallel relationships. Yet it would be unwarranted to take the relations between G and C, a and C, or a, d, and g and group them around a main key as a tonal center. And some relationships, for example the contrast between the verse endings on E-major and F-major chords (mm. 6–10), completely resist any attempt at a "functional" interpretation. The dominant, subdominant, and parallel relationships among the component keys have no fundamental significance.

4. Monteverdi's procedure of uniting component keys into a "society" is consequently less definite in its linkages of sonorities and less subject to a norm than is tonal harmony. But on the other hand, the delimitation of the system, of secondary importance in major-minor tonality, forms a primary factor in Monteverdi's madrigals. The component keys are limited to six cadential degrees that can be labeled by the hexachord syllables. The cadential degrees of the ♮-system, of the untransposed scale, form the natural hexachord (**c–a**), those of the ♭-system, of the transposed scale, the soft hexachord (**f–d′**). The half-step interval between the mi- and fa-degrees appears as the characteristic relation by which a system can be recognized. In *O Mirtillo*, the system is still not completely determined by the F: IV–I–V–I and G: IV–I–V–I cadences (mm. 1–6) because it remains an open question whether the b♭ (F: IV) should be considered an essential tone in the ♭-system or an incidental tone in the ♮-system. Only the mi–fa contrast in mm. 6–10 unmistakably establishes the ♮-system. The system of component keys, whose individual members are determined by the positions in which they occur, is thus necessarily limited. Exceeding the ♮-system through cadences on B♭-major or b-minor chords would eliminate the potential for recognizing the system through the mi–fa contrast. By contrast, in major-minor tonality the system of keys that one can relate to a basic key is in principle unlimited. Only the particular method of linking the chords determines whether a relationship between remote keys, between C major and F♯ minor, does or does not make sense. In major-minor tonality, a normalization of the methods of linking chords corresponds with the indeterminacy in the boundary of the system. For Monteverdi, an indeterminacy in the methods of linking chords corresponds with a normalization of the system.

5. As mentioned, the system of component keys is "logically prior" to the establishment of a main key. Instead of the system of partial keys being determined by the main key, the main key is determined by the system of component keys, whose most obvious expression is

given by the mi–fa contrast. In major-minor tonality, the functions and characters of the component keys depend on the main key: F major is the subdominant of C major and the tonic parallel of D minor. By comparison, E major and F major in *O Mirtillo* are not characterized by their relation to G major. Instead, the primary degree of G major is recognizable as Mixolydian from its relation to the secondary degrees of E major and F major. The method of uniting six component keys includes the possibility of renouncing the establishment of a main key, since the society of component keys is capable of existing as a self-supporting system. Therefore it is uncertain whether the assertion that *O Mirtillo* represents the g-Mixolydian mode really addresses an essential feature of the composition.

6. The transformation of the modes into the component keys of a "closed society" and the transition from intervallic to chordal composition form the prerequisites to an expansion of chromaticism across an entire composition, a chromaticism that does not endanger the system of keys even though it can frequently make the melodic form of the modes unrecognizable.

(a) A d-mode, viewed in isolation, is transformed from Dorian to Mixolydian by the raising of its third degree. But as a component key in a system characterized as the ♮-system by the E-major and F-major degrees, the d-key is unaffected by chromatic alterations. The line "O anime" in *O Mirtillo* (mm. 36–41), in spite of the chords D–G at the beginning and A–D at the end seeming to change Dorian into major, unmistakably represents the d-degree of the ♮-system that was established in the middle of the line by the fa–mi formula ⎰.

(b) In a chordal system based on the relations between chordal roots that jointly form a hexachord, chromatic alterations of the chords' thirds are incidental and irrelevant to the presentation of the component keys. Indeed the mutability of the thirds, "*Terzfreiheit*" to use Heinrich Besseler's term, is a sign that the society of component keys is formed by relationships between chordal degrees, not by the melodic patterns underlying a particular modal type. The limits of the tonal system are based on the chordal system. The extreme chroma on the sharp side is **g♯**, the third of the mi-degree **e**. The third **d♯** is excluded because it presumes the root **b**, which is not included in the system of six chordal degrees. One could object that the **d♯** is missing because in an unequally tempered tuning it would clash with e♭, a tone that is indispensable for the transposed scale of the ♭-system. But limits were drawn to chromatic alteration based not only on considerations of tuning and temperament but also and above all on the nature of the chordal system. This can be determined from the fact that not only the triad **b–d♯′–f♯′**

was avoided, but also **b–d'–f♯'**, which the tuning system allowed, because it would have disturbed the chordal system. In the ♮-system, the additional mi–fa contrast of b–C would have caused the mi–fa contrast of E–F to lose its function of unequivocally characterizing the system.

(c) The notion that the technique of chromatic alteration includes a tendency toward major-minor tonality is true and false at the same time. It is true to the extent that the minor chords whose thirds are raised generally form either a verse ending or a "secondary dominant" to the immediately following chord. Thus the "principle of the dominant," so important in tonal harmony, is operative in chromatic alterations. But on the other hand, the thesis is also false since in the system of six component keys—no less than in the modal polyphony of the 15th and 16th centuries—chromatic alterations are irrelevant to the characterization of the underlying key, mode, or system. The "principle of the dominant," even though it establishes chordal connections, has no "tonal" significance. For that reason there is no internal contradiction if the chromatic alterations in Monteverdi's chordal technique coincide with the norms of tonal harmony in some places but thwart them in others. In the third verse from *O Mirtillo* (mm. 8–10), one finds **f♯'** and **b'** where in tonal harmony one would expect to find **f'** and **b♭'**.

Example 103

The raising of **f'** to **f♯'** is motivated by three considerations. First, the "*relatio non harmonica*" **g♯'–f'** is avoided in the transition from the second to the third verse. Second, the E-major chord is linked to the D-major chord through contrary motion with a half-step connection in one of the voices ( ) [**g♯'–a'** in *canto*, **e–d** in *basso*]. And third, the D-major chord forms a "secondary dominant" to the G-major chord. The "principle of the dominant"—as one cofactor among many—is thus operative. But on the one hand, it does not exclude the notion that the $\begin{smallmatrix} \end{smallmatrix}$ progression establishes a close relationship between chords, a notion incompatible with the norms of tonal harmony. And on the other hand, it has no significance for the structure of the chordal system since the chromatic alteration of the d-minor chord to D-major does not influence the F-major verse ending's function of representing the fa-degree of the ♮-system in relation to the E-major mi-degree.

7. It is difficult if not impossible to unambiguously determine whether and under what limitations the ♮-system allows an incidental **b♭** in addition to **f♯**, **c♯**, and **g♯**. A B♭-chord as the cadential degree at the end of a verse unquestionably presumes a change of system, a transition to the ♭-system. And to nearly the same extent a Phrygian cadence on **a** ( ) appears as a sign of the ♭-system by virtue of the mi–fa contrast that it represents. But on the other hand, as was shown in Josquin's motets, the 16th-century tradition suggests understanding an f-mode with a B♭-chord on its fourth degree as an altered Lydian, not as a transposed Ionian mode. From this perspective the B♭-chord could be included as a supplementary chord, even if not as a cadential degree in the ♮-system. Doubts about the meaning of the B♭-degree can thus not be dismissed as mere inadequacies in our understanding. They should instead be understood as expressions of an indeterminacy in the subject itself. The beginning and the ending of *O Mirtillo*, the transposition of an F-cadence to G

$$\text{Measures 1–2:}\quad B^\flat - F^{\underline{6}} \; C - F$$
$$\text{Measures 3–5:}\quad C - G^{\underline{6}} \; D - G$$

and the transposition of a double verse from G major to D major

$$\text{mm. 56–62:}\quad G - C - A - d - C - F \;\|\; B^\flat - C - G \;|\; d - C^6 \; G^{\underline{6}} \; D - (G)$$
$$\text{mm. 62–69:}\quad D - G - E - a - G - C \;\|\; G - G - D \;|\; a - G^{\underline{6}} \; D^{\underline{6}} \; A - D,$$

admit of no less than four irreconcilable interpretations that all suffer from one defect or another.

(a) Under the assumptions of tonal harmony, the transposition of the F-major cadence to G major (mm. 1–5) would be understood as a change of key, thus as a whole-step transposition from the ♭-system system to the ♯-system. But if the G-major degree in m. 5 is not to sacrifice its identity with the other G-cadences in the composition, then mm. 3–5 must be related to the ♮-system as a Mixolydian cadence. Thus the F-major and G-major cadences are not analogous. The dominant third of the F-cadence, **e**, is diatonic and essential; the dominant third of the G-cadence, **f♯**, chromatic and incidental.

(b) On the other hand, the interpretation of the main key as Mixolydian is put into question by the concluding passage. If the double verse in mm. 56–62 is to be considered g-Mixolydian and its transposition at the upper fifth in mm. 62–69 as d-Mixolydian, then it must be assumed that the transposition is based on a change from the ♮-system to the ♯-system. But first, the hypothetical ♮-system (and analogously the ♯-system) includes an optional fa-degree (B♭-major; in the ♯-system, F-major). And second, the characteristic mi-degree is missing (E-major; in the ♯-system, B-major).

(c) Of course the result of an attempt to proceed from the given set of chords, basing mm. 56–62 on the ♭-system with the mi–fa contrast A–B♭ and mm. 62–69 on the ♮-system with the mi–fa contrast E–F, would be no less contradictory. One would be forced to classify the G-mode and the transposed D-mode as "Dorian," even though the G- and D-chords are always presented with major thirds.

(d) Even the idea of breaking up the double verses and ascribing mm. 56–60 to the ♭-system, mm. 60–66 to the ♮-system, and mm. 66–69 to the ♯-system comes to naught. The identity of the D-major chord at the beginning, middle, and end of the double verse in mm. 62–69 forces itself so inescapably on one's musical consciousness that the demand for hearing a change of system, thus imputing a different position and meaning in the system to the D-major chord at the beginning and in the middle than at the end, pales to a fiction.

8. A harmonic analysis that neglects the other features of compositional technique would be incomplete even as an analysis of harmony. Many features of harmony stand out more clearly or only become recognizable at all when one studies the reciprocal relationships by which harmony is bound up with a composition's rhythm and form.

The rhythm of *O Mirtillo* is determined by the declamation of the text, and the madrigal's form is determined by the arrangement of the verses. The composition should be understood as a musical presentation of speech — in fact a presentation less of the ideas expressed than of speech itself. The individual verses of the madrigal, which include eleven or seven syllables and can be subdivided into half verses (4 + 7, 5 + 6, or 6 + 5 syllables), relate to each other as independent and self-contained musico-linguistic unities, even though they do not always form independent units of meaning. The musical structure is thus paratactical rather than syntactical.

The fact that the verses or half verses appear as autonomous structures instead of as the result of previous verses is based on the large-scale rhythm. The length of the verses varies between 3/2, 4/2, and 5/2. And the 5/2 or 3/2 groupings cannot be reduced to extensions or contractions of 4/2 groupings. "Asymmetrical" arrangements of 4 + 5 or 5 + 4 half-note values are the norm, "symmetrical" arrangements the exception. "Asymmetry" does not, however, exclude the impression of a balance between the parts, of a rhythmic correspondence. To be perceptible, rhythm does not need to be regular. Of course "asymmetrical" groupings lack the factor of allowing for "nested binary subdivision" [*potenzierte Zweigliedrigkeit*] that characterizes "symmetrical" rhythmic periods. By "nested binary subdivision" is meant the schema $\{[(1+1)+(1+1)]+[(1+1)+(1+1)]\}$, where two one-measure motives combine into a phrase half, two phrase halves into a complete phrase, and two phrases into a period. What is critical is less the external symmetry of the number of measures, a symmetry which can be deformed, than the principle that the second phrase is divided, analogously to the first, into two phrase halves that are in turn divisible into two complementary motives. (The analogy in the division is the prerequisite for being able to reduce irregular phrases to regular phrases.)

As the counterpart of a subordinating rhythmic structure—the norm of "nested binary subdivision" in which single two- and four-measure groupings are set forth as halves requiring completion—there is a subordinating harmony. A subordinating harmony combines the contrast of an F- and a G-major cadence with an expectation of a C-major cadence, a cadence that reconciles the contrast and represents a superordinate key that accommodates both the F- and G-major cadences as cofactors, as its subdominant and dominant. But at the beginning of *O Mirtillo*, the F- and G-major sections stand apart harmonically as well as rhythmically. Neither do the cadential degrees represent harmonic functions in C major nor do the "asymmetrically" juxtaposed verse halves, which include both 4/2 and 5/2 lengths, combine as the antecedent and consequent phrases of a period. As with the cadential elements, the rhythmic elements can exist on their own and are not interdependent. A large-scale rhythm in which verses of unequal length and structure are set off from each other as independent, self-substantiated structures corresponds to a grouping of component keys that do, in fact, form a system but are not, as secondary keys, the result of a primary key. The rhythm, just like the harmony, is coordinate rather than subordinate.

. . .

The principle of taking six component keys whose cadential degrees form a hexachord and combining them into a "closed society" facilitates the transition from modality to major-minor tonality because the component keys can, without compromising the sense of the system, be not only modes but also major or minor keys. It is a matter of indifference whether the component G-key appears in Mixolydian or major form so long as its significance consists only in representing the sol-degree of the key-system c–d–e–f–g–a = ut–re–mi–fa–sol–la.

To be sure, the relationship between the main key, the society of component keys, and the change of system—the substitution of e♭ for e or b♭ for b—is frequently ambiguous. The five madrigals on texts from Guarini's *Il Pastor fido* (IV, 9)—*Ecco Silvio*, *Ma se con la pietà*, *Dorinda, ah dirò*, *Ecco piegando*, and *Ferir quel petto*[4]—are united into a cycle by a common key, g-Dorian in the ♭-system. But the Dorian character of the g-mode is not always unquestionably well established. The ♭-system alternates with the ♮-system or the ♭♭-system even in the final passages of several of the madrigals.

Thus it seems that either the unity of the key must be sacrificed or the g-key in the ♭-system must be identified with the g-key in the ♭♭-system. In the second case, the change of system appears as a secondary factor in the face of a g-key in which Aeolian and Dorian are melded together. The opposite interpretation, the contention that the beginning and end of a composition can be modally divergent, could be supported by Christoph Bernhard's theory of "*alteratio modi*" [change of mode].[5]

It was, however, precisely this indeterminacy, this lack of clarity, that was one of the preconditions for the rise of the key system of major-minor tonality.

A major or minor key's circle of closely related keys includes in its core set six keys whose cadential degrees—just like those of a "society" of component keys circa 1600—form a hexachord. On the one hand, the degrees of the soft hexachord, f–g–a–b♭–c–d, function in D minor as Tp–S–D–Sp–Dp–T, in F major as T–Sp–Dp–S–D–Tp. And on the other hand, a major or minor key's circle of closely related keys is based on modulations between three transposition systems: the S and Sp keys are in the ♭♭-system, the T and Tp keys are in the ♭-system, and the D and Dp keys are in the ♮-system. Not only the circle of closely related keys or cadential degrees but also the alternation between the three transposition systems reoccurs in major-minor tonality, though in a different function.

In major-minor tonality, a change of key and a change of system are tied together by a correlation: F major and D minor presume the ♭-system, B♭ major and G minor the ♭♭-system. By contrast, around

1600 the two factors were independent of each other: a transition to the ♭♭-system was not limited to the keys of G minor and B♭ major, but also included F major, C major, and D minor. There is a notion that a tendency toward major-minor tonality was the primary or even the sole force behind the alteration or coloration of the modes through switching e♭ and e♮, or b♭ and b♮. Yet this is a prejudice that suppresses, through a gross simplification, the complexities involved in the transition from modality to major-minor tonality. C-Mixolydian was indeed changed to Ionian by b♮, and g-Dorian to Aeolian by e♭, but C-Mixolydian was also changed to Dorian by e♭ and g-Dorian to Mixolydian by b♮. In modal transformations caused by a change of system, a precedence of Ionian or major and Aeolian or minor is scarcely detectable.

Ecco Silvio, the first madrigal from the cycle of texts from Guarini's *Il Pastor fido*, dramatically demonstrates the precedence, circa 1600, of the system of component keys over the characterization of a primary key. The first verse ends on a B♭-major chord (m. 6) and, transposed up a fifth, on an F-major chord (m. 11). But the second verse ends on an A-major chord (mm. 15–16). Instead of establishing a primary mode, the beginning of the madrigal, which at the same time forms the opening of the entire madrigal cycle, establishes the ♭-system characterized by the fa–mi contrast between the Lydian B♭-degree and the Phrygian A-degree. The third and fourth verses, with cadences on F-major (m. 18) and B♭-major chords (m. 21), run through the ♭-system's set of chords in a circle of fifths extending from A major to E♭ major: A–d–g–C–f / B♭–E♭–B♭–f–B♭. (The "foreign" E♭-major chord is included as IV in the B♭-major cadence.) The system is thus set forth in two ways: "intensively," through the characteristic cadential degrees of verses one and two, and "extensively," through the chordal sequence of lines three and four.

The fifth verse ends on a d-minor chord (m. 24), the sixth on a g-minor chord (m. 28), and the seventh on a C-major chord (m. 30). It consequently seems as though the g-degree, representing the primary mode, is in no way set off from the society of component keys, since the disposition of cadences in the first seven lines, B♭–F–A–F–B♭–d–g–C, places no noticeable accent on the g-degree. But the cadences of lines 4, 5, and 6 do form the primary degrees of the g-mode according to the modal norm as formulated by Zarlino: B♭-major is the "*clausula tertiaria*," d-minor the "*clausula secundaria*," and g-minor the "*clausula primaria*." And it is not out of the question that the arrangement of the cadence degrees according to the III–V–I schema was perceived as a sufficient emphasis of the g-degree.

But there is obviously yet another notion underlying the disposition of cadences. The fact that it includes all the degrees of the soft hexachord in the first seven verses signifies that the distribution of degrees to verse endings—just like the accentuation of the characteristic degrees in lines one and two and the running through of the set of chords in lines three and four—forms a means of representing the ♭-system. The closed system, the society of component keys, is the primary factor and the main key is secondary.

The final part of the madrigal (mm. 46–82) is based on a technique of transposition that may make clear the difficulties connected with the concept of a change of system.

Section:	a¹	b¹	a²	b²	c¹	d¹	c²	d²
Measure:	51	54	61	64	69	73	78	82
Cadence:	F	g	B♭	c	d	a	g	d
System:	♭		♭♭		♮		♭	

Sections a² and b² are transpositions up a fourth of sections a¹ and b¹, while sections c² and d² are transpositions up a fourth of sections c¹ and d¹. The transition to the ♭♭-system is marked by the E♭-major chord (mm. 55–56), and the abrupt turn toward the ♮-system is marked by an e-minor (m. 66) and an E-major chord (m. 71). Neither the E♭-major chord nor the e-minor and E-major chords are cadence degrees at the end of verses. Yet the insignificant appearance of these characteristic chords in the course of a verse is nonetheless sufficient because the change of system is combined with the transposition of sections of the form.

On the other hand, it cannot be dismissed as pure chance that in the closing part of the madrigal—just as in the opening part—the arrangement of cadences includes all the degrees of the soft hexachord, f–g–a–b♭–c–d. The ♭–♭♭–♮–♭ schema of the change of systems is filled out by component keys that taken together can be understood as a complete presentation of the ♭-system. And thus they fulfill the same function that they did in the madrigal's first seven verses. Of course the uncertainty of whether to posit a change of system or advocate a persistence of the ♭-system does not signify a lifeless contradiction between interpretive principles that cancel each other out. Instead, it means that the ♭♭-system and the ♮-system are subordinate to the ♭-system situated at the beginning and the end. And the grouping of secondary systems around a primary system can be interpreted as the prototype of the relations between primary and secondary degrees in major-minor tonality.

The direct relationships between the individual component keys are, of course, still not defined functionally. Instead of being connected to each other as relative major and minor, B♭ major and G minor are separated by a change of system [see diagram above]. And the fifth-relation is not sufficiently specific (d–a, g–d) since it is characteristic of many other modes as well. Hence what stands out is the whole-step interval between component keys (F–g, B♭–c), which as a self-contained relationship admits of no harmonically tonal interpretation. The fact that a relationship exists between the g-Dorian and f-Ionian degrees that is meaningful on its own—and does not need to be indirectly justified by the mediation of a d-minor degree forming the dominant to G minor and the parallel of F major—is not a special case in Monteverdi's madrigals, not something limited just to *Ecco Silvio*. Rather, it seems that around the year 1600 the antithesis between Ionian and Dorian was conceived as the paradigm of a "major-minor contrast." (For 17th-century theorists like Johann Lippius and Johann Crüger, Ionian and Dorian, not Ionian and Aeolian, formed the primary and most characteristic modes of the major and minor groups, the "*modi naturaliores*" and "*molliores*" [the more "natural" (i.e., major) modes and the "softer" (i.e., minor) modes]).

The major-minor contrast at the interval of a whole-step can be considered a distinguishing feature of a modal disposition of cadences. With minor keys or "*modi molliores*," Zarlino's I–III–V formula allows no differentiation to be made between modal and tonal dispositions of cadences. Even in the tonal harmony of the 18th century, just as in the modal harmony of the 16th century, it is the tonic parallel [♭III] and not the subdominant that forms the third cadential degree in minor keys, tonic and dominant naturally being the other two. By comparison, the major-minor contrast at the interval of a whole-step is a criterion of a modal disposition of cadences. In tonal minor, the dominant parallel [♭VII] is a remote secondary key that can only relate to the tonic indirectly, not directly.

In the second madrigal of the cycle, *Ma se con la pietà*, as in *Ecco Silvio*, it is the presentation of the system or the presentation of the change of systems that appears to stand in the foreground in relation to the characterization of a main key.

Verse:	a	b	c^1	c^2+d^1	d^2	d^3
Measure:	4	7	11	15	19	22
Cadence:	E♭	B♭	d	A–d	C–g	C–g
System:	♭♭			♭		

The ♭♭-system is set forth by its characteristic chords, the fa-degree E♭-major (mm. 4 and 9) and the mi-degree d-minor (m. 11). The E♭-chord does occur at the end of a verse, but it does not form the goal of a cadence. Rather it appears as a dependent part of a B♭-cadence that encompasses two verses: B♭–E♭–c–F–B♭–E♭–F–B♭ (mm. 1–7). The transition to the ♭-system is recognizable both in the transposition a fifth higher of the bass of the third verse (c^1 and c^2) and in the abrupt contrast between the fa-degree of the ♭♭-system, E♭ major (m. 9), and the mi-degree of the ♭-system, A major (m. 14). G minor, the main key, is presented late and unpretentiously in variants of the fourth verse (d^2 and d^3), in particular as g-Dorian in the ♭-system, not as g-Aeolian in the ♭♭-system. Verses d^2 and d^3 are divided into half verses, and the first half of each pair ends with a C-major cadence so that the Dorian character of the g-cadence is unmistakable.

To be sure, the precedence of the change of system in relation to the individual keys and the modal characterization of the component keys as b♭-Ionian, d-Phgrygian, d-Aeolian, and g-Dorian is not unambiguously established. The verse endings on B♭-major, d-minor, and g-minor chords would satisfy Zarlino's III–V–I norm of a disposition of cadences for the g-mode. Thus it is not out of the question that they ought to be understood as *clausula tertiaria*, *secundaria*, and *primaria* in spite of the change of system and in fact independent of it. And the hypothesis that the presentation of the main key of G minor is set above the change of system would include the possibility of understanding the B♭-cadence with an E♭-major chord, and the Phrygian d-cadence with a c-minor chord in first inversion, as cofactors of the g-key. But the very uncertainty of whether to attribute precedence to the change of system or to the III–V–I cadence schema is a sign of an internal contradiction that is resolved only by major-minor tonality.

The second, middle part of the madrigal is based on a twofold transposition up a fifth, concerning which, of course, it remains uncertain whether or not it implies a change of system.

e^1	f^1	e^2	g^1	g^3	f^2	g^2	g^3	g^4
27	29	33	35	40	42	44	47	51
F	B♭	C	F	G	C	F	F	C
♭♭		♭		♮		♭		♮

The ♭♭-system and the ♮-system are not completely determined. So the B♭-major (m. 29), F-major (m. 35), and C-major cadences (m. 42) can therefore be interpreted either as Ionian in the ♭♭-, ♭-, and ♮-systems, or as Lydian, Ionian, and altered Mixolydian in the ♭-system. The fa-degree e♭ of the B♭-cadence and the *subsemitonium* b of the C-cadence would be essential according to the first interpretation, but incidental according to the second. Yet it is precisely this indeterminacy between a changing and a unified system that points forward to major-minor tonality. A functional interpretation of B♭ major, F major, and C major as subdominant, tonic, and dominant keys would include both factors, the change of system and the unity of system. As secondary systems, ♭♭ and ♮ would relate to the primary ♭-system. Of course the tonal centering in *Ma se con la pietà* is limited to a faint hint that is insufficient to justify a functional interpretation of B♭ major, F major, and C major as the subdominant, tonic, and dominant keys. Even this "relative tonic" of F major relates to the main key of G minor not functionally but through a major-minor contrast at the interval of a whole step.

In the third, concluding part of the madrigal, not only the set of chords but also the change between the ♭♭- and ♭-systems also permits or seems to permit a functional interpretation. But this should not blind one to the fact that those features prefiguring major-minor tonality occur in a context based above all on the amalgamation of independent component keys into a system that is primarily self-supporting and only secondarily related to a single tonal center.

h^1	$h^2 + i^1$	k^1	i^2	k^2	k^3
54	58	61	63	66	68
a	d	F	a	d	g
♭	♭♭	♭			♭♭

The Phrygian cadences that conclude verses h^1, $h^2 + i^1$, and i^2—the clausulas and —resist the attempt to fit them, as iv–V progressions, into the "dominant key" of D minor and the "tonic key" of G minor. Instead of being cofactors (iv–V) of a minor key, they are self-substantiated as Phrygian cadences and as mi-degrees of the ♭- and ♭♭-systems. And in their immediate context they are not related to D and G minor but are linked to G minor and C major by progressions in contrary motion with a half-step connection in one of the voices (mm. 54–55: ; mm. 58–59:), progressions that evade a functional interpretation.

In the cycle's third madrigal, *Dorinda, ah dirò*, the question of the unity or change of system is also left up in the air.

Measure:	4	10	13	15	18
Cadence:	d	d	g	c	g
System:	♭♭	♭		♭♭	

The ♭♭-system is marked by the fa–mi contrast of E♭-major and d-minor chords (mm. 3–4) and the transition to the ♭-system by the A-major chord. Yet the relevance of the change of system is questionable. A denial of the change of system for the purpose of forcing an interpretation of the c-key [m. 15] as Mixolydian with an incidentally flatted third would certainly be a distortion. Yet the alternative, the assertion that the change of system [♭♭ to ♭] reinterprets d-Phrygian as d-Aeolian and g-Dorian as g-Aeolian is no less flawed. If the unity of key is to be fundamental to the musical context then one must admit that the identity of the d- or g-degrees is not negated by the variation of their "modal coloring." The change of system is therefore secondary.

This explanation is, of course, self-contradictory. The degrees are defined as degrees of a system—in *Dorinda, ah dirò* the ♭-system—so that "identity of degree" and "independence from a change of system" are irreconcilable concepts. The contradiction—not a mere dilemma of the theory but a feature of the problem itself—means only that the positions of the degrees are vague. The cadences on g-minor, d-minor, and c-minor chords are no longer unequivocal elements in a "closed society" of partial keys.

The fact that the relations between the component keys in *Dorinda, ah dirò* are clearly evident as a fundamental feature—more clearly than in other madrigals—can be understood as a kind of compensation. As long as the component keys, as a closed and firmly outlined society, form a self-supporting system, it is possible, without a loss of precision, to treat the relationships between them—the dominant, subdominant, and parallel relationships or the major-minor contrast at the interval of a whole step—as secondary factors. But in *Dorinda, ah dirò* the accent falls on the interrelationships because the positions in the system have grown indistinct. The d–g–c–g disposition of cadences is primarily based on the fifth-relations between the component keys, not on their position within the system. And an interpretation of d–g–c–g as dominant-tonic-subdominant-tonic is not out of the question.

. . .

The fact that individual chord progressions evade a functional interpretation proves little against the interpretation of key relationships. Chord and key relations are not necessarily subject to the same principle. In theory, the "noncongruity" of stages of development might be perceived as disorder. But in history it is more the rule than the exception. Tonal harmony did not step forward as a complete whole but arose from scattered beginnings.

On the other hand, it ought not to be denied that speaking of a "subdominant key" would be an overstatement as long as the individual chord progression still cannot be functionally defined. Since the features of tonal harmony are cofactors in a system, they receive the full measure of their significance only in a closed context. To define them in isolation with concepts that presume the complete system is something of an anticipation, albeit an unavoidable one. The description of a transition is impossible without terminological anticipations. And since such overstatement is unavoidable, there is no recourse but to admit it so as to counteract it.

. . .

The fifth and final madrigal of the cycle, *Ferir quel petto*, is untouched by the tendencies that facilitate the transition to major-minor tonality. It is single-mindedly based on the idea that the component keys form a self-supporting system that establishes musical coherence without requiring a main key as a tonal center.

a^1	a^2	b	c	d	e^1	e^2	f^1	f^2	g^1	f^3	f^4	g^2
3	5	8	12	18	23	26	28	31	32	35	37	39
d—a		F	C	g	B♭—c		F—g		d		C—d	d
♭♭	♭				♭♭		♭		♭♭	♮		♭♭

The changes between the ♭-, ♭♭-, and ♮-systems—the analysis is limited to the madrigal's first two parts—are clearly marked though not fully determined. The fa-degree, E♭ major, marks the ♭♭-system and the mi-degree, A major, marks the ♭-system. The change to the ♮-system can be detected only by the transpostion up a fifth of the double verse f^1/f^2, not by a characteristic chord.

Since the ♭♭-system and the ♮-system are not fully determined, they appear as secondary systems of the primary ♭-system. But this centering around the ♭-system does not serve the purpose of maintaining the unity of the key. Rather, it counterbalances the development of an excessive wealth of "modal colorings" of cadence degrees. The main key of G minor is merely a cofactor, not the *"fundamentum relationis"* [basis of relationship], of the system of keys. It sets itself off from its context not "intensively," as the center of a network of relationships, but only "extensively," by the ostinato-like repetition of the g-minor chord, a chord on which the harmonic motion comes to a halt for six measures (mm. 13–18).

The principle underlying the disposition of cadences is that of *"varietas"* [variety], the principle of extending to the utmost the wealth of degrees and "modal colorings" that are possible within the limits of an 11-tone scale restricted to the chromatic tones b♭, f♯, c♯, and e♭. In the first part of the madrigal, all the degrees of the soft hexachord are set forth as cadential degrees without any of them being repeated (d–a–F–C–g–B♭). And the changes between the ♭-, ♭♭-, and ♮-systems that dominate the second part could primarily be motivated by the intention of showing the cadences in ever-changing "modal colorings": the c- and d-degrees are transferred from the ♭-system to the ♭♭- and ♮-systems, the f- and g-degrees from the ♭-system into the ♭♭-system.

. . .

The attempt to describe a transition must depend on concepts of which it is uncertain whether and to what degree they are appropriate for the intermediate state they are meant to describe. The available single categories derive from systems that stand at the very beginning or end of a development. If used to describe a change that is accomplished not in one fell swoop but by the subtlest transitions and scarcely noticeable reinterpretations, then through qualifications and restrictions the categories lose the fixed outlines that they had in the closed system in which they originated. On the other hand, it would not make sense to coin neologisms that ascribe an independence to the intermediate state that it never in fact had. The transition between systems is not itself a system.

The following analysis of Monteverdi's *sestina* cycle[6] should be understood as an attempt to characterize this intermediate state as one of ambiguity. In contrast to its status in logic, in aesthetics ambiguity is a legitimate property, not a disturbing deficiency. But in the analysis of the *sestina* cycle the twofold interpretation is less the mark of a feature of the music itself than an expression of a methodological embarrassment. Or more precisely, the methodology itself is ambiguous. So it must be left an open question whether the work is intrinsically ambiguous and thus directly accessible to the methodology or whether it exists in an intermediate state that is overinterpreted by the concept of ambiguity.

The *sestina* cycle, a funeral lament on a text by Scipione Agnelli, dates from 1610, five years after the appearance of the fifth book of madrigals, and it was published as the sixth book of madrigals in 1614. It is Monteverdi's last set of madrigals without a thoroughbass.

A conspicuous feature of the first madrigal, *Incenerite spoglie*, is the slow and uniform "harmonic rhythm," that is, the time intervals between changes of chord. A section in the dominant key area of A minor, which stretches for twelve measures (mm. 13–24), is restricted in its chordal resources to just three degrees: a, d, and E. And each individual chord fills out one or two measures. The measure thus forms the unit of harmonic motion.

The slow and uniform harmonic rhythm is based on the character of the text (not on its declamation, the rhythm of which is independent of the harmony). But the fact that this uniformity coincides with a restriction of the chords to just a-minor, d-minor, and E-major—which can be interpreted as tonic, subdominant, and dominant—may be taken as a sign of the stage of development that this *sestina* cycle represents in the prehistory of major-minor tonality. In other words, two characteristic features of tonal harmony are brought into relation with each other.

Of course the importance attached to the uniformity of harmonic rhythm in tonal harmony only becomes recognizable if one analyzes harmony not in isolation but with a view to its formal functions. The fact that harmonic relationships establish a correlation between measures, groups of measures, or periods takes for granted the fact that the parts being harmonically related are comparable. And while a correspondence or similarity in the actual length of units is not a necessary condition, it is still the simplest presumption of comparability. (The importance of harmonic rhythm is proved negatively by the phenomenon of the "passing chord." In a group of four 3/4 or 4/4 measures, measures whose harmonic content is shaped by the chordal functions S–T–D–T, a third-inversion dominant chord on the last beat of the subdominant measure appears as a passing chord whose dominant function is only weakly characterized [e.g., $IV-V_2^4 \mid I^6- \mid V_3^4- \mid I-$]. Since the chord is between the subdominant and the tonic, and thus "regular," its passing character is inexplicable as long as the harmony is studied separately. To comprehend why this chord appears as a passing chord, one that can be disregarded in a harmonic analysis, it is necessary to consider the formal function of harmony in creating relationships between comparable parts. The chord is perceived as a passing chord because taking it literally as a harmonic function would disturb the harmonic rhythm.)

The final part of *Incenerite spoglie* (mm. 25–50) is based on three themes or verse melodies (a: "Con voi . . . "; b: "E notte e giorno . . . "; c: "In duolo . . . ") with overlapping presentations.

a^1	a^2+b^1	a^3+c^1	$a^4+b^2+c^2$	b^3+c^3	c^4	c^5	c^6
28	31	34	37	40	44	47	50
G	C	a	d	G	C	a	d

The disposition of cadences G–C–a–d is repeated unchanged despite the variation in thematic content. Thus it is a "harmonic pattern." But it is far from certain how this pattern should be understood. The attempt at a modal interpretation would be questionable since it is uncertain and in fact unlikely that the modal major-minor contrast between keys a whole step apart—the contrast of G major and A minor, C major and D minor—could be rearranged as G–C–a–d without becoming ineffective. Yet at the same time a functional interpretation as (D)–Dp–D–T is an exaggeration. One need not deny that individual dominant and parallel relationships are operative between G and C, C and a, and a and d. Yet it may be doubted whether the "pull toward the tonic," the dynamic factor of the harmony, is so decisively characterized that it amalgamates the G–C–a–d disposition of cadences into a unified whole that must be related to the tonal center of D minor as (D)–Dp–D–T.

The fact that the transition to tonal harmony is connected with changes in musical form is shown in the third and sixth madrigals of the *sestina* cycle, *Darà la notte il sol* and *Dunque amate reliquie*. Their beginnings and endings correspond. The first double verse in both madrigals is transposed from the ♭-system to the ♮-system (*Darà la notte il sol* mm. 1–5 = 6–10; *Dunque amate reliquie* mm. 1–10 = 11–20), the last, on the contrary, from the ♮-system to the ♭-system (*Darà la notte il sol* mm. 43–48 = 49–54; *Dunque amate reliquie* mm. 53–61 = 62–71). The keys underlying these sections are the tonic D minor in the ♭-system and the dominant A minor in the ♮-system. The fact that there is no ♭ in the key signiture does not mean that the d-key is Dorian. As a sign of a change of system, the ♭ notated as an accidental is still an essential, not an incidental, degree. And it is exactly in the transformation of the d-mode that the transition to minor-mode tonality can be seen more clearly than in that of the a-mode, which must be classified as Aeolian as long as it occurs in conjunction with a d-mode interpretable as Dorian.

In contrast to Monteverdi's earlier madrigals, the musical form in *Darà la notte il sol* and *Dunque amate reliquie* is hypotactical, not paratactical [i.e., subordinate, not coordinate, in structure]. The individual verses are not juxtaposed as independent, self-contained entities but become part of a larger context that includes them as subordinate cofactors.

The fact that the arrangement of the verses loses its importance becomes evident in the suppression of caesuras. For example, in *Darà la notte il sol*—to cite an extreme case—the next-to-the-last verse is linked with the last verse in such a way that the end of the one and the beginning of the other together form the penultima and ultima of a 6–8 cadence (mm. 44–45 and 50–51).

The form is established through harmonic relationships. In madrigals like *O Mirtillo*, the juxtaposition of self-contained verses is matched by a society of keys whose members, instead of being subordinated to a main key, were in a coordinate relationship with each other. By comparison, in *Darà la notte il sol* and *Dunque amate reliquie*, the formal hypotaxis is based on harmonic subordination. The middle part of *Darà la notte il sol* (mm. 20–49) is no less than a full and forceful exposition of D minor. The component keys are set out in four sections whose chordal vocabulary is limited to the sections' relative tonics and dominants. The keys are the subdominant (mm. 20–23), the tonic (mm. 24–31d), the subdominant (mm. 32–37), and the dominant (mm. 38–49). The harmony is based on subordinate, hierarchical relationships. And in this hypotactical structure the individual verses lose their independence. They become cofactors in a tonally based, superordinate entity.

A functional interpretation is, to be sure, not the only one possible. In fact, in the opening parts of both madrigals it seems that the accent falls less on the setting out of the key than on the presentation of the system. The ♭-system is characterized by a fa–mi contrast where the two degrees are in close proximity (*Darà la notte il sol*, mm. 4–5: B♭–g–A; *Dunque amate reliquie*, mm. 3–4: B♭–d–A). And the disposition of chords is unmistakably based on the principle of variety. At the beginnings of both *Darà la notte il sol* and *Dunque amate reliquie*, all the degrees of the soft hexachord are set forth without any of these chords returning until all the others have appeared:

Darà la notte il sol: d – G – C – F – B♭– g – A

Dunque amate reliquie: F – B♭– d – A – G – C

But the principle of variety and the demands of tonal harmony are not irreconcilably opposed. The beginning of *Darà la notte il sol* and the end of *Dunque amate reliquie* can be interpreted in two ways: as a presentation of the system and as a characterization of the key. The chords form a chain that scarcely differs from the circle of fifths, the model instance of tonal harmony in Rameau's system.

Darà la notte il sol:	d	G	C	F	B♭	g	A			
	i	IV	VII	III	VI	iv	V			
Dunque amate reliquie:	D	g	C	F	B♭	D	G	e⁶	A	d
	I	iv	VII	III	VI			ii	V	i

In *Darà la notte il sol*, the fourth degree appears of course not as the subdominant but as the secondary dominant of the seventh degree [C], with which the first verse concludes. Thus the verse retains a remnant of independence. The fourth degree is substituted for the second degree because the diminished fifth, the bass leap from the sixth to the second degree [B♭–E], was considered a "*relatio non harmonica*" and therefore something to be avoided. In *Dunque amate reliquie* the diminished triad on the second degree is replaced by a minor chord [e⁶], and the contrast between B♭ = VI and e = ii is softened by the interpolated D and G chords.

The principle of variety is thus reinterpreted without being abandoned. In Monteverdi's earlier madrigals this principle spent itself in the function of making a complete presentation of the system that underlay the chords and defined them as mi, fa, or la degrees. By comparison, the circles of fifths in *Darà la notte il sol* and *Dunque amate reliquie* set out the chordal resources of a single key, not of a system that is indifferent to individual keys. The F-major chord is the tonic parallel of D minor, not merely the ut-degree of the soft hexachord. Nevertheless, the tonal interpretation must be limited. Since one of the constituent features of a circle of fifths, the uniformity of harmonic rhythm, is missing, the "pull toward the tonic," the dynamic factor of tonal harmony, is only weakly characterized.

It would be utopian to expect all the cofactors in a composition to represent always the same stage of development in the history of harmony, thus to expect that the relations between verse endings would always be based on the same principle as the relations between chords or the tonal relations between entire sections. In historical reality, flawless uniformity, reminiscent of formal logic, is more the exception than the rule. Yet on the other hand, the reappearance of the same principle in different dimensions is a support and justification of an interpretation of single factors. And it may serve as a corroboration of the functional interpretation of smaller details in the *sestina* madrigals that the disposition of keys in the entire cycle represents an enlarged image of the T–S–D–T cadence. The fourth madrigal (*Ma te raccoglie*) places the subdominant key of G minor, the fifth madrigal (*O chiome d'or*) the dominant key of A minor, in contrast with the D-minor tonic.

Unlike the other madrigals in the cycle, *Ma te raccoglie* is notated with a signature of one ♭. Yet while the tonic is G minor, the composition ends with a d-cadence. The subdominant significance of G minor within the larger cycle is thus exhibited directly instead of being detectable only indirectly from the key relations between the separate compositions. The tonic is set forth as G minor in the ♭♭-system, while the dominant D minor is presented in the ♭-system. At the beginning, however, it seems as though the accent falls more on the system and the change of system than on the key and key relationships. In mm. 1–42, authentic cadences are avoided. The individual verses end with plagal cadences, half cadences, or Phrygian cadences (mm. 2–3 and 4–5: E♭–B♭; 8–9: g–D; 10–11: d–A; 15–16 and

18–19: g–D; 24–25: c–G; 27–28: g–D; 32: c–D; 34–35 and 39: g–A; 41–42: c–D). By means of the half cadences g–D and d–A and the Phrygian cadences c–D and g–A [E♭^{c}–d$^{\sharp 3}$ and B♭^{g}–a$^{\sharp 3}$, to use the notation suggested earlier] special attention is called to the characteristic chords of the ♭♭- and ♭-systems, the fa and mi degrees. And so it is uncertain in mm. 31–35 and 38–42 whether the transpositions should be understood as a change of system (♭♭/♭) with Phrygian cadences or as a change of key (G minor/D minor) with half cadences on the dominant (iv–V). Nevertheless the context permits one to conclude that in *Ma te raccoglie* the Phrygian cadence forfeits its independence and becomes a cofactor in the minor key (iv–V). The chain of half cadences that precedes the Phrygian cadences of mm. 31–35 and 38–42 can be understood as I–V in G minor, D minor, G minor, C minor, and G minor. A modal interpretation would be a distortion inasmuch as the disposition of cadences g–d–g–c–g = T–D–T–S–T is unequivocally functional. The "tonal integration" of the Phrygian cadence is thus doubly prepared by the external form and the internal relationships of the preceding cadences. These cadences, just like the Phrygian cadences, are half cadences and yet they have a functional relationship.

Even more clearly marked than the subdominant g-key in *Ma te raccoglie* is its counterpart, the dominant a-key in *O chiome d'or*. And the forceful presentation of the key is joined with a conception of form in which the stringing together of verses, the typical madrigal structure, pales to a secondary feature alongside the method of establishing musical coherence through repetition and variation.

a^1	a^2	b^1	b^2	a^3
1–7	8–14	15–18	19–22	23–30
A minor	A minor	G major	C major	A minor

Section b^2 is a simple transposition of b^1. But sections a^2 and a^3 are variants of a^1, variants overlaid on verses different than those used in the model. And the fact that a^2 and a^3, in spite of the divergences resulting from the disparity of the texts, can be recognized as variants of a^1 is based primarily on the recurrence of the harmonic foundation. The formal unity is based on the harmony. The text has a differentiating function.

The component key of G major (mm. 15–18) is ambiguous. It can be related to the a-minor tonic either directly, as a major-minor contrast at the interval of a whole step, or indirectly, as the dominant of the tonic parallel C major. The one interpretation would be "modal," the other functional. That the G-major key is established by the chord progression G–C–D–G = T–S–D–T may suggest a functional interpretation not only of the chord relationships but also the key relationships. The assumption, however, that the various dimensions of harmonic relationships are based on the same principle is a hypothesis that allows no certain conclusions to be drawn.

The last section of *O chiome d'or*, as in *Ma te raccoglie*, demonstrates the relation of the key of the composition to that of the cycle by transposing a sequence of chords, i–v–VI–III–iv–i, from A minor to D minor (mm. 44–53).

. . .

The genesis of harmonic minor can be detected not so much directly in the reinterpretation of the a-key, but more indirectly in the alteration of the d-key. And the fact that the d-key in the *sestina* cycle is notated without a flat in the signature—thus in the ♮-system—and still assumes the form of a minor key is a clearer sign of the transition to major-minor tonality than if it had the "regular" ♭-signature. This is because the ♭-signature leaves open the possibility of interpreting the d-key as a transposed Aeolian. In the completed system of major-minor tonality, the d-key with a ♭-signature is easily recognizable as minor. But in the intermediate state characterized by the juxtaposition of modal and harmonically tonal features, it is this very self-assertion against the given "Dorian" key signature that serves as a criterion of harmonic minor. It is, to be sure, not a property of minor itself, but a proviso for its being unmistakable.

If the transition to minor can be discerned in the d-key, so can the transition to major be detected in the G-key. But the reshaping of Mixolydian into major was more problematical than that of Dorian into minor. And with Monteverdi it was accomplished only late and not without hesitation—in the seventh book of madrigals, which appeared in print in 1619. His caution may seem surprising, but it becomes understandable when one considers the prevailing understanding of the tonal system in the 16th and still in the early 17th centuries. The substitution of the ♭-system for the ♮-system or the ♭♭-system for the ♭-system was justified by a tradition that extended back a century, so contrasting the d-minor tonic key with the g-minor subdominant key seemed unobjectionable. But in G major, it was awkward and even considered illegitimate to form the D-major dominant key because of the abnormal nature of the transition to the ♯-system, the stabilization of f♯ as a diatonic, essential degree. The semblance of being problematical and uncertain clung not to the dominant chord, whose f♯ could be explained as an incidental *subsemitonium modi*, but probably to the dominant key. And portions of the G-major compositions in Monteverdi's seventh book of madrigals are marked by an uncertainty between d-Dorian and D major that gives a "modal coloring" to D major.

The form of *Tornate*, a duet *"a doi tenori"* [for two tenors],[7] is based on repetitions of individual sections, repetitions that establish a closed form. Given this form, one would expect a tonally subordinating type of harmony rather than a juxtaposition of independent component keys.

Sections:	a^1	a^2	b^1	c^1	c^2	c^3	c^4	b^2	b^3
Measures:	1–9	9–15	15–23	24–28	29–34	35–40	39–49	49–56	56–64
Cadences:	G-a	a-G	C-G	E-C	E-C	a-C	C-G-d-G	C-a	D-G

Yet set against the G-major chord in mm. 1–2 are Phrygian E-cadences in mm. 3–4 and 5–6 that demonstrate the precedence of the system over the key—the precedence of the ♮-system in which G represents the Mixolydian sol-degree. (Even the d-Dorian cadences in mm. 10–12 and 41–42 characterize the G-key as Mixolydian.) The component keys of G and a (mm. 1–15) form a major-minor contrast at the interval of a whole step, a contrast that is self-contained instead of requiring a reconciliation through C or D. And in any case, the C degree is missing that would make possible an interpretation of A minor as the subdominant parallel in G major.

In a similarly sharp contrast—one that excludes a functional interpretation and can only be explained through the independence of the individual members in the society of six component keys—the component keys E major (mm. 24–26 and 29–32: E–a–E) and C major (mm. 26–28 and 32–34: C–F–G–C) seem to oppose each other in sections c^1 and c^2. Nevertheless, it is possible, without forcing the point, to interpret the E–a–E cadence functionally as a half cadence in the relative key of A minor. On the one hand, the T–S–D–T cadence characterizes the C-key as major. And on the other hand, in sections b^1, b^2, and b^3—which precede and follow the c-sections—the component keys are functionally interrelated: C major and G major (b^1) as subdominant and tonic, C major and A minor (b^2) as subdominant and subdominant parallel, and D major and G major (b^3) as dominant and tonic. The G-key, set forth as the Mixolydian mode in the a-sections, converts itself to major in the b-sections.

The "modal coloring" of the G-key, partially structural in *Tornate*, shrinks to a scant remainder in the duet *O viva fiamma*.[8] A chain of nine 6–8 cadences forms the opening of this work. As 3/2 groupings they cross the notated but fictive 4/4 meter: G–D–a–e–b–D–a–C–G (mm. 1–14). The themes or melodic lines set forth in the upper voice and imitated in the lower voice each span two 3/2 groups and are thus divided, even if in a rudimentary form, into antecedent and consequent phrases. The entries overlap: the first consequent phrase in the upper voice forms a D-cadence with the first antecedent phrase in the lower voice; the second antecedent phrase in the upper voice forms an a-minor cadence with the first consequent phrase in the lower voice, and so forth. The melodic shape of the lines depends on the harmonic construction. The *dux* on the cadential degrees b and D is answered by the *comes* on D and a, the *dux* on a and C by the *comes* on C and G, and so at the caesura between antecedent and consequent phrases the harmonic interval between the voices varies.

From the viewpoint of the development of the Mixolydian into major, the sequence of cadences appears at the same time "regressive" and "progressive." It is "regressive" because it is based on the idea of *varietas*, the principle of expanding a system's wealth of cadences without regard for a primary key. But it is also "progressive" since the system it characterizes is the ♯-system. Accordingly, even though a key signature is lacking, the composition is based on a scale that permits forming the D-major dominant key in G major.

In the closing section, a double verse spanning fourteen measures is transposed from D major (mm. 44–57) to G major (mm. 58–71). The correspondence between the keys is, to be sure, clouded by an imperfect placement of accidentals in the D-major section. In m. 45, f′ is notated and f♯′ appears only in m. 48, while in m. 48 c is notated and c♯″ appears only in m. 53, so that it seems as if the dominant key is interspersed with modal remnants. But these divergences are compositionally unmotivated—the harmonic conception is functional. Both the dominant and tonic keys are divided into component keys according to the schema T–D–T, and the component keys are marked by the cadences T–S–D–T (G major and D major), T–D–T (D major and A major), and T–S–D–T (G major and D major). The harmony thus exhibits a subordinate structure with the relations between chords being subject to the same general rule as the relations between phrases and periods. And in relation to the clarity with which Monteverdi realized the hierarchical principle of tonal harmony, the "modal coloring" appears as a secondary factor. Instead of expressing a modal conception of key, the divergences in the notation betray an aversion to writing key signatures that were illegitimate according to traditional norms. One is almost tempted to ascribe to the "modal detail" the effect of the picturesque vestige of the past that it received in 19th-century harmony.

. . .

Modifying the Dorian mode into major is not the only way for the d-key to become a cofactor of G major. In the duet *Soave libertate*,[9] the d-key is indirectly related to G as the subdominant parallel of the subdominant key of C major. The major character of the G-key is clear at the beginning (mm. 1–18) and at the end of the composition (mm. 61–73). And the middle section (mm. 19–60) can freely be related to the tonal center of C major. The C–d–G–C–a or C–a–d–G–C schema returns several times: in mm. 26–32 and 50–56 as a series of cadences, in mm. 56–60 as a series of cadences (C–a–d) and as a chord progression (d–G–d). The interpretation of the d-degree as the subdominant parallel may seem questionable if the term is taken literally, since the relationship between C major and D minor is not mediated by F major. But the concept of the subdominant parallel is problematical even in the unquestionably harmonically tonal I–vi–ii–V–I chord progression, of which the C–a–d–G–C disposition of keys appears as its enlarged copy. It is uncertain whether the function of the d-degree is based on its interchangeability with the subdominant F major or in the convincing nature of the a–d–G–C circle of fifths. Nevertheless, the divergence between the explanations does not alter the fact that the d-cadences in *Soave libertate* are integrated into the key of G major through the mediation of the subdominant key, C major.

In the early 17th century the notion that the dominant key, D major, would presume the ♯-system (with f♯ as an essential degree) was not as self-evident as it appears to us. Not only c♯, the "*subsemitonium modi*," but also f♯ could be explained as an accidental—as a chromatic alteration of the third at the end of a verse or as a modification induced by such a cadential third in the effort to avoid a cross relation or indirect melodic chromaticism. Only the parallel key, E minor, led to a consolidation of the ♯-system since its dominant, the B-major chord, represented the ♯-system's characteristic mi-degree.

On the other hand, in the duets *Ecco vicine o bella Tigre*[10] and *Perchè fuggi*,[11] in which he conspicuously and forcefully sets forth the B-major chord and the key of E minor, Monteverdi shows a preference for flatting the third of G major. The juxtaposition of extremes might seem strange, but it loses the appearance of bizarre randomness if the B-major chord is understood as a sign of a change of system. The contrasting of G minor and E minor means that the transition to the ♯-system, to the upper fifth, is counterbalanced by a turn toward the ♭-system, to the lower fifth.

The fact that the change of system from ♮ to ♭ compensates for the change from ♮ to ♯ does not prove, however, that the system—as the embodiment of a society of independent component keys—took precedence over the tonic key. On the contrary, the change of system is based on the tonic key of G major—more evidently in *Perchè fuggi*, more covertly in *Ecco vicine o bella Tigre*. The ♯-system forms the precondition for a modulation to the relative minor, E minor, and the ♭-system is expressed or intimated not by a B♭-major chord or a g^6–A Phrygian cadence, but by a coloring of the tonic third.

In *Perchè fuggi*, G minor and E minor form the extremes of a circle of fifths of minor keys.

Sections:	a^1	a^2	b	c	d^1	d^2
Measures:	46–49	50–53	54–60	60–62	63–64	65–66
Keys:	g	d	a	B(e)	a	G

The half cadence a–B (mm. 60–62) stands at the end of one verse, the e-minor chord at the beginning of the next.

Sections b, c, and d together form a part "B" that, transposed up a fourth, is repeated and supplemented by a coda that might well be characterized as a "development section."

b	c	d^1	d^2	d^3	d^4	d^5	d^6
67–73	73–75	76–77	77–79	79–80	80–82	82–84	85–90
d	E(a)	d	G	C	G	a	g

In the relations between parts "A" (mm. 46–53), "B¹" (mm. 54–66), and "B²" (mm. 67–90), one can see the ♭–♯–♮ schema of a change of systems that might be characterized as a contrast (♭–♯) and reconciliation (♮). But the flatting of the G-major third in the final verse (mm. 85–90)—a chromatic alteration that, if the unity of the key is not be be abandoned, cannot be conceived as a sign of a change of system—indicates that even the g-minor area of mm. 46–49 is intended merely as a coloring of the tonic key.

In *Ecco vicine o bella Tigre*, G minor and E minor are fully and forcefully expounded: G minor at the beginning (mm. 1–8) and the end (mm. 75–78) and E minor in the middle section (mm. 37–68). On the other hand, G major, the tonic key, is only fleetingly intimated—by a D–G–D cadence (mm. 25–32) of which it is not even certain whether it should be related to D or G as a tonic. G minor and E minor are joined together as the extremes of the g–d–a–e sequence of keys, a circle of fifths of minor keys. The g–d–a disposition of cadences at the beginning of the composition (mm. 1–23) is reversed to a–d–g at the end (mm. 69–78).

The change of systems ♭–♮–♯ forms the basis for the key sequence g–d–a–e. Yet it is not the ruling principle. The fact that it is precisely the keys of G minor and E minor that represent the ♭- and ♯-systems hardly admits of any other explanation but that G major, even though it is weakly characterized, represents the composition's relational center. One could even assert, though not without some exaggeration, that the tonic key could outwardly have disappeared since it was made functionally recognizable by the contrast between E minor and G minor, a contrast whose reconciliation—G major—must have been conceived at the same time.

· · ·

Tonality is a cofactor of musical form. And it is an unavoidable coincidence that compositions whose harmonic techniques are tonally oriented also depart the most decisively from the traditions of the 16th century in their form.

Although a key signature is lacking, the G-key in the trio *Vaga su spina ascosa*[12] is modified from Mixolydian to major without a trace of modality left over. The determining factor of its structure, both in detail and overall, is the alternation of tonic and dominant chords or tonic and dominant keys. But functional harmony—in contrast to the juxtaposition of independent component keys that formed the principle of harmony in Monteverdi's fifth book of madrigals—is a system of hierarchical relationships. And so it is no accident that a composition that is tonally based tends toward a form that is based on repetitions and correspondences instead of a simple seriation of verses.

a^1	a^2	b	c^1	d^1	e	f^1
1–9	9–17	17–21	22–29	29–34	35–40	40–45
G–D	G–D	G	D	D	G–a–C	C

$c^2 + f^2$	$d^2 + f^3$	d^3	d^4	d in augmentation
46–51	51–58	59–63	63–67	68–74
D	D	G	D	G

The individual sections mostly span two verses, less often one (f^1) or three (e and $d^2 + f^3$).

As suggested by the above diagram, the relationships between the sections are primarily based on musical factors. To be sure, the text as well as the melody stays the same in the repetition of a^1 as a^2 and in the reprise of d^1 as d^3 and d^4. But many relationships—for example the association of c^2 with c^1, of d^2 with d^1, and of f^2 with f^1—are independent of the text. And in some sections (c^1 and e) melodies are repeated over different verses. (Section b is developed from section a: the first verse of b, "*ch'a l'alba si diletta*," is a variant of "*su spina ascosa*" from m. 2, and the sixteenth-note figure in the second verse derives from m. 7.) Thus the form arises out of relationships that, pointedly expressed, seem to be imposed on the text from the outside and that constitute a structure that can stand on its own without the text's support. One can hardly imagine a sharper contrast to the principle of form prevailing in the fifth book of madrigals—the technique of stringing together self-contained verses.

Some of the features that characterize *Vaga su spina ascosa*, the reprise form and the method of linking sections melodically, recur in other works from the seventh book of madrigals. And a technique that is weakly indicated in *Vaga su spina ascosa*, the procedure of following the exposition and repetition of one section (a^1 and a^2) with an elaboration of a particular motive (b) taken out of its original context, is extensively developed in *Perchè fuggi*.

1. An extreme case of the close melodic linkage of sections is *O viva fiamma*, a duet "*a doi soprani*" [for two sopranos][13] whose tonal structure has already been analyzed. All the melodic lines can be reduced to a single pattern that appears in eight variants (x^{1-8}) and in inversion (y). In the final section the inversion and the basic form appear in augmentation. The text on which the composition is based is a sonnet with the rhyme scheme *abba / abba / cde / cde*. But the musical form is independent of that of the text. The paired arrangement of melodic lines in the first section (mm. 1–14) is in conflict with the cross rhyme of the poem.

Text:	a	b	b	a	/	a	b	b	a
Melody:	x^1	x^1	x^2	x^2		x^3	x^3	x^4	x^4

Moreover, the text and the composition diverge even in the proportions of the sections. In contrast to the precipitous exposition of the two quatrains in just 14 measures, one finds the broad exposition of the first terzett in 26 measures. The process of treating different verses musically alike is broken up by the opposite technique of repeating verses and musically differentiating them (line 9 = x^5 and x^6, line 10 = x^7 and x^8, line 11 = y).

x^5	x^6	$x^7 + y$	x^8	$x^7 + y$	$x^7 + y$
13–17	16–19	20–25	25–27	27–31	32–38

In the final section the lively declamation in eighth notes changes to quieter motion in quarter notes and is then further drawn out in half notes. The ascending fourth y, the inversion of the basic melodic shape x, forms the melodic motive of verse 12 (mm. 39–43), and variant x^4

(mm. 10–13) provides the melodic point of departure for verses 13 and 14 (mm. 44–57 = 58–71). Motive y is presented in doubled time values while those of x^4 are quadrupled. The coloratura of mm. 49–50 (= 63–64) derives from variant x^5 (mm. 14–15 and their repetition).

. . .

The rhythmic augmentation in *O viva fiamma* is not a special case. It also serves the function of a written out ritardando in other compositions: *Non è di gentil core*[14] (mm. 81–91), *O come sei gentile*[15] (mm. 78–88 = 68–73), *Dice la mia bellissima Licori*[16] (mm. 69–73 = 64–65), *Ah, che non si conviene*[17](mm. 61–64 = 57–58), *Ecco vicine o bella Tigre*[18] (mm. 75–78 = 72–74), *Soave libertate*[19] (mm. 68–73 = 65–67), *Vaga su spina ascosa*[20] (mm. 68–74, bass = 65–67), *Parlo miser o taccio*[21] (mm. 89–96 = 79–80 = 72).

. . .

2. The tendency toward a closed form, the correlate of the transition toward tonal harmony, has a most decisive realization in *Non è di gentil core*[22] (and similarly in *Tornate*[23]). The basic outline of *Non è di gentil core* is a four-part reprise form, a–b–c–a, expanded to

a^1	b^1	b^2	c	a^x	a^1	a^2
1–13	14–25	25–42	43–56	57–66	67–78	78–91

Section a^x leads back to the reprise of a^1. A partial motive from a^1 (mm. 4–5 = 70–71: "chi non arde d'amor") is anticipated in a^x in augmented form with a different text ("dunque non è").

3. The turn toward closed form is connected with a radical change in the technical aspects of musical structure. In sharp contrast to the compositional principle of the fifth book of madrigals, motives, not verses, form the substance of a composition. Verses are set one after the other but motives are "worked out." And in *Non è di gentil core*, sections a^2 and b^2 are precisely "workings out" of a^1 and b^1 [*Durchführungen*, a term used here with the sense of "development" sections of sonatas, but connoting as well the "expositions" of fugues and "settings" of cantus firmi]. A motive from a^1 (m. 69: "chi non arde"), taken out of its orignal context, is worked out in a^2 in both original and augmented forms. And similarly in b^2, the melody for the first verse of b^1 (mm. 14–16) is divided into motives that are individually sequenced (mm. 25–32). Of course the melody of this verse is no "theme," even though it comprises several motives. Instead of forming an unbroken melody, the motives are loosely set one after the other. And

in dismantling the verse what comes to the fore is less the splitting of a theme than the sense that detachment itself is the motives' characteristic feature. The feature that distinguishes Monteverdi's compositional technique in *Non è di gentil core* from that of the fifth book of madrigals, the lack of a closed melodic form, at the same time differentiates it from the working-out technique of the 18th century as well.

The ability to reverse "exposition" and "development" [*Durchführung*] demonstrates that the motive, not the verse, forms the substance of compositional technique. In *Tu dormi*,[24] it is the setting out and sequencing of individual motives that precedes their consolidation into complete verse melodies, not the exposition of verse melodies that precedes their division into motives.

Soprano:	a					a	a	b	c		d	
Alto:		b		b		b		a	b		c	d'
Tenor:			c		c	d	b		a	b	c	d"
	1–2	2–3	3–4	4–5	5–6	7–9	10	11	12	13	13–14	14	14–17
	A	D	G	C	F	A	D	G	C	A	D	G	A

In the first section (mm. 1–9), the component motives a, b, c, and d are scattered among the voices. Only in the second section (mm. 9–17) do motives a and b unite into a first verse, and motives c and d into a second.

The composition is based on chords. The progression V^6–I, represented by the thoroughbass progression from the *subsemitonium* to the tonic, forms the common basis of the various motives. And even the connection between consecutive motives is based on the harmony. It depends primarily on progression by fifths (V^6–I in A, V^6–I in D, V^6–I in G, etc.). The melodic amalgamation of the component motives into verse melodies appears as a secondary factor. While the relationship between motives a and b is the same in the alto as in the soprano (soprano mm. 10–11: A–D–G; alto mm. 11–12: D–G–C) it is not the same in the tenor (mm. 12–13: G–C–A), where the verse melody is split by the harmonic caesura between the end of one circle of fifths (C) and the beginning of the next (A). Thus the work's harmonically tonal foundation is the correlate of composition with motives. It guarantees a strong stability and coherence across the longer stretches of music preserved from fragmentation by motivic techniques.

In relation to the verse, to the "theme," the motive is the logically prior and sometimes even the temporally prior. It thus seems as though the distinction between "exposition" and "development"—more precisely, "exposition of thematic material" and "development of fragmented motives"—is invalidated. If the distinction is to be preserved, then it must be based on harmonic considerations, on the contrast between "closed" and "open" types of harmony.

The duet *Perchè fuggi*[25] has seven sections:

a^1	a^2	a^3	b	c^1	c^2	c^3
1–11	11–25	26–45	46–53	54–66	67–80	80–90

Section a^2 is an extension of a^1, a thorough exposition of the motives that were presented—and already developed through sequences—in a^1. The motives in sections a^1 and a^2 form loose complexes instead of fixed verse melodies or themes. Nevertheless, the working out of motives in a^3 appears as a development section. In contrast to the tightly closed set of chords in sections a^1 and a^2—limited to the tonic G, the subdominant C, the dominant D, and the dominant-of-the-dominant A—in section a^3 Monteverdi presents a circle of fifths extending from B to F (B–E–A–D–G–C–F). The development section, by its "open" harmony, contrasts with the exposition. The uniform course of modulation is interrupted and articulated by a G-cadence (mm. 34–38) that calls to mind the tonic. The motives from a^1 and a^2, the ascending fourth progression ("*perchè fuggi*") and the falling third ("*o cruda*"), are given different texts in the development section (ascending fourth progression: "*perchè un bacio ti tolse*"; falling third: "*un bacio*" and "*corsi, corsi*"). Instead of developing from the text, the musical form—the organization into exposition, extension, and development—is thus externally imposed on the text.

The notion that the motive takes precedence over the verse does not, to be sure, have universal validity. The opposite extreme, the primacy of the verse, is demonstrated in *Io son pur vezzosetta Pastorella*.[26] A snippet from the first verse, "*son pur vezzosetta*," is detached and sequenced (mm. 7–10). Yet its effect is not that of an independent motive but of a fragment that must be referred back to the verse it came from in order to be musically comprehensible.

The normal situation falls midway between these extremes. The motives underlying the second section of *S'el vostro cor Madonna*[27] (mm. 18–30), (a) "*tal hor si rivolgesse*," (b) "*e una stilla*," and (c) "*al mio languir*," are indeed presented in poetic sequence, but they make sense on their own and present no obstacle to their separation.

Tenor:	a	b	c	a	b	b	b	
Bass:			a	b	c	c	c	b	c
Measure:	18	19	20	21	22	23	24	25	26–27
Key:	g		c		F	g	a	d	g

The forward progress of the music depends less on the melodic connection of the motives than on the disposition of the chords. The component keys, characterized by V^6–I or by I–V^6–I, form a closed tonal context. The exposition of the motives is based on the tonic and the subdominant, the development section is based on the sequence F–g–a, a result of the chromatic fourth-progression in the bass (e–f–f♯–g–g♯–a), and the closing section is based on the dominant and the tonic. The correlation between motivic technique and tonal harmony is complete.

NOTES

NOTES TO INTRODUCTION

[1. François-Joseph Fétis, *Traité complet de la théorie et de la pratique de l'harmonie contenant la doctrine de la science et de l'art*, Paris, 1844, sec. 70; the term "tonality" (*tonalité*) was coined by Castil-Blaze (1784–1857, a.k.a. François Henri Joseph Blaze) to signify the fundamental tones of a key: the tonic, the fourth, and the fifth (*cordes tonales* as distinct from *cordes melodiques*). The term appeared in his *Dictionnaire de musique moderne* (Paris: Au magazin de musique de la Lyre moderne, 1821).]

NOTES TO CHAPTER 1, PAGES 7–18

1. Hugo Riemann, *Musik-Lexicon*, 7th ed. (Leipzig, 1909), s.v. Tonalität. Ernst Kurth gives a similar definition: "The concept of 'tonality' signifies the unified relationship of chords to a central tonic and hence comprises two different assumptions: first, the existence of unifying factors, and second, the existence of, or at least the hypothetical ability to reconstruct, a tonal center" [Der Begriff "Tonalität" bedeutet die einheitliche Beziehung der Klänge auf eine zentrale Tonika und enthält daher zweierlei Voraussetzungen; einmal das Vorhandensein zusammenschleißenden Momente, zweitens das Vorhandensein oder zumindest die ideele Rekonstruierbarkeit eines tonartlichen Zentrums] (*Romantische Harmonik und ihre Krise in Wagners Tristan*, Bern, 1920, p. 273).
   2. F. J. Fétis, *Traité complet de la théorie et de la pratique de l'harmonie*, 2d ed. (Brussels and Paris, 1844), p. xi.
   3. J. Ph. Rameau, *Nouveau système de musique théorique* (Paris, 1726), p. 59: "Therefore we well observe that the title of perfect cadence is attached only to a dominant that progresses to the main tone, because this dominant, which is naturally contained within the harmony of the main tone, seems, when it progresses to it, to return as if to its source" [Remarquons donc bien que le titre de *Cadence parfaite* n'est annexé à une *Dominante* qui passe au *Son principal*, qu'en ce que cette *Dominante* qui est naturellement comprise dans l'Harmonie du *Son principal*, semble retourner comme à sa source, lorsqu'elle y passe]. H. v. Helmholtz, *Die Lehre von den Tonempfindungen*, vol. 2 (Braunschweig, 1863), p. 448: "If I proceed from **c–e–g** to **g–b–d'**, then I turn toward a chord which was already part of the first chord, and whose entry has therefore been well prepared" [Wenn ich von c–e–g fortschreite zu g–h–d, so wende ich mich zu einem Klange hin, welcher schon in dem ersten Accorde mitgehört, und dessen Eintritt daher wohl vorbereitet worden ist]. H. Riemann, *Musikalische Syntaxis* (Leipzig, 1877), p. 14: "In f-major, c* is a sonority contained within the overtones of the tonic f*" ("c*" is Riemann's symbol for a C-major triad) [In f-Dur ist c* Partialklang der Tonika f*].
   4. Fétis, *Traité complet*, pp. 11f.

5. Ibid., p. 249.

6. Moritz Hauptmann, *Die Natur der Harmonik und der Metrik* (Leipzig, 1853), p. 21.

7. Fétis, *Traité complet*, p. iii.

8. Ibid., p. 251; see also pp. 21f.

9. Ibid., p. 26; see also pp. 34, 81, 88, and 235.

10. Hugo Riemann, *Geschichte der Musiktheorie*, 2d ed. (Berlin, 1920), p. 523.

11. Hugo Riemann, *Musik-Lexicon*, s.v. Tonalität. Riemann formulates this more cautiously in the foreword to the seventh edition of his *Handbuch der Harmonielehre* (1917, p. xvii). He sets out "the direct designation of third-sonorities [e.g., E-major and A♭-major triads in a C-major context] by 3* and III* instead of by (D)[Tp] or °Sp (3 is the upper third, III the lower third), for example, c* e* g* c* = T 3* D T and c* a♭* f* c* = T III* S T" [die direkte Bezeichnung der Terzklänge mit 3* und III* statt mit (D)[Tp] bzw. °Sp (3 is Oberterz, III Unterterz), z. B. c* e* g* c* = T 3* D T und c* as* f* c* = T III* S T]. He adds, "but I caution against the assumption that I am paving the way toward the replacement of the functional symbols D and S by 5 and V. On the contrary, I want the exceptional use of the symbols 3 and III to give expression to the problematical aspects of the scale-denying third-sonorities" [Ich warne aber vor der Annahme, daß ich damit den Weg auch zur Ersetzung der Funktionszeichen D und S durch 5 und V anbahne. Vielmehr will ich im Gegen-Teil durch die ausnahmsweise Anwendung der Zahlen 3 und III das problematische der die Skala verleugnenden Terzklänge zum Ausdruck bringen].

12. Fétis, *Traité complet*, p. 22.

13. Ibid., p. vii.

14. Ibid., p. 249.

15. Ibid., p. iii.

16. Hugo Riemann, *Geschichte der Musiktheorie*, p. 470.

17. Ibid., p. 470.

18. Ibid., p. 471.

19. Fétis, *Traité complet*, p. xii.

20. Ibid., p. 248.

21. Ibid., p. 174.

22. Ibid., p. 166.

23. Ibid., p. 152.

24. Ibid., p. 165.

25. Fétis, *Biographie universelle des musiciens*, 2d ed. (Paris, 1862), vol. 3, s.v. Fétis.

26. Ibid., s.v. Fétis.

27. M. F. Meyer, "The Musician's Arithmetic," in: The University of Missouri Studies, January 1929.

28. H. H. Dräger, "Die 'Bedeutung' der Sprachmelodie," *Congress Report* (Hamburg, 1956), p. 73.

29. J. Handschin, *Der Toncharakter* (Zurich, 1948).

30. Ibid., p. 7.

31. Ibid., p. 264.

32. H. Lang, "Begriffsgeschichte des Terminus 'Tonalität,'" (Ph.D. diss., Freiburg i. Br., 1956); W. E. Thomson, "A Clarification of the Tonality Concept," (Ph.D. diss., Indiana University, 1952).

33. Ernst Krenek, *Music Here and Now* (New York, 1939), p. 108.

34. Edward E. Lowinsky, *Tonality and Atonality in Sixteenth-Century Music* (Berkeley, 1961), pp. xii and 39.

Notes to Chapter 1, pages 18–22

1. H. Hüschen's study on the concept of harmony in antiquity and the Middle Ages ("Harmoniebegriff im Musikschrifttum des Altertums und des Mittelalters," *Congress Report* [Cologne, 1958], pp. 143–50) should be supplemented by two observations. First, according to Hüschen, the concept of harmony has "undergone great changes in definition corresponding to the changing subject matter" (p. 143) [dem wechselnden Begriffsinhalt entsprechend sehr verschiedene Begriffsbestimmungen erfahren]. Yet strictly speaking, what changed was not the subject matter and definition of the concept—"harmony" was always a joining together of disparate or contrasted elements—but only the concept's range and application. It was not that the concept of harmony was given diverse definitions, but that diverse musical circumstances were defined as "harmony."

Second, Hüschen's asserted equation of *harmonia* with *musica* (p. 145) is problematical. A narrowing and shrinking of the Greek μουσικη τεχνη to ‛αρμονικη τεχνη means either an abstraction not only from language but also from rhythm, or a subsumption even of rhythm, the arrangement of time values, under the concept of harmony.

2. Isidor of Seville (cited in H. Hüschen's article "Harmonie" in *MGG*, vol. 5, col. 1610). The sentence does not mean that *harmonia* is defined as *modulatio*. Quite the reverse, it means that *modulatio* is recognized as a type of harmony. In *modulatio*—the *modus movendi* (manner of moving)— numerical proportions are represented not only by intervals but also by rhythms. "Whatever is pleasant in *modulatio* is accomplished by number through the measured dimensions of the tones; whatever rhythms are especially pleasing, whether in *modulatio* or in any rhythmic motions, are all brought about by number" [Quidquid in modulatione suave est, numerus operatur per ratas dimensiones vocum; quidquid rhythmi delectabile praestant sive in modulationibus, seu in quibuslibet rhythmicis motibus, totum numerus efficit] (*Scholica Enchiriadis*, GerbertS, vol. 1, p. 195; cf. H. H. Eggebrecht, "Ars musica," *Die Sammlung* 12 (1957): 314).

3. Tinctoris, Coussemaker, vol. 4, pp. 179 and 147.

4. Anonymous 1, Coussemaker, vol. 1, p. 297; cf. H. Hüschen, "Harmoniebegriff," *Congress Report* (Cologne, 1958), p. 149.

5. Hugo Riemann, *Geschichte der Musiktheorie*, 2d ed. (Berlin, 1920), p. 333.

6. Gafurius, *De harmonia* (Milan, 1518), bk. 3, chap. 10.

7. Ibid., bk. 3, chap. 11.

8. Prosdocimo de' Beldemandi, *Tractatus de contrapunctu*, Coussemaker, vol. 3, p. 197.

9. *Ars perfecta in musica magistri Philippoti de Vitriaco*, Coussemaker, vol. 3, p. 28.

10. Carl Dahlhaus, "War Zarlino Dualist?" *Mf* 10 (1957): 286–90.

11. G. Zarlino, *Istitutioni harmoniche* (Venice, 1558), bk. 2, chap. 7.

12. Ibid., bk. 3, chap. 29.

13. D. P. Walker, *Der musikalische Humanismus im 16. und frühen 17. Jahrhundert* (Kassel, 1949), p. 43.

14. Zarlino, *Istitutioni*, bk. 3, chap. 1. A frequently recurring definition of *compositio* [composition, as opposed to improvisation] in German music treatises of the 16th and 17th centuries also combines the concept of harmony with the demand for *varietas*. "To compose, however, is to unite with just concords the diverse parts of harmony" [Componere vero est diversas harmoniae partes discretis concordantiis in unum coadunare] (N. Wollick, *Opus aureum*, Cologne, 1501; cited by E. T. Ferand in his article "Composition," *MGG*, vol. 7, col. 1434).

15. D'Alembert, *Eléments de musique théorique et pratique suivant les principes de M. Rameau, éclaircis, développés et simplifiés* (Lyons, 1766), pp. 1f. [repr. of *Elements musique théorique et pratique* (Paris, 1752)].

Notes to Chapter 1, pages 23–38

1. Hugo Riemann, *Geschichte der Musiktheorie*, 2d ed. (Berlin, 1920), p. 474.

2. J. Ph. Rameau, *Traité de l'harmonie réduite à ses principes naturels* (Paris, 1722), p. 127.

3. J. Lippius, *Synopsis musicae novae* (Erfurt, 1612), fol. 6v.

4. Th. Campion, *A New Way of Making Foure Parts in Counterpoint* (London, ?1613–14); cited in R. W. Wienpahl, "English Theorists and Evolving Tonality," *Music and Letters* 36 (1955): 386.

5. H. Baryphonus, *Pleiades Musicae* (Magdeburg, 1630), pp. 163ff.

6. Michel de Saint-Lambert, *Principes de clavecin* (Paris, 1702), p. 23.

7. *Roger North on Music*, Transcribed from the Manuscripts and edited by John Wilson (London, 1959), p. 91.

8. Riemann, *Geschichte der Musiktheorie*, p. 485.

9. Rameau, *Traité*, p. 33.

10. Ibid., p. 185.

11. Rameau, *Génération harmonique, ou Traité de musique théorique et pratique* (Paris, 1737), pp. 171f.

12. Rameau, *Nouveau système de musique théorique, où l'on découvre le principe de toutes les règles nécessaires à la pratique* (Paris, 1726), p. 39; *Traité*, p. 64.

13. Rameau, *Génération harmonique*, p. 172: "In addition, the tonic can descend by fifth to its subdominant, ascend by fifth or third to a tonic-dominant,

or else descend by fifth, third, or seventh to a simple dominant, which, if one wishes, can equally be made into a tonic-dominant" [La Tonique peut d'ailleurs descendre de Quinte sur sa Soudominante, monter de Quinte, ou de Tierce, sur une Dominante-tonique, sinon descendre de Quinte, de Tierce, ou de Septiéme sur une simple Dominante, qu'on peut rendre également Dominant-tonique, si l'on veut]. Thus *simples Dominantes* are the IV^7, vi^7, and ii^7 chords.

14. Ibid., p. 171; see also *Traité*, p. 68.

15. Rameau, *Traité*, pp. 71f.

16. Ibid., p. 248.

17. Rameau, *Génération harmonique*, p. 173.

18. Rameau, *Nouveau système*, p. 33.

19. Rameau, *Traité*, p. 204.

20. Riemann, *Geschichte der Musiktheorie*, p. 482.

21. Rameau, *Nouveau système*, p. 62.

22. Rameau, *Génération harmonique*, p. 171.

23. Ibid., pp. 171f.

24. Riemann, *Geschichte der Musiktheorie*, p. 523.

25. Rameau, *Nouveau système*, p. 31.

26. Ibid., p. 42.

27. Riemann, *Geschichte der Musiktheorie*, p. 488.

28. Simon Sechter, *Die Grundsätze der musikalischen Komposition* (Leipzig, 1853).

29. Ibid., pt. 1, p. 11.

30. Ibid., pt. 1, p. 18.

31. Ibid., pt. 1, p. 32.

32. Rameau, *Nouveau système*, pp. 56f.

33. Rameau, *Génération harmonique*, p. 175.

34. Sechter, *Grundsätze*, pt. 1, p. 17.

35. Ibid., pt. 2, p. 22.

36. Ibid., pt. 3, p. 80.

37. Ibid., pt. 3, p. 96.

NOTES TO CHAPTER 1, PAGES 38–47

1. Simon Sechter, *Die Grundsätze der musikalischen Komposition* (Leipzig, 1853), pt. 1, p. 13.

2. August Halm, *Harmonielehre* (Leipzig, 1902), p. 15.

3. J. Ph. Rameau, *Traité de l'harmonie réduite à ses principes naturels* (Paris, 1722), p. 129.

4. J. Ph. Rameau, *Nouveau système de musique théorique, où l'on découvre le principe de toutes les règles nécessaires à la pratique* (Paris, 1726), p. 59.

5. Rameau, *Traité*, p. 56.

6. Arnold Schönberg, *Harmonielehre* (Leipzig and Vienna, 1911), p. 35.

7. Heinrich Schenker, *Neue musikalische Theorien und Phantasien, Band I: Harmonielehre* (Stuttgart, 1906), p. 44.

8. H. H. Dräger, "Die 'Bedeutung' der Sprachmelodie," *Congress Report*, Hamburg, 1956, p. 73.

9. J. Handschin, *Der Toncharakter* (Zurich, 1948), p. 108.

10. Rameau, *Traité*, p. 64.

11. Rameau, *Nouveau système*, p. 39.

12. Moritz Hauptmann, *Die Natur der Harmonik und der Metrik* (Leipzig, 1853), pp. 25f.

13. Halm, *Harmonielehre*, pp. 30f.

14. Ibid., p. 15.

15. Hauptmann, *Die Natur*, p. 241. Friedrich Neumann also stresses the reciprocal relationship between harmony and meter (bar-rhythm): "Now when the tonic substitutes for the dominant in the third of four measures of dominant harmony [D–D–T–D], then, seen harmonically, it has a dual aspect. Taken unconditionally, it would be a tonal point of rest against which the dominant appears as a tension-forming contrast. But in relation to the length of the dominant section the dominant becomes, on rhythmic grounds, the superior function and the tonic to some extent appears in a plagal, foreground relationship of tension to the dominant" (*Die Zeitgestalt*, Vienna, 1959, p. 138) [Wenn nun im 3. Takt des dominantischen Viertakters die Tonika mit der Dominante wechselt, so zeigt sie harmonisch gesehen ein doppeltes Gesicht. Absolut genommen wäre sie tonaler Ruhepunkt, dem die Dominante als spannender Kontrast gegenüber tritt. Im Zusammenhang der dominantischen Länge aber wird die Dominante aus rhythmischen Gründen zur übergeordneten Funktion, und die Tonika tritt zu ihr in ein gewissermaßen plagales, vordergründiges Spannungsverhältnis].

16. J. B. Mercadier, *Nouveau système de musique théorique et pratique* (Paris, 1776), p. xvi.

17. Ernst Kurth, *Die Voraussetzungen der theoretischen Harmonik und der tonalen Darstellungssysteme* (Bern, 1913), pp. 125f.

18. Ibid., pp. 124f.

19. Ibid., p. 120.

20. Ibid., p. 121.

21. *Quatuor principalia* (Pseudo-Tunstede), Coussemaker, vol. 4, p. 280.

22. Anonymous 5, Coussemaker, vol. 1, p. 366.

23. Heinrich Schenker, *Neue musikalische Theorien und Phantasien, Band III: Der freie Satz*, 2d ed. (Vienna, 1956), p. 65.

NOTES TO CHAPTER 1, PAGES 47–59

1. H. v. Herzogenberg, "Tonalität," *Vierteljahrsschrift für Musikwissenshaft* 6 (1890): 571.

2. Hugo Riemann, "Ideen zu einer 'Lehre von den Tonvorstellungen,' " *Jahrbuch Peters* 21/22 (1914/15), p. 1.

3. Ibid., p. 2.

4. Ibid., p. 5.

5. Ibid., p. 18.

6. Ibid., p. 19.

7. Hugo Riemann, *Handbuch der Harmonielehre*, 6th ed. (Leipzig, 1912), p. 214.

8. Hugo Riemann, *Musik-Lexikon*, 7th ed. (Leipzig, 1909), p. 441, s.v. Funktionsbezeichnung.

9. Reprinted in Riemann, *Präludien und Studien III* (Leipzig, 1900–1901), p. 1.

10. Cited in W. Gurlitt, "Hugo Riemann (1849–1919)," *Abhandlungen der geistes- und sozialwissenschaftlichen Klasse der Akademie der Wissenschaften und der Literatur in Mainz*, 1950, no. 25, p. 8.

11. Moritz Hauptmann, *Die Natur der Harmonik und der Metrik* (Leipzig, 1853), pp. 25ff.

12. Riemann, *Präludien und Studien III*, p. 3.

13. Upper-case letters indicate tones that have been defined as roots or fifths while lower-case letters indicate thirds.

14. H. v. Helmholtz, *Die Lehre von den Tonempfindungen*, vol. 2 (Braunschweig, 1863), p. 448.

15. Ibid., p. 448.

16. Hugo Riemann, *Musikalische Syntaxis* (Leipzig, 1877), p. 38.

17. Hugo Riemann, *Vereinfachte Harmonielehre* (London, 1893).

18. Riemann, *Musik-Lexikon*, p. 441.

19. Ibid., p. 441. Riemann's definition of secondary degrees is self-contradictory. One the one hand, he explains the root of ii in major as a *sixte ajoutée*, as a sixth added to the subdominant harmony. On the other hand, he symbolizes this chord as "°a," and "°a" means that the tone **a** is the *centre harmonique* of the chord **d–f–a**. "°a" is thus the formula for a minor chord, which is to be understood as a "sonorous unity" and not as an "apparent consonance": "In C major, Sp = the subdominant with a sixth and without a fifth = **f–a–d′** = (°a)" (*Handbuch der Harmonie- und Modulationslehre*, 7th ed., Berlin, c1919, p. 69).

The definition of the *Leittonwechselklang* (**e–g–b** in relation to **c–e–g**) is similarly schizophrenic. The term *Leittonwechsel* can be divided into its component parts. *Leitton* means the leading-tone interval between **b**, the reference tone of **e–g–b**, and **c**, the reference tone of **c–e–g**. *Wechsel* refers to the change from major to minor (*Handbuch der Harmonie- und Modulationslehre*, p. 113). On the other hand, Riemann explains the *Leittonwechselklang*, whose name implies that it forms a sonorous unity [*Klangeinheit*], as an "apparent consonance": the *Leittonwechselklang* is a seventh chord (**c–e–g–b**) with a "suppressed root" (**c**). The contradiction is already indicated in Moritz Hauptmann's system. According to Hauptmann, the major system, the tonal system of the major key, is composed of roots and fifths (upper-case letters) as well as thirds (lower-case letters): F–a–C–e–G–b–D. Hauptmann symbolizes the relationship of a fifth (F–C) by the Roman numerals I–II, the relationship of a third (F–a) by I–III (*Die Natur der Harmonik und der Metrik*, Leipzig, 1853, p. 26).

The secondary chords in C major, a–C–e and e–G–b, are defined in three ways (*Die Natur*, pp. 34–36): (1) as the combination of components of two major chords—III I III; (2) as a fifth and a major third that have in common the same upper tone— $\begin{smallmatrix} & \text{I} & \text{II} \\ \text{I} & & \text{III} \end{smallmatrix}$; and (3) as a minor chord with the fifth as its *centre harmonique*—II III I. Hauptmann terms the chord's second meaning "positive," the third "negative": reading minor chords from the top down presumes, as "negation," the very "position" that it denies. "Dualism"—the thesis that the fifth is the *centre harmonique* of the minor chord—is for Hauptmann not a "principle" but a cofactor in a dialectic. "Negation of negation" is represented by the minor chord in a minor key: A–c–E instead of a–C–e . The "internal division" of the minor chord in the major system—the contradiction that the chord's root and fifth (II and I) are thirds of the system (lower-case letters) and vice versa (a–C–e = II III I)—is resolved in the minor system (A–c–E = II III I). Hauptmann's theory does not permit an unequivocal definition of the function of the secondary chords. Yet rather than being a deficiency, the ambiguity—as "internal division"—is a factor in the dialectic. "Too much here depends on the particular placement, on the prominence of one or the other chordal interval to enable one to establish in the abstract a universally valid definition of the substitution of secondary chords for primary chords" (*Die Natur*, p. 375) [Es hängt hier zu Vieles ab von der besonderen Stellung, von dem Hervortreten des einen oder anderen Accordintervalls, als daß eine allgemein gültige Substitutionsbestimmung der Nebenaccorde für die Hauptaccorde sich abstract könnte festsetzen lassen]. Riemann, however, insisted on an equivocal definition: in C major, **d–f–a** is "Sp" and nothing else. The fact that the subdominant harmony with *sixte ajoutée* is at the same time defined as "°**a**"—as a "sonorous unity"—is a relic from Hauptmann's dialectical theory and, in Riemann's nondialectical system, a contradiction composed of part theoretical deficiency, part error.

On the other hand, Hauptmann's own dialectic is flawed. The varying meanings of a minor chord in the major system are not cofactors in a self-coherent process but are tied to separate events. The tonic parallel of a major key is, when between the tonic and the subdominant, a passing chord or the result of a suspension (= III I III); when in a sequence of fifth progressions, an independent degree and a "sonorous unity" (= II III I); and when used as a deceptive cadence, a triad with a divided root $\begin{smallmatrix} \text{I} & \text{II} \\ \text{I} & \text{III} \end{smallmatrix}$. The functions that this chord can fulfill are distributed across diverse situations instead of "changing into one another" in the course of a dialectic.

20. Ernst Kurth, *Die Voraussetzungen der theoretischen Harmonik und der tonalen Darstellungssysteme* (Bern, 1913), pp. 110f.

21. Tl = tonic *Leittonwechselklang* [i.e., **e–g–b** derived from **e–g–c′**].

22. H. Federhofer, *Beiträge zur musikalischen Gestaltanalyse* (Graz, 1950), p. 13.

23. Opus 2, no. 1, Adagio, m. 12; Opus 2, no. 2, Allegro vivace, the 15th to the 10th measure before the recapitulation.

24. Opus 2, no. 2, Rondo grazioso, the 11th to the 14th measures of the a-minor episode; Opus 2, no. 3, Allegro con brio, mm. 69–70.

25. Opus 2, no. 1, Prestissimo, the 1st to the 10th measures of the development section.

26. Hugo Riemann, *Handbuch der Harmonie- und Modulationslehre*, 7th ed. (Berlin, c. 1919), p. 202.

NOTES TO CHAPTER 1, PAGES 59–65

1. Cited in W. Gurlitt, "Hugo Riemann (1849–1919)," *Abhandlungen der geistes- und sozialwissenschaftlichen Klasse der Akademie der Wissenschaften und der Literatur in Mainz*, 1950, no. 25, p. 8.

2. H. v. Helmholtz, *Die Lehre von den Tonempfindungen*, (Braunschweig, 1863), vol. 2, p. 358.

3. "Dogma is really nothing more than the systematic explanation of a particular attitude, of a distinct style, of a particular way of looking at things" [Dogmatik ist eben gar nichts anderes als die systematische Explikation einer besonderen Haltung, eines bestimmten Stils, einer besonderen Blickweise] (Erich Rothacker, "Die dogmatische Denkform in den Geisteswissenschaften und das Problem des Historismus," *Abhandlungen der geistes- und sozialwissenschaftlichen Klasse der Akademie der Wissenschaften und der Literatur in Mainz*, 1954, no. 6, p. 14).

4. Moritz Hauptmann, *Die Natur der Harmonik und der Metrik* (Leipzig, 1853), p. 21.

5. H. v. Helmholtz, *Tonempfindungen*, p. 382.

6. Ibid., pp. 361 and 383.

7. Ibid., p. 361.

8. Ibid., p. 359.

9. J. Ph. Rameau, *Traité de l'harmonie réduite à ses principes naturels* (Paris, 1722), p. 58.

10. H. Erpf, *Studien zur Harmonie- und Klangtechnik der neueren Musik* (Leipzig, 1927), p. 20.

NOTES TO CHAPTER 2, PAGES 67–71

1. Cf. H. H. Eggebrecht, "Studien zur musikalischen Terminologie," *Abhandlungen der geistes- und sozialwissenschaftlichen Klasse der Akademie der Wissenschaften und der Literatur in Mainz*, Wiesbaden, 1955, p. 20. The sources cited by Eggebrecht should be augmented by a passage from Anonymous 13 (14th century): "Moreover, it should be known that from the thirteen species previously mentioned thirteen chords are made: three perfect, four imperfect, and six dissonant" (Coussemaker, vol. 3, p. 496) [Encore est à scavoir que de ces XIII espèces devant dites sont fais XIII acors, III parfais et IIII imparfais et VI dissonans].

2. In his *Traité de l'harmonie* (Paris 1722, p. 58), Rameau cites an "Exemple de Zarlin, auquel nous ajoûtons la basse fondamentale" [An example of Zarlino, to which we add the fundamental bass]. Rameau adds the bass **D–G–C** to the three sonorities ⟨music example⟩ . Yet the suspension and resolution of the dissonant seventh by leaps in the bass is at variance with 16th-century rules of counterpoint.

In his *Handbuch der Musikgeschichte*, 2d ed., vol. 2, pt. 1 (1920), p. 437, Hugo Riemann attempts a functional harmonic interpretation of the chromatic motet *Mirabile mysterium* by Jacobus Gallus. But even in the opening measures he is forced to give different interpretations to the same theme. While e–f♯–g–g♯–a in the first voice are to be taken as root, suspension, third, suspension, and root, the analogous tones in the second voice, b–c♯–d–d♯–e, are interpreted as fifth, third, root, third, and root.

3. Hugo Riemann, *Geschichte der Musiktheorie*, 2d ed. (Berlin, 1920), p. 485.

4. Heinrich Besseler, *Bourdon und Fauxbourdon* (Leipzig, 1950), p. 14.

5. Ernst Kurth, *Grundlagen des linearen Kontrapunkts* (Bern, 1917), p. 438: "Instead of *proceeding from the chord*, counterpoint *arrives at the chord*" [Der Kontrapunkt *geht nicht vom Akkord aus*, sondern *gelangt zum Akkord*].

6. Ibid., p. 107.

7. Preface to the third edition (1922) of the *Grundlagen des linearen Kontrapunkts*.

8. The difference between Rameau's theory of fundamental progressions and Riemann's theory of functions—between the reduction of the penultimate g–b–e' (before f–c'–f') to a V^7 chord with "suppressed root," and the explanation of it as a *Leittonwechselklang*—is trivial. That is, since Riemann allows the secondary chords to be formed by the addition of a "nonharmonic tone" and the omission of a note "from the harmony proper," he likewise understands secondary chords as latent seventh chords.

9. Simon Sechter, the systematizer of the theory of fundamental progressions, cites the inaudible nature of the "suppressed root" to justify resulting part-writing errors: "Since the seventh above the absent root is not perceived as a seventh, one could even hear this tone as two different voices and allow the one to ascend to the fifth above the tonic while the other correctly descends to the third" (*Die Grundsätze der musikalischen Komposition* Leipzig, 1853, pt. 3, p. 144) [Da die Sept bei abwesendem Fundamente nicht als solche gefühlt wird, so läßt man sie auch wohl in zwei Stimmen hören, und läßt eine davon in die Quint der Tonica steigen, während die andere richtig in die Terz der Tonica herab geht].

NOTES TO CHAPTER 2, PAGES 71–83

1. Smits van Waesberghe, *A Textbook of Melody* (Rome: American Institute of Musicology, 1955), pp. 76–85.

2. Ibid., p. 76.

3. Smits van Waesberghe's terminology could be augmented by the expressions "fundamental fifth" (d–a), "lower contrasting fifth" (c–g), "lower contrasting sonority" (c–e–g), "upper contrasting fifth" (e–b), and "upper contrasting sonority" (e–g–b).

Ernest H. Sanders ("Tonal Aspects of 13th-Century English Polyphony," *Acta musicologica* 37 [1965]: 19–34) emphasizes the "tonal unity" (p. 34) of those English compositions from the second half of the 13th century based on a *pes* [ground bass] instead of a cantus firmus. "What gives these pieces their English sound is, in addition to the frequency of the major mode, the stress on the chords of the tonic and supertonic, their emphasis on triads and $^6_3$- chords, with the latter functioning most prominantly as penultimate chords at cadence points, and a predilection for trochaic rhythms and regular periodicity" (p. 22). Yet it appears that one must differentiate two techniques with antithetical characters, even though they often alternate with one another in the same piece, as for example in the composition from the Worchester Fragments reproduced by Sanders (pp. 28–30, *Suspiria—Peroris*). The one is the operation of a "functional unit" and a "functional contrast" (**c–e–g** and **B–d–f–a**), to use Smits van Waesberghe's terms (sections A1 and B). The other is the method of erecting perfect consonances over the individual notes of the *pes*, consonances that are juxtaposed without a functional relationship (sections D1 and D2). According to the theory of Smits van Waesberghe, the first technique appears as melodic tonality transferred to the tonality of sonorities. From the second technique there arose, by means of the interpolation of six-three chords (which can already be observed in the Worchester Fragments), the characteristic method of 14th-century composition, that of developing a principle of connecting sonorities from the "tendency" of imperfect consonance toward perfect consonance—a principle, to be sure, that is tonally indifferent.

4. The system of thirds is not presupposed as dogma but as a hypothesis. First, modifications are unavoidable. And second, the range of validity of this system of thirds, which Smits van Waesberghe sets forth as a natural law of all melody, must be restricted to the Middle Ages. Otherwise, one would be forced to consider a melodic style based on the chordal system of tonal harmony an aberration of the musical imagination.

5. Smits van Waesberghe, *Melody,* p. 78.

6. In the Middle Ages, the whole step was bound up with notions of perfection and simplicity, stability and clarity, and even of masculinity and firmness. The half step was associated with notions of imperfection, complication and obscurity, of weakness and femininity (Johannes Affligemensis, Gerbert, vol. 2, p. 258 = CSM I, 137; Aribo Scholasticus, Gerbert, vol. 2, p. 213 = CSM II, 56; Engelbert von Admont, Gerbert, vol. 2, p. 324).

7. Gerbert, vol. 3, p. 80. The demand for connection by half step is also probably behind the observation of Anonymous 1 (second half of the 13th century) that the minor third (in the interval progression 3–1) is a better consonance than the major third: "For a minor third is a better consonance than the major third, especially when two voices advance together" (Coussemaker, vol. 1, p. 296) [Est autem semiditonus consonantia melior ditono maxime cum due voces simul proferantur].

8. Franco, in S. M. Cserba, *Hieronymus de Moravia O. P.: Tractatus de Musica* (Regensburg, 1935), p. 252; Anonymous 1, Coussemaker, vol. 1, p. 301.

9. "Likewise understand that in every rhythmic mode a [perfect] consonance should always be used at the beginning of a perfection, whether it be a long, a breve, or a semibreve" (Cserba, *Hieronymus de Moravia*, p. 254) [Item intellegendum est, quod in omnibus modis utendum est semper concordantia in principio perfectionis, licet sit longa, brevis vel semibrevis].

10. "Note that from the unison, octave, or double octave one should never ascend or descend with the plainchant by exactly the same quantity unless the plainchant ascends or descends beyond a third" (Anonymous 5, Coussemaker, vol. 1, p. 366) [Nota quod ab unisono vel octavo vel quintodecimo numquam ascendendum vel descendendum est cum plano cantu per consimilem quantitatem nisi planus ascendat vel descendat ultra tertium gradum]. "And one should never set or sing two fifths or two octaves one after the other, either ascending or descending with one's tenor, because they are perfect" (Anonymous 13, Coussemaker, vol. 3, p. 497) [Et ne doilt on point faire ne dire II quintes ne deux doubles l'une après l'autre ne monter ne descendre avec sa teneur car ils sont parfais].

11. "We should never ascend or descend in a like series of perfect consonances above or below the voice we are counterpointing . . . The reason is that the same thing would be sung by two voices . . .; that is not the intent of counterpoint" (Prosdocimo de' Beldemandi, 1412; Coussemaker, vol. 3, p. 197) [Insimul cum cantu supra vel infra quem contrapunctamus nunquam ascendere vel descendere debemus cum eadem combinatione perfecte concordante . . . Et ratio huius est quoniam idem cantaret unus quod alter . . . quod contrapuncti non est intentio].

12. "The discant may well have two fifths with the countertenor; this occurs when the countertenor is above the tenor in the high octave [a–g']" (Anonymous 11, Coussemaker, vol. 3, p. 465) [Discantus bene habere potest duas quintas cum contratenore et hoc quum contratenor est supra tenorem in acutis].

13. According to Franco, the triplum is alternately related to the tenor and to the duplum, so that not only an irregular progression with the duplum can be legitimized by a regular progression with the tenor, but also, conversely, an irregular progression with the tenor can be legitimized by a regular progression with the duplum. "But he who would work with a triplum must consider the tenor and discant, so that if he makes a discord with the tenor he should not make a discord with the discant, and vice versa. And he should proceed further by concords, ascending or descending now with the tenor, now with the discant" (Cserba, *Hieronymus de Moravia*, p. 254) [Qui autem triplum voluerit operari, respiciendum est tenorem et discantum, ita quod si discordat cum tenore, non discordet cum discantu vel e converso. Et procedat ulterius per concordantias nunc ascendendo cum tenore vel descendendo, nunc cum discantu].

14. According to A. Machabey (*Genèse de la tonalité musicale classique des origines au XVe siècle*, [Paris, 1955]) the main features of tonal harmony are already prefigured in the 13th century. "The melodic cadence and the harmonic cadence are mutually related. The generalization of melodic leading tones, and the establishment and concatenation of the chords that become characteristic of the closing grouping, not only bring about the unification of the different modes but also reinforce the notion of the tonic, the directing force of all polyphony" (p. 142) [La cadence mélodique et la cadence harmonique sont corrélatives; la généralisation des sensibles mélodiques, la constitution et l'enchainement des accords qui deviennent caractéristiques du group conclusif,

non seulement déterminent l'unification des différents modes, mais encore renforcent la notion de tonique, directive de toute polyphonie]. First, the citation of Franco (Coussemaker, vol. 1, p. 154) on which Machabey supports his interpretation of 13th-century chordal technique (pp. 136, 138) derives from the pseudo-Franconian, 14th-century *Compendium discantus*. Second, the principle of connection by half step merely brings about a "Lydian" or "Phrygian" stylization of the cadences, not an assimilation of the modes—a coalescing of Dorian, Phrygian, and Aeolian into minor, and of Lydian, Mixolydian, and Ionian into major. Third, a consciousness of the tonic would be less supported than thwarted by musica ficta: the fact that successions such as (*Desolata mater ecclesia*, m. 2) and (mm. 13–14) are possible in close proximity reveals that the principle of contrasting sonorities, as opposed to tonal harmony, was guided not by the principle of subordination but by the mere addition of chordal contrasts. And fourth, Machabey's description of the "genèse de la tonalité musicale classique" suffers from a methodological defect. To be in a position to say that tonal harmony originated in the 13th to 15th centuries, Machabey cites separate factors—the leading tone (p. 207), the rootlike character of the tenor when it is the lowest voice (pp. 182ff.), fifth-progressions of the lowest voice (pp. 226, 245ff., 263), and pieces that begin or end with imperfect consonances (pp. 186, 209, 267)—that together form a system in the 17th century, that of tonal harmony, but which in the 13th through the 15th century did not (or at least not in the same way as later) mutually cohere.

15. Anonymous 13, Coussemaker, vol. 3, pp. 496–97.

16. Pseudo-Franco, *Compendium discantus*, Coussemaker, vol. 1, p. 154.

17. *De discantu et consonantiis*, Gerbert, vol. 3, p. 306.

18. Thr. Georgiades, *Englische Diskanttraktate aus der ersten Hälfte des 15. Jahrhunderts* (Würzburg, 1937), pp. 64f. and 72f.

19. "In like manner, if the cantus firmus should ascend by a half step, for example from **e** to **f**, and the discantus is at the octave, for example on **e'**, and should descend a major third stepwise from the octave, a fifth will result. If, on the other hand, the cantus firmus should descend by a half step and the discant is at the fifth, the discant should conversely ascend a major third stepwise, that an octave may result" (Cserba, *Hieronymus de Moravia*, p. 191) [Item si firmus cantus ascendat per semitonium, puta de E gravi in F grave, et discantus sit in diapason, puta in e acuto, descendat in ditonum per secundam a duplo et habebit diapente. Si autem e converso descendat per semitonium et discantus sit in diapente, e converso in ditonum (should be added: per secundam) debet ascendere, ut habeat diapason].

20. Coussemaker, vol. 1, p. 359.

21. Gerbert, vol. 3, p. 80.

22. Following Simon Tunstede (if he can be taken as the author of the *Quatuor principalia*), the same situation is expressed by the term "imperfect": "Imperfect consonance is justly named by virtue of its instability. This con-

sonance moves from place to place and is not by itself found among any fixed proportions. Such are the minor third, the major third, and the major sixth" (Coussemaker, vol. 4, p. 280) [Imperfecta concordantia ab instabilitate sua merito denominatur, quae de loco movetur in locum et per se inter nullas certas invenitur proportiones. Tales enim sunt semiditonus, ditonus et tonus cum diapente].

23. "Some discords are called perfect, some imperfect, others medial. They are called perfect when two voices do not unite in any way according to the sufferance of the voices, so that according to the ear one would be incompatible with the other. And these are of three types, namely the semitone, tritone, and major seventh. Discords are called imperfect when two voices are so united, that according to the ear they may in some way be compatible, yet not be consonant. And there are two types, namely the major sixth and minor seventh . . . Discords are called medial when two voices are so united that they partially pertain to perfect dissonances and partially to imperfect dissonances. And these are of two types, namely the whole tone and the minor sixth" (Coussemaker, vol. 1, p. 105) [Discordantiarum quedam dicuntur perfecte, quedam imperfecte, quedam vero medie. Perfecte dicuntur, quando due voces non iunguntur aliquo modo secundum compassionem vocum, ita quod, secundum auditum, una non possit compati cum alia. Et iste sunt tres species, scilicet semitonium, tritonus, ditonus cum diapente. Imperfecte dicuntur, quando due voces iunguntur ita, quod secundum auditum vel possunt aliquo modo compati, tamen non concordant. Et sunt due species, scilicet tonus cum diapente et semiditonus cum diapente . . . Medie dicuntur, quando due voces iunguntur ita, quod partim conveniunt cum perfectis, partim cum imperfectis. Et iste sunt due species, scilicet tonus et semitonium cum diapente].

24. On the one hand, Franco (Cserba, *Hieronymus de Moravia*, p. 250) combines the "imperfect" and "medial discords," and on the other hand, he numbers the minor sixth among the "perfect discords." Thus the minor sixth relates to the fifth as an oblique-motion dissonance with a half-step connection instead of relating to the fourth as a contrary-motion dissonance with half- and whole-step connections.

25. Coussemaker, vol. 3, p. 497.

26. Hugo Riemann (*Geschichte der Musiktheorie*, 2d ed., Berlin, 1920, pp. 126f.) interprets *notes appendans* as "intervals with double connection by second in contrary motion" [Intervalle mit doppeltem Secundanschluß in Gegenbewegung], *notes non appendans* as "intervals that lack or have in only one voice a connection by second, regardless of whether in parallel or contrary motion" [Intervalle mit fehlendem oder nur in einer Stimme vorhandenem Sekundanschluß, gleichviel ob in Parallel- oder Gegenbewegung], and *notes désirans appendans* as "intervals with complete connection by second in parallel motion" [Intervalle mit vollkommenem Sekundanschluß in Parallelbewegung]. First, the expression *notes appendans*, if it were to indicate an interval—thus one tone of the cantus firmus and one of the discant—would only make sense in the plural. But the Anonymous also uses the singular. Second, Riemann's interpretation is incompatible with the tenet that the 5–8 interval succession

over a descending second or third in the cantus firmus is a progression *sur notes appendans*. Third, Riemann is forced to lay aside, as "totally corrupt" [*ganz verdorben*], the second part of the explanation of *notes appendans* requiring the 5–8 progression and to leave this part out of his version of the text. And fourth, an explanation that considers only the differences between parallel and contrary motion, and between single and double connection by second, while neglecting the antithesis between imperfect and perfect consonance, fails to do justice to the 14th-century concept of counterpoint.

27. In the 14th century the 5–8 interval progression did decline in importance in comparison with the 6–8 progression, yet it still preserved its cadential character.

28. Georgiades, *Englische Diskanttraktate*, p. 59. On page 58 he refutes Riemann's dating of Anonymous 13 (Riemann: 13th century; Georgiades: 14th century).

29. "If the tenor descends, as in **d–c**, **e–c**, **a–f**, or **a–g**, the first [interval] should be a fifth, placed so that it is on *notes appendans*" [Se la teneur descent, si comme Re Ut ou Mi Ut ou La Fa ou La Sol, la première doilt estre quinte, mes que se soit sur notes appendans].

NOTES TO CHAPTER 2, PAGES 83–94

1. Bernhard Meier, "Die Harmonik im cantus-firmus-haltigen Satz des 15. Jahrhunderts," *AfMw* 9 (1952): 27–44.

2. W. Korte, *Die Harmonik des frühen 15. Jahrhunderts in ihrem Zusammenhang mit der Form-technik* (Münster, 1929); Thr. Georgiades, *Englische Diskanttraktate aus der ersten Hälfte des 15. Jahrhunderts* (Würzburg, 1937), pp. 109f.; Heinrich Besseler, *Bourdon und Fauxbourdon* (Leipzig, 1950).

3. Korte, *Die Harmonik,* p. 12.

4. Ibid., p. 5.

5. In Riemann's symbolization: DD and SS [V of V and IV of IV].

6. *DTÖ*, vol. 27, p. 78.

7. Korte, Die Harmonik, pp. 18–22.

8. Korte relies on a version of the theory of functions formulated by H. Erpf (*Studien zur Harmonie- und Klang-technik der neueren Musik* [Leipzig, 1927]). Erpf recognizes the major subdominant in minor and the minor dominant in major, though only as "analogous forms" (p. 20). Yet it hardly seems reasonable to transfer to a rudimentary and preliminary stage of tonal harmony the categories supposedly legitimized by the differentiations of a late stage of development—19th-century harmony. A functional analysis of early 15th-century works runs into complications that would be justified only if the simple functional relationships—as a foundation for the more complex—were clearly expressed.

9. Besseler, *Bourdon und Fauxbourdon*, p. 41 and Appendix 1; analysis on pp. 40–43.

10. Ibid., p. 42.

11. Rudolf von Ficker, "Zur Schöpfungsgeschichte des Fauxbourdon," *Acta musicologica* 23 (1951): 116; Ernst Apfel, "Der Diskant in der Musiktheorie des 12. bis 15. Jahrhunderts" (Ph.D. diss., Heidelberg, 1953). On the other hand, Ernest H. Sanders ("Die Rolle der englischen Mehrstimmigkeit des Mittelalters in der Entwicklung von ʾCantus-firmus-Satz und Tonalitätsstruktur," *AfMw* 24 [1967]: 35) argues against the thesis that the countertenor in three-voice compositions of the early 15th century simply filled out a discant-tenor framework and thus was not a "*Harmonieträger*." He maintains that while "some of the old functions and tendencies" still led "a certain pro forma existence" (evidently he means the cadential function of the tenor progression

e–d and the tendency of imperfect toward perfect consonance: , they

nonetheless had "lost their basic character and original significance" [aber ihr Wesen und ihre ursprüngliche Bedeutung eingebüßt (hätten)]. Furthermore, "the position taken by R. von Ficker and E. Apfel also seems doubtful in view of the fact that functional cadences already occur in a series of Machaut's chansons" [R. v. Fickers und Apfels Standpunkt scheint auch bedenklich angesichts der Tatsache, daß Dominantkadenzen schon in einer Reihe von Machauts Chansons vorkommen]. Yet the subject under discussion is not whether one encounters chord progressions in the 14th and 15th centuries that sound like functional cadences to a 20th-century listener, but whether their interpretation as functional cadences can be historically justified.

"Moreover, the question remains unanswered why the double-leading-tone cadence was not retained" [Außerdem bleibt die Frage unerklärt, wieso die Doppelleittonkadenz nicht beibehalten wurde]. This statement suggests that only the assumption of "functional tonality" could explain the displacement

of the double-leading-tone cadence ( ) by the tritone cadence

( ). But in the first place, the interpretation of **e–g–c♯′** as a dominant—

more precisely as a fragment of a dominant seventh chord—is wrong inasmuch as the dominant seventh it takes for granted was foreign to composers of the 15th and even the 16th centuries (Sanders would also have to make clear why the **g** progresses to **a** and not to **f**). And in the second place, it is not improbable that the obsolescence of the double-leading-tone cadence can be attributed to a growing sensitivity to the tritone cross-relation between the leading tone to the fifth (**g♯**) and the following root (**d**).

"Moreover, when compositions from this period contain, between cadences, characteristic chord progressions and widely leaping roots, it seems equally impossible to credit the contemporaneous listener with the ability or even the intention of distinguishing between the voices in such a way that he could pick out the 'two-voice framework'" [Und wenn außerdem Kompositionen dieser Zeit zwischen Kadenzen Passagen mit markanten Akkordfortschreitungen und einem weitschrittigen Fundament enthalten, scheint es ebenso unmöglich, dem damaligen Hörer die Fähigkeit oder gar die Absicht zuzutrauen, die Stimmen so auseinanderzuhalten, daß er die "Gerüststimmen" erkennen konnte]. Yet not only does Sanders ignore the possibility that the voices were set off from each other by timbral differentiation, but he also imputes a meaning to von Ficker and Apfel's hypothesis that it never had or at least does not need to have. What was at issue was the progression from an imperfect to a perfect consonance (𝄢), a move that was felt to be just as compelling and manifest as was the resolution of the dominant seventh chord to the tonic triad in the 18th and 19th centuries. The effect of this progression was supplemented but not altered by the countertenor, regardless of whether in filling out the discant-tenor framework it resulted in a double-leading-tone, octave-leap, or fourth-leap cadence (**g♯–a, A–a, A–d**).

Arnold Salop ("Jacob Obrecht and the Early Development of Harmonic Polyphony," *JAMS* 17 [1964]: 288–309) gives a surprising twist to the thesis that harmonic tonality originated in the 15th century. On the one hand, he regards the leaping countertenors of Dufay's chansons—the "bearers of the harmony" that according to Besseler represent one of the crucial factors of "functional tonality"—as simply extra voices added to discant-tenor frameworks (p. 290), thus denying their primarily harmonic character. On the other hand, he observed in Obrecht the tendency, at the beginning of a composition, to firmly establish the tonic by means of several cadences, so that later cadences on different degrees could be related, as deviations, to the tonal center still present in the listener's mind: ". . . a practice similar, in a sense, to that of the late baroque, and probably deserving the designation 'tonal' generally applied to the music of the later period. This is tonality, not in the sense of major or minor key, or in the sense of specific functional operations (such as dominant-tonic)—such associations reflect exceedingly narrow viewpoints—but in the sense of 'loyalty to a tonic,' as Willi Apel puts it" (p. 304). One ought not belittle Salop's right to use the word "tonality" in such a way, since to him it seems appropriate for the purpose of his study. But as to the matter at hand, those phenomena that Salop has in mind clearly pertain not to the harmonic tonality that forms the subject of our studies, but to nothing other than the representation of mode through a dispositon of cadences. The difference comes to light even in his remarks on details of compositional technique: "Obrecht's harmonic practice is implemented by the two factors discussed earlier, the designed bass and the tritone drive to the cadence" (p. 304). The pregnant, "designed" bass striving for the cadence on the basis of its melodic outline (not as a *Harmonieträger*) is more the antithesis of a bass in tonal harmony than its prototype. And Salop seems to overrate the "tritone drive." Even in Obrecht the progression of the tritone to the fourth (𝄢) is no less common than its resolution to the sixth (𝄢).

12. The assumption that the major chord must be understood as a directly perceived sonorous unity is necessary only if the chord is to be attributed to the "natural model" of the overtone series. If, however, one considers the proposition that the perfect fifth and major third are the fundamental intervals

of major and minor chords, and views it not as a musical fact of nature but as a hypothesis meant to explain the historical system of tonal harmony, then one can have chords result from the combining of intervals, rather than conversely, as with Riemann, having intervals result from the dismantling of chords.

13. Besseler, *Bourdon und Fauxbourdon,* p. 43. The chromatic alteration of thirds is not excluded from tonal harmony, but it is tied to conditions that are not always satisfied in *Helas, ma dame*: a tonic triad with raised third must progress to the subdominant, and a subdominant triad with raised third must progress to the major dominant.

14. It is questionable whether the e♭ in the signature of the countertenor applies to the upper octave as well. In mm. 4 and 29 one should probably read e′ rather than e♭′.

15. Coussemaker, vol. 3, p. 93: "In learning to compose chansons or motets with three voices, namely tenor, discant, and countertenor, the first thing to note is that when there is a unison on the tenor's first tone, then the counter-tenor may be placed at the third, fifth, sixth (this sixth sounds harsh), octave, or tenth below the tenor . . ." [Ad sciendum componere carmina vel motetos cum tribus, scilicet cum tenore, carmine et contratenore primo notandum est, quod quando unisonus habetur super principalem tenorem tunc tertia sub tenore vel quinta sub vel sexta sub (quae sexta tunc non dulce sonat) vel octava sub vel decima sub potest poni in contratenore . . .].

16. Coussemaker, vol. 3, p. 72: "Whenever an imperfect third, that is, one with less than two full tones, is immediately followed by a perfect fifth or any other type of perfect interval, and the upper voice ascends only a single tone, then that imperfect third should be perfected by the hard ♮ [i.e., sharped] . . ." [Quandocumque tertia imperfecta id est non plena de tonis immediate post se habet quintam vel sive etiam aliam quamcumque speciem perfectam, ascendendo solam notulam, illa tertia imperfecta debet perfici ♮ duro . . .].

17. The instructions for the perfecting and imperfecting of intervals can be compared with the thoroughbass rule that the first tone of a descending fourth in the bass be accompanied by a $^6_5$ chord and the first tone of a descending fifth by a seventh chord—both are similarly rigorous and overemphatic but likewise characteristic of the musical perception of their times.

18. Ernst Kurth, *Die Voraussetzungen der theoretischen Harmonik und der tonalen Darstellungssysteme* (Bern, 1913), pp. 119ff. According to Kurth, the antithesis between major and minor is attributable to "leading-tone tensions": "Only on this basis is the establishment of the minor mode supportable. That is to say, if the third of the major triad is that chord member that carries a latent tension, namely in an upward direction, then the minor triad represents a correction of this leading-tone tendency through the flatting of the third, by means of which, however, there already penetrates into this flatted third a downward directed leading-tone tension" (pp. 121f.) [For Kurth, just as the third of the major dominant strives upward toward the tonic, so the third of the minor subdominant was felt to strive downward toward the fifth scale degree.] [Darauf allein kann sich eine Mollbegründung stützen; wenn nämlich

die Terz des Durdreiklangs derjenige Teilton ist, der latente Spannkraft, und zwar in der Richtung nach oben, in sich trägt, so stellt der Molldreiklang eine Korrektur dieser Leittontendenz durch Abwärtsalterierung dar, wodurch aber in die Terz bereits wieder abwärtsgerichtete Leittonspannung eindringt]. First, however, "leading-tone tension" cannot be a prerequisite to, and basis of, the "dissonant energy" of major and minor thirds because the leading-tone tension itself originated in connection with the "tendency" of an imperfect consonance to progress to perfect consonance. And second, the leading-tone tension of **e** and **b** was originally connected not with major thirds [**c–e** and **g–b**] but with the tendency of minor thirds to progress to unisons (𝄢 and 𝄢).

19. In Johannes Gallicus's striking description of the primary interval progressions, the half-step connection appears as a secondary factor in relation to the dependence of imperfect consonances on perfect consonances: "And even when imperfect concords have been separated from their perfect concords, they cleave onto them by some natural instinct, retaining for instance a certain imperfect concord between high and low pitches until they return to their perfect concords by step and half step or by step and more than a step . . ." (Coussemaker, vol. 4, p. 385) [Sed etsi quando separatae fuerint a suis perfectis, naturali quodam instinctu semper ad illas hunelent (?haerescunt) quandam videlicet imperfectam inter gravem et acutum sonum retinentes concordiam, donec ad suas perfectas per tonum etiam ac per semitonium aut per tonum ad plus et tonum redeant . . .].

20. H. Riemann, *Verloren gegangene Selbstverständlichkeiten in der Musik des 15. bis 16. Jahrhunderts* (Langensalza, 1907), and *Handbuch der Musikgeschichte*, 2d ed., vol. 2, pt. 1 (1920), pp. 35–39.

21. Cf. K. Dèzes, "Prinzipielle Fragen auf dem Gebiet der fingierten Music" (Ph.D. diss., Berlin, 1922).

22. Besseler, *Bourdon und Fauxbourdon,* pp. 158ff.

23. Cf. Besseler, *Bourdon und Fauxbourdon,* pp. 32ff; R. W. Wienpahl, "The Evolutionary Significance of 15th Century Cadential Formulae," *Journal of Music Theory* 4 (1960): 131–52.

24. A. Berardi, *Il Perchè musicale* (Bologna, 1693), p. 38.

25. According to Ernst Apfel, the source of major-minor tonality is a secondary form of the parallel cadence, 𝄢 . Apfel views "tonality" and the "compositional treatment of sonorities" [*Klangtechnik*] as being one and the same: "The structure and the movement of sonorities forms the so-called tonality. For both, the lowest voice of the composition is crucial. Even in the 13th to the beginning of the 15th centuries the prevailing progression of sonorities by seconds (the neighbor-tone relationship of sonorities: double and triple leading-tone cadences) forms a type of 'tonality,' though a short-winded type to be sure" ("Spätmittelalterliche Klangstruktur und Dur-Moll-Tonalität," *Mf* 16 [1963]: 153) [Aufbau und Bewegung der Klänge bilden die sogenannte Tonalität. Entscheidend für beides ist die tiefste Stimme des Satzes. Auch die

im 13. bis beginnenden 15. Jahrhundert vorherrschende Sekundfolge der Klänge (Nachbarschaftsverhältnis der Klänge: Doppel- und Tripelleittonkadenz) bildet eine Art "Tonalität," allerdings eine sehr kurzatmige]. In contrast to Besseler, Apfel does not yet accept the cadences ♭♭♭ and ♭♭♭ as chord progressions. The countertenor bassus may well be the lowest voice. "Nevertheless, as an added voice it does not function as the bearer of the sonorities, even when it finds itself below the tenor. The two-voice framework can exist without it" ("Die klangliche Struktur der spätmittelalterlichen Musik als Grundlage der Dur-Moll-Tonalität," *Mf* 15 [1962]: 217) [Als Füllstimme hat er jedoch, auch wo er sich unter dem Tenor befindet, keine Klangträgerfunktion. Die beiden Gerüststimmen können ohne ihn existieren]. Only in the cadences ♭♭♭ , ♭♭♭ , and ♭♭♭ , where the diminished fifth between tenor and discant could not stand alone, would the bass be a necessary support for the upper voices. Moreover, the diminished fifth implies a tendency toward the major mode—it presumes the flatting of the Lydian fourth degree and the sharping of the Mixolydian seventh (Apfel, "Die klangliche Struktur," p. 219). Therefore the diminished fifth between tenor and discant, the function of the bass as the "bearer of the sonorities," and the tendency toward the major mode appear as different aspects of the same thing.

26. Coussemaker, vol. 3, p. 295.

27. Ibid., p. 296: "Exceptions are made to this rule, the first of which is that the tenor may behave like the discant [in ascending at a cadence], as in mi-fa, fa-sol, sol-la [e.g., **e–f, f–g, g–a**]. Then the countertenor bassus can behave like the tenor, that is, making its penultimate tone a sixth below the tenor and its final pitch an octave below" [Ab ista enim regula fiunt exceptiones, quarum prima talis, quod cantus firmus teneat modum suprani, sicut: fa mi, mi fa; sol fa, fa sol; la sol, sol la; tunc contratenor bassus potest tenere modum tenoris, hoc ist facere suam penultimam sextam bassam subtus tenorem ultimam vero octavam bassam].

28. Pietro Aaron, *Toscanello in musica*, 2d ed. (Venice, 1529), bk. 2, chap. 18.

29. G. Zarlino, *Istitutioni harmoniche* (Venice, 1558), bk. 3, chap. 51.

30. H. Riemann, *Geschichte der Musiktheorie,* 2d ed. (Berlin, 1920), p. 357.

31. Cf. S. Hermelink, "Zur Geschichte der Kadenz im 16. Jahrhundert," *Congress Report* (Cologne, 1958), p. 133.

32. Alfred Einstein, *The Italian Madrigal*, 3 vols. (Princeton: Princeton University Press, 1949), 3:21–23.

33. Cf. M. Ruhnke's article "Intervall" in *MGG*, vol. 7, col. 1344ff.

34. Anonymous 13: "But with imperfect consonances—thirds and sixths—one can rightly ascend or descend two or three tones or more if necessary" (Coussemaker 3:497) [Mais par accors imparfais, tierces et sixtes, peut-on bien monter ou descendre II ou III notes ou plus se besoing est]; *Optima introductio in contrapunctum pro rudibus*: "And we can have two types of imperfect

consonances ascending in order three, four, or more degrees when necessary and descending two, three, four, or more degrees as long as there always follows a type of perfect consonance" (Coussemaker, vol. 3, p. 12) [Et possumus duas species imperfectas ordinare ascendendo vel tres aut quatuor vel plures si necesse fuerit, descendendo autem duas vel tres vel quatuor vel plures semper speciebus perfectis sequentibus]; Anonymous 11: "Several thirds and sixths can follow one another provided that no more than four or five occur in a row and that they are immediately followed by a type of perfect consonance; this happens when the tenor ascends or descends by single degrees" (Coussemaker, vol. 3, p. 463) [Plures tertiae et plures sextae possunt sequi una post alteram ita tamen quod non fiant ultra quatuor vel quinque et post illas immediate sequatur perfecta species et hoc fit quum tenor ascendit vel descendit per simplices gradus]. Whether the criterion of the nearly free admission of parallel imperfect consonances suffices to banish the *Optima introductio* from the 14th to the 15th century (see Manfred Bukofzer's article "Discantus" in *MGG*, vol. 3, col. 572) seems questionable in view of its scant difference from the rule of Anonymous 13.

35. Gerbert, vol. 3, p. 353. As an analogue to the terminology of rhetoricians, who labeled as "figures" or "ornaments" their artistic deviations from the rules of grammar, the expression *ornatus* could, of course, infer that a phenomenon is exceptional—an artistic license. Thus the *ricchezza dell'harmonia* was still not a foregone conclusion.

36. Zarlino, *Istitutioni harmoniche*, bk. 3, chap. 31.

37. Ibid., chap. 38.

38. In the theory of consonance, one had to set aside its definition as "fusion" (where the inability of musically untrained subjects to differentiate individual pitches is a measurable phenomenon). This was because a theory in which the greater or lesser difficulty of differentiating the individual components of a sonority passes for a criterion of the degree of consonance lays itself open to the charge that it would make the consonant character of an interval dependent upon its particular orchestration. Carl Stumpf, who had first seen the possibility of an operational definition of consonance in his experiments with musically untrained subjects, later characterized fusion as mere "homogeneity" [*Einheitlichkeit*].

NOTES TO CHAPTER 2, PAGES 94–111

1. Pietro Aaron, *Toscanello in Musica*, 2d ed. (Venice, 1529), bk. 2, chap. 16.

2. Coussemaker, vol. 3, p. 93.

3. Johannes Nucius, *Musica poetica*, chap. 6: "If the tenor and discant should sound a unison, how are the remaining voices to be added?" [Si tenor et discantus unisonum sonuerint, quomodo addendae sunt reliquae voces?].

4. Nucius, *Musica poetica*, chap. 7.

5. Tinctoris, Coussemaker, vol. 4, p. 29: "Hence when a certain mass or chanson or whatever other composition might be made from diverse parts of

diverse modes, if someone were to ask exactly of which mode is such a composition, the person asked should respond exactly according to the nature of the tenor, for it is the principle part of all composition as the basis of the whole relationship" [Unde quando missa aliqua vel cantilena vel quaevis alia compositio fuerit ex diversis partibus diversorum tonorum effecta, si quis peteret absolute cuius toni talis compositio esset, interrogatus debet absolute respondere secundum qualitatem tenoris, eo quod omnis compositionis sit pars principalis ut fundamentum totius relationis]. (See also E. Lowinsky, "Conflicting Views on Conflicting Signatures," *JAMS* 7 [1954]: 194.)

6. Anonymous 11, Coussemaker, vol. 3, p. 465.

7. G. Zarlino, *Istitutioni harmoniche* (Venice, 1558), bk. 3, chap. 58; Hugo Riemann, *Geschichte der Musiktheorie*, 2d ed. (Berlin, 1920), p. 423.

8. Johann Lippius, *Synopsis musicae*, chap. 1.

9. Thomas Morley, *A Plaine and Easie Introduction to Practicall Musicke* (facs. repr. in Shakespeare Association Facsimiles, No. 14 [London, 1937], p. 129).

10. Zarlino, *Istitutioni harmoniche*, bk. 3, chap. 58.

11. Morley, *A Plaine and Easie Introduction*, p. 126.

12. Coussemaker, vol. 3, p. 466.

13. Ibid., vol. 4, p. 448.

14. Manfred Bukofzer (*Geschichte des englischen Diskants und des Fauxbourdons nach den theoretischen Quellen* [Strasbourg, 1936]) speaks of "four-voice harmonic composition," claiming that with the examples on Bukofzer's page 296 and following, Guilelmus has taken "the final step toward a homogeneous 'pure composition' [i.e., the Renaissance style]" (p. 97) [den letzten Schritt zum homogenen "reinen Satz"]. But Bukofzer is mistaken if he thinks that "the design of the voices already presumes a four-voice conception" [die Stimmerfindung schon die Vierstimmigkeit voraussetzt].

15. Coussemaker, vol. 3, pp. 295f.

16. Ibid., p. 289.

17. Cf. Ernst Apfel, "Zur Entstehungsgeschichte des Palestrinasatzes," *AfMw* 14 (1957): 42.

18. Coussemaker, vol. 4, p. 448.

19. Ibid., p. 450.

20. Edward E. Lowinsky ("On the Use of Scores by Sixteenth-Century Musicians," *JAMS* 1 (1948): 21n20) distinguishes three types of "simultaneous conception": (1) the polyphony of the 16th century in which all the voices, even if they did not originate at the same time, are related to each other; (2) chordal composition; and (3) discant-bass composition. "And finally there is that mixed form—partly simultaneous, partly successive—that appears in the frottola; here the soprano and bass are simultaneously conceived while the alto and tenor are later additions." First however, even discant-tenor composition of the 15th century is a "mixed form." And second, frottolas are based less often on a discant-bass framework than on a discant-tenor framework.

21. Marius Schneider, *Die Anfänge des Basso continuo und seiner Bezifferung* (Leipzig, 1918), pp. 30–46. The designation "theory of harmony" is anach-

ronistic inasmuch as Tomás de Santa Maria regards four-voice sonorities not as direct unities—as chords—but as combinations of intervals.

22. Ibid., p. 44n2.

23. Morley, *A Plaine and Easie Introduction*, p. 143.

24. Burmeister, *Musica poetica* (Rostock, 1606), facs. repr. (Kassel, 1955), p. 18.

25. *Ars discantus per Johannem de Muris*, Coussemaker, vol. 3, p. 72.

26. Burmeister, *Musica poetica*, p. 19; cf. M. Ruhnke, *Joachim Burmeister* (Kassel, 1955), p. 108.

27. Burmeister, *Musica poetica*, p. 24.

28. G. Coperario, *Rules how to compose* (A Facsimile Edition of a Manuscript from the Library of the Earl of Bridgewater, circa 1610, now in the Huntington Library, San Marino, California. With an Introduction by Manfred F. Bukofzer. Los Angeles, 1952), fol. 4v.

29. Coperario, fol. 32v; Bukofzer comments (p. 13): "The real difference between the two types lies not in the way they are approached, as Coperario believes, but in their respective resolutions to either a six-four combination or a five-three combination." But even Bukofzer's interpretation is one-sided. Below a suspended second or seventh in the upper voices, the bass can change pitches or keep the same pitch not only from the preparatory consonance to the dissonance, but also from the dissonance to the resolution. Since Coperario writes down only the two extremes of the four ways of handling the bass, which differ not only in the way the suspension is prepared but also in the way it is resolved, he could have in mind that the one goes with the other.

30. Cf. Carl Dahlhaus, "Zur Theorie des klassischen Kontrapunkts," *KmJb* (1961): 43–57.

31. Otto Gombosi, "Italia: Patria del Basso ostinato," *Rassegna Musicale* 7 (1934): 25: "The baroque manner no longer wanted to experience the Dorian tonality in the Passamezzo: exchanging the first two steps transforms the Dorian into the relative major" [La forma barocca non vuole più saperne della tonalità dorica del Passamezzo: scambiando i primi passi doppi trasforma il dorico nel maggiore parallelo].

32. *The Complete Works of Claudio Monteverdi*, ed. F. Malipiero, 1926ff. Vol. 2, p. 9, system 1, m. 1; vol. 2, p. 10, sys. 3, m. 1; vol. 2, p. 29, sys. 2, m. 4; vol. 2, p. 31, sys. 3, m. 5; vol. 2, p. 33, sys. 2, m. 1; vol. 2, p. 65, sys. 2, m. 6; vol. 2, p. 97, sys. 2, m. 5; vol. 2, p. 97, sys. 3, m. 2.

33. Ibid., vol. 3, p. 76, sys. 3, m. 1.

34. Ibid., vol. 3, p. 87, sys. 1, m. 4.

35. Ibid., vol. 8, p. 260, sys. 1, m. 3.

36. Ibid., vol. 2, p. 63, sys. 2, m. 3.

37. Arnold Schering, *Geschichte der Musik in Beispielen* (Leipzig, 1931), No. 184, p. 217.

38. P. Hamburger, *Subdominante und Wechseldominante* (Wiesbaden, 1955), pp. 139ff.

39. E. E. Lowinsky, *Tonality and Atonality in Sixteenth-Century Music* (Berkeley and Los Angeles, 1961), p. 15.

40. The Complete Works of Josquin, Motets, vol. 1, p. 1.

41. Joanambrosio Dalza, *Tastar de corde* and *Recercar*, in O. Körte, *Laute und Lautenmusik bis zur Mitte des 16. Jahrhunderts* (Leipzig, 1901), p. 132.

42. Dalza, p. 132, mm. 20–30.

43. Lowinsky, *Tonality and Atonality*, pp. 63f.

44. Ibid., p. 62.

45. Ibid., pp. 18f.

46. Ibid., p. 65.

NOTES TO CHAPTER 2, PAGES 111–21

1. Hermann Finck, *Practica musica* (Wittenberg, 1556), fol. C1; Ambrosius Wilphlingseder, *Erotemata musices practicae* (Nürnberg, 1563), bk. 1, chap. 7; Fredericus Beurhusius, *Erotematum musicae libri duo* (n.p., 1580), bk. 1, chap. 9; Lucas Lossius, *Erotemata musicae practicae* (Nürnberg, 1563), bk. 1, chap. 6; Peter Eichmann, *Praecepta musicae practicae*, 1604, fol. G2.

2. Hugo Riemann, *Geschichte der Musiktheorie*, 2d ed. (Berlin, 1920), p. 120.

3. Coussemaker, vol. 1, p. 202.

4. Ibid., p. 360; Riemann, *Geschichte*, p. 191; Thr. Georgiades, *Englische Diskanttraktate aus der ersten Hälfte des 15. Jahrhunderts* (Würzburg, 1937), p. 77; Ernst Apfel, "Zur Entstehung des realen vierstimmigen Satzes in England," *AfMw* 17 (1960): 86n.

5. Gafurius, *Practica musicae* (Milan, 1496), bk. 3, chap. 2. The sentence immediately following says that a sixth added to a third will equal an octave, and that the octave, together with the fifth, forms a "harmonic proportion" (6:4:3). "If this mean tone [of the fifth, i.e. the third] is raised the interval of a sixth, then it will enclose the higher of the outer tones [of the fifth] as a harmonic mean, perfecting the equal-sounding and composite octave" [Huius quidem medietatis chorda se in acutum exachordi interuallo fuerit intensa: acutiorem ipsas extremitates harmonica medietate conclaudit: diapason compositam perficiens aequisonantiam].

6. Gafurius, *De armonia*, bk. 3, chap. 12.

7. Riemann, *Geschichte*, pp. 389ff.

8. Carl Dahlhaus, "War Zarlino Dualist?" *Mf* 10 (1957): 286.

9. Zarlino, *Istitutioni harmoniche* (Venice, 1558), bk. 3, chaps. 31 and 60.

10. Ibid., chap. 60: "One sees that after the minor third contained between the terms 6 and 5 [m3 = 6:5], there immediately follows the perfect fourth placed between the terms 8 and 6 [p4 = 8:6 = 4:3]" [Se vede, che dopo il semidituono, contenuto tra questi termini 6 and 5 segue immediatamente la Diatessaron, posta tra questi termini 8 et 6].

11. Ibid., chap. 60: "In the above mentioned ordering, the major third would not be placed below the perfect fourth unless some other interval intervened between them; the reason being that these two consonances, arranged one on top of the other contrary to their natures, have that interval placed above which ought to be located below, and below, that which ought to remain above" [. . . non se trova nell' ordine nominato, che'l Ditono sia posta senz' alcun mezzo avanti la Diatessaron; la onde essendo queste due consonanze accomodate l'una

dopo l'altra contra la loro natura, essendo posta nell'acuto quella, che doverebbe esser collocata nel grave et nel grave quella, che doverebbe tener
l'acuto].

12. Johann Lippius, *Synopsis musicae novae* (Erfurt, 1612), fol. F4.

13. Ibid., fol. F5.

14. Ibid., fol. H4.

15. Ibid., fol. F6.

16. Heinrich Baryphonus, *Henrici Baryphoni Pleiades musicae* (Magdeburg,
1630), pp. 164f.

17. Thomas Campion, *A New Way of Making Foure Parts* (circa 1613); cited
in R. W. Wienpahl, "English Theorists and Evolving Tonality," *M & L* 36
(1955): 386.

18. Andreas Werckmeister, *Harmonologia musica* (Frankfurt, 1702), pp. 3ff.

19. Zarlino, *Istitutioni harmoniche*, bk. 3, chap. 10.

20. Lippius, *Synopsis*, fol. E7.

21. Glen Haydon's presentation of the development of the six-four chord
from the 13th to the 17th century (*The Evolution of the Six-Four Chord: A
Chapter in the History of Dissonance Treatment* [Berkeley, 1933]), so discriminating in its description and classification of this phenomenon, suffers from
an overestimation of the chordal character of this interval combination. In tonal
harmony, the six-four chord is a consonance when it is an inversion of the
tonic triad, and a dissonance when a double suspension resolving to the
dominant. And whether it was the one or the other in mensural music is the
question that Haydon attempts to answer: "The thesis that the six-four chord
at any moment in the periods studied, is treated as a purely consonant
combination cannot successfully be defended. On the contrary, all the examples
cited give overwhelming proof that the six-four chord is treated exclusively as
a dissonance . . . At no time does one find both free entrance and free quitting
of the six-four chord, i.e., the six-four both approached and quitted by a
skipwise progression of all the parts" (pp. 133f.). Nevertheless, just as it is
undeniable that the six-four was never conceived as a consonance, so is it faulty
to assert that it was a dissonance. It was not a chord that was dissonant as
a whole, but a combination of two intervals that were independent of each
other and treated differently: the fourth as a dissonance that had to be prepared
and resolved, the sixth as a consonance not subject to rules of progression.

a. The sixth can be held while the fourth is resolved: $\begin{smallmatrix}6&6\\4&3\end{smallmatrix}$.

And the fifth in the progression $\begin{smallmatrix}6&5\\4&3\end{smallmatrix}$, apparently a parallel to

the resolution of the fourth in the third, is, in the 15th century, often nothing
other than an ornamental neighbor note resulting from the under-third cadence:

b. The unprepared fourth on a strong beat, found in Dufay and still in Ockeghem, is, as Haydon rightly emphasizes, not a prototype of the consonant six-four chord but rather a remnant of an older manner of dissonance treatment—a remnant severed in the 16th century by a more discriminating contrapuntal technique. "Even the presence of a relatively large number of these accented unprepared six-four chords in the music of Dufay and his contemporaries is scarcely sufficient ground for reaching the conclusion that the six-four chord in its modern sense was consciously used by the composers of that period" (p. 20). The apparent modernism is an archaism.

c. The fourth over a held tone, , should be related primarily as a consonance to the sixth, not as an irregular dissonance to the tied voice. The held tone, which in three-voice works of the 15th century is generally given to the countertenor (the supplemental voice added to the discant-tenor framework), is more an added tone than a bass tone.

d. It need hardly be mentioned that a six-four sonority in which the bass or the fourth is a passing tone does not represent a chord. The dissonant passing tone, not unusual in the 15th century, became obsolete in the 16th century (without becoming entirely suppressed [Haydon, p. 68]), only to return to favor as a modernism in the 17th century.

22. "This same nature sees to it lest three voices should come together without some perfect consonance: for look how above the bass **A** are set the third **c** and fifth **e**, or above the bass **c** the third **e** and fifth **g**; the thirds **A–c** and **c–e** are below, and the thirds **c–e** and **e–g** above, joined in perfection with the fifths **A–e** and **c–g**. On the other hand, above the bass **A** are placed the fourth **d** and sixth **f**: or above the base **c** the fourth **f** and sixth **a**. In these examples, the sixth **A–f** and the third **d–f**, or the sixth **c–a** and the third **f–a**, are supported by the fourth **A–d** or **c–f**" [Eadem natura providit, ne tres voces convenire possint sine perfecta aliqua consonantia . . . Ecce enim super A bassum dentur tertia C et quinta E aut super C bassum tertia E et quint G; sunt in priori A C et C E, in posteriori C E et E G tertiae, colligatae perfectione quintae A E et C G. Rursus super bassum A imponantur D quarta et F sexta: aut super bassum C quarta F et sexta a. In his exemplis sexta A F et tertia D F, aut sexta C a et tertia F a fulciuntur quarta A D, aut C F] (Andreas Papius, *De consonantiis, seu pro diatessaron libri duo* [Antwerp, 1581], p. 107). The dispute over the consonant and dissonant character of the fourth was a significant theme of the musical "querelle des anciens et modernes" [quarrel between the ancients and the moderns]—though neglected in D. P. Walker's treatment of the *Musikalischen Humanismus im 16. and frühen 17. Jahrhundert* (Kassel, 1949).

23. Andreas Werckmeister, *Die nothwendigsten Anmerckungen und Regeln / wie der General-Baß wol könne tractiret werden* (Aschersleben, 1698), fol. B2 (par. 26), and *Harmonologia musica*, p. 49.

24. Werckmeister, *Hypomnemata musica oder Musicalisches Memorial*

(Quedlinburg, 1697), p. 7. "The odd numbers are completely unfit to serve as a root which can produce a natural harmony; for 3:4 would have a fourth above the fundamental, and 5 with its following 6 [5:6] the minor third; all this turns on its head what is natural" [Die Ungeraden Zahlen dienen gar nicht zur Wurtzel / welche eine harmoniam naturalem geben können; Denn 3.4. giebet eine quartam zum fundament / 5. giebet mit ihr folgenden 6. die tertiam minorem; ist alles ein verkertes Wesen der Natur] (*Hypomnemata musica*, p. 6; *Harmonologia musica*, p. 26).

25. W. Schönsleder, *Architectonice musices universalis . . . Autore Volupio Decoro* (n.p., 1631), pt. 1, chap. 4. In his *Rules how to compose* (circa 1610, fols. 4–9), G. Coperario develops chord progressions over 10 bass progressions: the ascending and descending major second, minor third, fourth, fifth, and octave. He describes the voice leading of the upper voices as intervals above the bass ("If the bass rise a 2, Canto demands a 10, next an 8") and limits himself to the $\frac{5}{3}$ chord. But he takes into consideration neither the principle of doubling the bass nor the method of connecting chord tones by the smallest melodic interval.

26. Johann Crüger, *Synopsis musica*, Berlin 1630, chap. 8 (the theory of chords); 2d ed. (1654), p. 65 (Tabula naturalis).

27. Francesco Bianciardi, *Breve regola per imparar a sonare sopra il Basso con ogni sorte d'Istromento* (n.p., 1607); cited in F. T. Arnold, *The Art of Accompaniment from a Thorough-Bass* (Oxford, 1931), p. 77.

28. Lorenzo Penna, *Primi albori musicali*, 3d ed. (Bologna, 1679), bk. 3, p. 151: "When the bass moves down a fourth or up a fifth it is given a minor third, though in some cases it can be given the major third; then it conforms with the nature of the composition" [Andando il basso di quarta in giù, ò il quinto in sù, se gli dia terza minore se bene in alcun caso se li può dar e la maggiore, dunque si conformi con la natura della composizione]. And on page 154: "When the bass descends by fifth or ascends by fourth, the following rules will be of use for these passages. First rule: that they be given the major third, because if they should happen to be given the minor third they will sound deformed" [Descendendo il basso di quinta, ò ascendendo di quarta, le regole seguenti serviranno per questi passi. Prima regola. Che se li dia la terza maggiore, perche se occorrerà darvi la terza minore, sarà segnata].

29. Franz Xaver Murschhauser, *Academia musico-poetica bipartita*, pt. 1 (Nürnberg, 1721) (a second part did not appear), p. 26.

30. Murschhauser, *Academia*, p. 29.

31. Hugo Riemann, *Handbuch der Harmonielehre*, 7th ed. (Berlin, 1919), p. 214: "Therefore all dominant relationships are major in nature, all sub-dominant relationships minor in nature, as is already revealed by the striving of a minor key to produce a major dominant and of a major key to produce a minor subdominant, while the opposite (a major subdominant in minor, a minor dominant in major) is out of the question" [Alle dominantischen Beziehungen sind daher eigentlich dur-artige, alle subdominantischen moll-artige, wie sich schon an dem Bestreben, der Molltonart eine Durdominante

und der Durtonart eine Mollsubdominante zu geben, offenbart, während das Gegenteil (Dursubdominante in Moll, Molldominante in Dur) ausgeschlossen ist].

32. Galeazzo Sabbatini, *Regola facile e breve per sonare sopra il Basso continuo* (n.p., 1628); cited in Arnold, *The Art of Accompaniment*, pp. 111f.

33. Penna, *Primi albori musicali*, bk. 3, p. 136. Angelo Berardi attests to the fact that the rule for chords of the sixth was not merely a trick of thoroughbass practice, but a principle of composition. He formulates it as a prescription for "Contrapunto semplice" [simple counterpoint]: "Above the mi-degree, endeavor to give it a minor sixth or third" [Sopra la voce del mi, procaci di darli la sesta minore, o terza] (*Miscellanea musicale* [Bologna, 1689], p. 113).

34. Matthew Locke, *Melothesia, or Certain Rules for playing upon a Continued-Bass*, (n.p., 1673); cited in Arnold, *The Art of Accompaniment*, p. 155.

35. J. Ph. Rameau, *Traité de l'harmonie* (Paris, 1722), pp. 204f.

NOTES TO CHAPTER 2, PAGES 121–35

1. J. Ph. Rameau, *Génération harmonique* (Paris, 1737), p. 171: "Only the tonic note carries the perfect, or natural, chord; to this chord the seventh is added in the case of dominants, and the major sixth in the case of subdominants" [La seule Note tonique porte l'Accord parfait, ou naturel; on ajoute la Septiéme a cet Accord pour les Dominantes, et la Sixte majeure pour les Sousdominantes]. For Rameau, the *dominante* is defined as the first tone of an ascending fourth in the bass, and the *sousdominante* as the first tone of a descending fourth. The rule of seventh chords can be transferred to chord inversions. Thus the first of two six-three chords above an ascending half step in the bass should be filled out to produce a four-three chord [e.g., when preceding **f–a–d′** (d⁶), **e–g–c′** becomes **e–g–a–c′** (a₃⁴)] (Michel de Saint-Lambert, *Nouveau traité de l'accompagnement* (n.p., 1707); cited in F. T. Arnold, *The Art of Accompaniment* (Oxford, 1931), p. 191.

2. Preface to his *Nuove Musiche*, 1601; cited in A. Solerti, *Le origini del melodramma* (1903), p. 60. Jacopo Peri requires that the quicker or slower motion of the bass should conform to the affect of the text (and not to the rules of counterpoint). Yet he defines the consonances and dissonances of the voice part not as chord tones and "nonharmonic" tones, but as "wrong and right proportions" [false e buone proporzioni], as intervals to the bass (Preface to Euridice, 1600; cited in Solerti, *Le origini*, p. 46).

3. Cf. H. H. Eggebrecht, "Arten des Generalbasses im frühen und mittleren 17. Jahrhundert," *AfMw* 14 (1957): 74; Eggebrecht, *Heinrich Schütz* (Göttingen, 1959), p. 38.

4. Adriano Banchieri, *Cartella musicale*, 3d ed. (Bologna, 1614), p. 103.

5. Ibid., p. 166.

6. Cf. Knud Jeppesen, *Der Palestrinastil und die Dissonanz* (Leipzig, 1925), p. 92 (passing tones) and p. 204 (suspensions).

7. Ibid., pp. 136ff.

8. "Yet they [dissonances] are used in florid song because there they are not sensed on account of the quickness of their syllables" [Usitantur tamen in cantu fractibili, eo quod in ipso propter velocitatem vocum earum non sentiuntur dissonantiae] (Prosdocimo de' Beldomandi; Coussemaker, vol. 3, p. 197). "A dissonance is felt or can be felt less strongly by reason of its short duration or quickness in pronunciation" [Dissonantia minus percipitur seu percipi potest ratione parvae morae seu velocitatis in pronunciando] (Anonymous 11; Coussemaker, vol. 3, p. 463).

9. Gafurius, *Practica musicae* (Milan, 1496), bk. 3, chap. 4.

10. "The dissonance of a second gives sweetness to the third below, while the dissonance of a seventh gives sweetness to the sixth; the dissonance of a fourth gives sweetness to the third above" [Dissonantia secunde dat dulcedinem tertie basse; dissonantia vero septime dat dulcedinem sexte; dissonantia quarte dat dulcedinem tertie alte] (Guilelmus Monachus; Coussemaker, vol. 3, p. 291).

11. "And in order that the composer could provide a greatly varied diet for the ears, a manner has been discovered of composing the dissonances between the consonances, and these said dissonances are made acceptible through the means and grace of the suspension" [Et acciò che il compositore possi usare assai varietà di cibo per gl'orecchi, si ha ritrovato un modo da comporre le dissonanze fra le consonanze e dette dissonanze si fanno passar con il mezzo et il favore della sincopa] (Vicentino, *L'antica musica ridotta alla moderna prattica* [Rome, 1555], facs. repr. [Kassel, 1959], fol. 29v).

12. Zarlino, *Istitutioni harmoniche* (Venice, 1558), bk. 3, chap. 42.

13. Jeppesen, *Der Palestrinastil*, p. 78.

14. Examples of this type of dissonance in the works of Palestrina are listed in P. Hamburger, *Studien zur Vokalpolyphonie* (Wiesbaden, 1956), pp. 54–61.

15. Zarlino, *Istitutioni harmoniche*, bk. 3, chap. 26.

16. Claude V. Palisca, "Vincenzo Galilei's Counterpoint Treatise: A Code for the Seconda Prattica," *JAMS* 9 (1956): 81–96.

17. Giovanni Maria Bononcini, *Musico prattico* (Bologna, 1678), p. 48.

18. J. Müller-Blattau, *Die Kompositionslehre Heinrich Schützens in der Fassung seines Schülers Christoph Bernhard* (Leipzig, 1926), p. 40.

19. Monteverdi, vol. 11 (*L'Orfeo*), p. 145, sys. 2, m. 2; likewise p. 77, sys. 3, m. 1; p. 146, sys. 5, m. 1.

20. Christoph Bernhard, in Müller-Blattau, *Die Kompositionslehre*, p. 86: "A *transitus inversus* occurs when the first part of a measure, in passing, is bad [=dissonant] and the second part is good [=consonant]" [Transitus inversus ist, wenn das erste Theil eines Tactes im Transitu böse, das andere gut ist].

21. Monteverdi, vol. 11, p. 10, sys. 2, m. 2; likewise p. 22, sys. 4, m. 1; p. 22, sys. 5, m. 3; p. 57, sys. 1, mm. 2–3; p. 80, sys. 4, m. 3; p. 125, sys. 4, m. 2; p. 140, sys. 3, m. 1; p. 141, sys. 4, m. 2; p. 143, sys. 1, m. 3; vol. 13 (*L'Incoronazione di Poppea*), p. 29, sys. 1, m. 2; p. 50, sys. 2, m. 3; p. 53, sys. 2, m. 3; p. 58, sys. 4, m. 4; p. 64, sys. 5, m. 4; p. 70, sys. 2, m. 1; p. 85, sys. 4, m. 3; p. 86, sys. 1, m. 3; p. 115, sys. 1, m. 2; p. 120, sys.

4, m. 4; p. 121, sys. 1, m. 1; p. 178, sys. 2, m. 2; p. 201, sys. 4, m. 1; p. 202, sys. 2, m. 3; p. 207, sys. 1, 1; p. 212, sys. 3, m. 3.

22. Bernhard (in Müller-Blattau, *Die Kompositionslehre*, p. 85) labels the resolution of an accented suspension by an ascending second an "inverted suspension" [umgekehrte Syncopatio].

23. Jeppesen, *Der Palestrinastil*, p. 169.

24. Monteverdi, vol. 11, p. 66, sys. 4, m. 1; likewise p. 114, sys. 1, m. 2, and p. 114, sys. 3, m. 3.

25. Ibid., p. 56, sys. 1, m. 3; likewise p. 143, sys. 3, m. 1. In his polemic against Monteverdi, Giovanni Maria Artusi denies that "a rest could be considered a consonance" (E. Vogel, "Claudio Monteverdi," *VjfMw* 3 (1887): 330).

26. In contrast to the "accented passing tone," which is presented over a held tone in the other voice, the "freely approached [i.e., unprepared] suspension" is a "note-against-note" dissonance (Monteverdi, vol. 11, p. 56, sys. 4, m. 2; p. 60, sys. 2, m. 2; p. 62, sys. 5, m. 3; p. 66, sys. 2, m. 2; p. 105, sys. 2, m. 1).

27. Bernhard (Müller-Blattau, *Die Kompositionslehre*, p. 87): "*Heterolepsis* is a taking up of another voice and is of two kinds. The first is when I leap or go from a consonance to a dissonance that could be made by another voice in passing" [Heterolepsis ist eine Ergreiffung einer anderen Stimme und ist Zweyerley. Erstlich wenn ich nach einer Consonantz in eine Dissonantz springe oder gehe, so von einer andern Stimme in transitu könte gemacht werden].

28. Monteverdi, vol. 11, p. 64, sys. 2, m. 2; likewise p. 21, sys. 3, m. 1; p. 60, sys. 1, m. 2; p. 64, sys. 2, m. 1; p. 64, sys. 3, m. 3; p. 79, sys. 2, m. 2; p. 142, sys. 3, m. 1; p. 142, sys. 3, m. 3.

29. Ibid., p. 59, sys. 3, m. 2; likewise p. 57, sys. 1, m. 2.

30. In the 16th century, the significance of the downward leap of a suspended seventh to a third or a fifth changed from that of an archaism to a modernism— from a feature of a preliminary stage of "classical" counterpoint to an expressive departure from the norms of the strict style. Jeppesen (*Der Palestrinastil*, p. 243) cites an example from Josquin's mass *Malheur me bat* and refers to Artusi. And other theorists from around 1600 also cite this dissonance figure: Pietro Pontio (*Ragionamento di musica*, 1588, pp. 80 and 82), Vincenzo Galilei (cf. Palisca, "Vincenzo Galilei's Counterpoint Treatise," pp. 90f) and Domenico Cerone (*El Melopeo y maestro*, 1613; cf. R. Hannas, "Cerone, Philosopher and Teacher," *MQ* 21 [1935]: 415).

31. Bernhard (Müller-Blattau, *Die Kompositionslehre*, p. 89). Bernhard classifies the irregularly resolved suspension—one resolved by a leap or an ascending second—not only as *heterolepsis* but also as (1) *syncopatio catachrestica* [misused suspension] (p. 77), because it contradicts the norm, as (2) *ellipsis* (p. 84), because the regular consonance of resolution is lacking, and as (3) *mora* [delay] (p. 85) or *retardatio* (p. 151), because the consonance is delayed by the dissonance. Yet only the interpretation as *heterolepsis* can be deemed a fitting explanation.

32. Monteverdi, vol. 11, p. 61, sys. 2, m. 1; likewise p. 77, sys. 4, m. 1.

33. Ibid., p. 9, sys. 3, m. 2; likewise p. 57, sys. 3, m. 3; p. 60, sys. 4, m. 3; p. 62, sys. 2, m. 1; p. 66, sys. 2, m. 1.

34. Ibid., p. 142, sys. 5, m. 4; likewise p. 141, sys. 4, m. 3.

35. Ibid., p. 119, sys. 2, m. 2; likewise p. 114, sys. 3, m. 3.

36. Ibid., p. 101, sys. 2, m. 2; likewise p. 142, sys. 1, m. 3.

37. Ibid., p. 19, sys. 2, mm. 1–2; likewise p. 61, sys. 3, m. 3; p. 140, sys. 4, m. 2.

38. Cf. Jeppesen, *Der Palestrinastil*, pp. 136ff.

39. Monteverdi, vol. 11, p. 56, sys. 1, m. 1; likewise p. 142, sys. 3, m. 2; p. 142, sys. 4, m. 2.

40. Ibid., p. 56, sys. 2, m. 2; likewise p. 19, sys. 3, m. 1; p. 62, sys. 4, m. 2; p. 116, sys. 4, 1; p. 139, sys. 4, m. 1; p. 144, sys. 1, m. 2.

41. Monteverdi, vol. 8, pp. 305–9.

42. J. D. Heinichen, *Der Generalbaß in der Composition* (Dresden, 1728).

43. J. Mattheson (*Der vollkommene Capellmeister* [Hamburg, 1739], facsimile reprint [Kassel, 1954], p. 320) explains the bass note of the second seventh as an anticipation: "For the eighth [resolution of a seventh], the one seventh, in the case of tied notes, occasionally takes the other seventh, so that in a certain manner this dissonance is thus resolved in its like interval. The bass is thereby more of an anticipation, and strides ahead earlier than it should"

[Fürs **achte** nimmt sich auch die eine **Sept** in gebundenen

Fällen bisweilen der andern an, so daß auf gewisse Weise diese Dissonantz alsdann durch ihres gleichen gelöset wird. Der Baß nimmt dabey mehr voraus, und schreitet eher fort, als er sollte].

44. Monteverdi, vol. 13, p. 40, sys. 1, m. 2; p. 109, sys. 1, m. 2; p. 244, sys. 1, m. 2; p. 244, sys. 3, m. 3; p. 244, sys. 4, m. 1.

45. Monteverdi, vol. 11, p. 3, sys. 3, m. 1; likewise p. 13, sys. 2, m. 2; p. 30, sys. 3, m. 2; p. 77, 1, m. 3.

46. Monteverdi, vol. 7, pp. 52–57.

47. Galeazzo Sabbatini, *Regola facile e breve per sonare sopra il Basso continuo* (1628); cited in F. T. Arnold, *The Art of Accompaniment*, pp. 125f.

48. Monteverdi, vol. 8, p. 282, sys. 1, mm. 2–4.

49. Ibid., p. 309, sys. 1, mm. 1–2.

50. According to the theory of fundamental progressions, the bass **f** preceding **g** would be interpreted as supporting a d^6 chord. Thus, besides **e′** in the upper voice, the **c′** in the inner voice would also be a passing tone.

51. Jeppesen, *Der Palestrinastil*, p. 235. Jeppesen erroneously interprets the (relatively) accented passing tone in the alto as the reference tone of a suspension in the soprano, and the [subsequent] unaccented passing tone in the soprano as a resolution of the suspension by an "ascending step" [Sekundschritt nach oben].

52. Ernst Kurth, *Die Voraussetzungen der theoretischen Harmonik und der tonalen Darstellungssysteme* (Bern, 1913), p. 53.

53. The distinction between a chordal dissonance and a nonharmonic tone

is compromised by the systematizing force not only of the theory of fundamental progressions but also by the theory of functions. On the one hand, the distinction is made empty by Simon Sechter's consequent "schematization of thirds" [the piling up of thirds]. Sechter understands the fourth and sixth to be octave displacements of the eleventh and thirteenth, and interprets a suspended fourth preceding the third of the dominant not as a nonharmonic tone but as the eleventh of the chord (*Die Grundsätze der musikalischen Komposition* [Leipzig, 1853], pt. 3, p. 830). On the other hand, in Riemann's theory of functions—which reduces the concept of harmony to the tonic, subdominant, and dominant sonorities—the suspended fourth preceding the third of the dominant, together with the seventh of the dominant seventh chord and the root of the tonic parallel (in major), is subsumed under the concept of "nonharmonic tones." But the attempt to subsume chordal dissonances, nonharmonic tones, and those tones of secondary chords that deviate from the tones of primary chords, under a single concept robs music theory of essential terminological differentiations.

54. The downward stepwise resolution of the seventh has a different motivation in tonal harmony than it had in older counterpoint. As intervallic dissonance, the seventh was resolved to the sixth and not to the octave because the direct transition from a dissonance to a perfect consonance was perceived as harsh and abrupt. Dissonance (**d–c′**) was to be followed by imperfect consonance (**d–b**), and imperfect consonance by perfect consonance (**c–c′**). In contrast, as chordal dissonance, the seventh is resolved stepwise downward and not upward because a mode of listening emphasizing the "dynamic" impulse of the ii^7–V and IV^7–V chord progressions seeks to interpret the resolution of dissonance as a result of that impulse; but only the tone below the seventh—not the tone above—differentiates the chords.

55. Arnold Schönberg (*Harmonielehre* [Leipzig and Vienna, 1911], pp. 132–40) even counts the descending second among the "stronger" root progressions. He interprets the second-progression d–C as a double fifth-progression (d–G–C). But one can also interpret it as a descending progression of a fourth (F–C) with a "supposed third" (d) under the first root (F), and thus view it as a "weaker" root progression.

56. G. Zarlino, *Istitutioni harmoniche* (Venice, 1558), bk. 3, chap. 42: "In singing a syncopated semibreve, the syllable is held firm and it is heard much like a suspension or a reluctance to speak" [. . . nel cantar la Semibreve sincopata se tiene salda la voce & se ode quasi una suspensione o taciturnità].

57. Paul Hamburger, *Subdominante und Wechseldominante* (Wiesbaden, 1955), p. 151.

58. Ibid., pp. 139ff.

59. Hamburger (pp. 155f.) cites examples from the 16th century without considering that they contradict his hypothesis.

60. Schönberg's polemic against the concept of "nonharmonic" tones (*Harmonielehre*, pp. 344–87) is poorly substantiated. It is based on four arguments: 1. "Since 'harmony' is the simultaneous sounding of tones, there is no such thing as nonharmonic tones" (p. 355) [Harmoniefremde Töne gibt es nicht,

denn Harmonie ist Zusammenklang]; his objection concerns only the terminology, not the facts of the matter. 2. The argument that "nonharmonic" tones are not entirely but only "relatively without influence" can be turned around: while their significance for harmonic progression may be indisputable, it is less than that of chordal dissonances, so that one cannot give up all claim to the distinction. 3. The objection that sonorities originating in "nonharmonic" tones can later become consolidated as autonomous chords (p. 352) does not mean that the differentiation between "chordal dissonances" and "nonharmonic tones" is superfluous. Just the reverse: the differentiation is essential if the historical modifications of sonorities are to be described. 4. According to Schönberg (pp. 353f.), the "change of harmony" is an insuffient criterion by which to distinguish chordal dissonances from nonharmonic tones, since a suspended ninth **d'/c**, thus a nonharmonic tone, could not only be resolved to the octave **c'/c** but also—through a "change of harmony"—to the tenth **c'/A**. The example is a borderline case which does not, however, signify that the criteria break down, but only that two interpretations are possible. Either the dissonance is a chordal dissonance and the first tone in the bass is a supposed third [E^7 with a **c** bass moving to A minor], or it is a nonharmonic tone and the second tone in the bass is a supposed third [C major with a major ninth moving to A minor].

NOTES TO CHAPTER 2, PAGES 135–41

1. The compositional technique of monody, in which this correlation is suspended, forces the thoroughbass player to read the vocal part as well.

2. Michel de Saint-Lambert (*Nouveau traité de l'accompagnement*, 1707) still interprets the figure "2" as $\frac{5}{2}$, not $\frac{4}{2}$ (F. T. Arnold, *The Art of Accompaniment*, p. 175).

3. Hugo Riemann, *Zur Reform der Harmonie-Lehrmethode*, in *Präludien und Studien III* (Leipzig), p. 56.

4. F. Blume, *Das monodische Prinzip in der protestantischen Kirchenmusik* (Leipzig, 1925), pp. 64–75; H. H. Eggebrecht, "Arten des Generalbasses im frühen und mittleren 17. Jahrhundert," *AfMw* 14 (1957): 69–73.

5. Marius Schneider, *Die Anfänge des Basso continuo und seiner Bezifferung* (Leipzig, 1918), pp. 172f.

6. Giulio Caccini, *Le Nuove Musiche*, 1601; facs. repr. 1934, p. 23.

7. Preface to *Le Nuove Musiche* (cited in A. Solerti, *Le origini del melodramma*, 1903, p. 57).

8. Arnold (p. 45) comments: "It is, of course, possible that Caccini intended the 11 in question to be prepared by taking the preceding 6 on ♯ c as $\frac{6}{3}$." Yet the diminished fifth, as a "note-against-note" dissonance, would scarcely be a less irregular figure than the abbreviation of a suspended fourth.

9. Monteverdi, vol. 7, p. 35, sys. 3, m. 4; p. 37, sys. 3, m. 1; p. 76, sys. 1, m. 1.

10. Ibid., p. 38, sys. 1, m. 3.

11. Ibid., p. 37, sys. 1, m. 2; p. 42, sys. 1, m. 2.

12. Ibid., p. 50, sys. 1, m. 1.

13. Ibid., p. 8.

NOTES TO CHAPTER 2, PAGES 141–51

1. Alfred Einstein, *The Italian Madrigal* (Princeton, 1949), vol. 3, pp. 178–81.

2. "The bilateral, polar formation of the dominant relation [here meaning both IV and V] is likewise one of those ultimate givens for which an 'explanation' is simply not to be had" (H. Erpf, *Studien zur Harmonie- und Klangtechnik der neueren Musik* [Leipzig, 1927], p. 19) [Die zweiseitige, polare Ausbildung des Dominantverhältnisses ist ebenfalls eine jener letzten Gegebenheiten, für die eine "Erklärung" schlechthin nicht zu geben ist].

3. E. Kirsch, *Wesen und Aufbau der Lehre von den harmonischen Funktionen* (Leipzig, 1928), p. 6.

4. Hugo Riemann (*Handbuch der Harmonielehre* [Berlin, 1917], 7th ed., p. 166) interprets the secondary dominant on the supertonic (ex. 52c) as a "chromatic alteration of subdominant harmony" [chromatische Veränderung der Subdominantharmonie].

5. J. Ph. Rameau, *Traité de l'Harmonie* (Paris, 1722), pp. 204f.

6. Monteverdi, vol. 8, p. 303.

7. Monteverdi, vol. 7, p. 49, sys. 2, mm. 1–2.

8. Hans Zingerle, *Die Harmonik Monteverdis und seiner Zeit*, pp. 6–10.

9. Monteverdi, vol. 7, p. 182, sys. 3, m. 4; Zingerle, ex. 33.

10. Zingerle recognized that in order to interpret the chords C–A in a tonal context—as I – V/ii—they must be "separated from each other by a caesura" (p. 13). In Carissimi's oratorios *Jephta*, *Judicium Salomonis*, *Baltazar*, and *Jonas* (ed. Friedrich Chrysander in *Denkmäler der Tonkunst*, vol. 2, 1869) the chords G and F (p. 5, sys. 1, m. 1; p. 20, sys. 5, m. 2; p. 53, sys. 41, m. 1; p. 58, sys. 1, m. 2; p. 60, sys. 2, m. 4; p. 63, sys. 4, m. 4) or G and d (p. 34, sys. 3, m. 1; p. 38, sys. 3, m. 1; p. 53, sys. 2, m. 3; p. 56, sys. 2, m. 2; p. 67, sys. 2, m. 4; p. 84, sys. 5, m. 3; p. 104, sys. 4, m. 4; p. 107, sys. 4, m. 2) are, except in two sequences (p. 3, sys. 2, m. 1; p. 74, sys. 1, m. 3), separated from each other by formal caesuras.

11. Monteverdi, vol. 7, p. 42, sys. 2, m. 2.

12. Ibid., p. 49, sys. 1, m. 1; likewise p. 41, sys. 1, m. 2; p. 41, sys. 2, m. 2.

13. Ibid., p. 11, sys. 1, m. 4.

14. Ibid., p. 49, sys. 3, m. 3; similarly p. 98, sys. 1, m. 1; p. 132, sys. 3, m. 2; p. 177, sys. 1, m. 3.

15. Ibid., p. 48, sys. 3, m. 2.

16. Moritz Hauptmann, *Die Natur der Harmonik und der Metrik* (Leipzig, 1853), p. 70.

17. Monteverdi, vol. 2, p. 33, sys. 3, m. 4; p. 37, sys. 2, m. 3; p. 61, sys. 1, m. 4; p. 73, sys. 2, m. 3; p. 78, sys. 2, m. 1.

18. Monteverdi, vol. 7, p. 4, sys. 2, m. 3.

NOTES TO CHAPTER 3, PAGES 153–61

1. Carl Dahlhaus, "Die Termini Dur und Moll," *AfMw* 12 (1955): 280ff.
2. Ibid., "Die Termini," p. 294.
3. J. Mattheson, *Der vollkommene Capellmeister* (Hamburg, 1739), facs. repr. (Kassel, 1954), Preface, p. 14.
4. Ibid., p. 15.
5. Within the fourths of the fourth-fifth-octave framework (**c-f-g-c′**, **d-g-a-d′**, or **e-a-b-e′**), the whole tones are inserted either at the bottom (Ionian mode [**c-d-e-f**, **g-a-b-c′**]), at the top (Phrygian mode [**e-f-g-a**, **b-c′-d′-e′**]), or one at the bottom and one at the top (Dorian mode [**d-e-f-g**, **a-b-c′-d′**]).
6. The sense that a sharp or flat must express either a chromatic alteration or a transposition is, as will be shown, "modern" and inadequate to the conceptions of the 15th and 16th centuries.
7. The simultaneous appearance of diverse modes in a polyphonic composition causes the individual modes to lose their distinctive characters, so that what comes to the fore is not the individual modes but their common foundation, the diatonic scale.
8. Hugo Riemann, *Geschichte der Musiktheorie*, 2d ed. (Berlin, 1920), p. 523.
9. Jacques Handschin, *Der Toncharakter* (Zurich, 1948), p. 260.

NOTES TO CHAPTER 3, PAGES 162–91

1. Theodore Kroyer, *Die Anfänge der Chromatik im italienischen Madrigal des 16. Jahrhunderts* (Leipzig, 1902), p. 1.
2. Moritz Hauptmann marks the roots and fifths of the system by upper-case letters, the thirds by lower-case letters (*Die Natur der Harmonik und der Metrik* [Leipzig, 1853], p. 11).
3. Jacques Handschin, *Der Toncharakter* (Zürich, 1948), pp. 254f.
4. Hugo Riemann, *Geschichte der Musiktheorie*, 2d ed. (Berlin, 1920), pp. 111f.; Joseph Smits van Waesberghe, *A Textbook of Melody* (Rome, 1955), pp. 66f.
5. H. Stephani, *Zur Psychologie des musikalischen Hörens* (Regensburg, 1956), pp. 8f.
6. Handschin, *Der Toncharakter*, pp. 254f.
7. Otto Gombosi, *Die Tonarten und Stimmungen der antiken Musik* (Copenhagen, 1939).
8. Handschin, *Der Toncharakter*, p. 342.
9. Adam of Fulda, *Musica*, Gerbert, vol. 3, p. 343.
10. Carl Dahlhaus, "Die Termini Dur und Moll," *AfMw* 12 (1955): 280ff.
11. Pseudo-Tunstede, *Quatuor principalia*, Coussemaker, vol. 4, p. 225.
12. Odo of Saint-Maur characterized b♭ as "nona prima" [the first ninth] and b♮ as "nona secunda" [the second ninth]. (The counting begins at **A**.)
13. Handschin, *Der Toncharakter*, pp. 53ff.
14. Dahlhaus, "Die Termini," pp. 286ff.

15. *Introductio secundum Johannem de Garlandia*, Coussemaker, vol. 1, p. 166.

16. Rudolf von Ficker, "Beiträge zur Chromatik des 14. bis 16. Jahrhunderts," *StzMw* 2 (1914): 8.

17. *Ars contrapunctus secundum Philippum de Vitriaco*, Coussemaker, vol. 3, p. 26; see also Anonymous 2, Coussemaker, vol. 1, p. 312.

18. Riemann, *Geschichte der Musiktheorie*, p. 229n.

19. *Ars nova*, Coussemaker, vol. 3, p. 18.

20. Tunstede, Coussemaker, vol. 4, p. 222.

21. Adam of Fulda, Gerbert, vol. 3, p. 343.

22. Hieronymus of Moravia, *Tractatus de musica*, ed. S. Cserba (Regensburg, 1935), p. 173.

23. Riemann, *Geschichte der Musiktheorie*, p. 279.

24. *Ars contrapunctus secundum Philippum de Vitriaco*, Coussemaker, vol. 3, p. 26.

25. Ibid., p. 18.

26. Prosdocimo de' Beldomandi, *Libellus monochordi*, Coussemaker, vol. 3, p. 257.

27. Riemann, *Geschichte der Musiktheorie*, p. 309.

28. Anonymous 11, Coussemaker, vol. 3, p. 427.

29. J. Wolf, *Musica practica Bartolomei Rami de Pareia* (Leipzig, 1901), p. 29.

30. Cited in von Ficker, *Beiträge zur Chromatik*, p. 8.

31. Francesco Salinas, *De musica libri VII* (Salamanca, 1577), p. 115.

32. Ibid., p. 121.

33. Ernst Kurth, *Die Voraussetzungen der theoretischen Harmonik und der tonalen Darstellungssysteme* (Bern, 1913), pp. 119ff.

34. Riemann, *Geschichte der Musiktheorie*, p. 332.

35. Wolf, *Musica practica Bartolomei Rami de Pareia*, p. 98.

36. Ibid., p. 98.

37. Ibid., p. 99.

38. Hauptmann, *Die Natur*, p. 43.

Notes to Chapter 3, pages 192–212

1. H. Schmid, "Byzantinisches in der karolingischen Musik," *Report of the Eleventh International Congress of Byzantine Studies* (Munich, 1958), p. 16n1.

2. U. Bomm, *Der Wechsel der Modalitätsbestimmung in der Tradition der Meßgesänge im 9. bis 13. Jahrhundert* (Einsiedeln, 1929).

3. Aurelian of Réôme, Gerbert, vol. 1, p. 44b.

4. E. L. Waeltner, "Die 'Musica disciplina' des Aurelianus Reomensis," *Congress Report* (Cologne, 1958), pp. 293f.

5. Aurelian of Réôme, Gerbert, vol. 1, p. 43a.

6. Hermannus Contractus, Gerbert, vol. 2, p. 132b.

7. Ibid., p. 130a.

8. Ibid., p. 128a.

9. Ibid., p. 130a.

10. Guido d'Arezzo, Gerbert, vol. 2, p. 5b.

11. Ibid., p. 11b.

12. Ibid., p. 11b.

13. Ibid., p. 12a.

14. Ibid., p. 5b.

15. Ibid., p. 7b.

16. Ibid., p. 10b.

17. Knud Jeppesen, *Kontrapunkt. Lehrbuch der klassischen Vokalpolyphonie*, 2d ed. (Leipzig, 1956), p. 55.

18. Ibid., p. 55.

19. Ibid., p. 55.

20. G. Reichert, "Kirchentonart als Formfaktor in der mehrstimmigen Musik des 15. und 16. Jahrhunderts," *Mf* 4 (1951): 36.

21. Ibid., p. 40.

22. The fact that it is precisely **c'** and **a** that stand out as *repercussae* seems to have provoked the idea that polyphonically presented modes are really major or minor keys that end on the dominant or subdominant instead of the tonic.

23. While one need not accept all of Jacques Handschin's thesis that the modes are a mere "superstructure" [*Überbau*] erected over the diatonic system, still it can hardly be denied that a change of mode implies a lesser modification in tones' characters than does a modulation, a change of key.

24. Bernhard Meier, "Die Handschrift Porto 714 als Quelle zur Tonartenlehre des 15. Jahrhunderts," *Musica Disciplina* 7 (1953): 180.

25. S. Hermelink, *Dispositiones Modorum. Die Tonarten in der Musik Palestrinas und seiner Zeitgenossen* (Tutzing, 1960), pp. 55ff.

26. Bernhard Meier, "Bemerkungen zu Lechners 'Motectae Sacrae' von 1575," *AfMw* 14 (1957): 84.

The discant was considered the primary voice in cantilena-style composition of the 15th century. Of course Leo Treitler has pointed out ("Tone System in the Secular Works of Guillaume Dufay," *JAMS* 18 [1965]: 131–69) that in the chansons of Dufay, the discant's fifth-fourth structure characterizing the mode (e.g., **a–d'–a'**) is almost always supplemented by complement (**d–a–d'**) or analogous (**A–d–a**) structures in the lower voices. "With this observation we have stated the compositional principles on which Dufay's distinctive harmonic style rests: (1) each voice is internally consistent in that it is dominated by a single pentachord-tetrachord-pair, and (2) the same pentachord-tetrachord-pair, in one or another of its simple or compound dispositions, controls all the voices of a given piece—in a word, all the voices are in the same tonality" (p. 153).

Treitler emphasizes the influence of melodic structure on tonal [*klangliche*] structure without mentioning, however, that the "tetrachord-pentachord principle" regulating the "tonality" is in a problematical relationship with the disposition of cadences, a factor that also characterizes the tonality. Clausulas on secondary degrees either negate the fifth-fourth structure of the basic mode (an e-clausula in a d-mode suggests that the partitioning of the octave prevailing in the preceding section was **A–e–a** instead of **A–d–a**), or, supposing that the fifth-fourth structure is preserved, such clausulas have the effect of random and abrupt modulations without a basis in the melodic-tonal structure of the composition. And this second possibility is by no means out of the question in Dufay's case, however strange it may seem to a listener accustomed to perceiving cadences as the structural framework of the tonality.

In the discant of *Pour l'amour* (Treitler, pp. 151–53), the **c′–f′** tetrachord is supplemented by the **f′–a′** trichord (instead of the **f′–c″** pentachord). The lower voices form the regular **c–f–c′** fourth-fifth structure. The countertenor is the supplementary voice to a discant-tenor framework that can stand on its own. The progression ♮ should thus be understood as an a-clausula, even if the countertenor places an **f** or a **d** below it (mm. 12 and 29). The disposition of clausulas is quite diverse:

Clausula Degree:	f	(c)	(a)	c	d	a	(f)	f
Measure:	5	7	12	17	23	29	33	37

Yet to a degree, the melodic-tonal structure (in the sense of Treitler's thesis) is defined by the predominance of the basic keynote. Thus instead of clausulas on secondary degrees operating as the goal and outcome of melodic-tonal progressions, they have the effect of being surprising detours designed more to demonstrate a wealth of tonal resources than to establish tonal coherence.

27. Tinctoris, *Liber de natura et proprietate tonorum*, Coussemaker, vol. 4, p. 29a–b.

28. P. Aaron, *Trattato della natura e cognizione di tutti gli toni di canto figurato* (Venice, 1524), chap. 2.

29. G. Zarlino, *Istitutioni harmoniche* (Venice, 1558), bk. 4, chaps. 28 and 31.

30. Martin Agricola, *Questiones vulgatoriores in musicam* (n.p., 1543); cited in B. Meier, *AfMw* 14, p. 84, n. 1.

31. Zarlino, *Istitutioni*, bk. 4, chap. 31.

32. Gallus Dressler, *Praecepta musicae practicae* (n.p., 1562); cited in B. Meier, *AfMw* 14, p. 84, n. 2.

33. Michael Praetorius, *Syntagma musicum III* (Wolfenbüttel, 1619), facs. repr. (Kassel, 1958), pp. 36ff.

34. Cyriacus Schneegaß, *Isagoges musicae libri duo* (Erfurt, 1591); cited in B. Meier, *AfMw* 14, p. 84, n. 3.

35. Aaron, *Trattato*, chap. 2.

36. Zarlino, *Istitutioni*, bk. 4, chap. 31.

37. Meier, *AfMw* 14, pp. 83ff.

38. Zarlino, *Istitutioni*, bk. 4, chap. 13.

39. Ibid.

40. Ibid.

41. Meier, *AfMw* 14, pp. 83ff.

42. The Complete Works of Palestrina (Haberl), vol. 9.

43. F. Gafurius, *De harmonia musicorum instrumentorum opus* (Milan, 1518), fol. 88; cited in L. Kunz, *Die Tonartenlehre des römischen Theoretikers und Komponisten Pier Francesco Valentini* (Kassel, 1937), p. 30.

44. J. Gallicus, *Vera quamque facilis ad cantandum atque brevis introductio*, Coussemaker, vol. 4, p. 359b.

45. Ibid., p. 359b.

46. Glarean, *Dodekachordon* (Basel, 1547), bk. 2, chaps. 18 and 25.

47. Boethius, *De institutione musica*, bk. 2, chap. 12.

48. Glarean, *Dodekachordon*, bk. 2, chaps. 18 and 25.

49. J. Burmeister, *Musica poetica* (Rostock, 1606), facs. repr. (Kassel, 1955), pp. 42f.

50. J. Müller-Blattau, *Die Compositionslehre Heinrich Schützens in der Fassung seines Schülers Christoph Bernhard* (Leipzig, 1926), p. 93.

51. Zarlino, *Istitutioni*, bk. 4, chap. 8.

52. Ibid., chaps. 18–29.

53. Zarlino, *Dimostrationi harmoniche* (Venice, 1571), bk. 1, rag. 5, def. 8; idem, *Istitutioni harmoniche*, 3d ed. (n.p., 1573), bk. 4, chaps. 18–29.

54. F. Högler, "Bemerkungen zu Zarlinos Theorie," *ZfMw* 9 (1926–27): 518.

55. D. P. Walker, *Der musikalische Humanismus im 16. und frühen 17. Jahrhundert* (Kassel, 1949), p. 30, n. 92.

56. S. Calvisius, *Melopoiia sive Melodiae condendae ratio* (Erfurt, 1602), chap. 17, fol. 5r–v.

57. J. Lippius, *Synopsis musicae novae* (Strasbourg, 1612), fol. 1, 1v.

58. Calvisius, *Melopoiia*, chap. 17, fol. 5r–v.

59. A. Banchieri, *Conclusioni nel suono dell' organo* (Bologna, 1609), pp. 40f. and 43.

60. Praetorius, *Syntagma musicum III*, pp. 36ff.

61. Lippius, *Synopsis*, fol. 1, 1v.

62. L. Penna, *Terzo libro delli Primi Albori Musicali* (Bologna, 1679), pp. 120f.

63. Aaron, *Trattato*, chaps. 4–7.

64. Ibid., chap. 3.

65. Ibid., chaps. 4–7.

66. Palestrina, vol. 9.

67. Palestrina, vol. 27.

68. Palestrina, vol. 2, p. 81; vol. 5, pp. 63 and 72; vol. 10, p. 80; vol. 14, p. 66; vol. 15, p. 44.

69. Aaron, *Trattato*, chap. 1.

NOTES TO CHAPTER 3, PAGES 212–34

1. A. Schmitz, "Die Kadenz als Ornamentum musicae," *Congress Report* (Bamberg, 1953), pp. 114–20.

2. G. Reichert, "Kirchentonart als Formfaktor in der mehrstimmigen Musik des 15. und 16. Jahrhunderts," *Mf* 4 (1951): 35–48.

3. Bernhard Meier, "Die Handschrift Porto 714 als Quelle zur Tonartenlehre des 15. Jahrhunderts," *Musica Disciplina* 7 (1953): 175–97.

4. S. Hermelink, *Dispositiones Modorum. Die Tonarten in der Musik Palestrinas und seiner Zeitgenossen* (Tutzing, 1960).

5. R. Jakoby, "Untersuchungen über die Klausellehre in deutschen Musiktraktaten des 17. Jahrhunderts" (Ph.D. diss., Mainz, 1955).

6. Schmitz, *Die Kadenz*, p. 115.

7. Seth Calvisius, *Melopoiia sive Melodiae condendae ratio* (Erfurt, 1602), chap. 18; Schmitz, *Die Kadenz*, p. 115.

8. Calvisius, *Melopoiia*, chap. 18.

9. Ibid., chap. 14.

10. G. Zarlino, *Istitutioni harmoniche* (Venice, 1558), bk. 4, chap. 18: "Then I will show how one can normally set this mode's initial tones and where . . . one can make the cadences" [Dipoi mostrarò dove regolarmente si possa dare principio ad esso Modo; & dove . . . si possa far le Cadenze].

11. J. Müller-Blattau, *Die Kompositionslehre Heinrich Schützens in der Fassung seines Schülers Christoph Bernhard* (Leipzig, 1926), p. 106.

12. Müller-Blattau, *Die Kompositionslehre*, p. 108.

13. Ibid., p. 79.

14. Calvisius, *Melopoiia*, chap. 18.

15. J. Nucius, *Musices poeticae sive de Compositione Cantus Praeceptiones* (Neiße, 1613), chap. 8; Nucius forms alternating alto and bass voices to the Phrygian discant-tenor clausula.

16. Ernst Apfel, "Die klangliche Struktur der spätmittelalterlichen Musik als Grundlage der Dur-Moll-Tonalität," *Mf* 15 (1962): 212–27.

17. J. Lippius, *Synopsis musicae novae* (Strasbourg, 1612), fol. G 2v and H 3r.

18. Zarlino, *Istitutioni*, bk. 3, chap. 53: "The cadence is therefore a certain act that the voice parts of the composition perform singing together" [La Cadenza adunque è un certo atto, che fanno le parti della cantilena cantando insieme].

19. L. Finscher, "Tonale Ordnungen am Beginn der Neuzeit," *Musikalische Zeitfragen* 10 (1962): 91–96.

20. Cited in Jakoby, *Untersuchungen*, pp. 28f.

21. Zarlino, *Istitutioni*, bk. 4, chap. 18–29.

22. Ibid., bk. 3, chap. 53: "And although the cadence is most necessary, it should be used only when one arrives at a clausula or period contained within the prose or verse" [Et benche la Cadenza sia molto necessaria . . . non è però da usarla se non quando se arriva alla Clausula, overo al Periodo contenuto nella Prosa, o nel Verso].

23. R. O. Morris, *Contrapuntal Technique in the Sixteenth Century*, 7th ed. (Oxford, 1958), p. 15.

24. Reichert, *Kirchentonart*, pp. 44f.

25. Hermelink, *Dispositiones modorum*, pp. 109ff.

26. Cited in Meier, *Die Handschrift*, p. 179.

27. P. Aaron, *Trattato della natura e cognizione di tutti gli toni di canto figurato* (Venice, 1525), chaps. 4–7.

28. Ibid., chap. 8.

29. J. Tinctoris, *Liber de natura et proprietate tonorum*, Coussemaker, vol. 4.

30. The Complete Works of Palestrina (Haberl), vol. 9.

31. Tinctoris, *Liber*.

32. The simultaneous appearance of different modes neutralizes their individual characters, so that what comes to the fore is not their differences, but the modes' common basis, the diatonic scale.

33. See below [in particular, chap. 4].

34. Zarlino, *Istitutioni*, bk. 4, chap. 30.

35. Hermelink, *Dispositiones modorum*, p. 56, n. 16.

36. See above [in particular, chap. 3, sec. 3].

37. Hermelink, *Dispositiones modorum*, p. 55.

38. Zarlino, *Istitutioni*, bk. 4, chap 18.

39. L. Kunz, *Die Tonartenlehre des römischen Theoretikers und Komponisten Pier Francesco Valentini* (Kassel, 1937), p. 83.

40. Zarlino, *Istitutioni*, bk. 4, chap. 18.

41. See above [in particular, chap. 2, sec. 5].

42. As mentioned, the cadential degrees match the melodic structural tones of the mode.

43. Zarlino, *Istitutioni*, bk. 4, chap. 30.

44. Hermelink, *Dispositiones modorum*, p. 57.

45. P. Benary, *Die deutsche Kompositionslehre des 18. Jahrhunderts* (Leipzig, 1961), p. 34.

46. G. M. Artusi, *L'arte del contrapunto*, 2d ed. (1598), p. 73.

47. Zarlino, *Istitutioni*, bk. 4, chap. 18.

48. A. Banchieri, *Conclusioni nel suono dell' organo* (Bologna, 1609), p. 39.

49. Ibid., pp. 39 and 41.

50. Zarlino, *Istitutioni*, bk. 3, chap. 31.

51. Kunz, *Die Tonartenlehre*, p. 80.

52. Ibid., pp. 67ff.

53. Ibid., p. 86.

54. Calvisius, *Melopoiia*, chap. 14.

55. Lippius, *Synopsis*, fol. I 3.

56. J. Burmeister, *Musica poetica* (Rostock, 1606), facs. repr. (Kassel, 1955), p. 52.

57. Müller-Blattau, *Die Kompositionslehre*, p. 94.

58. See also U. Siegele, "Bemerkungen zu Bachs Motetten," *Bach-Jahrbuch* (1962): 39–42: Zur Ordnung der Modulation.

59. Th. Morley, *A Plaine and Easie Introduction to Practicall Musicke* (London, 1597), ed. R. A. Harman (London, 1952), p. 249.

60. A. Berardi, *Il Perchè musicale* (Bologna, 1693), pp. 38–43.

61. Aaron, *Trattato*, chap. 1.

62. L. Penna, *Terzo libro delli Primi Albori Musicali* (Bologna, 1679), pp. 120–22.

NOTES TO CHAPTER 3, PAGES 234–47

1. J. Handschin, *Der Toncharakter* (Zurich, 1948), p. 260.
2. G. Zarlino, *Istitutioni harmoniche* (Venice, 1558), bk. 3, chap. 31.
3. Ibid., bk. 3, chap. 10.
4. Ibid., chap. 10.
5. Arnold Schönberg, *Harmonielehre* (Leipzig and Vienna, 1911), pp. 170ff.
6. Edward E. Lowinsky, *Tonality and Atonality in Sixteenth-Century Music* (Berkeley and Los Angeles, 1961).
7. P. Aaron, *De institutione harmonica* (Venice, 1516), bk. 1, chap. 30; idem, *Trattato della natura e cognizione di tutti gli toni di canto figurato* (Venice, 1524), chap. 1.
8. This assertion is based on a statistical study of the four-voice motets from Willaert's *Musica nova*.
9. Franklin B. Zimmerman, "Advanced Tonal Design in the Part-Songs of William Byrd," *Congress Report* (Cologne, 1958), p. 322.
10. *English Madrigal School*, ed. E. H. Fellowes, vol. 14 (London, 1920).
11. "O Lord, how long wilt Thou forget," *English Madrigal School*, p. 26.
12. "O Lord, who in Thy sacred tent," *English Madrigal School*, p. 32.
13. Zimmerman, "Advanced Tonal Design," p. 324.

NOTES TO CHAPTER 4, PAGES 249–80

1. Motet no. 65, *Werken van Josquin des Prez*, Motets, vol. 4, p. 33.
2. Motet no. 11, vol. 1, p. 41.
3. Motet no. 10, vol. 1, p. 35, mm. 26–39.
4. Motet no. 36, vol. 2, p. 51, mm. 28–39.
5. Willi Apel, "The Partial Signatures in the Sources up to 1450," *Acta mus.* 10 (1938): 1ff.; R. H. Hoppin, "Partial Signatures and Musica Ficta in Some Early 15th-Century Sources," *JAMS* 6 (1953): 197ff.
6. Motet no. 65, vol. 4, p. 33.
7. A. Smijers's method of placing a single ♭ in the signatures of all the voices, even alto and bass, and using accidentals to change e to e♭ is a questionable editorial practice. If, in the original, the prescribed e♭′ is raised to e♮′ in f-clausulas, then in the edition, this chromatic alteration, based as it is on the intervention of the editor, appears as the original text—as a missing ♭ before e′ (mm. 129, 133, 135, 138, 140, 143). The edition suggests that what is incidental—changing e♭′ to e♮′—is essential, and what is essential—the e♭′ called for in the signature—is incidental. And in two places the raising of e♭ can hardly be justified (mm. 128 and 132).
8. Motet no. 54, vol. 3, p. 95.
9. Motet no. 43, vol. 2, p. 118.
10. Motet no. 7, vol. 1, p. 29.
11. Motets, vol. 1, app., p. 172.
12. Motet no. 22, vol. 1, p. 110.
13. Motet no. 50, vol. 3, p. 47.
14. Motet no. 45, vol. 3, p. 1.

15. Motet no. 49, vol. 3, p. 37.

16. H. Glarean, *Dodekachordon* (Basel, 1547); B. Meier, "The Musica Reservata of Adrianus Petit Coclico and its Relationship to Josquin," *Musica Disciplina* 10 (1956): 69.

17. Glarean, *Dodekachordon*, bk. 3, chap. 24: "Concerning this man (i.e., Josquin), if cognizance of the twelve modes and the true science of music had joined with his native ability and keen spirit, for which he was distinguished, then nature could have produced nothing more exalted and magnificent in this art. So versatile was his artistic spirit, so armed was he with natural acuity and power, that there was nothing in this field he could not have accomplished. But as a rule he lacked moderation and the judgment that comes with study" [Cui viro (sc. Josquin), si de duodecim Modis ac uera ratione musica, noticia contigisset ad nativam illam indolem, & ingenii, qua uiguit, acrimoniam, nihil natura augustius in hac arte, nihil magnificentius producere potuisset. Ita in omnia uersatile ingenium erat, ita naturae acumine ac vi armatum, ut nihil in hoc negocio ille non potuisset. Sed defuit in plaerisque Modus, & cum eruditione iudicium].

18. Edward E. Lowinsky, *Tonality and Atonality in Sixteenth-Century Music* (Berkeley and Los Angeles, 1961), pp. 15ff.

19. Pietro Aaron, *Trattato della natura e cognizione di tutti gli toni di canto figurato* (Venice, 1524).

20. Motet nos. 31, 37, 43, and 63.

21. Motet nos. 32, 34, 52, and 70.

22. Motet no. 52, vol. 3, p. 75.

23. Motet no. 70, vol. 4, p. 83.

24. Motets, vol. 3, p. xxxiv.

25. Motet no. 31, vol. 2, p. 3.

26. Meier, *The Musica Reservata*, p. 75.

27. Motet no. 37, vol. 2, p. 58.

28. Meier, *The Musica Reservata*, pp. 77 and 84.

29. Motet no. 32, vol. 2, p. 11.

30. Motet no. 34, vol. 2, p. 29.

31. Rolf Dammann, "Spätformen der isorhythmischen Motette im 16. Jahrhundert," *AfMw* 10 (1953): 20–22.

32. In some sources O is given, in others O2 (vol. 2, pp. x–xii).

33. The *apparatus criticus* lists no mensuration signs differing from the notated ¢ in the Complete Edition.

34. Peter Wagner, *Gregorianische Formenlehre* (Leipzig, 1921), p. 310.

35. Motet no. 43, vol. 2, p. 118.

36. Motet no. 63, vol. 4, p. 16.

37. Glarean, *Dodekachordon*, p. 115.

38. Motet nos. 2, 8, 9, 10, 13, 14, 17, 18, 23, 24, 25, 26, 27, 30, 33, 35, 40, 45, 48, 49, 50, 51, 52, 54, 59, 60, 69, 70.

39. Motet nos. 4, 7, 11, 15, 16, 19, 29, 31, 32, 34, 37, 39, 41, 43, 44, 47, 61, 62, 63, 64, 66.

40. Glarean, *Dodekachordon*, p. 115.

41. Motet no. 12, vol. 1, p. 48.
42. Motet no. 5, vol. 1, p. 24.
43. Motet no. 22, vol. 1, p. 110.
44. Motet nos. 1, 3, 21, and 28.
45. Motet no. 28, vol. 1, p. 147.
46. Motet no. 21, vol. 1, p. 105.
47. Motets, vol. 1, p. 175.
48. Motet no. 3, vol. 1, p. 14.
49. Motet no 1, vol. 1, p. 1.
50. Motets, vol. 1, p. 171.
51. Ibid., p. 157.
52. Motet no. 38, vol. 2, p. 77.
53. Motet no. 42, vol. 2, p. 111.
54. Motet no. 20, vol. 1, p. 95.
55. Gioseffo Zarlino, *Istitutioni harmoniche* (Venice, 1558), bk. 4, chap. 23.
56. Motet no. 1, vol. 1, p. 1.
57. Motet no. 68, vol. 4, p. 61.
58. Motet no. 53, vol. 3, p. 86.
59. Lowinsky, *Tonality and Atonality*, pp. 20–25.
60. Ibid., p. 24.
61. Ibid., p. 21.
62. Motets, vol. 3, pp. xxxvf.
63. In the alto of m. 79, the **f'** should be replaced by **g'**, in the discant of m. 94 the **b♭'** by **a'**, in the alto of m. 99 the **c″** by **b♭'**, and in the discant of m. 196 the **b♭'** by **c″**.

NOTES TO CHAPTER 4, PAGES 280–89

1. Ottaviano Petrucci, *Frottole*, books 1 and 4, ed. by Rudolf Schwartz, *PÄM* 8 (1935).
2. Ibid., p. 1.
3. Edward E. Lowinsky, *Tonality and Atonality in Sixteenth-Century Music* (Berkeley and Los Angeles, 1961), pp. 8f.
4. Ibid., p. 6.
5. Ibid., p. 14.
6. Cantus-tenor composition can be distinguished from cantus-bass composition according to four criteria. First, unsupported fourths that cannot be explained as passing tones or suspensions must be avoided between cantus and tenor. Second, a suspended fourth in which the lower voice (the tenor) is the dissonance and progresses to a (diminished) fifth assumes a supporting bass. Such a suspended fourth is a secondary dissonance, the interval left over between a suspended seventh in the lower voices and a tenth between the outer voices: . Third, chains of thirds or sixths terminating in a unison or octave at the end of a verse must be recognizable as a basic form of

cantus-tenor composition. And fourth, although the sixth was acknowledged as an independent consonance, it was, in contrast to the third, perceived as unstable and avoided at the ends of verses. A sixth between tenor and cantus at the end of a verse requires the support of a lower third or fifth in the bass.

7. Petrucci, *Frottole*, p. 4, no. 6.

8. Ibid., p. 9, no. 12.

9. Ibid., p. 11, no. 15; the tenor part is erroneously notated with a mezzo-soprano clef instead of an alto clef.

10. Ibid., p. 16, no. 23; the instrumental coda (mm. 20–28) violates the principle of cantus-tenor composition.

11. Ibid., p. 18, no. 26.

12. Ibid., p. 22, no. 31; as in *Vale, diva mia*, the principle of cantus-tenor composition is abandoned in the instrumental coda.

13. Ibid., p. 24, no. 33; in the cadences, the cantus relates primarily to the tenor (g-Dorian clausula), the alto to the bass. In order to count *Poi che'l ciel* (p. 16, no. 24) also among the works with a cantus-tenor framework one must first correct a printing error: the tenor part should be read a third lower in mm. 21–27 (beginning with the first whole note).

14. Ibid., p. 10, no. 14.

15. Ibid., p. 12, no. 17; the octave-leap cadence in mm. 18–19, though stemming from the tradition of cantus-tenor composition, does not change the fact that *La fortuna* is based on a cantus-bass framework.

16. Ibid., p. 15, no. 22, mm. 10–12.

17. Ibid., p. 17, no. 25, mm. 13–16.

18. Ibid., p. 5, no. 7, mm. 24–27.

19. Ibid., p. 24, no. 34, mm. 20–22.

20. *Non ual aqua* (ibid., p. 14, no. 20), mm. 1–3; *Se ben hor non scopro* (p. 14, no. 21), mm. 10–13; *Se mi e grave* (p. 15, no. 22), mm. 1–4; *Crudel, come mai potesti* (p. 17, no. 25), mm. 1–2.

21. In the cadences of Cara's *Glie pur* (ibid., p. 8, no. 11), one can infer from the fact that the alto is an essential voice and the tenor is an added voice that the voice designations have been mistakenly interchanged.

22. Ibid., p. 18, no. 27.

23. Ibid., p. 10, no. 13.

24. Ibid., p. 6, no. 9.

25. Ibid., p. 3, no. 4.

26. Ibid., p. 11, no. 16.

NOTES TO CHAPTER 4, PAGES 289–323

1. Giovanni Maria Artusi, *L'Artusi overo delle imperfettioni della moderna musica* (Venice, 1600).

2. The Complete Works of Monteverdi, vol. 5, p. 5.

3. Artusi, *L'Artusi*, fol. 48b.

4. Monteverdi, vol. 5, p. 14.

5. J. Müller-Blattau, *Die Kompositionslehre Heinrich Schützens in der Fassung seines Schülers Christoph Bernhard* (Leipzig, 1926), p. 108; 2d ed. (Kassel, 1963).

6. Monteverdi, vol. 6, p. 46.

7. Monteverdi, vol. 7, p. 81.

8. Ibid., p. 47.

9. Ibid., p. 85.

10. Ibid., p. 71.

11. Ibid., p. 76.

12. Ibid., p. 104.

13. Ibid., p. 47.

14. Ibid., p. 8.

15. Ibid., p. 35.

16. Ibid., p. 58.

17. Ibid., p. 62.

18. Ibid., p. 71.

19. Ibid., p. 85.

20. Ibid., p. 104.

21. Ibid., p. 116.

22. Ibid., p. 8.

23. Ibid., p. 81.

24. Ibid., p. 123.

25. Ibid., p. 76.

26. Ibid., p. 41.

27. Ibid., p. 90.

BIBLIOGRAPHY

Aaron, Pietro. *De institutione harmonica*. Venice, 1516.

———. *Toscanello in musica*. 2d ed. Venice, 1529.

———. *Trattato della natura e cognizione di tutti gli toni di canto figurato*. Venice, 1524.

Abraham, Lars Ulrich. *Der Generalbaß im Schaffen des Michael Praetorius und seine harmonischen Voraussetzungen*. Berlin, 1961.

Adam of Fulda. *Musica*. (Gerbert III).

Agricola, Martin. *Questiones vulgatoriores in musicam*. 1543.

Albersheim, Gerhard. "Die Tonstufe." *Musikforschung* 16 (1963).

D'Alembert, Jean le Rond. *Eléments de musique Théorique et pratique suivant les principes de M. Rameau, éclaircis, développés, et simplifiés*. Paris, 1752.

Anonymous 1. (Coussemaker I).

Anonymous 4. (Coussemaker I).

Anonymous 5. (Coussemaker I).

Anonymous 11. (Coussemaker III).

Anonymous 13. (Coussemaker III).

Apel, Willi. "Accidentien und Tonalität in den Musikdenkmälern des 15. und 16. Jahrhunderts." Ph.D. diss., Berlin, 1936.

———. "The Partial Signatures in the Sources up to 1450." *Acta musicologica* 10 (1938).

Apfel, Ernst. "Der Diskant in der Musiktheorie des 12. bis 15. Jahrhunderts." Ph.D. diss., Heidelberg, 1953.

———. "Die klangliche Struktur der spätmittelalterlichen Musik als Grundlage der Dur-Moll Tonalität." *Musikforschung* 15 (1962).

———. "Spätmittelalterliche Klangstruktur und Dur-Moll Tonalität." *Musikforschung* 16 (1963).

———. "Zur Entstehung des realen vierstimmigen Satzes in England." *Archiv für Musikwissenschaft* 17 (1960).

———. "Zur Entstehungsgeschichte des Palestrinasatzes." *Archiv für Musikwissenschaft* 14 (1957).

Aribo Scholasticus. (Gerbert II).

Arnold, Frank Thomas. *The Art of Accompaniment from a Thorough-Bass*. Oxford, 1931.

Ars contrapunctus secundum Philippum de Vitriaco. (Coussemaker III).

Ars discantus per Johannem de Muris. (Coussemaker III).

Ars perfecta in musica magistri Philippoti de Vitriaco. (Coussemaker III).

Artusi, Giovanni Maria. *L'arte del contrapunto*. 2d ed. 1598.

———. *L'Artusi overo delle imperfettioni della moderna musica*. Venice, 1600.

Aurelian of Réôme. *Musica disciplina*. (Gerbert I).

Banchieri, Adriano. *Cartella musicale*. 3d ed. Bologna, 1614.

———. *Conclusioni nel suono dell' organo*. Bologna, 1609.

Baryphonus, Heinricus. *Pleiades musicae*. Magdeburg, 1630.

Bawden, J. L. *Aspects of Tonality in Early European Music*. Philadelphia, 1947.

Benary, Peter. *Die deutsche Kompositionslehre des 18. Jahrhunderts*. Leipzig, 1961.

Bengtsson, Ingmar. "On Relationships between Tonal and Rhythmic Structures in Western Multipart Music." *Svensk tidskrift för musikforskning* (1961).

Berardi, Angelo. *Miscellanea musicale*. Bologna, 1689.

———. *Il Perchè musicale*. Bologna, 1693.

Besseler, Heinrich. *Bourdon und Fauxbourdon*. Leipzig, 1950.

———. "Tonalharmonik und Vollklang." *Acta musicologica* 23 (1951).

Beswick, Delbert M. "The Problem of Tonality in Seventeenth Century Music." Ph.D. diss., North Carolina, 1950.

Beurhusius (a.k.a. Friedrich Beurhaus). *Erotematum musicae libri duo*. 1580.

Beyer, Paul. *Studien zur Vorgeschichte des Dur-Moll*. Kassel, 1958.

Bianciardi, Francesco. *Breve regola per imparar a sonare sopra il Basso con ogni sorte d'Istromento*. 1607.

Blume, Friedrich. *Das monodische Prinzip in der protestantischen Kirchenmusik*. Leipzig, 1925.

Boethius. *De Institutione musica*. Roman, early sixth century.

Bomm, Urbanus. *Der Wechsel der Modalitätsbestimmung in der Tradition der Meßgesänge im 9. bis 13. Jahrhundert*. Einsiedeln, 1929.

Bononcini, Giovanni Maria. *Musico prattico*. Bologna, 1678.

Bukofzer, Manfred. "Discantus." In *Die Musik in Geschichte und Gegenwart*. Kassel, 1949–68.

———. *Geschichte des englischen Diskants und des Fauxbourdons nach den theoretischen Quellen*. Strasbourg, 1936.

———. *Music in the Baroque Era*. New York, 1947.

Burmeister, Joachim. *Musica poetica*. Rostock, 1606.

Caccini, Giulio. *Le Nuove Musiche*. 1601.

Calvisius, Seth. *Melopoiia sive Melodiae condendae ratio*. Erfurt, 1602.

Campion, Thomas. *A New Way of Making Foure Parts in Counterpoint*. London, ?1613–14.

Castil-Blaze (a.k.a. François Henri Joseph Blaze). *Dictionnaire de musique moderne*. Paris, 1821.

Cerone, Domenico. *El Melopeo y maestro*. 1613.

Chailley, Jacques. "La révision de la notion traditionelle de tonalité." *Congress Report*. Cologne, 1958.

Compendium discantus. (Coussemaker I).

Coperario, Giovanni. *Rules how to compose*. c. 1610.

Coussemaker, Charles-Edmond-Henri de. *Scriptorum de musica medii aevi nova series*. 4 vols. Paris, 1864.

Crüger, Johann. *Synopsis musica*. Berlin, 1630.

Cserba, Simon M. *Hieronymus de Moravia O. P.: Tractatus de Musica*. Regensburg, 1935.

Dahlhaus, Carl. "Die Termini Dur und Moll." *Archiv für Musikwissenschaft* 12 (1955).

————. "War Zarlino Dualist?" *Musikforschung* 10 (1957).

————. "Zur Theorie des klassischen Kontrapunkts." *Kirchenmusikalisches Jahrbuch* (1961).

Dammann, Rolf. "Spätformen der isorhythmischen Mottette im 16. Jahrhundert." *Archiv für Musikwissenschaft* 10 (1953).

Danckert, Werner. "Melodische Funktionen." In *Festschrift Max Schneider*. Leipzig, 1955.

De discantu et consonantiis. (Gerbert III).

Dèzes, Karl. "Prinzipielle Fragen auf dem Gebiet der fingierten Music." Ph.D. diss., Berlin, 1922.

Dräger, Hans-Heinz. "Die 'Bedeutung' der Sprachmelodie." *Congress Report*. Hamburg, 1956.

Dressler, Gallus. *Praecepta musicae practicae.* 1562.

Eggebrecht, Hans Heinrich. "Ars musica." *Die Sammlung* 2 (1957).

————. "Arten des Generalbasses im frühen und mittleren 17. Jahrhundert." *Archiv für Musikwissenschaft* 14 (1957).

————. *Heinrich Schütz.* Göttingen, 1959.

————. "Studien zur musikalischen Terminologie." *Abhandlungen der geistes- und sozialwissenschaftlichen Klasse der Akademie der Wissenschaften und der Literatur in Mainz* (1955).

Eichmann, Peter. *Praecepta musicae practicae.* 1604.

Einstein, Alfred. *The Italian Madrigal.* Princeton, 1949.

Engelbert of Admont. (Gerbert II).

Erpf, Hermann. *Studien zur Harmonie- und Klangtechnik der neueren Musik.* Leipzig, 1927.

Federhofer, Helmut. *Beiträge zur musikalischen Gestaltanalyse.* Graz, 1950.

Ferand, Ernest Thomas. "Composition." In *Die Musik in Geschichte und Gegenwart.* Kassel, 1949–68.

Fétis, François-Joseph. *Biographie universelle des musiciens.* 2d ed. Paris, 1862.

————. *Traité complet de la théorie et de la pratique de l'harmonie contenant la doctrine de la science et de l'art.* Paris, 1844.

Ficker, Rudolf von. "Beiträge zur Chromatik des 14. bis 16. Jahrhunderts." *Studien zur Musikwissenschaft* 2 (1914).

————. "Zur Schöpfungsgeschichte des Fauxfourdon." *Acta musicologica* 23 (1951).

Finck, Hermann. *Practica musica.* Wittenberg, 1556.

Finscher, Ludwig. "Tonale Ordnungen am Beginn der Neuzeit." *Musikalische Zeitfragen* 10 (1962).

Franco of Cologne. (Coussemaker I and Cserba).

Friedheim, Philip. "The Relationship between Tonality and Musical Structure." *Music Review* 27 (1966).

Gafurius, Franchinus. *De harmonia musicorum instrumentorum opus.* Milan, 1518.

————. *Practica musicae.* Milan, 1496.

Gallicus, Joannes. *Vera quamque facilis ad cantandum atque brevis introductio.* (Coussemaker IV).

Georgiades, Thrasybulos. *Englische Diskanttraktate aus der ersten Hälfte des 15. Jahrhunderts*. Würzburg, 1937.

Gerbert, Martin. *Scriptores ecclesiastici de musica*. 3 vols. St. Blasien, 1784.

Glarean, Heinrich. *Dodekachordon*. Basel, 1547.

Gombosi, Otto. "Italia: Patria del Basso ostinato." *Rassegna musicale* 7 (1934).

――――. "Key, Mode, Species." *Journal of the American Musicological Society* 4 (1951).

――――. "Studien zur Tonartenlehre des frühen Mittelalters." *Acta musicologica* 10–12 (1938–40).

――――. *Die Tonarten und Stimmungen der antiken Musik*. Copenhagen, 1939.

Guido d'Arezzo. *Micrologus*. (Gerbert II).

Guilelmus Monachus. *Regula ad componendum cum tribus vocibus non mutatis*. (Coussemaker III).

Gurlitt, Wilibald. "Hugo Riemann (1849–1919)." *Abhandlungen der geistes- und sozialwissenschaftlichen Klasse der Akademie der Wissenschaften und der Literatur in Mainz* (1950, no. 25).

Halm, August. *Harmonielehre*. Leipzig, 1902.

Hamburger, Paul. *Studien zur Vokalpolyphonie*. Wiesbaden, 1956.

――――. *Subdominante und Wechseldominante*. Wiesbaden, 1955.

Handschin, Jacques. *Der Toncharakter*. Zurich, 1948.

Hannas, Ruth. "Cerone: Philosopher and Teacher." *Musical Quarterly* 21 (1935).

Hauptmann, Moritz. *Die Natur der Harmonik und der Metrik*. Leipzig, 1853.

Haydon, Glen. *The Evolution of the Six-Four Chord: A Chapter in the History of Dissonance Treatment*. Berkeley, 1933.

Heinichen, Johann David. *Der Generalbaß in der Composition*. Dresden, 1728.

Helmholtz, Heinrich von. *Die Lehre von den Tonempfindungen*. Braunschweig, 1863.

Hermannus Contractus. (Gerbert II).

Hermelink, Siegfried. *Dispositiones Modorum. Die Tonarten in der Musik Palestrinas und seiner Zeitgenossen*. Tutzing, 1960.

――――. "Zur Geschichte der Kadenz im 16. Jahrhundert." *Congress Report*. Cologne, 1958.

Herzogenberg, Heinrich von. "Tonalität." *Vierteljahrsschrift für Musikwissenschaft* 6 (1890).

Hibbard, Lloyd. " 'Tonality' and Related Problems in Terminology." *Music Review* 22 (1961).

Hieronymus of Moravia. *Tractatus de musica*. Edited by S. Cserba. Regensburg, 1935.

Högler, Fritz. "Bemerkungen zu Zarlinos Theorie." *Zeitschrift für Musikwissenschaft* 9 (1926–27).

Hoppin, Richard H. "Partial Signatures and Musica Ficta in Some Early 15th-Century Sources." *Journal of the American Musicological Society* 6 (1953).

Hüschen, Heinrich. "Harmoniebegriff im Musikschrifttum des Altertums und des Mittelalters." *Congress Report*. Cologne, 1958.

Introduction secundum Johannem de Garlandia. (Coussemaker I).

Jakoby, Richard. "Untersuchungen über die Klausellehre in deutschen Musiktraktaten des 17. Jahrhunderts." Ph.D. diss., Mainz, 1955.

Jeppesen, Knud. *Kontrapunkt. Lehrbuch der klassischen Vokalpolyphonie.* 2d ed. Leipzig, 1956.

―――. "Eine musiktheoretische Korrespondenz des frühen Cinquecento." *Acta musicologica* 13 (1941).

―――. *Der Palestrinastil und die Dissonanz.* Leipzig, 1925.

Johannes Affligemensis. (Gerbert II).

Kirsch, Ernst. *Wesen und Aufbau der Lehre von den harmonischen Funktionen.* Leipzig, 1928.

Körte, Oswald. *Laute und Lautenmusik bis zur Mitte des 16. Jahrhunderts.* Leipzig, 1901.

Korte, Werner. *Die Harmonik des frühen 15. Jahrhunderts in ihrem Zusammenhang mit der Form-technik.* Münster, 1929.

Krehbiel, James Woodrow. "Harmonic Principles of J.-Ph. Rameau and His Contemporaries." Ph.D. diss., Indiana University, Bloomington, 1964.

Krenek, Ernst. *Music Here and Now.* New York, 1939.

Kroyer, Theodore. *Die Anfänge der Chromatik im italienischen Madrigal des 16. Jahrhunderts.* Leipzig, 1902.

Kunz, Lucas. *Die Tonartenlehre des römischen Theoretikers und Komponisten Pier Francesco Valentini.* Kassel, 1937.

Kurth, Ernst. *Grundlagen des linearen Kontrapunkts.* Bern, 1917.

―――. *Romantische Harmonik und ihre Krise in Wagners "Tristan."* Bern, 1920.

―――. *Die Voraussetzungen der theoretischen Harmonik und der tonalen Darstellungssysteme.* Bern, 1913.

Lamm, Robert Carlson. "The Evolution of the Secondary Dominant Concept." Ph.D. diss., Indiana University, Bloomington, 1954.

Lang, Hermann. "Begriffsgeschichte der Terminus 'Tonalität.' " Ph.D. diss., Freiburg i. Br., 1956.

Lippius, Johann. *Synopsis musicae novae.* Erfurt, 1612.

Locke, Matthew. *Melothesia, or Certain Rules for playing upon a Continued-Bass.* 1673.

Lossius, Lucas. *Erotemata musicae practicae.* Nürnberg, 1563.

Lowinsky, Edward E. "Awareness of Tonality in the 16th Century." *Congress Report.* New York, 1961.

―――. "On the Use of Scores by Sixteenth-Century Musicians." *Journal of the American Musicological Society* 1 (1948).

―――. *Tonality and Atonality in Sixteenth-Century Music.* Berkeley, 1961.

Machabey, Armand. *Genèse de la tonalité musicale classique des origines au XVe siècle.* Paris, 1955.

Marchettus of Padua. *Lucidarium.* (Gerbert III).

Mattheson, Johann. *Der vollkommene Capellmeister.* Hamburg, 1739.

Meier, Bernhard. "Bemerkungen zu Lechners 'Motectae Sacrae' von 1575." *Archiv für Musikwissenshaft* 14 (1957).

————. "Die Handschrift Porto 714 als Quelle zur Tonartenlehre des 15. Jahrhunderts." *Musica disciplina* 7 (1953).

————. "Die Harmonik im cantus-firmus-haltigen Satz des 15. Jahrhunderts." *Archiv für Musikwissenschaft* 9 (1952).

————. "The Musica Reservata of Adrianus Petit Coclico and its Relationship to Josquin." *Musica Disciplina* 10 (1956).

————. "Wortausdeutung und Tonalität bei Orlando di Lasso." *Kirchenmusikalisches Jahrbuch* 47 (1963).

Mercadier, Jean Baptiste. *Nouveau système de musique théorique et pratique*. Paris, 1776.

Meyer, M. F. "The Musician"s Arithmetic." In *The University of Missouri Studies*. January (1929).

Mitchell, William John. "Chord and Context in 18th-Century Theory." *Journal of the American Musicological Society* 16 (1963).

Morley, Thomas. *A Plaine and Easie Introduction to Practicall Musicke*. Facs. repr., London, 1937.

Morris, Reginald Owen. *Contrapuntal Technique in the Sixteenth Century*. 7th ed. Oxford, 1958.

Müller-Blattau, Joseph. *Die Kompositionslehre Heinrich Schützens in der Fassung seines Schülers Christoph Bernhard*. Leipzig, 1926.

Murschhauser, Franz Xaver. *Academia musico-poetica bipartita*. Nürnberg, 1721.

Musica enchiriadis. (Gerbert II).

Neumann, Friedrich. *Die Zeitgestalt*. Vienna, 1959.

Nucius, Johannes. *Musica poetica*. Neisse, 1613.

Odington, Walter. (Coussemaker I).

Optima introductio in contrapunctum pro rudibus. (Coussemaker III).

Palisca, Claude V. "Vincenzo Galilei's Counterpoint Treatise: A Code for the Seconda Prattica." *Journal of the American Musicological Society* 9 (1956).

Papius, Andreas (a.k.a. André de Pape). *De consonantiis*. Antwerp, 1581.

Penna, Lorenzo. *Primi albori musicali*. 3d ed. Bologna, 1679.

Pfrogner, Hermann. *Die Zwölfordnung der Töne*. Zurich, 1953.

Philipp de Vitry. *Ars nova*. (Coussemaker III).

Pontio, Pietro. *Ragionamento di musica*. 1558.

Praetorius, Michael. *Syntagma musicum III*. Wolfenbüttel, 1619.

Prosdocimo de' Beldemandi. *Libellus monochordi*. (Coussemaker III).

————. *Tractatus de contrapunctu*. (Coussemaker III).

Quatuor principalia. (Coussemaker IV).

Radcliffe, Philip F. "The Relationship of Rhythm and Tonality in the Sixteenth Century." *Proceedings of the Musical Association* 57 (1951).

Rameau, Jean-Phillipe. *Génération harmonique, ou Traité de musique théorique et pratique*. Paris, 1737.

————. *Nouveau système de musique théorique, où l'on découvre le principe de toutes les règles nécessaires à la pratique*. Paris, 1726.

————. *Traité de l'harmonie réduite à ses principes naturels*. Paris, 1722.

Reichert, Georg. "Kirchentonart als Formfaktor in der mehrstimmigen Musik des 15. und 16. Jahrhunderts." *Musikforschung* 4 (1951).

————. "Tonart und Tonalität in der älteren Musik." *Musikalische Zeitfragen* 10 (1962).

Riemann, Hugo. *Geschichte der Musiktheorie.* 2d ed. Berlin, 1920.

————. *Handbuch der Harmonie- und Modulationslehre.* 7th ed. c. 1919.

————. *Handbuch der Musikgeschichte.* 2d ed. 1920.

————. "Ideen zu einer 'Lehre von den Tonvorstellungen,' " *Jahrbuch Peters* 21/22 (1914–15).

————. *Musik-Lexicon.* 7th ed. Leipzig, 1909.

————. *Musikalische Syntaxis.* Leipzig, 1877.

————. *Präludien und Studien III.* Leipzig, 1900–1901.

————. *Vereinfachte Harmonielehre.* London, 1893.

————. *Verloren gegangene Selbstverständlichkeiten in der Musik des 15. bis 16. Jahrhunderts.* Langensalza, 1907.

Rogers, Helen Olive. "The Development of the Concept of Modulation in Theory from the 16th to the Early 18th Century." Ph.D. diss., Indiana University, Bloomington, 1955.

Rothacker, Erich. "Die dogmatische Denkform in den Geisteswissenschaften und das Problem des Historismus." *Abhandlungen der geistes- und sozialwissenschaftlichen Klasse der Akademie der Wissenschaften und der Literatur in Mainz (1950, no. 6).*

Ruhnke, Martin. "Intervall." In *Die Musik in Geschichte und Gegenwart.* Kassel, 1949–68.

Sabbatini, Galeazzo. *Regola facile e breve per sonare sopra il Basso continuo.* 1628.

Sachs, Curt. "The Road to Major." *Musical Quarterly* 29 (1943).

Saint-Lambert, Michel de. *Nouveau traité de l'accompagnement.* 1707.

————. *Principes de clavecin.* Paris, 1702.

Salinas, Francesco. *De musica libri VII.* Salamanca, 1577.

Salop, Arnold. "Jacob Obrecht and the Early Development of Harmonic Polyphony." *Journal of the American Musicological Society* 17 (1964).

Salzer, Felix. *Strukturelles Hören. Der tonale Zusammenhang in der Musik.* Wilhelmshaven, 1960.

Sanders, Ernest H. "Die Rolle der englischen Mehrstimmigkeit des Mittelalters in der Entwicklung von Cantus-firmus-Satz und Tonalitätsstrucktur." *Archiv für Musikwissenschaft* 24 (1967).

————. "Tonal Aspects of 13th-Century English Polyphony." *Acta musicologica* 37 (1965).

Santa Maria, Tomàs de. *Arte de tañer fantasia.* 1565.

Schadler, Friedrich. "Das Problem der Tonalität." Ph.D. diss., Zurich, 1950 (1939).

Schenker, Heinrich. *Neue musikalische Theorien und Phantasien, Band I: Harmonielehre.* Stuttgart, 1906.

————. *Neue musikalische Theorien und Phantasien, Band III: Der freie Satz.* 2d ed. Vienna, 1956.

Schering, Arnold. *Geschichte der Musik in Beispielen.* No. 184. Leipzig, 1931.

Schmid, Hans. "Byzantinisches in der karolingischen Musik." *Report of the Eleventh International Congress of Byzantine Studies.* Munich, 1958.

Schmitz, Arnold. "Die Kadenz als Ornamentum musicae." *Congress Report*. Bamberg, 1953.

Schneegaß, Cyriacus. *Isagoges musicae libri duo*. Erfurt, 1591.

Schneider, Marius. *Die Anfänge des Basso continuo und seiner Bezifferung*. Leipzig, 1918.

Scholica enchiriadis. (Gerbert I).

Schönberg, Arnold. *Harmonielehre*. Leipzig and Vienna, 1911.

Schönsleder, Wolfgang. *Architectonice musices universalis . . . Autore Volupio Decoro*. 1631.

Sechter, Simon. *Die Grundsätze der musikalischen Komposition*. Leipzig, 1853.

Siegele, Ulrich. "Bemerkungen zu Bachs Motetten." *Bach-Jahrbuch* (1962).

Smits van Waesberghe, Joseph. *A Textbook of Melody*. Rome, 1955.

———. "Zur Entstehung der drei Hauptfunktionen in der Harmonik." *Congress Report*. Lüneburg, 1950.

Solerti, Angelo. *Le origini del melodramma*. 1903.

Stephani, Hermann. *Zur Psychologie des musikalischen Hörens*. Regensburg, 1956.

Thomson, William Ennis. "A Clarification of the Tonality Concept." Ph.D. diss., Indiana University, 1952.

Tinctoris, Johannes. *Difinitorium*. (Coussemaker IV).

———. *Liber de arte contrapuncti*. (Coussemaker IV).

———. *Liber de natura et proprietate tonorum*. (Coussemaker IV).

Treitler, Leo. "Tone System in the Secular Works of Guillaume Dufay." *Journal of the American Musicological Society* 18 (1965).

Trumble, Ernest Lorenz. "Early Renaissance Harmony." Ph.D. diss., Indiana University, Bloomington, 1954.

Vicentino, Nicola. *L'antica musica ridotta alla moderna prattica*. Rome, 1555.

Vogel, Emil. "Claudio Monteverdi." *Vierteljahrsschrift für Musikwissenshaft* 3 (1887).

Waeltner, Ernst Ludwig. "Die 'Musica disciplina' des Aurelianus Reomensis." *Congress Report*. Cologne, 1958.

Wagner, Peter. *Gregorianische Formenlehre*. Leipzig, 1921.

Walker, Daniel Pickering. *Der musikalische Humanismus im 16. und frühen 17. Jahrhundert*. Kassel, 1949.

Werckmeister, *Andreas*. *Harmonologia musica*. Frankfurt, 1702.

———. *Hypomnemata musica oder Musicalisches Memorial*. Quedlinburg, 1697.

———. *Die nothwendigsten Anmerckungen und Regeln / wie der General-Baß wol könne tractiret werden*. Aschersleben, 1698.

Wienpahl, Robert W. "The Emergence of Tonality." Ph.D. diss., University of California, 1953.

———. "English Theorists and Evolving Tonality." *Music & Letters* 36 (1955).

———. "The Evolutionary Significance of 15th Century Cadential Formulae." *Journal of Music Theory* 4 (1960).

———. "Zarlino, the Senario, and Tonality." *Journal of the American Musicological Society* 12 (1959).

Wilphlingseder, Fredericus. *Erotemata musices practicae*. Nürnberg, 1563.

Wilson, John, transcr. and ed. *Roger North on Music*. London, 1959.

Wolf, Johannes. *Musica practica Bartolomei Rami de Pareia*. Leipzig, 1901.

Wollick, Nicolaus. *Opus aureum*. Cologne, 1501.

Zarlino, Gioseffo. *Dimostrationi harmoniche*. Venice, 1571.

———. *Istitutioni harmoniche*. Venice, 1558.

Zimmerman, Franklin B. "Advanced Tonal Design in the Part-Songs of William Byrd." *Congress Report*. Cologne, 1958.

Zingerle, Hans. *Die Harmonik Monteverdis und seiner Zeit*. (Edition Helbling, n.d.).

Index

Aaron, P., 90, 94–95, 201, 209, 211–12,
  221–22, 232, 243, 261, 287
accidentals, 87, 155, 238–39, 246, 249–50,
  275
accompaniment, a norm of thoroughbass, 145
accord: *dérivé*, 9; *parfaite*, 8, 27ff., 35
Adam of Fulda, 87, 92, 170–71, 175–76
affinalis, 229–30
Agnelli, S., 307
Agricola, M., 201
Alcuin, 193
D'Alembert, J., 21
alteratio: *modi*, 215, 299; *toni*, 160
alternation, principle of, 81
alto clausula, 117
ambitus, 154, 192, 203–4, 211, 222–23, 226,
  243, 265, 271, 275, 291; schema, 199–201
Anonymous 1, 19, 335n.7
Anonymous 2, 360n.17
Anonymous 4, 78
Anonymous 5, 330n.22, 336n.10
Anonymous 11, 92, 95–96, 123, 336n.12,
  353n.8
Anonymous 13, 78, 81ff., 92, 333n.1,
  336n.10, 339n.28, 344n.34
Anonymous 1 de Lafage, 182
Anonymous Coussemaker IV, 96, 98
answer: at the fifth, 204; at the fourth, 204
antecedent phrase, 298, 315
antepenult, 96–97, 107–8, 139, 143, 273
anticipatio transitus, 129
anticipation, 126, 129–30, 139
antiphon, 265, 271–72
antiphonary of Lucca, 265
Apel, W., 252
Apfel, E., 216, 340n.11, 343n.25
Aribo scholasticus, 335n.6
Aristides Quintilianus, 170
arithmetic division, 205, 227, 228–29, 232
arithmetic proportion, 20, 114
armonia piena, 187
Arnold, F. T., 352n.34, 357n.8
Artusi, G. M., 228, 289, 354nn.25, 30
atonality, 17–18; triadic, 17
attraction, 14; points of, 154, 224, 232

Aurelian, 192–93
authentic-plagal combination, 204

Bach, J. S., 69
Banchieri, A., 122, 207, 223
Baryphonus, H., 23, 115, 136
bass clausula, 137, 139
basse fondamentale, 23, 29, 39, 58, 67ff.,
  71, 73, 88, 93, 100, 103, 117
basso continuo, 23, 104
Beethoven, L. van, 57
Benary, P., 365n.45
Berardi, A., 231–32, 352n.33
Bernhard, Chr., 125ff., 206, 215, 230, 299,
  353n.20, 354nn.22, 27, 31
Besseler, H., 3, 75, 84–85, 294
Beurhusius, F., 348n.1
Bianciardi, F., 119
binary division, nested, 298
bitonality, 249, 252
bitonus, 190
Blume, F., 357n.4
Boethius, A.M.S., 205ff.
Bomm, U., 360n.2
Bononcini, B. M., 124, 231
Borrono, P., 110–11
Brumel, A., 110
Bukofzer, M., 3, 344n.34, 346n.14,
  347nn.28, 29
Burmeister, J., 100, 206, 229–30
Burtius, N., 205
Byrd, W., 244ff.

Caccini, G., 121, 139
cadence, 158, 185, 199, 212–13, 216ff., 221,
  229–30, 239–40, 256; authentic, 119, 311;
  divergent, 263; double leading-tone, 176,
  181, 340n.11; extended, 106; fourth-leap,
  89–90, 340n.11; impeded, 274; octave-
  leap, 89–90, 340n.11, 369n.15; parallel,
  89–90; perfect or complete, 101, 108, 111,
  274; plagal, 119, 311
cadence: *irrégulière*, 41; *parfaite*, 26–27, 41,
  63